DISCRIMINATION IN THE CONSTITUTIONS OF THE WORLD

DISCRIMINATION

IN THE

CONSTITUTIONS OF THE WORLD

A Study of the Group Rights Problem

Eschel Rhoodie M.A., Ph. D.

BRENTWOOD

By the Same Author

Penal Systems of the Commonwealth
The Third Africa
Het Omstrede Land
The Paper Curtain
South West: The Last Frontier in Africa
Het Derde Afrika
Southern Africa in Perspective (with Dale, Potholm and others)
The Real Information Scandal

In Preparation

Discrimination Against Women: The Legal Environment

Published and printed in the United States by Brentwood Communications Group, 2605 Cross Country Plaza, Columbus, Georgia 31906, USA.

ISBN 0-916573-03-6
Library of Congress Catalog Card Number 84-070124

This book is set in Century Textbook.
First printed in 1984.

DISCRIMINATION IN THE CONSTITUTIONS OF THE WORLD

List of Contents

PREFACE

This book is a study of the group rights problem and of prescriptions concerning race, religion, ethnicity and sex in 157 constitutions of the world up to 1980.

There are now 166 "recognized" nation-states, but only 159 of them have traditional, one document or entrenched constitutions. The United Kingdom, New Zealand, South Africa and Israel have all enacted a number of basic, fundamental, organic acts and laws which collectively serve as their constitutions. In Bhutan, the hereditary monarchy does not have a written constitution or even a series of organic laws defining the powers and functions of the major political institutions. Libya (the Socialist People's Libyan Arab *Jamahiriya*) is ruled by decrees and the philosophy expounded in "The Green Book on Political Rights." Saudi Arabia and Oman both claim that the Koran is their constitution.

In 1940, there were only seven independent Muslim countries; now there are 40. In at least one, Iran, the rigorous application of fundamental Islamic laws have all but obliterated the constitutional laws dating back to 1906. A new constitution adopted on December 3, 1979 established Shi'ite Islam as the official state religion, places supreme power in the hands of the Muslim clergy and names Ayatollah Ruhollah Khomeini as the nation's religious and political leader for life.

Often such a switch to Muslim laws may not be perceived as religious discrimination against non-Muslims but *de facto* it leads to discrimination against non-Muslims in other areas eg. the right to democratic elections. After the Shariat Muslims laws were officially introduced into Pakistan in late 1978 by the President, General Zia, he stated that "Islam includes no provision for Western type elections."

The United States Constitution of 1789 is by far the world's oldest -- and the only survivor of the eighteenth century. There are eight constitutions which date from the 1800's, and three of these were recently revised or replaced: The Liberian constitution of

1820, the British North America Act of 1867 which serves as Canada's constitution, and the 1873 Swiss constitution. The other nineteenth century constitutions are from Norway (1814), Argentina (1853), Andorra and Luxembourg (1868), and Columbia (1886).

There are only six other constitutions which, as amended, have been in continuous existence since the pre-World War II period: Australia (1901), Mexico (1917), Finland (1919), Liechtenstein (1921), Lebanon (1926) and Ireland (1937).

On the other hand, there have been 127 new constitutions since 1960 -- 34 of them since 1978. And only 16 date from the 1940's and 1960's.

The most important of the new "replacement" constitutions are those of the People's Republic of China, Panama, Spain and Sri Lanka in 1978; Ghana, Iran, Nigeria and Peru in 1979; Afghanistan, Chile, Vietnam and South Korea in 1980 and Canada in 1982. New nations -- and thus new constitutions -- since 1978 include Dominica, St. Lucia and St. Vincent in the Caribbean; Kirabati, Seychelles and Tuvalu in the Pacifica, Antigua and Barbuda (one country) and Zimbabwe in Africa. Namibia (South West Africa), the former German colony ruled by the Republic of South Africa since 1918, is slated for independence in 1985, the last of the former European colonies in Africa to achieve independence.

In my view, the constitutions of the nations of the world provide a basic expression of the values and goals of society. They are extremely important documents fulfilling important functions.

According to conventional definition, a constitution is the framework which structures the assemblage of laws, institutions and customs which govern a nation and its peoples including the document(s) that legitimizes governmental authority and prescribes political conduct. But a constitution is also an ideological manifesto, a written manifestation of national purpose, the formulation of the rights of people and therefore a nation's showpiece. It tells the world what a nation is and what it stands for.

As Professor Albert Blaustein, Chairman of the New York International Consortium of Constitutional Consultants said: "It is a brief to the world court of public opinion; what is most solemn of all government documents is also -- inevitably -- a nation's most significant public relations presentation."

Constitutions are used by numerous political systems and ideologies ranging from the super democracies such as the United States to oppressive Communist regimes such as the Soviet Union. They cater to a multitude of political needs fulfilling many functions. They entail a commitment to an ideology, such as in the Soviet Union, Syria, China, East Germany, Mocambique and Cuba. They have a nationalistic function such as in Iraq, Korea and Equatorian Guinea. Or a party political function such as in Tanzania, Mali, Vietnam, Mali, Gabon, and Mauritania. They have a structuring function in that they show which expectations are legitimate. They have a rationalising function, expressing political wishes, aims and convictions in legal terms. They have a public relations function, such as when new states present themselves to the world and serve as tangible proof of the right to international association. They have a registration function recording the results of political development. They have a symbolic function, serving as the symbol of democracy, freedom and justice such as in the United States, Costa Rica and France. Lastly, they have a barrier function by impeding hasty political change; serving as a barrier to new revolutionary political forces. Its general functions are to contain important legal pronouncements, converting power into law, setting up state institutions; provides information about the nature of the state; regulate behaviour and decision making processes and provide indications of how legal and political problems should be solved. [1]

Constitutions are important documents for the following reasons: They are the result of a decision making process at the highest political level; they constitute the nucleus of a country's public law; they contain a number of values and norms that

---

1. Van Marseveen, Henc and van der Tang, Ger: *Written Constitutions*, Oceana Publications, New York, 1978, pp. 273-280.

represent beliefs held throughout the world; they are one of the channels through which development at international level are affected at national level; they provide information on the organization of the state and the formal grant of powers and they provide an easy means of comparing political systems.

A constitution can be the most important instrument for transforming politics into law. For this very reason a society suffering the stresses of its multi-national, multi-racial population structure and looking towards satisfying the legitimate aspirations of groups (ethnic, religious or linguistic) can look to its constitution or to the modification of its constitution to convert sound political sense into constitutional law which would be respected by all groups.

While the vast majority of constitutional scholars (for so many reasons) have not perceived the significance of group rights, they have been the subject of major constitutional debate since the earliest constitutions. Three major provisions of the United States Constitution of 1789 are concerned with slavery; diverse religious guarantees are set forth in the Swiss Constitution of 1789; linguistic differences and rights arising out of those differences constitute a feature of the Belgian Constitution of 1831, etc. Group rights can even be traced back to the Magna Carta in 1215 when the barons were guaranteed rights as barons; and even further back to the rights of the family as a group in the Old Testament of the Bible.

Group rights, in fact, antedate individual rights and when peoples' representatives have met in constituent assemblies they have recognized such rights. In Henc van Marseveen and Ger van der Tangs' *Written Constitutions* (a computerized comparative study of 1978), it is shown that some 27 percent of all constitutions provide for the rights of ethnic communities or minority groups. In addition some 30 percent refer to the protection of different languages and 18 percent to religious or ethnic requirements for membership of the central executive.[2] Yet, despite this, the literature on human rights has been dominated by concern for

2. Van Marseveen and van der Tang, op. cit., p. 292.

individual human rights. Locke, Rousseau and Jefferson (and their intellectual heirs) have concerned themselves almost exclusively with the rights of the individual as an individual. And this has been the universal theme from Tom Paine's *The Rights of Man* to the 1948 Universal Declaration of Human Rights.

Conventional wisdom teaches that the emergence of human rights parallels the development of individualism. From what I have read this has been a three stage process. The eighteenth century witnessed the first serious recognition of individual claims against the state. This was followed in the nineteenth century by the granting of voting rights and the recognition of the right of the individual to participate in the governance of the state. And the twentieth century saw the acceptance of positive rights bestowed upon the individual by the state -- the development of economic and social human rights to enhance the development of the individual and to fulfill the idea of individual rights.

Thus it is that scholars have not appreciated the significance of group rights developments -- either in the formative period of constitution writing from 1787 to World War I, in the breakup of Austria-Hungary and the Ottoman Empire and the minorities provisions of the Czechoslovakian and Yugoslavian constitutions between the great wars, or in the Third World constitutions and the various documents of the United Nations following World War II.

There are also a number of almost personal, perhaps even Freudian, reasons why constitutional scholars have parroted individual rights dogma. The fact is that these scholars, with scant exception, have been well-educated, free-thinking, white men and usually lawyers and professional writers by trade. Thus their disregard for group rights which might have been advanced by women, or blacks, or clerics; and thus the lawyers emphasis on due process and *habeas corpus* and the professional writers' emphasis on freedom of speech and press.

So long as constitutional thought was based upon the American Constitution and the French Declaration of the Rights of Man, this conventional wisdom manifested by scholarly pre-occupation with individual rights, might be condoned. But this was before we knew of Nazi genocide. Beginning with the breakup of British India in 1947, followed by the complicated Nigeria and Malaysia-Singapore experiences, together with the multi-dimensional documents of the United Nations on colonialism, race, genocide, etc., we witnessed the slow beginnings of well-documented constitutional literature on group rights. Apart from the important field of group rights, this study will, hopefully, also contribute to the equally important field of comparative constitutional law and as a source and guide in development of human rights research.

There is a special benefit for South Africa (the most oft-discussed and disputed multi-ethnic state in the world) in any analysis of the group rights problem as it has been approached, constitutionally, elsewhere. While there has been a strong emphasis during the past two decades on racial groupings and on the concept of "nation" [*Volk*] for the Whites and "nations" (Zulu, Xhosa, Tswana, etc.) for the Blacks, government thinking may now be forced by demographic and political circumstances into a stand based purely on *group rights,* in which *racial* considerations would no longer be paramount. The recommendations of a multi-racial Presidential council led to a referendum in 1983 which brought about the first significant constitutional reform in the field of group rights since formation of the country in 1910. For the first time, groups such as the Coloureds (mixed-blood) and Asians (mostly Indians) will join Whites in the legislative decision making process. The country's white conservative Prime Minister stated categorically that South Africa's greatest problem may not be one of racism. "It was one of minorities and not only White and Coloured minorities but also Black minorities," he said. In those chapters dealing with the constitutions of India, Belgium, the Soviet Union, Yugoslavia (particularly the latter) the political theorists in South Africa will come across remarkable similarities in terminology and attitudes about the multi-national society, protection of group rights and prescriptions for minorities.

Seeking constitutional solutions of formulae for race, religious, ethnic and cultural conflict is to most scholars a vexing business and in the late seventies has become one of the most important challenges to scholars in law, political science, sociology and allied disciplines. Failure to inspire or achieve the proper constitutional responses could mean another Lebanon, Ethiopia or Cyprus where the Turkish Cypriots in 1983 declared unilateral independence. New countries are still being formed. In 1945, there were 70 nation states. After World War II up to 1983, a total of 94 new states came into being. There will be more. Constitutions all over the world are also continually being revised, sometimes in part or in whole. In September, 1980, General Kenan Evren and the army seized power in Turkey and in 1983 a new constitution was voted in by 92 percent of the electorate, providing for a one chamber 400 member democratically elected legislature. Partial revision in 1980-1981 took place in dozens of states, Mauritania, Gabon, Belgium, Egypt and Afghanistan, to name but a few.

There may be no constitutional science, as yet, but there is a constitutional art or technology which can be practised by those who are knowledgeable about constitutions and who accept, or even just recognise, that group rights today are even more important than individual rights. After all, only some nine percent of the 157 states whose constitutions were examined were homogeneous from an ethnic point of view and in more than 63 states the population is divided into five or more significantly different ethnic communities. In total, there are 892 clearly recognizable ethnic groups living within the borders of these 157 states. Other, qualified, researchers have pointed out that out of 164 significant violent conflicts between 1958-1976 a mere 15 were military conflicts. In fact, the most significant violence the world has experienced this century, World Wars I and II, Korea and Vietnam excluded, has found its *casus belli* in religious and ethnic disputes such as the 3,600 killed and 230,000 made homeless in the clash of 1983 between Hindus and Moslems in India's state of Assam where a seccessionist movement is gathering power. This fact, alone, makes it worth while for everyone to look again at the group rights problem and how this is dealt with, or could be dealt with in the constitution of their own country.

There are few countries in the world which can afford to look the other way when it comes to group rights issues within their borders. There are only 12 contemporary states which can be considered ethnically homogeneous. In nearly 30 percent of the countries of the world, the largest group comprises less than 50 percent of the population. And in more than 60 states the population is divided into at least five significant ethnic groupings.

The majority of researchers among the academic community are no longer pretending that ethnicity and group rights is something blown up by sectional interests or conservative research institutes. And if the academic community is beginning to consider the group rights problem worthy of its attention then the governments of the world cannot be far behind. The ideal of every statesman, every serious politician or administrator, is surely to head a successful society, however, as Charles Manning wrote in his thought provoking book, *The Nature of the International Society,* "in so far as society functions with success this is . . . because it is formed of individuals so emotionally and psychologically constituted as to lend themselves to social co-existence."

It is the worst kind of intellectual dishonesty to pretend that in most countries of the world ethnic stress is not a major social, legal and political problem. Yet all too often, notably in Africa and Asia, government policies have been dedicated to the pursuit of abstractions such as the notion that a state deeply divided by racial, tribal, linguistic and other cultural schisms should in fact be governed as one nation when "unity," in reality, is a paper legacy of history when individuals, in Europe, arbitrarily created nation states all over the world in pursuit of colonial empires. It is only in Rousseau's atomistic nation (*The Social Contract*) and Aldous Huxley's *Brave New World* where everyone is expected to have uniform chromosomes, abilities and opinions. Recognising group rights and the existence of disparate groups in many states, and which have no hope of pulling together, is getting one's feet on the ground. It may be a rocky terrain but at least the rocks have more substance than Rousseau and Huxley's wishful utopias.

PART I

INTRODUCTION

CHAPTER I
OBJECTIVES, SCOPE OF RESEARCH AND ORGANIZATION OF MATERIALS

The primary objective in 1976 when the research began was a study of the group rights problem and prescriptions concerning race, religion, ethnicity and sex in the then 160 existing constitutions of the world. Eventually 157 constitutions were read and analyzed.

In addition, I looked at the concept of differences among peoples. In this increasingly nationalistic and increasingly pluralistic world, there is a growing awareness of ethnical, cultural, linguistic, and traditional differences among peoples. Academically we hardly ever speak of "melting pots" any longer. The concepts which are now being followed are those of ethnocentrism and ethnicity, even of a "new nationalism" rooted in group rights.[3] There is a belated recognition in the intellectual community of what at least most realistic politicians already knew -- that differences in race, religion, sex and ethnic inheritage are meaningful and must be studied. A work which has become widely read for this very reason is that of Moynihan, P. and Glazer, N.: *Ethnicity,* Harvard University Press, 1976.

Such a study as I undertook during 1976-1980 necessarily also involves the legal order, the rule of law. And most important in any analysis of law and political sciences the study of *constitutions*. For constitutions provide the framework of the various societies in

3. Cf. Blaustein, Albert: "The New Nationalism," paper read at the Eleventh International Congress on Comparative Law, Caracas, Venezuela, August 29 -- September 5, 1982.

which live people of different ethnic backgrounds, different races, different religions and, of course, different sexes. How shall the heightened conscience of separate identities be satisfied, be reconciled, be ordered? What has already been done in constitutionalism? What provision is made for group rights? What discrimination or prescriptions exist in the world's constitutions?

That was the scope of this study.

I wished to briefly refer to the problems involved under the traditional headings of race, religious and sex "discrimination" -- and, if necessary, to go further in these respects.

First, I wanted to by-pass, if not avoid, the perjorative label of "discrimination". This study was not to be a tome or file on racism/racialism and other evils. Constitutions and other legal documents often make racial, religious and sexual classifications which are beneficial to minorities and/or to others not in the power structure: prescribed parliamentary representation for non-voting aborigines in Australia and New Zealand; authorization for Moslems to have plural wives; alimony provision for women only, etc.

The study focussed briefly on differences between and among people but more extensively on *constitutional classification* based on such differences.

Second, I wished to go beyond race-religion-sex to include other differences which are becoming even more important in the constitutional sense. Basques are not racially different from Spaniards; Kurds and Iraquis all worship Allah; Quebecois differ from other Canadians only in language, etc. My concern was therefore also with **ethnicity** and how this is recognized and provided for in constitutions which distinguish people on the basis of culture, traditions, level of development, etc.

Third, I wanted to look beyond the language of race-religion-sex-ethnicity in making a comprehensive study. Constitutional language on literary requirements, for example, may have the outward appearance of equality. But as used in two South

American constitutions, for example, they are designed to disenfranchise the native Indian population.

This is an important area of study.

A *constitution* provides the basic expression of the values and goals of a state; it provides valuable insights into the official norms of society. While some constitutions are but convenient facades behind which the rights and duties of people are manipulated, in most countries this is the exception rather than the rule. Even the 1936 Soviet constitution -- the prime example of a constitution as an instrument of propaganda -- prescribes a framework of ideals, albeit ideals, not practices.

Finally, this study was designed to provide factual, organized and classified data on how constitutions treat differences among people. This was not to be a vehicle for social commentary, a forum for value judgments in a prean for human rights. It is designed to provide source materials which can be used by policy makers in meeting the problems of plural societies and the issues of ethnicity and group rights. Only in the introduction and conclusions are some recommendations and editorialising, based on the wisdom gained from this study and on the language of the constitutions itself.

My study has been source oriented -- not so much empirical as pragmatic and inductive. It has, I trust, been completely value free and without pre-conceptions. While I have read and studied the literature in the field, I have relegated it to a secondary status. I have let the constitutions speak for themselves.

I have attempted a frame of mind of academic neutrality. How different, for example, would have been the approaches had I undertaken this study for a particular government or an activist organization in the field of human rights. How could the researcher avoid the role of self-appointed advocate while in the service of known patrons? My neutrality has encouraged objectivity. It has removed the pressure to meet the preferences and standards and fashions and preconceptions current among so many academicians in the West.

In one way the project departs slightly from the stated objecti in that the category of "race" is expanded to include cultural, ethnic and similar factors which are appropriate to a broader view of this disputed term.

I have, as previously stated, reviewed all constitutional prescriptions which make distinctions based on race, ethnicity, religion or sex because the word "discriminate" is perjorative and, in normal usage, implied that the distinction made or imposed is unjust or unfair. I have found that many constitutions do make distinctions which respond to the plural characteristics of their societies, while others rested upon attitudes grounded in individual preferences, upon the preferences of members of a particular class, of race and religion.

In Zambia and Malawi the constitution now provides that in order to become President of the state one has to be a member of "the Party." To become King of Nepal, one has to be not only a Hindu but also of strict Aryan descent and culture. In Syria, the candidate for President must not only be Muslim, he must also be Syrian and Arab Syrian. These countries are thus as racist, and religious and politically restrictive in their constitutions, than the much maligned Republic of South Africa.

It was never and is still not my intention to fasten normative judgments upon certain constitutions or to determine which are "good" or "bad", but simply to identify the divergencies and to attempt to explain them.

In undertaking the study I assumed that constitutional texts provide a valuable insight into the official norms of a society. I do not believe that a constitution is always a facade or merely a convenient facade. But I also assumed that while it may not always be just a convenient facade any scholar should beware of the gap between constitutional objectives and reality when analyzing constitutions, particularly of Third World Countries. A sound knowledge of major political events in those countries has become almost a pre-requisite for the constitutional scholar. For example, in the preamble to the Syrian constitution the following appears:

"Freedom is a sacred right and popular democracy is the ideal formulation which insures for the citizen the exercise of his freedom which makes him a dignified human being . . . freedom can only be preserved by its free citizens . . ." Coming from a state known for its despotic government, intolerance of the religious beliefs of others and whose occupying military forces have been a significant factor in denying the neighbouring Lebanese citizens their freedom of choice, the preamble smacks of cynical propaganda. Another example. An article in the constitution of Uganda states: "No person shall be subject to torture or to inhuman or degrading punishment or other like treatment." Given the record of Presidents Milton Obote en Idi Amin in Uganda the past fifteen years in torture and punishment of Blacks and Asians, this becomes a ludicrous statement. [4]

I did not provide an empirical analysis of the implementation of written constitutional rights and liberties since this was beyond the scope of my research. Furthermore, the data necessary for such a study is either uncollected, unavailable, scattered and more often that not unreliable. I could not quantify the degree or extent of the realization of constitutional assertions of rights and liberties, nor did I think it appropriate to try and do so. Where I have referred to a gap between policy and practice it was merely to recognise the problem that rights normally associated with constitutional rights are being abused is undeniable. [5]

I was able to do a considerable amount of research by mail. Fortunately, the publications of the five volumes *Case Studies in*

---

4. See in this respect Loewenstein, K.: "Reflections on the Value of Constitutions in our Revolutionary Age," in Zurcher, A.J. Ed.: *Constitutions and Constitutional Trends Since World War II*, 1951, pp. 191-224.

5. Cf. Kurt Glaser and Stefan Possony's *Victims of Politics*, N.Y., Columbia University Press, 1979, to which further reference is made in this chapter and the five volume *Case Studies on Human Rights*, Marthinus Nijhof, The Hague, 1976 (Editors W. Veenhoven and W. Crum Ewing) probably the best work of its kind ever published up to 1984. To a lesser extent one can also consult *Ethnic Conflict in the Western World*, Cornell University Press, London, 1977, edited by Milton Esman; the second part of Alvin Rabushka en Kenneth Shepsle's *Politics in Plural Societies*, Charles Merril Co., Columbus, Ohio, 1972, and *Comparative Human Rights*, edited by Richard Claude, Johns Hopkins University Press, Baltimore, 1976, notably Part II.

Human Rights under editorship of Veenhoven and others, minimised correspondence to a great deal. Few would dispute that the more than one hundred contributors to this monumental 3,000 page work are all experts in their field. In addition, it is easily the most comprehensive and detailed analysis of *de facto* and *de jure* discrimination that has ever been published, covering fifty different countries and dealing with religious, linguistic, racial, ethnic, social, sexual and economic discrimination. [6]

I made use of a team of post-graduate law and political students in the USA, France, Switzerland and Israel to fill in the gaps, for photocopying and the mechanical extraction of material, for scrutinising material in Arabic, Portuguese, French and other languages which I cannot read and for cross checking. They obtained reliable material in Washington, New York, Boston, Quebec, London, The Hague, Paris, Geneva, and Jerusalem. I personally read at the library of the International Court of Justice in The Hague, at Leiden University in Holland, [7] at the University of Ecuador in Quito, the University of Costa Rica in San Jose, and other centres of learning in the USA, Israel, Britain and Switzerland. While the vast majority of English language literature in this field can be found in the university libraries of Princeton and Rutgers University in the USA, research assistants have taken advantage of the collections at Harvard and the Library of Congress, Washington, D.C. I also did some research at New York public library, the United Nations library in New York City and the libraries of the University of Pretoria and the Pretoria Public Library in South Africa. [8]

---

6. Cf. also Glaser and Possony, op. cit, which is more concise.

7. The Department of Constitutional Law at the Erasmus University, Rotterdam, has become quite well known following the publication in 1978 of Henc van Marseveen and Ger van der Tang's Computerized Study of Written Constitutions.

8. In South Africa excellent sources of information are the Institute for the Study of Plural Societies at the University of Pretoria which has produced first class works such as Professor Nic Rhoodie (editor) *Intergroup Accommodation in Plural Societies*, MacMillan Press, London, 1978; the Africa Institute in Pretoria, the only institute of its kind on the African continent; the Institute of Foreign and Comparative Law of the University of South Africa and the law faculties at the various other universities.

The American Jewish Committee have done much research in the field of religious discrimination. There was also much material available in Israel where I often visited between 1974-1978. The Russian Institute at Columbia University and the Institute of Latin American Studies at the same university also had much material on this subject. My team covered the Anti-Slavery Society, Amnesty International and Minority Rights Groups in London, the *Centre Nationale de la Recherche Scientifique,* International Association of Democratic Jurists and the *Societte de Legislation Comparee* in Paris; the International Red Cross, the International Labour Organization, the U.N. High Commission for Refugees, the International Commission for Jurists and the World Jewish Congress, all in Geneva.

ORGANIZATION OF MATERIALS:

The *patterns* which I have developed are pres ed in two parts.

First (in Part II) are the conceptual *Group Patterns* which cut across all the constitutions and encompass materials under such headings as ''Affirmative Action,'' ''Institutional Arrangements'' and ''Slavery.''

The third part of the study is devoted to *National Patterns,* studying the co-ordinated, integrated, national responses to the totality of race, religions, sex and ethnic classifications.

Part IV covers the conclusions.

Part V covers the bibliography.

What has taken by far the longest period of time (aided by several assistants) has been the preparation of, at first, two major annexes to the commentary.

Both annexes were inevitable; both could have been the starting points for the total study. They contain *essential* material for any student of group rights, political science or comparative international law.

The first *annex* listed every provision of every constitution dealing with the subjects of racial, religious, sex and other ethnic discrimination. To this end, I have done precisely what other scholars have done who have been involved with similar projects. I (supported by research assistants), have studied carefully the fifteen volumes of *Constitutions of the Countries of the World,* edited by Albert P. Blaustein and Gisbert H. Flanz, published in Dobbs Ferry, New York, since 1971. (Cited as *Blaustein* throughout the study). This is a loose-leaf edition continuously in the process of being updated, and I have tried to get the latest constitution wherever possible, stopping approximately at the end of 1980 . For example, I included the constitution of the Peoples Republic of China of March 5, 1978.

The Blaustein-Flanz collection has proven to be the basic source for all similar studies. A comparative constitutional study was made by Dr. Giuseppe Turi, head of the legal department of the *Regie de la Langue Francaise* of the Government of Quebec. The result was his volume, *Les Dispositions Juridico -- Constitutionnelles de 147 E'tats en Matiere de Politique Linguistique.* This was published in 1977 by the International Center for Research on Bilingualism in Quebec. (While Turi covered only 147 countries, the present study encompasses 157. In addition, the Turi study is limited to linguistic provisions.) [9]

Another detailed examination of the contents of the Blaustein set was pursued by Professors H. Th. J.F. van Maarseveen and G.F.M. van der Tang, professors of constitutional law at the Erasmus University of Rotterdam. Their computerized study, *On Written Constitutions,* was published by Oceana Publications, Dobbs Ferry, New York in 1978. This excellent study is much more broadly focused than is my survey, but it is not especially concerned with discriminatory provisions.

In extracting the applicable constitutional provisions, I

---

9. The work by Peaslee: *Constitutions of Nations,* Marthinus Nijhof, The Hague, though in its third edition was published in 1970 and the summaries of states have not been updated since 1965.

proceeded on a country-by-country basis. In other words, I and my assistants read each constitution, marking articles and sections which were appropriate, and then made photocopies of the material.

To facilitate the country-by-country research, various assistants and foreign scholars provided aid. Prior to final checking I had one assistant read through all of the Latin American constitutions, another to extract material from constitutions in the Arabic world, another for Anglophone Africa, another for Francophone Africa, and so forth. During a visit of six weeks to Costa Rica in early 1979 I enlisted the services of a top constitutional law professor at the University of Costa Rica. And he provided a valuable check list. Similarly, two scholars at the Indian Law Institute at New Delhi provided the basic information on all the entities making up the former British Raj. This was particularly valuable since it must be recalled that until the early twentieth century the British Raj was defined officially as "India-Burma-Ceylon and Federated Malay States. In addition they provided an introduction to constitutional provisions (and analysis) to Pakistan, Bangladesh and Singapore as well as Sri Lanka (formerly Ceylon), Burma and Malaysia, though India was the more important. [10]

Alas, many travel *cum* interviews abroad proved to be virtually worthless. This is especially true concerning the personnel and agencies connected with the United Nations. While some attention must be given to U.N. studies and some respect must be accorded their massive efforts to collect and organize data, the quality of the work is poor. This is not very important business at the U.N. and the personnel at the Human Rights Division in Geneva were singularly unimpressive. The same can be said for UNESCO personnel and activities in Paris and the ILO in Geneva.

While other agencies have been staffed by much more able personnel and individuals far more co-operative, the simple truth is that the gleanings were minimal. All one could obtain from

---

10. See S.R. Mohan Das, "Discrimination in India," in *Veenhoven,* Vol. II, p. 157.

Amnesty International and the Minority Rights Group were copies of their very limited selected and politicized literature and viewpoints. Ditto the International Committee of Jurists and such organizations as the International Committee of the Red Cross and the International Labor Organization were completely barren -- the same may be said for another dozen sources explored, too numerous and too unimportant to be listed here. And one can only cull selected items from the masses of data published. There were no guideposts and there was little guidance for us in this comprehensive effort.

Particularly disappointing were the representatives of The World Council of Churches, The World Jewish Congress and other religious entities. They have next to nothing. But they have offered my assistants their co-operation and assistance to whatever we want to do next in this area, for they are anxious to obtain the results of this type of study.[11]

Thus I concluded that there were no shortcuts. All I learned was that few others had done anything really useful and that I would have to do the job by myself. And thus, as noted above, I and my research assistants had to read all of the constitutions and collect and co-ordinate those of significance.

Having extracted all of the applicable provisions, the next step was color coding -- in five classifications. The photocopies of these constitutional provisions were fastened to 4'' x 6'' cards. Everything which might be classified as *General* was fastened to a blue card; every reference to *Race* was placed on a pink card; provisions on *Sex* were on white cards; provisions on *Religion* were on yellow cards; and green cards were used for the classification *Other Ethnic.* Then these cards were filed together by country in alphabetical order.

The question then was whether the constitutional provisions

---

11. In preparation is a study dealing specifically with religious discrimination in the world and discrimination against women, provisionally entitled *The Legal Environment of Women.*

should be prepared by country or by topic. The latter alternative was chosen. The material was then broken down under the four headings or classifications noted above. This may have been a mistake. For it is often useful to analyze provisions on religious discrimination together with provisions on sex discrimination, etc.

When it came to the production stage for this book, economic considerations took over. The annex which I had prepared and which contained all the extracts from the 157 constitutions dealing with recognition, protection, privileges, differentiation and discrimination in respect of languages, race, religion and sex ran into more than 300 pages of text and will therefore have to await publication at a later date. Including this mass of data with the material already in this book would have resulted in a massive tome with a prohibitive price tag for the average scholar. In fact, by itself, it is four complete "books" following the pattern of Turi's work on *Les Dispositions Juridico-Constitutionnelles De 147 Etats En Matiere De Politique Linguistique.* As noted above, this was published in 1977 by The International Center for Research on Bilingualism in Quebec. And to do this job he (and his staff) went about the task of extracting all of the applicable sections on linguistic matters from the Blaustein compilation. (There appear to be serious omissions in the Turi compilation.)

With four Turi equivalents, routine sub-categories and classifications can be and should be made by scholars. Interesting provisions can be highlighted and comparisons should be made. Here are some examples of materials to be compared, contrasted, etc. on sex: Article 191 of the Yugoslav Constitution of 1974 provides that "It is a human right freely to decide on family planning." It is quite obvious that this is the right to abortion since Article One continues with, "This right may only be restricted for reasons of health." On the other hand, Chapter One, Article One, Section One of the Constitutional Act, Number 3 enacted in Chile in 1976, has this provision: "The law protects the life of the unborn child." One can also make note of the interesting Article 75 of the Sudan Constitution of 1973 which provides that pregnant women may not be executed.

And the astute researcher can see the implications of sexual discrimination in Article 49 of the Swiss constitution of 1874, as amended. It reads:

> 3. The holder of the paternal or tutorial authority shall determine the religious education of children in conformity with the foregoing principles until they have completed their sixteenth year.

My study has thus gone far beyond routine analysis. Under *Group Patterns*, I have organized the various materials under such headings as slavery, affirmative action, etc. and have provided illustrations of racial, religious, sex and ethnic classifications under such headings. I have then followed this with selected *National Patterns* providing models for studies yet to be made.

While I did not perform the routine task of presenting *Group Patterns* under such headings as race and sex, there is a section on religion to serve as an example of such analysis and as a guideline for studies to come. Further, there is a *Group Patterns* under the heading of indigenous peoples -- one of the many headings under which racial matters could and should be classified.

It had been hoped that the study might encompass research into historic constitutions, the examination of state and provincial constitutions, the constitutions of dependencies and special territories. And, finally, model and utopian constitutions. Certainly, there were some potential benefits lost from my inability to perform such tasks. And I am sure that some fruitful insights were missed. Yet, it was simply too much to undertake such research in addition to the study of 157 current national constitutions. With certain particular exceptions, the research did inevitably require me to examine the draft constitution of Nigeria and make appropriate references to the earlier constitutions of Germany, the Soviet Union and Yugoslavia.

Important in understanding both *Group Patterns, National Patterns* and the *Conclusions* is the fact that this has been an inductive study. I did not deduce from existing literature and existing generalities. And, as a result, my conclusions have, in substantial measure, run counter to conventional wisdom. I repeat that the study has been source-oriented -- empirical and pragmatic and inductive. It has been completely value-free and without preconceptions. While I have been reading the literature in the field, I have relegated it to a secondary status. I have let the constitutions speak for themselves.

In gathering, assembling, and analyzing the basic data, I had to go beyond the three classifications of race, religion, and sex. Thus, I have provided and studied constitutional extracts which are general in character and have devised the category of "Other Ethnic" as well.

In analyzing the materials on race, it was necessary to consider caste, tribes, indigenous peoples, cultural, and ethnic minorities, etc.

In a world where racism is scorned and where everyone denies being a racist, there is a natural tendency to classify peoples of another color or physiognomy under some other heading. Thus such words as "indigenous peoples" when Paraguayans are talking about Amerindians, or when South Africans are talking about Bushmen, or when the situation of the pygmies is being considered by the people of Zaire.

In addition, classifications which may have had their base in other "differences" between peoples may eventually take on a racial characterization. For example, the caste system of India resulted in isolation and restrictive breeding practices dating back to 1500 B.C. True, the origins of the caste system are obscure and its principal manifestations have been in occupational separateness. But after 3500 years of selective breeding it is probably not important whether caste is predicated upon occupational, ethnic, or racial differences. And caste must be considered in any study of race.

Discriminatory practices based upon racial classifications are often hidden and require references to constitutional provisions on property, voting, and literacy requirements, as well as provisions pointing up cultural, ethnic and linguistic distinctions.

For religion, every kind of religious preferment, disability or regulation was included. Provisions touching upon the establishment of religion, support of religion, religious education, distinctions among religions and the rights of non-believers were examined.

On sex, all mention of the special status of women, of marriage, the family, of female labor, and professional activity were given attention. Women's rights to property, and rights after divorce or widowhood were likewise scrutinized.

DEFINITIONS:

To foster consistency and, more important, to sharpen and clarify the distinctions used in this study, a series of *definitions* have been developed. These definitions guided the selection of relevant extracts from the constitutions which comprise the annexes. They are also the result of a study of these extracts. They will also serve as guidelines in further research which must be done in these areas in future years.

Constitution -- a constitution is the framework which structures the assemblage of laws, institutions and customs which govern a nation and its peoples. It legitimizes governmental authority for, as Thomas Paine wrote, a government without a constitution is power without right. The constitution is also an ideological manifesto and the formulation of the rights of people. "Written constitutions (are) to liberty what a grammar is to language," wrote Paine.

Group -- An entity composed of individuals/persons who share common perceptions of their racial, ethnic,[12] religious, social, economic or political position. To constitute a group, no political party or other organization need exist so long as the members of the assemblage identify themselves in a common or collective manner.

12. The term ethnic refers to a social group, sharing some aspects of a common culture, but is defined primarily by *descent*. Cf. Glazer, N.: "Ethnicity: A World Phenomenon," in *Dialogue*, U.S. Information Service, Washington, Vol. 8, 1975, No. 314.

Minority -- Any racial, tribal, linguistic, religious, caste or nationality group which perceives itself as being inferior in status to other (i.e., dominant) groups within the society, without regard to objective conditions. Thus, the Flemings and the Walloons of Belgium are both minority groups. The Flemings see themselves as collectively economically deprived and the Walloons see themselves as a numerical minority. In this sense women may also be regarded and treated as a minority group even though they constitute a numerical majority in most nations. Many religious groups are minorities in the same sense, and so are various ethnic groups. For example, while they constitute a numerical majority, the Asian Indians of Fiji are a minority since they consider themselves politically dominated.[13] Some groups, such as Gypsies, are often denied official recognition as separate ethnic groups, but they are nonetheless a minority whether the government recognizes them or not. No one can be certain of the number of minority groups which can be found in any country at any given time, since subjective attitudes and perceptions are continually changing. Minority status may be based upon race, language, caste, nationality, tribe, religion, sex or even sexual preferences. In the 157 countries examined there are 892 clearly recognizable groups.[14]

Rights -- In a constitutional study, rights must be defined (and thus limited) to legal rights. These are rights which constitute claims upon government, legitimized by recognition as constitutional or basic law, and politically enforceable by the institutions and processes of government.

So-called natural, immutable or God-given rights are beyond the purview of the study. On the other hand, under my definition, it is not necessary that a right actually be enforced or enjoyed to be classified as a legal right. Recognition in a fundamental document is the test. Rights, in this sense, encompass both rights *against* the state and special treatment of "affirmative action" rights derived *from* the state.

---

13. Fiji maintains dual voting roles to assure Fidjian control.

14. Cf. Murdoch, G.P.: *Ethnographic Atlas,* 1967.

Race -- Racial groups are those which may be distinguished by physical differences, such as skin color, physiognomy, type of hair or other differences, which are subjectively perceived by members of the group or others (outsiders) as significant. Racial groups may be difficult to demonstrate scientifically, but are nonetheless operative in the real day-to-day life of a society, eg. The Maoris in New Zealand, the Coloured in South Africa, Surinamers in the Netherlands.

Linguistic Groups -- Shared common language is another manifestation of group identity. Even where language distinctiveness may or may not indicate cultural and other differences, it may still be a decisive factor in national life. Linguistic groups are significant both in Quebec, where they parallel cultural differences, and in Wales, where they do not. The fact that so many Argentinians speak Italian constitutes a language group, but not a language problem, while language groups and language problems are synonymous in India.

Religious Groups -- Religion is a major manifestation of group identity. The professed rights of religious groups include both freedom of religion and freedom from religion. Religion as a source of group identity has been significant in dividing nations, as in Lebanon, or in unifying them, as in Denmark.

Caste -- Castes are groups distinguished and divided from other elements of society according to hierarchical lines. Caste distinctions are the result of racial, tribal/occupational, or some other classification in the past. Caste exists today, however, as the result of the perpetuation of practices which include societal control of breeding. Since stratification of society along caste lines is genetic, it tends to be persistent. Caste results in relationships of social inferiority to superior elements of society.

Nationalities -- A nationality is a group whose members have adopted the principles of political nationalism. This is usually manifested by the development of separate autonomous states within the plural nation-state, or of independence from the nation-state. In a sense, the Quebecois, the Basques, and the

Palestinians are all groups which fit the definition of nationalities. Even though such a group has neither attained nationhood nor autonomy, the leadership of such a group seeks one or the other status. The Republic of South Africa refers to its Black homelands as "National States" and though rejected internationally for purely political reasons, the fact of independence, in terms of international law, does not depend on recognition. Four of the homelands are now independent and possess all the formalities of independent statehood except recognition.[15]

Indigenous Peoples -- Indigenous peoples are the descendants of the inhabitants of territories now occupied (and usually dominated) by later settlers of a different culture. The definition also includes groups living in remote parts of a nation-state never settled by outsiders, but isolated from other major elements of the country's population. Usually, these indigenous people are the descendants of conquered populations. Usually, also, they are organized into tribal groupings, to the extent that they have not been assimilated into the rest of the population or to the extent they live in simpler, more primitive, separate social structures.

Discrimination -- Recognition, perception and identification of differences between people on racial, linguistic or other ethnic grounds and the provision of differential status, treatment, protection or penalty based on such differences, categorically rather than individually, either by a constitutional provision, act of parliament or government decree. There can, of course, be discrimination without any constitutional, legal or government input eg. the social discrimination practiced by the upper classes in India in the face of laws forbidding application of the caste

---

15. See: Convention on Rights and Duties of States, signed at Montev[illegible] December 1933. 49 Stat. 3097, T.S. 881, 165 L.N.T.S. 19. "Article 1: The state as a person of international law should possess the following qualifications: (a) a permanent population; (b) a defined territory; (c) government and (d) capacity to enter into relations with the other states." In every respect the national states of Venda, Transkei, Ciskei and Bobhuthatswana meet the foregoing requirements. Cf. O'Connell, D.P.: *International Law,* Vol. 1, 1970, 2nd. ed., p. 130 on the legal aspect of recognition.

system. Discrimination against women in British, American, South African, Australian and French Society. Often such collective social action carry as much weight as a law of parliament. Discrimination can be both positive i.e. protective, or negative i.e. injurious to the group concerned. In constitutional language differentiation is a better term to use in discussing the positive aspects of discrimination. The separate voters role for the native Fidjians on Fidji and for the Maoris in New Zealand is a differentiation which has brought both groups greater political power and other advantages, not less. On the other hand, the voteless black majority Hutu in Burundi are the victims not of differentiation but of discrimination against them by a black minority (the Watutsi) of different ethnic origin, and even of selective genocide.[16] I am using Burundi merely to illustrate that discrimination is not solely confined to a white-black political relationship but also occurs in black and brown societies. *Apartheid de jure* and *de facto* relationship is not confined to South Africa, it is visible and active in several African and Asian states, for example, the Sudan, most Muslim states, Madagascar (against the Merina people of the plateau) in Shri-Lanka (against the Tamils) in Egypt (against the Copts) in Mauritania (against the Blacks) In Burundi (against the Hutu) in Liberia (against the inland tribes) and Burma, against the Indians.[17]

Plural State or Society -- a country within whose internationally recognized boundaries live, on a permanent basis, different racial, linguistic, religious and ethnic groups, nationalities or communities and who find themselves within those borders not by choice but as a legacy of imperialism, colonialism or as result of big power geographical dispensations following major wars, eg. South Africa, Nigeria, Poland, Belgium, Sudan, South West Africa-Nambia, Israel, Cyprus, Yugoslavia.

These definitions shall avoid the ambiguity and vagueness

---

16. Glazer, K. and Possony, S.: Op. cit., p. 285 and Hunt, C.L. and Walker, L.: *Ethnic Dynamics,* The Dorsey Press, 1974, p. 199.

17. Glazer and Possony, op. cit., pp. 283-284.

which surrounds much constitutional interpretation. For example, the Indian constitution, which is one of the most explicit of all constitutional documents, has been difficult to apply, partially because of the vagueness of its terms. For example, frequent reference is made to the so-called ''backward classes'' which have been long neglected and must now be constitutionally protected. In Articles 15(4) and 340 of the Indian constitution the term would logically mean ''educationally'' backward. Elsewhere in the constitution ''backward classes'' carries the legal meaning of social or economic deprivation. There is even a ''Backward Classes Commission,'' which has been charged with developing criteria to determine which groups were ''backward'' and those entitled to receive aid. But the commission could not agree on any objective tests to define ''backwardness.'' Undoubtedly the caste characteristics of Indian life which are so pervasive warranted correction by means of a constitutional mandate, but terms such as ''backward classes'' obscure the real issues.

The definitions here should also advance discussions on group rights.

THE BIBLIOGRAPHY

The second major compilation was the bibliography.

I have read exhaustively. And the more I have read, the more I could have used the ''tip of the iceberg'' analogy. For I could not possibly prepare a comprehensive study discoursing comprehensively on the constitutional treatment of racial, religious, sex and ethnic discrimination. There is just too much. But what I did was to provide a sound foundation for everything which should be done in this area in the future. That is why the bibliography is so long. It is important to explain its nature.

Because there are so many references to two particular works, a ''short-cut'' citation has been utilized in this study.

For Blaustein, Albert P., and Gisbert H. Flanz, *Constitutions of the Countries of the World,* 15 volumes, Dobbs Ferry, New York, Oceana Publications, Inc., 1971 -- I refer merely to *Blaustein.*

For *Case Studies on Human Rights and Fundamental Freedoms*, William A. Veenhoven, Editor-in-Chief, 5 volumes, The Hague, Nijhoff, 1975; I use *Veenhoven.*

The bibliography is divided into five parts.

Part I lists those special sets, books, and articles which are most significant in understanding and working with the problems of race, religion and sex classifications in the world's constitutions. This is the "basic" or "select" library on the subject for basic research ahead.

Part II is an annotated bibliography of key materials *essential* to this study or to any study in this area. But while important, none of these items meets the test of being "basic." (All of the Part I materials have also been incorporated alphabetically into the Part II listing as well -- with the entries in capital letters).

Part III is a "Negative Bibliography," and a very unusual one. It is a contribution almost never found in studies of this type. In the process of doing legal research on such a broad topic as this, numerous entries in indexes and the bibliographies of others have necessarily been checked. Those listed in Part II have been found wanting; they have little value in so far as the objective of this book is concerned. In many other fields of research the works and essays listed in *Part III* may be of considerable significance but because they may appear attractice to subsequent research in the area which this book has covered, they are listed here as a caveat and time saver.

While the work of Professors Glazer and Possony (*Victims of Politics: The State of Human Rights*) are the most important ones currently available and essential reading to go with this study, *Part II* also lists the names of many books and articles which contribute significantly to obtaining a perspective of the extent of ethnic conflict and to evaluation of the various efforts (or lack of efforts) which have been made constitutionally, and on the level of state and provincial legislation, to accommodate group rights.

Among many outstanding publications listed in *Part II* is *The Anti-Slavery Reporter*, a periodical almost basic to any comprehensive study of racial, religious and sex discrimination. In the latter field *The Columbia Human Rights Law Review* recently devoted an entire issue to an international symposium on "Law and the Status of Women" covering 15 countries. To grasp the extent of ethnicity read Walker Connor's "Nation Building or Nation Destroying" in *World Politics.* In the field of languages there is Karl Deutsch's contribution "The Political Significance of Linguistic Conflicts" in *Multilingual Political Systems,* or Andre Donneur's *La Solution Territoriale au Probleme de Multilinguisme* in the same book. On a wider scale there is an excellent summary of comparative data on the world's constitutions in selected areas by Ivo Duchacek [*Power Maps: Comparative Politics of Constitutions*] though of only secondary value in a study on racial, religious and sex discrimination. Ethnicity is fully discussed from a sociological and policy view point by J. Clayden "The Transnational Protection of Minorities" in *The Canadian Yearbook of International Law.* To realise the extent to which ethnicity and group rights problems can lead to the violence there is Christopher Hewit's article "Majorities and Minorities: A Comparative Survey of Ethnic Violence" in *Annals of the American Academy of Political and Social Science.* An excellent bibliography of the sources for studies in African constitutionalism is that of Paul Karksson in *African Law Studies.* In the field of religion there is a good study on the problems and laws relating to religious freedom by McDougal, Laswell and Chen in *The Michigan Law Review.*

Part II also contains scores of first class essays dealing with individual countries where constitutional provision for group rights have been made or are being attempted eg. India, Belgium, the Lebanon, Cyprus, Yugoslavia, South Africa, Malaysia, the Philippines, Fidji, Spain, and the problems of national minorities in the Soviet Union, to name but a few. Some works go beyond a mere analysis of the problem and, like this book, propose new approaches, even solutions, often idealistically, such as Dunkwart Rustow's "Language, Nations and Democracy" in *Multilingual Political Systems* in which he postulates that for linguistic nationalism to succeed political boundaries must be reshaped to coincide with language boundaries. **Part I** is therefore for the overview, basic to all research in the field of group rights. **Part II** is for more specific research in select areas of the subject.

CHAPTER II
GENERAL INTRODUCTION

Seeking constitutional solutions or formulae for race, religious, ethnic and cultural conflict is to most scholars a vexing business.[18] In the late 1970's, this has become the most important of all challenges to the ingenuity of scholars in law, political science, history, sociology and their allied disciplines. Women's rights, too, have become a world wide concern.

This has become the era of ultra-nationalism as exemplified by events in Iran and of (national) identity. The age of colonialism is at an end. Each former colony has demanded (and has been given) the borders which had been claimed by the former occupying power. Namibia (South West Africa) is the last significant area in Africa awaiting independence.[19] The older nations at the same time have become no less nationalistic. There is no nation today, like the Germany and Korea of thirty-odd years ago, which would permit its partition: -- neither Cyprus, nor Ethiopia, nor Spain nor any other nation where separation would appear to be an acceptable solution to existing conflict to the governments concerned.

Nationalism has been buttressed by growing identity with or love for specific lands or territories. Five hundred thousand

18. Cf. Rabushka A. and Shepsle, K.: op. cit., p. 213.

19. The further segmentation of South Africa, the establishment of additional so called independent national states is continuing but these states have no support in any country abroad. This does not subtract from the merits of the argument that internal de-colonisation in South Africa has historical and legal precedents elsewhere in the world.

Cypriots are of Greek descent and only 120,000 have Turkish forbears. The "easy" solution would "appear" to be a population transfer, giving the Turkish Cypriots adequate funds to begin new lives in Turkey. But this is not to be. The ethnic Turks of Cyprus are Cypriots, not Turks; they will not forego their native land regardless of the sums which might be offered. Such a forced transfer was Stalin's solution to the Soviet nationalities problem, a brutal, but successful solution possible only in wartime. Instead, the Cypriot Turks in 1983 opted for an independent status in Eastern Cyprus and were immediately recognized by Turkey.

So, too, the Palestinians in Gaza and the so-called West Bank. Some 800,000 Jews left the greater "Arab nation" to settle in Israel. There was at the same time a displacement of 700,000 Arab "Palestinians." An agreed-upon population exchange would "appear" to be the simplest and most logical solution to the "Palestinian Problem." But that is also not to be. The Palestinians demand the specific lands they once occupied. Some dream of a solution through renewed warfare.

There is also at the same time -- encouraged by the studies of eminent scholars -- a growing awareness and recognition of ethnic and cultural identity. [20] The very definition of the concept of ethnicity is now the subject of much study. [21] The Catalans and Basques of Spain demand autonomy, Scotland and Wales are toying with devolution; there is a strong separation movement in Quebec, Corsica, The Azores, etc. The Kurds of Iraq seek statehood; the native Fijians join to resist the Indian majority of Fiji; Malaysia's ethnic Chinese want guarantees from the Malay majority, many in Assam would like to see that state secede from India, etc.

---

20. See for example: Van Dyke, Vernon: "The Individual The State and Ethnic Communities in Political Theory," *World Politics,* Princeton University Press, pp. 344-369. Also Moynihan P. and Glazer, Nathan: *Ethnicity,* Harvard University Press, 1976 and Connor, Walker: "Nation Building or Nation Destroying," *World Politics,* Vol. 34, 1972.

21. See Isajiw, Wsevolod W.: "Definitions of Ethnicity" in *Ethnicity,* Vol. I, 1974, pp. 111-124.

There is also a fast-growing women's movement, demanding equal rights in what has been and continues to be a male-dominated world.[22]

All of this could have only one result: internal conflict. Not conflict in progressive, homogeneous Denmark, perhaps; not conflict in all-white, all-Catholic, all Spanish-speaking Costa Rica, perhaps. But conflict which affects a majority of the world's population -- the people who live in the plural societies, i.e. in the multi-racial, multi-lingual, multi-ethnic states.

Conflict has not been confined to those areas such as the Lebanon where common sense indicates that the ultra-disparate nature of the various ethnic and religious groups are almost guaranteed to produce strife. It also happened in the tiniest of states. During the late seventies Britain granted independence to the Gilbert and Ellice Islands Colony, which most university students in political science will have great difficulty in locating on the map. Before independence the islands split into separate dependent territories. With independence in 1978 and 1979 they became the microstates of Tuvalu and Kiribati respectively. The main reason for this ''separate development'' was because the population of Kiribati is Micronesian and the population of Tuvalu is Polynesian.[23] This makes the South African government's reasons for separate states for the various black peoples in that area appear highly respectable. Differences in race, religion, customs, culture, religion and social structure are infinitely more compelling reasons for separation of states. If the Micronesians had been black and the Polynesians white, or the Polynesians Hebrew speaking and the Micronesians Arabs their reasons for separation would have begun to approach the depth of the problem in South Africa.

Of course, there is still a minority who profess the Jeffersonian

---

22. Cf. Glaser, K. and Possony, S.: *Victims of Politics,* New York, Columbia University Press, 1979, p. 261.

23. For more details on colonial entities consult Blaustein, A.P. and Blaustein, E.B.: *Constitutions of Dependencies and Special Sovereignties,* 6 Vols., 1975–.

view of government as best which governs least. They would argue that racial justice, religious freedom and cultural identity do not require government interference. But this is a small minority indeed. Should the state not be seen as the best legalk source for the protection of group rights, not as the chief threat to rights.?[24]

Thus, the task of accommodating ethnic and cultural rights and demands, while preserving the status quo of group or national identity, means a search for constitutional solutions, perhaps even constitutional legerdemain. Failure to achieve the proper constitutional responses means another Lebanon, another Ethiopia, another Cyprus. This is perhaps what the Zulu chief Gatsha Buthelezi is trying to impress upon whites in South Africa.

More than anyone else South Africa with its plural society should study the constitutional pattern of other nations to review and analyze all provisions dealing with the rights of racial, linguistic, ethnic and cultural minorities. There can be much to learn. In future discussions on accommodating the various peoples of South Africa, politically, culturally or socially, it will be the rights of *groups,* whether they be racial, sexual, religious or linguistic that will be the main talking point. Economically, the word is already out -- free enterprise -- the integration of the economically active population regulated by free market forces will become the order of the day. Only the intellectually (and politically) dishonest will maintain that government policy under Mr. P.W. Botha is still vigorously directed towards implementing the Verwoerdian concept of *grand apartheid* i.e. political independence for each of the black nations each in his own geographically consolidated homeland with economic interdependence in a common market. The grand concept was abandoned overnight after his predecessor's departure in 1979. Economic integration and political accommodation in a form yet to be fully spelled out is now the ultimate goal. For future's sake, such a policy begs a careful look at *group rights* since the Zulus, numerically and

---

24. Cf. Van Dyke, V.: "Human Rights and the Rights of Groups," *American Journal of Political Science,* Vol. 18, 1974, pp. 725-741.

politically the most powerful of the Black nations, flatly refuse to accept independence (a) on principle (b) in a homeland fragmented into a dozen areas.

Understanding and solving group rights is a problem that cannot be tackled without a proper knowledge of that subject. All too long group rights have been neglected by politicians and constitutionalists who, as a result of their education and both legal and liberal academic tradition, have emphasized (at least in the West) the formulation of constitutional mandates or individual rights as the basic statements on the rights of man. This liberal conception argues Professor Vernon van Dyke, is unduly limited.[25] It follows that this calls for corrective action and (as my study of the subject and of the 157 existing constitutions of the world also show) *group rights are really more important than individual rights when it comes to causing or preventing human conflict and in settling significant political or ideological disputes.*

Researchers have pointed out that out of 164 significant violent conflicts involving states between 1958-1976 a mere 15 were military conflicts, the most significant violence after 1945 has found its *casus belli* in ethnic disputes.[26] Greeley concluded that the conflicts that have occupied mankind over the past three decades "have had precious little to do with ideological divisions . . . the principle conflicts are not ideological but tribal."[27]

We live in a world of plural societies. For even the most homogeneous nations of the world have a group called women whose claims of rights are often in conflict with the power establishment. The ideal constitution for the plural society should therefore incorporate provisions on group rights, both to protect and safeguard race, religious, sex, ethnic, linguistic and cultural rights and to foster their development and growth. There is even

25. "The Individual, The State and Ethnic Communities in Political Theory," in *World Politics,* p. 343.

26. Said, A.A. and Simmons, L.R.: eds. *Ethnicity in International Context,* Transaction Books, New Brunswick, New Jersey, 1976, p. 16.

27. Greeley, A.: "The Rediscovery of Diversity," *The Antioch Review,* Fall, 1971, p. 343.

much to argue that groups, ethnic communities, have a morally justifiable claim to such protection.[28] While it is true that many of the world's 159 constitutions do indeed make provision for group rights (as will be amply illustrated), such formulations are all too often absent, inappropriate or poorly phrased or left to government at state level, eg. in India.

Such conclusions lead inevitably to recommendations for more work and more efforts on the subject. This calls first for a concerted public information and public relations program -- including instruction at the universities -- to create an awareness of the plural society-group rights situation. This should have a three pronged objective: (1) to create an awareness of each nation's own minorities, groups or other ethnic problems; (2) to create an awareness of the scope of such problems in other nations; and (3) to create an awareness of *comparative* discrimination -- an appreciation of the degree to which group rights are safe-guarded and fostered in other nation-states.

This must in turn be followed by more study, research and reports. Yet to be organized for research are the electoral laws, statutes, administrative dictates and judicial decisions on group rights. Yet to be organized are university courses on the subject. And finally must come case studies on the efficacy of group rights efforts which will point up the direction for further efforts.

To understand these conclusions and recommendations, it is necessary to explore and explain the history and literature on *les droits de l'hommes.* It must be emphasized at the outset that the recognition of individual human rights has had an impressive history in the western world,[29] which has been taught to and received at least the lip-service approval of the Third World.[30]

---

28. Cf. Ginsberg, Morris: *On Justice in Society,* Ithaca, Cornell University Press, 1965, and Van Dyke, V.: "Justice as Fairness for Groups," *American Political Science Review,* Vol. 69, 1975, pp. 607-614.

29. Cf. Claude, R.P.: op. cit., pp. 7-39.

30. Ernest Lefever in "Limits of Government in the Third World," Nic Rhoodie, Editor, op. cit., p. 21 advance the thesis that Western style democracy has not only failed to take root but will not succeed in future either.

There is no similar history cum literature for the concepts of group rights to meet the needs of a world driven by racial, religious, ethnic, linguistic, cultural and caste divisions, at the same time besieged by a womankind moved by a heightened awareness of their common concerns and natural rights.

While the *idea* of individual human rights has had an impressive history, it is, in terms of constitutional law, only of recent development in the long span of human development. Constitutionally speaking it is but 200 years old, dating from the American and French Revolutions which proclaimed liberty as the common property of the entire citizenry. [31] The American Revolution was fought in the name of Americans as individuals, resisting the control of a distant sovereign. When, in 1791, they came to frame their Bill of Rights, they were formulating protections against their new sovereign -- the government which they themselves had just created. These rights which they insisted upon were protections of individual expression in writing, speaking, assembling, praying, etc. They sought individual security against the instrumentalities of their state in the form of due process of law, right to counsel, open trials and trial by jury. The French Revolution went a step further using the protections of individual human rights to destroy the feudal institutions which controlled society. [32]

The American and French concepts of individual rights are based on the philosophies of Locke, Rousseau and Jefferson and such intellectual heirs as Tom Paine, author of *The Rights of Man.* The fact that their works were studied and argued by the men who made the American and French Revolutions is only one reason for the acceptance and development of the individual rights approach. Also important was the concurrent development of a new economic structure, built on the ruins of feudalism. That system was capitalism, a system which encouraged the growth of a highly individualistic middle class which soon assumed the reins of

---

31. See A.J. Carlyle, *Political Liberty, a History of the Conception in the Middle Ages and Modern Times,* Oxford University Press, Oxford, 1963.

32. Cf. F.L. Huillier, "Histoire et droits de l'Homme" 6 *Revue des Droits de l'Homme* 81 (1973).

government. Those nations which first experienced the simultaneous collapse of feudalism and the rise of capitalism were the first to put provisions on individual human rights into their constitutions: France in 1791, followed by the Netherlands in 1798, Belgium in 1831, and Switzerland and Italy in 1848. Constitutions as documents derive their form and characteristics from the same period that witnessed the birth of the political and legal culture of the capitalist bourgeois era.[33]

With the Russian Revolution of 1917 came another economic system and with it another constitutional approach to the rights of man. The constitutionalists of communism promulgated provisions on socio-economic rights -- which are fundamentally collectivist and therefore anti-individualistic.[34]

By way of illustration: The French Declaration of the Rights of Man and Citizen, 1789, proclaimed on behalf of individual rights that ''property being a sacred and inviolable right, no one can be deprived of it, unless a legally established public necessity evidently demands it, under the condition of a just and prior indemnity.''[35] On the other hand, the collectivist model, the Soviet Constitution of 1936, provides for a state ''network of sanatoriums, holiday homes and clubs for the accommodation of working people.''[36]

Collectivist concepts, in terms of socio-economic rights have not been restricted to the left. The Spanish Labor Charter, passed by the Franco regime, proclaimed that ''the state shall enter the social sphere with the resolve to place wealth at the service of the Spanish people and to subordinate its economy to this purpose.[37] Ironically, the Spanish Basic Law also entitled each worker ''to a

---

33. Cf. Carl J. Friedrich. ''Political Theory of New Democratic Constitutions,'' in Arnold J. Zurcher, ed. *Constitutions and Constitutional Trends Since World War II*, New York University Press, New York, 1951.

34. Article 17.

35. Article 119.

36. Van Marseveen, H. and van der Tang, G.: op. cit., p. 3.

37. Fuero del Trabajo 1938/1947, Part I, converted into the Basic Law of Spain by a referendum in 1947.

yearly holiday with full pay to enable him to take a well-earned rest,'' at institutions to be established by the state.[38]

The Universal Declaration of Human Rights in 1948 -- whose drafting was dominated by Mrs. Eleonor Roosevelt and her egocentric, American-oriented view of the world -- was the last important constitutional document to preach the philosophy of individual human rights. True, it does recognize socio-economic rights. It does provide in Article 25 that ''everyone has the right to a standard of living adequate for the health and well-being of himself and of his family.'' But it does not spell out state responsibility.

A clear formulation of cultural rights has had to await the International Covenant on Economic, Social and Cultural Rights which went into effect on March 23, 1976.

One reason for the growing recognition of group rights has been the growing acceptance of state responsibility. Even highly capitalist West Germany places ''marriage and the family under the special protection of the State.''[39] Note also that the constitutions of both Catholic Ireland[40] and Catholic Venezuela[41] have placed the power of the state behind Motherhood and the Family, based at least in part upon the social doctrines of two papal encyclicals which are somewhat critical of capitalism and individualism.[42]

A more important reason for the constitutional recognition of group rights has been the population composition of the 84 nations which have attained independence since World War II. The chronological checklist begins with Lebanon in 1943. India was no. 7 in 1947; Indonesia was no. 15 in 1949; Malaysia was no. 21 in 1957; Cyprus was no. 35 in 1960; Nigeria was no. 39 in 1960, etc.,

38. Part II (5).

39. Bonn Basic Law, Article 6.

40. Irish Constitution of 1937, Article 41.

41. Constitution of Venezuela, Article 74.

42. *Rerum Novarum* (1891) and *Quadragesimo Anno* (1931).

etc. For these new nations, the concepts of individual rights as inherited from the west and/or the concept of social rights as inherited from the east were not enough. For these new nations have been plural societies. They have been divided from within by ancient rivalries of race, religion, tribe, caste, language and culture, and often adhered to customs which consigned women to a special status in society. They required new formulations of rights if only to hold their fragile governments together. And the legal rights which were incorporated into their constitutions were group rights in which communities were seen as units.[43] Fiji is a prime example. Britain assumed the existence of three communities in Fiji and in the constitution of the political right of the individual is to participate in selecting those who represent, not individuals, but the community.[44]

The failures of their constitutional formulations have far exceeded their successes. Lebanon, Cyprus and Nigeria are prime examples of plural societies which could not survive under their constitutional structure. Indonesia has suffered through revolution and dictatorship; Malaysia and Singapore broke up their union; etc.[45] India's patchwork quilt constitution, already amended 42 times, is a sad example of moderate, perhaps even questionable success.

This is not to say that the plural society with its constitutional recognition of group rights is only a post-World War II phenomenon. Belgium, South Africa, Czechoslovakia and Yugoslavia are the prime examples of multi-racial, multi-ethnic, multi-linguistic societies with long histories of constitutional revision designed to reconcile the inevitably conflicting peoples within their borders. Significantly, however, the important constitutional developments are of recent origin.

It is less than a decade ago that Belgium, which had one of the

---

43. Cf. Van Dyke, V.: "One Man One Vote and Majority Rule as Human Rights," *Revue des Droits de l'Homme,* Vol. 6, Nos. 3-4, 1973, pp. 456-458.

44. Great Britain. *Fiji Independence Order,* 1970, Articles 45 and 68.

45. Cf. Van der Kroef, Justus: "Patterns of Intergroup Accommodation in South East Asia: Is Democratic Pluralism Possible?" in Rhoodie, Nic: op. cit., pp. 143-171.

world's first constitutions, finally promulgated a system of group rights to reconcile its Flemish-Protestant-poor population with its French-Catholic-prosperous citizenry. The 1971 Belgian constitution actually has a Flemish elected parliamentary caucus to legislate on cultural matters affecting the Flemish community and a French elected parliamentary caucus to legislate on French cultural matters. [46]

South Africa's latest constitution, promulgated in 1961, is now being revised, and so is Yugoslavia's latest constitution, dated 1974. And if Czechoslovakia's 1960 constitution is not being revised to change the group rights provisions designed to reconcile group conflict, it is only because there are no rights and there is no conflict permitted in a rigid, totalitarian communist society.

This new recognition of group rights has even caused some nations belatedly to recognize the fact that they are indeed plural societies. The end of Franco's Fascism has freed Spain's Basque and Catalan populations to assert their "differences," and has resulted in Madrid's recognition of the plural nature of the country. The result is an ongoing process of constitutional revision in which autonomy is being accorded to linguistic groups within the state. [47] Canada is also struggling with the framing of its new constitution, largely because the French speaking majority of Quebec is now asserting its linguistic rights. [48]

---

46. The Constitution states that Belgium comprises four linguistic regions: the French, the Dutch, the German and the bilingual region of Brussels (Heading I, Article 36). Three cultural communities are also recognized, each having significant powers vested in it (Heading II, Article 6b). Linguistic groups can make delaying motions in the parliament when, in the view of three-fourths of the members of the linguistic group, a proposed bill is of such a nature as to have a serious effect on the relations between communities (Heading III, Chapter I, Article 38). This power is in addition to the powers of linguistic groups within the parliament to legislate for their linguistic region.

47. For an excellent review of Spanish Basque ethnicity cf. Greenwood, D.J., "Continuity in Change, Spanish Basque Ethnicity as a Historical Process," in Esman, Milton, J.: op. cit., pp. 81-102.

48. Brazeau, J. and Cloutier, E.: "Interethnic relations and their issue in Canada," in Esman, Milton, J.: op. cit., pp. 204-227.

Switzerland is the only plural society which has a long-term constitution which can be described as a success. Short term successes are Austria and the Netherlands.[49]

The violent demonstrations in Belgium during 1982-1983 demonstrated the enormity of Britain's failure to recognize that Belgium was not one country inhabited by one people but a plural society of two different peoples. The Nationalist Volksunie Party in Flanders are fond of saying that "nations are made up of peoples and states are nothing but fantasies."[50]

The state of Belgium was forged by the British in 1830 not because of a desire on the part of the people but to serve Britain as a buffer against French expansionism. Its very existence served only British interests while creating a shotgun wedding between two distinct cultures, the Flemish speaking people and the French speaking Walloons.[51] The selfish attitude of Britain (repeated in dozens of other areas of the world, notably Africa,) created a problem for the state of Belgium which may end up in Belgium becoming the first European state since World War II to self destruct. In fact, tensions over the long and arduous battle to reach the present constitutional compromise between the Flemish and the Walloons were responsible for bringing down every government in Belgium between 1968-1980. Many scients will say: We told you so. The political theorists in white South Africa hardly command the ear and attention of the West which seems to believe that because South Africa practises ethnic discrimination, they are unable to grasp the roots of ethnic strife elsewhere. In fact these same theorists have always maintained that the natural community in which the individual can enjoy the maximum individual freedom is in the ethnic community. Because Belgium did not elect separate political development from day one, the present conflict has left the King reigning, in name only, over the state of Belgium. The current race towards a loose federation may very well end up into complete separation in the next ten years. Currently the

49. Lijphart, A.: *Democracy in Plural Societies,* Yale University Press, 1977, p. 2.

50 *The Atlanta Journal and Constitution,* June 26, 1983, 4-D, Col. 3.

51. Hunt, C.L. and Walker, L.: op. cit., pp. 26-31.

national government exercises enough power to maintain Belgium as an economic unit but it is no longer a cultural entity. Up to World War II French speaking population dominated the impoverished Dutch speaking Flemish. Now the tables have been turned. And ethnic arguments now embrace cultural self-determination and even secession.

What has gone wrong? Can the plural society solve its group rights problems by itself? What prescriptions can one expect from the outside?

What has been wrong in the first place is the failure to recognize the extent of group rights problems and issues. Britain did not do so in 1830 in Belgium and up to World War II, the French speaking element in Belgium also failed to see the dangers. How foolish today seem Sekou Toure's words at the time of Guinea's independence in 1958: ". . . in three or four years, no one will remember the tribal, ethnic or religious rivalries which, in the recent past, caused so much damage to our country and its population." [52] But it takes little wisdom, with the 20-20 vision of hindsight, to label Sekou Toure as foolish for failing to recognize the extent of differences within his nation back in 1958. In fact, he was no more foolish than those who wrote the constitutions of Ethiopia, Cyprus, Belgium and a hundred other states.

The prophecies of eminent scholars of the past two decades on the inevitability of the process of political integration and the weakness of ethnicity appear equally foolish when compared to modern trends where human rights in its perfect ideal manisfestation seems to demand a multiplication of micro-states. Today's thesis is that the greater the degree of autonomy the greater the extent of human rights with the proviso that human rights be viewed primarily as group rights. [53] Only 25 years ago experts

52. Sekou Toure, *Towards Full Reafricanization* Presence Africaine, Paris, 1959, p. 28.

53. Blaustein, Albert P.: "The New Nationalism," op. cit. Cf. Elie Kedourie (Professor of Politics at London School of Economics) in "The New Nationalism: Conflicts and Hopes," *Britanica Book of the Year,* 1978, pp. 24-29.

supported the statements of scholars such as Robert E. Park when he said that "In the relations of races . . . accommodations and eventual assimilation is apparently progressive and irreversible . . . the resulting changes assume the character of cosmic process."[54] Other scholars such as D.J. Grove even called this the most famous and influential statement on the assimilation of racial groups.[55] Some 25 years later others still made the same mistake. Cynthia H. Enloe wrote that religion, familialism, ethnicity were all obstacles which curb progress and blind individuals to their true capacities. "Groups founded on ethnic allegiance compete with the nation state and is intolerable because the nation state is the principal vehicle for development."[56] Precisely the opposite appears to be true and by 1978 the Declaration on Race and Racial Prejudice unanimously approved by UNESCO on November 29, 1978, even coupled group rights demands with self-determination and supported ethnic group rights provided they are not racially discriminatory.[57]

Today the task of evaluating group conflict is too important to be left exclusively to a nation's political leadership or any political group within the nation. The task is also too important to be solved by those who are emotionally involved and who are struggling for power and position. Those on the inside cannot see the forest for the trees, like the cuckolded husband, they are the last to know. Rhodesia (now Zimbabwe) is a good example of a state which did not timeously recognize the extent of its group rights problems. Its constitutional draftsmen (mostly British) were so busy trying to reconcile the minority rights of its white population that it ignored the long-standing tribal confrontations between and among its

---

54. Park, R.E.: *Race and Culture,* 1950, p. 150.

55. Grove, D.J.: *The Race Versus Ethnic Debate: A Cross National Analysis of Two Theoretical Approaches,* 1974, p. 4.

56. Enloe, C.H.: *Ethnic Conflict and Political Development,* 1973, pp. 261-262.

57. Other UN documents taking up this line are Capotorti F.: *Study of the Rights of Persons Belonging to Ethnic, Religious and Linguistic Minorities,* June 20, 1977, E/CN4/Sub. 2/384 and Cristescu, A.: *Historical and Current Developments of the Right to Self-Determination,* July 3, 1978, E/CN/4/Sub. 2/404.

black majority. Yes, it was taking the obvious steps to assure recognition of the group rights of its Matabele and Shona populations; but it neglected the specific rights of the Karanga, the largest of the Shona tribes.

Certainly, no one in authority in Kenya will listen to recommendations for group rights guarantees which can be incorporated into that nation's constitution today -- as long as its political establishment is tribally based.

Iran was another nation in need of an outsider. For this was another country where so many minority rights were solely dependent upon the life of its ruler.

In South Africa, ever in the world limelight, a dispensation decided upon at party political or cabinet level is no longer practical politics nor, in the long run, physically possible. The governing National Party's followers (but not the leaders) are still convinced that politics, as defined by the white man, will determine the state of affairs in the future. Perhaps. But more and more white Afrikaners are beginning to believe that eventually, and not in two decades, but in the present one, a new constitutional dispensation will have to be worked out, one in which all other ethnic communities, nationalities and races will have to participate, as *groups. Group rights* of Whites, non-Homeland Blacks, Coloureds, and Indians will then be the dominating consideration. This book is written as a guide to future conferences and is also intended, beyond the important academic objectives, to prove to white South Africans (and the world) that they are not unique, no worse, no better, than any other race, nation or ethnic community in their struggle to safeguard their identity. The crucial question is: How will they go about settling this crisis of identity?

The plural society cannot solve its group rights problems by itself. For even where group conflict is recognized, passions run so high that the rights which give rise to that conflict are denied. Clear thinking is at a premium. The person who is his own lawyer has a fool for a client.

To its credit, the government of Mr. P.W. Botha in white ruled South Africa, asked the opinion of at least certain other racial groups in the preparation of the new constitution for 1984 and elicited the support of private enterprise in its drive towards a better economic and political relationship between South Africa and the other states of Southern Africa. But while seeking the opinion of select groups the advisers and the decision makers remained party political men, and herein lies a great weakness.

Only an outsider can possess the perception that Cyprus is a multi-racial society whose constitution must be built on the basis of a Cypriot identity and include integrative features. Tensions and passions are so strong that internal leaders refuse to recognize the fact that constitution mandated parallel societies will not work. Only outsiders, acting as arbitrators as well as advisers can effect constitutional reconciliation.

Detachment, i.e., lack of emotional involvement, is not the only attribute of the constitutional adviser. More is involved than the "subordination of 'primordial sentiments' to the requirements of civil politics."[58] What the informed constitutional adviser also possesses is a philosophy of group rights, a theoretical foundation for group rights analysis. He will not be guilty of the *ad hoc* formulation which merely responds to group rights pressure. Because he possesses a philosophy, he has perspective.

The constitutional adviser(s) also possess the appropriate constitutional tools. He can bring all of the precedents to the constitutional conference. He (they) will know what has been written on a given subject in all of the other constitutions and which of the various formulations have been effective. They will know whether the ends can best be accomplished by specific precepts or by general statements subject to judicial dictates. They

58. Clifford Geertz, "The Integrative Revolution," in Clifford Geertz, ed. *Old Societies and New States: The Quest for Modernity in Asia and Africa*, Free Press of Glencoe, New York, 1963, pp. 105-107.

will know whether a given objective is best accomplished by inclusion in a bill of rights, or in an article on education, on voting, or by making it a non-amendable provision.

There is, of course, no one prescription. Just as no two plural societies are exactly alike, so no group rights formulations can be exactly alike.

No one electoral system is preferable to another and according to most scholars fair representation in a plural society is a difficult problem from any angle. [59]

There is no constitutional science. But there is a constitutional art, almost a technology, which can be practiced by those who are knowledgeable about constitutions and who recognize that group rights today are even more important than individual rights.

To a certain extent this study is unfortunately 15-20 years too late. It should have been a product of the early 1960's when it (and comparable studies) could have provided comparative guidelines for the new constitutions of the Third World.

For this is a study of constitutional provisions which could have provided new constitutional framers with the ideas, approaches, and even words for the constitutions they were drafting. Alas, such information was conspicuous by its absence in the preparation of most of the constitutions of most of the countries which came into being in the era which followed World War II.

Many of the constitutions of the new states were drafted by scholars in London and Paris; but more often they give the appearance of having been composed by second-level civil servants. And words are repeated in constitutions designed to

59. Cf. Laponce, J.A.: "The Protection of Minorities by the Electoral System," *Western Political Quarterly,* Vol. 10, No. 2, June 1957, pp. 318-339 and MacKenzie, W.J.: "Representation in Plural Societies," *Political Studies,* Vol. 2, No. 1, February 1954, pp. 54-69.

meet the needs of very different countries.

The situation which existed in India is unique; there was a history, an adequate amount of time and a more than adequate supply of lawyers and other would-be constitution writers to prepare a constitution draft with notes on precedents.[60]

But perhaps this study, while late, is yet timely.

For there are still new countries being formed and some existing countries (old ones like New Zealand, Oman and new ones like Djibouti) which do not have formal, one-document constitutions. And, of course, constitutions are being revised all the time.

It is particularly regretable that some of the lessons of this study could not have been conveyed to those who in early 1978 were preparing a constitutional settlement for Rhodesia/Zimbabwe. Perhaps there are lessons which can be incorporated into the future constitution of Namibia, of Angola and Mocambique, liberated of its hard-line Marxist political clique and whose notion of democracy is imposed by its real masters, the Soviet Union. Perhaps even for white ruled South Africa.

Learning about the realities of racial, religious, sex, and ethnic discrimination via a study of constitutional provisions is frustrating in several respects:

a. The first frustration is the obvious one. How can anyone ascribe the meaning or importance of a constitutional provision if it is not followed in practice? Let us use India for illustrative purposes. For India has, by far, the longest constitution of any in the world and the one which devotes most attention to problems of discrimination.

Article 17 of the Indian Constitution abolished "Untouchabil-

60. See, for example, the text of the Indian Draft Constitution of October, 1947, prepared by the "Constitutional Adviser." This is published in Vol. III, starting at p. iii, of *The Framing of India's Constitution*, published by The Indian Institute of Public Administration in New Delhi. B. Shiva Rao was chairman of the committee preparing this five-volume set.

ity,'' but there are still nearly 120 million persons who are in one way or another considered Untouchables and mistreated as such.[61]

b. No matter how carefully one reads and studies the world's constitutions, it is inevitable that some things will be missed. Again, India provides a useful example. Paragraph V of list III of the Seventh Schedule reads as follows: ''Marriage and divorce; infants and minors; adoptions; wills; intestacy, and succession; joint family and partition; all matters in respect of which parties in judicial proceedings were immediately before the commencement of this Constitution subject to their personal law.''

It is pursuant to this vital provision that family and property laws of Hindus and Muslims are governed by their respective religious laws. The key words are ''personal law'' covering matters of inheritance and large areas of contract law.

c. Constitutional provisions, even where self-executing and even where they are supported by the vast majority of the population, do not have full meaning in the absence of judicial analysis, which goes far beyond the scope of this study. Again, one can use India by way of illustration.

One of the bedrock provisions of the Indian Constitution is Article 46. It reads: ''The State shall promote with special care the educational and economic interests of the weaker sections of the people, and, in particular, of the Scheduled Castes and the Scheduled Tribes, and shall protect them from social injustice and all forms of exploitation.''

Pursuant to this provision, the then State of Madras apportioned seats in its medical and engineering colleges in accordance with the formula which provided quotas for Non-Brahmin Hindus, Backward Hindus, Brahmins, Harifans, Muslims, and Anglo-

61. Cf. Isaacs, H.R.: "The Ex-Untouchables," in Mahar, J.M. ed., *The Untouchables in Contemporary India*, University of Arizona Press, Tucson, 1972, p. 392.

Indians and Indian Christians. Based on purely academic qualifications, a certain Brahmin student would have been admitted, but admission was denied because of the quota system. The claim of the protesting student charged a violation of Article 29 (2) which provides that "No citizen shall be denied admission into any educational institution maintained by the State or receiving aid out of State funds on grounds only of religion, race, caste, language, or any of them."

The student won. The Supreme Court found that admission had been denied solely on the basis of her caste. It concluded that "the right to get admission into any educational institution (covered by Article 29[2]) is a right which an individual citizen has as a citizen and not as a member of any community or class of citizens." [62]

This was an important case, the culmination of a series on preference quotas in education and employment. Significantly, it was overturned within two months by the Constitution (First Amendment) Act, 1951. Among the provisions of that amendment was a new Article 15 (4) which read: "Nothing in this article or in clause (2) of Article 29 shall prevent the State from making any special provision for the advancement of any socially and educationally backward classes of citizens or for the Scheduled Castes and the Scheduled Tribes."

Granted, India has the most complicated assortment of constitutional provisions on this subject, and, granted again, India has the most complicated case law analyzing its constitutional structure. Yet the problem is not confined to India. And, as previously pointed out, a comprehensive analysis of the judicial relationship is beyond the scope of this study.

d. The more comprehensive the study of constitutional responses to discrimination, the more the researcher realizes the need for follow-up studies of national legislation on this subject. Constitutional provisions tend to be overbroad. Further, they are

---

62. *State of Madras v. Champakam Dorairajan,* A.I.R. 1951 S.C. 226, 1951 S.C.J. 313, 315.

usually not self-executing. This means that one must examine the legislative formulation in order to give meaning to what the constitution ostensibly provides.

In addition, many countries eschew constitutional formulations in setting forth specific policies involving racial, religious, sex and ethnic classifications. A good many of these, for example, are provided for in election laws. It would be literally impossible to count the vast number of these which exist in the complicated Indian structure. But perhaps the best illustration is provided by Iran under the Shah.

Based on population considerations alone, the non-Muslims of Iran would certainly not have any representation in its parliament. Yet since 1909, there have been a series of electoral laws providing that the tiny Jewish, Christian and Zoroastrian minorities have parliamentary representation. This aspect, too, is not covered in this study but the reader is referred to the massive and excellent world wide survey *Case Studies in Human Rights* published by Nijhof in Holland and to Glaser and Possony's first class work *Victims of Politics* as, currently, essential reading on the abuse of constitutions and legislation. [63] It is also realized that in one party states, or dictatorships, constitutional and legal prescriptions are at the mercy of the ruling party of the dictator. Problems of racial, religious, sex and other ethnic discrimination and classification cannot be met (let alone solved) by constitutional provisions directed specifically to an outlawing of inequality or mandates to advance the cause of the downtrodden. Nor can the problems be met by legislative or judicial amplification specifically directed to these issues.

The point is that group, religious, ethnic, etc. problems can sometimes best be solved by constitutional provisions which have nothing to do with human rights, legal guarantees or the language of equality. Indirect methods may prove most effective. A good

---

63. 5 Volumes, Marthinus Nijhof, The Hague, 1975 and Columbia University Press, New York, 1979 respectively.

example of this can be found in the Constitution of the United States, ratified in 1789. And references are made to it because this is the oldest of all modern constitutions and set the model for so many others. The reference which is important is Article V which reads as follows:

> The Congress, whenever two-thirds of both houses shall deem it necessary, shall propose amendments to this Constitution, or on the application of the legislatures of two-thirds of the several States, shall call a convention for proposing amendments, which, in either case, shall be valid to all intents and purposes, as part of this Constitution, when ratified by the legislatures of three-fourths of the several States, or by conventions in three-fourths thereof, as the one or the other mode of ratification may be proposed by the Congress, provided that no amendment which may be made prior to the year one thousand eight hundred and eight shall in any manner affect the first and fourth clauses in the Ninth Section of the First Article; and that no State, without its consent, shall be deprived of its equal suffrage in the Senate.

This is the prototype of similar constitutions which specify in advance those sections of the constitution which may not be amended. Note how the last clause precludes any governmental action, by amendment or otherwise, to change the system which has existed since 1789 of having the same number of senators from each state. This despite the fact that California's population is past the 25 million mark, and Wyoming's population totals a scant 300 thousand. Similar entrenched provisions may give substantial protection to minority groups in other nations. [64]

Constitutional formulations prohibiting amendments or delaying powers to amend or establishing some clauses as more

64. The now obsolete clause relating to amendments prior to 1808 was an early limitation denying congressional power to prohibit the importation of slaves until that date.

fundamental than others can all be used to thwart discrimination or to give appropriate effect to group rights. Similarly, depending upon the population structure of a nation, a percentage requirement for amendments or legislation may have the same effect.

This might also be accomplished by judicial mandate. Again, India provides an example. *Golak Nath v. State of Punjab*, A.I.R. 1967 A.C. 1643, is the principle case. Here the majority concluded that "henceforward" fundamental rights could not be curtailed by constitutional amendment. The court took the position that Article 368, concerned with constitutional amendments, was not the source of the amending power; it merely prescribed amending procedures. On the other hand, since the fundamental rights in the constitution were "inalienable," "transcendental" and "supreme," their abridgement was beyond the reach of any amending power. True, this is no longer the law of India. The 24th, 25th, and 26th Amendments of 1971 essentially overturned the *Golak Nath* case. And the validity of the amendments was sustained in a 10 to 3 overruling of *Golak Nath* in Kesavananda v. State of Kerala, A.I.R. 1973, S.C. 1461.

This final point suggests that provisions safeguarding various group rights may not always appear on the surface of the constitutional text. Subtle and indirect approaches may achieve more lasting success. It also suggests that some constitutional protections of group rights may have escaped the research net because of the hidden character of the provisions. I and my research assistants have combed as carefully through these texts as time would allow and believe that all of the critical provisions have been identified, isolated, and examined.

PART II

GROUP PATTERNS

CHAPTER III

INSTITUTIONAL ARRANGEMENTS

Institutional means for coping with diversity within a nation are virtually the same thing as means for the protection of group rights. Such devices as federalism, proportional representation, party competition and executive or legislative guarantees to particular groups have all been used as structural restraints upon popular majorities to protect the minority groups within a society. And so, to a greater or lesser extent, have there been measures which might lead to or facilitate the establishment of a *confiliation,* discussed in some detail in Part IV of the conclusion. Constitutional provisions, incorporating some of these features, have been used in many nations to safeguard the rights of religious groups, racial and ethnic minorities, and even women. No study of comparative constitutions could fail to take note of these arrangements, for they provide a fund of constitutional experience (both good and bad) for constitution drafters and for scholars in law, political science, anthropology, sociology, etc.

How group rights are managed, arranged and institutionalized depends to a considerable degree upon how the minority perceives its situation and the likelihood of obtaining its goals. The minorities may aspire to assimilation, separation or recognition of their special status. Physical factors such as size, location and concentration are also significant. Then there is the attitude of the dominant group; it may be tolerant of minorities (e.g. Thailand) or it may seek to dominate them. For cleavages between minorities and majorities are different in each nation and methods of accommodating these differences are profoundly dissimilar. To match a constitutional arrangement to the peculiar needs of a nation requires a skill at social engineering which is rarely encountered. What we need to know is why institutional arrangements work and why they do not. A comparative study of constitutions can assist in that quest; but it cannot yield all the answers.

FEDERALISM

Federalism is the most familiar means of promoting subnational diversity within a complex or multinational state. Federal states divide political power territorially, usually with spheres of responsibility defined in a written constitution. The national and sub-national units of government are "within a sphere, co-ordinate and independent," and neither government can "alter the scope of the other's power as laid down by the constitution." [1] Only 21 of the world's constitutions, however, are explicitly federal, and federalism is by no means a high barrier to national majorities aiming to restrict group rights. There are many multinational states, Belgium, South Africa, and Indonesia, for example, which prefer alternatives to federalism. Yet federalism remains a favored, long-time institutional technique for safeguarding group rights, even if some groups who have shared such experience (e.g., the French leadership in Quebec and the Biafrans of 1967-69) might prefer breaking up a federation arrangement in order to establish a separate nation-state for its group.

Federal states with internal territorial divisions corresponding closely to major ethnic, linguistic, and religious groupings are

---

1. K.C. Wheare: *Federal Government,* Oxford University Press, 1964, pp. 10 and 16.

rather rare. The Soviet Union, Yugoslavia, Czechoslovakia, Switzerland, Burma and Nigeria are the leading examples. Czechoslovakia became a federal system composed of the Czech and Slovak Republics by modifying its 1960 constitution in an amendment of January 1, 1969. The national legislature of Czechoslovakia is a bicameral federal Assembly. In the lower house, the Czechs have a majority based upon their greater numbers in the population than the Slovaks, Hungarians and other minority groups. The upper house, the Chamber of Nationalities, gives equal representation to the Czech Republic and the Slovak Republic, an institutional arrangement which gives legislative strength to the Slovaks who, in fact, are outnumbered by the Czechs 9.5 million to 4 million. The Swiss, Russian, Yugoslavian and Nigerian federal systems are commented upon in greater detail in the later chapter on "National Patterns."

All federal systems express diversity in the organization of their legislatures. Almost all are bicameral, with one of the chambers representing territorial subdivisions. Their model, of course, is the Constitution of the United States, which is composed of two houses of virtually coequal power. The members of the Senate originally were selected by their respective state legislatures but are now chosen by the voters of an entire state.[2] And the Senate does possess certain powers not conferred upon the other house, most notably the powers to ratify treaties and to confirm presidential appointments. Since each American state is guaranteed two senators, regardless of population,[3] the less populous areas have been given power equal to that of the more populous areas in Senate representation and voting. Alaska's 300,000 population has the same Senate representation as California's twenty-five million plus. However, in America the state boundaries were never drawn to coincide with religious, ethnic or racial patterns of distribution. A contrary philosophy guided the establishment of the cantonal boundaries of Switzerland. As a result the Swiss

2. U.S. Constitution, Amendment XVII (1913).

3. U.S. Constitution, Article I, Section 3 and Article V.

Council of States, unlike the United States Senate, represents real differences of religion, culture and language in that multinational society.

There are other federations with bicameral legislatures which do not provide for equality between the two houses. This is the situation in West Germany, India and Canada where the upper houses are politically inferior. In both India and Canada, the upper house has only a suspensive veto; new laws may be passed without its approval. In federal states employing cabinet systems of government, the lower house is the only chamber which can unseat a ministry, again underscoring the inequality of the two houses. The institutional arrangements which make an upper house inferior weaken the rights of minority groups. The French-Canadian experience provides a graphic example.

Few nations have attempted to federalize the executive branch of government. Yugoslavia, however, has recently adopted some measures to accomplish this below the presidential level. Switzerland has long indulged in the constitutional practice of always including at least one Italian-speaking member and one French-speaking member in its seven-person national council (cabinet). The 1965 Tanzanian Constitution provided for two Vice-Presidents, one of whom was designated as president of Zanzibar.[4] More experimentation along these lines would be fruitful in states with powerful executives.

Some constitution-makers, stopping short of creating a full-fledged federal system, have preferred to carve out regions within a country which would be awarded semi-autonomous powers. Italy is the best example. The Italian constitution of 1947 divided the country into twenty regions, with enumerated regional powers.[5] Taxing and other financial powers were authorized in each of the areas.[6] But the federal central government kept its

4. However, Zanzibar lacks a parliament and independent judges.

5. Constitution of Italy, Article 117 (1947).

6. *Id.*, Article 119 (1947).

prefects in each province, just as in the non-federal states. These prefects and the regional commissioners were given broad powers to suspend acts of the regional councils and had the authority to dissolve the regional legislative council and call for new elections in certain circumstances. Small wonder that Italian regional differences remain a source of friction under this peculiar division of national and regional powers.

Few states have gone as far as Burma in accommodating constituent nationalities. The first constitution of Burma (1947) identified specified nationality groups and assigned a fixed number of parliamentary representatives for each of them. As a result, the non-Burmese ethnic groups obtained a clear guaranteed majority in the upper house of the legislature. This constitutional arrangement at first won much praise for its role in preserving national unity. However, some fifteen years later, the constitutional guarantees were in shreds. When *Time Magazine* (April 9, 1965) made a survey of discrimination and discord in Asia it found that religious hatred and racial discrimination had reached new heights. The editors concluded that hatred among peoples in Asia, and Burma was quoted as an example, represented the greatest single cause of turmoil in Asia. The magazine had pointed out in an earlier survey (July 17, 1964) that during that year nearly 900,000 people had fled across national borders to escape religious persecution in Pakistan and in India. The worst fate, however, befell the Indians in Burma. When Premier Ne Win turned Burma into a one party state that year and began his drive towards socialism in Burma all Indians who had no citizenship were thrown out of the country. At the airports and dockyards Indian women were stripped of their jewelry and Hindu women forced to give up their *mangal sutra* necklaces, worn as a symbol of marriage. A decade later the situation repeated itself. Mid 1978 some 200,000 Muslims fled to Bangladesh because of Burmese persecution and discrimination. Burma claimed that the Muslim leaders were actively working to establish the Arakan region as a separate Islamic state.

PROPORTIONAL REPRESENTATION

A second favored institutional arrangement for protecting group rights is proportional representation in the national election system. The Weimar Republic constitution in pre-Hitler Germany pioneered the concept of incorporating group representation into fundamental law. Article 17 of the Weimar constitution provided that every state legislature should be "elected in universal, equal, direct and secret elections by all male and female citizens in accordance with the principles of proportional representation." In spite of the unhappy results of proportional representation in Weimar Germany, the West German Basic Law retained, in part, a system of proportional representation for members of its lower house. The East German Constitution of 1949 provides for proportional representation both in its legislature and cabinet, but the significance of such provisions in a communist dictatorship is minimal.

Mexico, a nation long dominated by a single party, the Institutional Revolutionary Party (PRI), has also constitutionally adopted a modified and limited version of proportional representation. The 1963 amendments to the Mexican constitution provide for some minor representation for national parties other than the PRI which have not obtained a majority in at least twenty electoral districts. The provision authorizes legislative seats for so-called "party deputies" in addition to seats for deputies who obtained majority victories in their electoral districts.

OTHER INSTITUTIONAL ARRANGEMENTS

There are other institutional techniques for responding to group rights which are examined in the country-by-country "National Patterns" analysis. But it must be emphasized at this point that no particular arrangement has proved superior to any other. Nor has any institutional technique been discredited or proved unworkable. While federalism has been an accepted approach since 1789, few nations have developed truly federal constitutions.

Proportional representation, a nineteenth century invention, is often discussed and advocated -- but has been incorporated into few constitutions. Before examining other techniques, it must also be pointed out that some states, such as Yugoslavia, India and Malaysia are still experimenting with a whole series of differing constitutional arrangements. It is these variations which are more interesting than any particular technique and which call for careful examination.

There are notable examples of extremely detailed institutional arrangements designed to deal with extremely sensitive social problems. For example, one must cite the "delicate" Lebanese technique designed to protect both the Christian and Muslim communities in that troubled nation during the 1950's and 60's. There were in Lebanon at that time 11 Christian communities, including an Armenian community. There were three different Muslim groups. And there was a Jewish community. In addition, the population included Palestinian refugees who were not granted Lebanese citizenship because their naturalization would have disturbed the delicate equilibrium among the older groups. The political system was in part based upon the concept of proportionate representation set forth in Article 95 of the constitution. Beyond the constitution, however, was an unwritten Pacte Nationale, agreed upon by the leaders of both the Muslim and Christian communities. Under this agreement, seats in parliament were divided among the various communities, with each election district allocated a predetermined seat according to religious persuasion. [7] Thus, in the five election districts of the city of Tripolis, there were four Muslim Sunnite seats and one Greek Orthodox seat. Voters had to choose one of the various religious representatives who were running, even if they themselves did not share the religion of their assigned representative.

---

7. Described in United Nations: *Human Rights Yearbook of the United Nations,* 1950, p. 186. Cf. Glazer and Possony, op. cit., p. 309.

The communal proportional representation system prescribed by Article 95 of the constitution carried over to non-elective offices as well. Within the bureaucracy and in almost every sector of national life, each of the religious-based communities was given formal or informal quotas. This complicated system, going so far beyond the traditional proportional voting systems, was the foundation of the precarious Lebanese political situation which eventually collapsed in 1976-77. The Lebanese experience points up the weakness and fragility of over-elaborate institutional arrangements designed to preserve a multiplicity of different customs, habits and rights of minorities.

Separate electoral rolls for each racial or ethnic entity and separate blocs of seats for a particular group are also favored means to provide communal representation. The Cyprus Constitution is another good example of separate electoral rolls for communal candidates. New Zealand has had such a system for its Maori indigenous minority since 1867 (76 ordinary seats for non-Maoris and four seats for Maoris). In India 15 percent of its parliamentary seats are continually reserved until 1985; 77 seats of the 522 seat total have been so reserved for the untouchables. Fiji also have separate rolls and separate seats.

Singapore, in a 1973 act which supplements its constitution, has developed an unusual arrangement to preserve the rights of its varied population. A special presidential council for minority rights has been established.[8] This council has the general function of considering and reporting on any matters touching upon the rights of any racial or religious community in this city-state. The council has the power to examine any existing law or proposed law to determine whether it is a ''differentiating measure.'' (This is defined as ''any measure which is or is likely in its practical application to be, disadvantageous to persons of any racial or religious community and not equally disadvantageous to persons of other such communities. . .'') Bills containing such

8. Section 81A., Constitutional Act of Singapore (1973).

differentiating features (as found by the council) must be discussed in the light of such features. Legislation may be delayed on that basis, and passage of a bill may even require a special two-thirds vote as a result. The mere discovery and mention of differentiating features may cause a bill to be withdrawn or changed. This presidential council is an unusual constitutional device, grafted onto the normal legislative process in such a way as to give weight and significance to minority feelings.

Many other ingenious constitutional arrangements can be found. Few are as complex as the Cyprus constitutional arrangement. This troubled island is split between two cultures and two religions. The constitution is a prime example of constitutional manipulation to preserve group rights. It is doubtful whether the constitution can endure. It will certainly have to be revised if the 1983 unilateral declaration of independence by the Cypriot Turks in the north survives.

In Cyprus, the numerical relationship between the Greek majority and the Turkish minority is approximately seven to three. Under the now almost defunct 1959 constitution, a presidential system was established with a Greek president and a Turkish vice president, each having veto power over major laws concerning foreign affairs, defense and security. The constitution provided for a six-to-four ratio of Greeks to Turks in the Cypriot army, and a seven-to-three ratio in the police force, in Parliament, and in the cabinet. In addition, one of the three key ministries Defense, Finance, and Foreign Affairs was always to be held by a Turk. The social system collapsed when fighting broke out in 1963, partly as a result of the proposal by the Greek president (President Makarios) to change the constitution. The Turkish minority feared for its rights. Yet, the constitution of 1950 continued to function, albeit in a limited fashion, until the Turkish sector seceded in 1983.

So rigid was the constitutional division between the Greek and Turkish communities that special constitutional provisions of intermarriage between spouses from each community were made.[9] The president of the House of Representatives must be Greek and the Vice-President a Turk.[10] Committee assignments are based upon nationality.[11] Schoolmasters, professors and clergymen must be hired with a view to proper representation in these professions for Greeks and Turks.[12] The Supreme Court consists of a Greek, a Turk, and a neutral judge who is president of the court.[13] Locating any neutrals on an island constitutionally split into two unequal parts would be hard. The Cyprus crisis highlighted the dangers of a power sharing system between numerically unequal partners.

RESTRICTING GROUP RIGHTS

One approach to the restriction of group rights, in the guise of preserving internal disintegration, is by restraining dissidents through constitutional fiat. For example, Article 51 of the 1963 Senegal Constitution prohibits regionalist propaganda or particularist or ethnic propaganda. Similar provisions are to be found in Chad[14] and the Ivory Coast[15] , and many other countries have likewise experimented with this kind of constitutional approach. In and of themselves such provisions seem an exercise in futility. No more feeble institutional arrangement can be imagined for dealing with minority rights. The 1964 constitution of Chad was abrogated in 1975 by the Malloun government and replaced with another constitution in 1978 of a provisional nature. Plans for a new constitution in 1980 were delayed indefinitely as result of war.

Fiji provides a graphic illustration of a constitutional attempt to discourage an important component group within a multi-ethnic state. While Article 32 of Fiji's constitution seems superficially to be no more than an effort to guarantee parliamentary representa-

9. Articles 111 and 22, Constitution of Cyprus.

10. Article 72.

11. Article 73.

12. Article 108.

13. Article 133.

14. Preamble, Chad Constitution.

15. Article 6, Constitution of the Ivory Coast.

tion to Fijians, Indians and those who are neither Indians or Fijians, it really does much more. Indians (descendents of imported laborers) constitute 51 percent of the population. Yet they are assigned the same number of seats in the lower house as Fijians who comprise 43 percent of the population. Europeans, who constitute only one percent of the population, together with the remaining five percent of the population, are given eight seats. This arrangement discriminates against Indians and their group rights. Fijians are also given a dominant position in the Senate. These provisions reflect a widespread fear of Indian influence in politics, stemming from the rapid growth of the Indian population and from the recognition of the hard-working qualities of the Indians. The constitutional arrangement keeps the Fijians in permanent control of the country as long as their alliance with the prosperous European community continue. The amendment procedure laid down in the constitution makes it impossible to change the representation scheme without the consent of the Fijians.[16] Very often the political arrangements prescribed by the constitution makes it impossible for groups or individuals to enjoy even basic rights. Mali's new "democratic" constitution of June 19, 1979 stated explicitly that the country remains a one-party state.

USE OF THE AMENDING PROCESS

A very useful constitutional arrangement in the process of preserving group rights is achieved through restrictions on the amending process. Selected constitutional provisions can be accorded a special significance, elevating them to a plane above the other parts of the constitution. As such they cannot be affected by the usual amending process and are either inviolate or subject to amendment by an exceptional majority. In Algeria the provisions regarding religion cannot be amended.[17] In the

16. Article 68(1) and (2), Constitution of Fiji.
17. Article 195, Constitution of Algeria (1976).

United States no state may have its boundaries changed by constitutional amendment, since its consent to such a change is required.[18] The rights of Mexican citizens cannot be restricted or suspended without special constitutional measures.[19] Tribal trust lands could not be infringed without satisfying the special provisions of the old Rhodesian constitution.[20]

The device of making a section of the constitution unamendable or of making it amendable only under special voting arrangements reveals the high priority of the values represented by some portions of a constitution. One example is the protection provided to the two major language groups in South Africa, Afrikaans and English. The Republic of South Africa Constitution Act of 1961 did not introduce any fundamental changes compared to the South African Act of 1909. The South Africa Act could be altered in any way by a majority in Parliament by ordinary legislative procedure with the exception of the sovereignty of Parliament itself, the franchise arrangements in the Cape Province and the protection of the two languages as official languages. These were known as the ''entrenched'' clauses which required a two-thirds majority of both Houses of Parliament (the Legislative Assembly and the Senate) in joint session. There is, of course, a risk in making such a rigid provision. The risk is that the constitution itself may have to be discarded before major changes in government can be made.

Another example is the protection of the lands of the indigenous population of Kiribati which became independent in 1979. Kiribati was formerly known as the Gilbert Islands -- a British protectorate, which explains why its constitution is at the same time the U.K. Kiribati Independence Order. The Order includes entrenched provisions to safeguard individual and land rights for the Barnabans who are defined as persons whose ancestors were born in Kiribati before 1900.

18. Article IV, Section 4, United States Constitution.

19. Article 1, Mexican Constitution.

20. Article 80(1) (b), Constitution of Rhodesia (1969).

CHAPTER IV

POLICIES AND CONSTITUTIONAL PRINCIPLES

Central to understanding of American constitutional law is the concept that fundamental rights and principles are enforceable in a court of law. And this is a widely-followed concept. Constitutional Act No. 3 of Chile, which was promulgated on September 11, 1976, carries this theme to its logical conclusion. While Chapter I of this act (following the pattern of most constitutions) provides a list of constitutional rights and guarantees, Chapter II is concerned with procedural remedies, giving everyone direct access to a Court of Appeals for the violation of any Chapter I rights.

But there is another type of constitutional pattern and formulation which is used to promote equality in matters dealing with race, religion and sex in which the courts play no role. In those constitutions which have developed such formulations there is a reference to "principles" rather than "rights."

Because such statements of "principles" are so little known to the constitutional lawyers of the West and because these have been discussed in such detail in the constitutional literature of India, many scholars have mistakenly classified them as Indian in origin.

But their beginnings are found in the 1937 Constitution of Ireland. This is freely acknowledged in the draft Constitution of

India prepared by the designated constitutional advisor. And not surprisingly, these principles appear also in the constitutions of Pakistan, Bangladesh, Sri Lanka, and Burma.

These lists of "principles" do not always bear the same title, but they have the same function. They are those "principles" which the State is directed to follow not only in achieving equality before the law, but in advancing group recognition and group rights.

Here are the names which have been given to the sets of "principles" in the five constitutions noted:

Ireland. 1937. Article 45. *Directive Principles of Social Policy.*

Republic of India. 1949. (As amended 1976). Article 36 to 51. *Directive Principles of State Policy.*

Islamic Republic of Pakistan. 1973. Articles 29 to 40. *Principles of Policy.*

Peoples Republic of Bangladesh. 1972. Articles 8 to 25. *Fundamental Principles of State Policy.*

Republic of Sri Lanka. 1972. Article 16 and 17. *Principles of State Policy.*

As pointed out in the Irish Constitution, these "principles" are designed for general guidance "and shall not be cognisable by any Court under any of the provisions of this Constitution." Here is the language of Article 37 of the Indian Constitution: "The provisions contained in this Part shall not be enforceable by any court, but the principles therein laid down are nevertheless fundamental in the governance of the country and it shall be the duty of the State to apply these principles in making laws."

And here is how it is restated in Article 8 (2) in the Constitution of Bangladesh. "The principles set out in this Part shall be fundamental to the governance of Bangladesh, shall be applied by the State in the making of laws, shall be a guide to the interpretation of the constitution and of the other laws of Bangladesh, and shall form the basis of the other laws of Bangladesh, and shall form the basis of the work of the State and of its citizens, but shall not be judicially enforceable."

These "principles" are thus designed to guide the executive, legislators and administrators in the making, interpreting and applying the law.

But to what ends?

The Irish provisions are the least detailed. They speak in terms of promoting the welfare "of the whole people." And about "a social order" of "justice and charity." More specifically, the State is instructed to "direct its policy toward securing" equal rights for women.

Article 39 of the Indian constitution speaks in greater detail about equality for women and continues with provisions on the right to work, the right to an education, the right to a living wage, etc. The best known article in this part of the constitution is Article 46, calling for affirmative action, which will be discussed in detail under Affirmative Action in II B. This Article reads as follows: "The State shall promote with special care the educational and economic interests of the weaker sections of the people, and, in particular, of the Scheduled Castes and the Scheduled Tribes, and shall protect them from social injustice and all forms of exploitation."

Pakistan's principles of policy are dominated by provisions encouraging the promotion of the Islamic way of life, such as those set forth in Article 31. There is, however, Article 33, calling upon the State to "discourage parochial, racial, tribal, sectarian and provincial prejudices among the citizens." Article 38 then calls upon the State to take other action to "secure the well-being of the people irrespective of sex, caste, creed, or race."

In language which reflects its Soviet influence, the fundamental principles of state policy of the Bangladesh Constitution emphasize the protection of the people from economic exploitation and pledges the State to "endeavor to ensure equality of opportunity to all citizens.'' (Article 19). Constitutional provisions dealing with discrimination on grounds of religion, race, caste, sex or place of birth are found in Articles 28 and 29 in the ''Fundamental Rights'' section.

The new Constitution of Sri Lanka also contains language based on the language of Soviet economic rights. But two provisions in the *Principles of State Policy* in Article 16 are applicable here. They are as follows: ''The State shall assist the development of the cultures and the languages of the people,'' and ''The State shall endeavor to create the necessary economic and social environment to enable people of all religious faiths to make a living reality of their religious principles.''

Sometimes the constitutional principles consist of pure ideology. For example the 1978 Constitution for China (containing 60 articles compared to the 30 of the 1975 constitution) identifies China as ''. . a socialist state under the dictatorship of the proletariat.''

The new 1980 constitution of Cape Verde Islands declares Cape Verde to be ''a sovereign, democratic, unitary, anti-colonialist and anti-imperialist republic'' -- the sort of language usually associated with editorials in *Pravda*, the official Communist newspaper published in Moscow. Mocambiques most recent constitution, adopted on August 14, 1978, sets as national objective ''. . . the construction of the material and ideological basis for a socialist society.'' On December 18, 1980, the National Assembly of Vietnam approved a new constitutional law defining the socialist republic as ''a state of proletarian dictatorship'' and identifies the Communist Party as ''the only force leading the state and society.''

CHAPTER V

AFFIRMATIVE ACTION

"Affirmative Action" is a code word. It is a symbol. An Americanism. Logically, the phrase has no place in the English language. Whoever heard of "negative action"? Yet, we all know what these words portend. We are all aware of the symbolic meaning of the phrase.

But there is a counterphrase which conveys the same meaning -- from the opposite point of view. And that phrase is "reverse discrimination".

But whether it is called affirmative action, positive discrimination (as it was known in Rhodesia -- Zimbabwe), or reverse discrimination, it plays an important role in the constitution framework of many nations. Many nations do see affirmative action provisions as a solution (or at least a partial solution) to problems of racial, religious, sex and ethnic discrimination, including the uplifting of backward peoples. Certainly, affirmative action has accomplished much to these ends. Just as certainly, however, it has created problems. And the first of these problems is the fact that affirmative action provisions are a necessary denial of the concept of equality, repeated over and over again in constitution after constitution. On January 15, 1978 Ecuador by referendum approved a new constitution which not only established a framework for social rights, but extended the vote to the illiterates. The vote of one illiterate mountain farmer cancelled the vote of the Head of the Department of Law at the University of Ecuador.

There is nothing new about the concept of affirmative action. Inequality may not be eliminated simply by acting to remove discrimination. But the banning of discrimination may be inadequate to remove the "badges of inferiority". Positive governmental and private action may be necessary to promote fair treatment of disadvantaged groups. The oldest example is found in the Swiss constitutional provision of 1874 (as amended) which states in Article 34 that "the Confederation shall institute maternity insurance by means of legislation." This concept is expanded in the Sri Lanka constitution which further protects women by providing that civil service positions may be reserved "for members of either sex." Thus, in the name of equality, women may be assured certain job preferences.

Preferential treatment on the basis of affirmative action principles may be offensive to other groups. In India in March, 1978, mass protests against the reserving of local government jobs for untouchables became quite violent. Resentment against special treatment for minority groups in America is also quite extensive. Public opinion polls in the United States show that almost 80 percent of those polled opposed affirmative action-type programs. A majority of Blacks oppose affirmative action. Some see in this action the spectre of "preferential treatment" for Blacks to right past wrongs. A veritable Pandora's box.

The most significant aspect of affirmative action from my point of view is that affirmative action rights are plainly and openly **group rights**. It is because of the disadvantaged position of women, Blacks, Hispanics, untouchables or other minority groups that special preferences are provided. Entitlement to an affirmative action right is based upon group membership. Quotas and other special arrangements are group-based. The majority is, in effect, discriminated against on behalf of members of the disadvantaged group. Moreover, individual rights and questions of individual merit are irrelevant to the concept of affirmative action, although some members of the disadvantaged may fare better than others in obtaining the benefits. Finally, the definition of the group is critical. Whether poor people, old people, this tribe of Indians or that tribe is entitled to affirmative action treatment is not objectively known in advance. The group members are entitled to affirmative action only after a constitution or a statute establishes their eligibility for special treatment.

Affirmative action programs seem to run counter to the formal principle of equal treatment under the law. The Rhodesian Declaration of Rights (1969) expressly recognized this inconsistency. Article ten, section two provided that "different treatment of persons or communities is warranted if such treatment is fair and will promote harmonious relations between such persons or communities by making due allowance for economic, social or cultural differences between them." Some constitutions even go so far as to engraft affirmative action ideas side by side with declarations of equal treatment. Yet the Rhodesian language clearly stated the problem and gave a sensible justification for enequal treatment though that does not justify negative unequal treatment, such as suppression of Blacks, only positive unequal treatment, to promote their interests .

The special problem of reverse discrimination was crystallized in the United States Supreme Court case of *Regents of the University of California v. Allan Bakke.* The case involved a 37 year-old white male applicant for admission to the medical school of the University of California at Davis. Alleging that his denial was based solely upon the fact that he was a member of the Caucasian race in violation of the Fourteenth Amendment to the U.S. Constitution, Bakke challenged the validity of an affirmative action admission program, "voluntarily" undertaken by the University of California in order to remedy the effects of past racial discrimination upon minority group applicants to the medical school.

The Bakke case was the most significant case in American race relations since the 1954 desegregation case, *Brown* v. *Board of Education.* The notion that a majority group member can successfully claim racial discrimination because minority group members enjoyed a special preference is difficult and vexing for American authorities. Many state and federal affirmative action plans do serve to advance the interest of minorities because of their disadvantages as members of a deprived group. Whether the equal protection clause of the Fourteenth Amendment to the U.S. Constitution bars institutions of higher learning from giving special preferences because of race was the immediate issue in the *Bakke* case. But how much of the superstructure of affirmative action programs will remain in the wake of *Bakke* and later decisions remains to be seen. In any event, the American constitutional provision intended to end race discrimination may be seen to prohibit some forms of positive as well as negative discrimination.

"All persons are equal before the law and entitled to the equal protection of the law." So reads Article 8 (1) of the Malaysian Constitution. And here is the wording of Article 26 of the 1975 constitution of one of the world's newest states -- in Africa: "All citizens of the People's Republic of Mozambique enjoy the same rights and are subject to the same duties, irrespective of colour, race, sex, ethnic origin, place of birth, religion, level of education, social position or occupation." From another part of the world, Latin America, is the following from Article 37 of a new 1974 constitutional revision. "All Nicaraguans are equal before the law. In Nicaragua privilege by reason of birth, social condition or race, or for any reason other than capacity of virtue, is not recognized."

Do the affirmative action provisions violate these equality provisions? Before answering, one should examine the particular provisions of Articles 8 (2) and 8 (3) of the Malaysian Constitution. The key words are set in italics.

(2) Except as expressly authorised by this Constitution,

there shall be *no discrimination against citizens* on the ground only of religion, race, descent or place of birth in any law or in the appointment to any office or in the administration of any law relating to the acquisition, holding or disposition of the property or the establishing or carrying on of any trade, business, profession, vocation or employment.

(3) There shall be *no discrimination in favor of any person* on the ground that he is a subject of the Ruler of any State.

The various constitutions themselves apparently find no contradiction between the general provisions on equality and the special statements on affirmative action. For example, Article 9 (5) explains that Article 8 does not invalidate or prohibit.

(c) any provision for the protection, well-being or advancement of the aboriginal peoples of the Malay Peninsula (including the reservation of land) or the reservation to aborigines of a reasonable proportion of suitable positions in the public service; . . .

Similarly, examine the language from Articles 25 and 26 of the Fundamental Rights of the Pakistan Constitution of 1973.

25. (1) All citizens are equal before law and are entitled to equal protection of law.

(2) There shall be no discrimination on the basis of sex alone.

(3) Nothing in this Article shall prevent the State from making any special provision for the protection of women and children.

26. (1) In respect of access to places of public entertainment or resort, not intended for religious purposes only, there shall be no discrimination against any citizen on the ground only of race, religion, caste, sex, residence or place of birth.

(2) Nothing in clause (1) shall prevent the State

from making any special provision for women and children.

Judicial reconciliation of the conflict between "equality" and "affirmative action" is found in a number of Indian cases. At issue in one case was Section 15 (1) and 15 (4), the latter having been added to the constitution by the First Amendment Act of 1951. Also involved were Article 14, Article 29 (2) and the affirmative action provisions of Section 16 (4). These read as follows:

> 14. The State shall not deny to any person equality before the law or the equal protection of the laws within the territory of India.
>
> 15. (1) The State shall not discriminate against any citizen on grounds only of religion, race, caste, sex, place of birth or any of them.
>
> (4) Nothing in this article or in clause (2) of article 29 shall prevent the State from making any special provision for the advancement of any socially and educationally backward classes of citizens or for the Scheduled Castes and the Scheduled Tribes.
>
> 29. (2) No citizen shall be denied admission into any educational institution maintained by the State or receiving aid out of State funds on grounds only of religion, race, caste, language or any of them.
>
> 16. (4) Nothing in this article shall prevent the State from making any provision for the reservation of appointments or posts in favour of any backward class of citizens which, in the opinion of the State, is not adequately represented in the services under the State.

Here is how Professor Galanter explains the legal analysis.

> Proceeding from the notion that Articles 15 (4) and 16 (4) are provisions of a special and exceptional character, rather than principles that can be given general operation, the Court finds these provisions should not be read as com-

pletely excluding or ignoring the fundamental rights of all citizens. It characterized the purpose of these special provisions not merely as conferring special privileges on the backward, but as serving the interests of the whole society by promoting the advancement of its weakest elements. Thus, any scheme for preference can be weighed in terms of the interests of the whole society. In considering reservations in institutions of higher education, it is necessary then, to balance the policy of advancing the backward against the national interest in the full utilization of talent. Lowering of the quality of graduates, says the Court, is the 'inevitable consequence of reservation.' But the need for technical, scientific and academic personnel 'is so great that it would cause grave prejudice to national interests if considerations of merit are completely excluded by wholesale reservation of seats in all technical, medical, or engineering colleges or institutions of that kind. Thus, special provisions for the backward must be 'within reasonable limits': 'the interests of the weaker sections of society which are a first charge on the States and the Centre have to be adjusted with the interests of the community as a whole.' [21]

Thus, the argument for reconciliation of this apparent conflict comes when the special provisions for disadvantaged peoples are not permitted, in Professor Galanter's words, "to hamper unduly other important national interests." [22]

Another problem with affirmative action programs is that they institutionalize segregation. Again people who make and interpret constitutions are faced with a problem in semantics. In modern terminology, "integration" is a desirable objective. At the same time, however, Americans who advocate integration tend to be in

---

21. Galanter, Marc: "Equality and Preferential Treatment: Constitutional Limits and Judicial Control," 14 *Indian Yearbook of International Affairs 257,* pp. 260-261.

22. Id. at p. 257.

the forefront of those denying either the desirability or the reality of the "melting pot." Adherents of group rights throughout the world are naturally opposed to the old American dream of a melting pot. But that does not mean necessarily that they support a constitutional framework which institutionalizes segregation.

In Chapter 2 of his work on the general subject, Professor Galanter explains some of the debate on Article 15. As originally promulgated, it did provide that "(3) Nothing in this article shall prevent the State from making any special provision for women and children." But, as explained by Professor Galanter,

> Professor K.T. Shah's proposal to amend Article 15 to allow the state to make special provision for the "advantage, safeguard, or betterment" of the Scheduled Castes and Scheduled Tribes was rejected by the Assembly. 7 CAD NO JPALC 665, 664. Dr. B.R. Ambedkar, chairman of the Drafting Committee, opposed the amendment as providing an opening for segregated facilities. 7 CAD 661. It should be noted that the Shah amendment is narrower in scope than Article 15 (4), which applies to Backward Classes as well as Scheduled Castes and Scheduled Tribes. [23]

A third serious problem which arises from affirmative action provisions is that they encourage "backwardness." India again provides an excellent example -- especially in the analysis of the caste situation. The language of V.K. Thiruvenkata Chari on this point is pertinent:

> **Caste.** The Preamble speaks of equality of status and opportunity and Article 46 specially refers to the promotion of educational and economic interests of the weaker sections of the people, and in particular of the scheduled castes and the scheduled tribles. The State is to protect them from social injustice and all forms of exploitation. Article 17 provides that 'untouchability' is abolished and its

---

23. Galanter, Marc: *Competing Equalities: The Indian Experiment with Compensatory Discrimination,* 1978, Chapter 2, note 25.

practice in any form is forbidden. Article 340 provided the appointment by the President of a Commission to investigate the conditions of socially and educationally backward classes and to make recommendations. The Report of the Backward Classes Commission (1956) is in the writer's opinion a major blow to the growth of democracy in India. The caste system has been the bane of Indian politics and untouchability the final disgrace. The election law makes it a corrupt practice to make systematic appeals to vote or refrain from voting on ground of caste, race, community or religion. But adult suffrage has by itself exaggerated the influence of caste, as political parties with an eye on success at the polls tend to choose candidates belonging to the predominant caste or sub-caste in the particular electorate. The Constitution exempts from the equality of Article 14 "any special provision for the advancement of any socially and educationally backward classes of citizens." The result has been a race for each sub-caste among the Hindus to claim that it is a backward class. It has been estimated that in the list compiled by the Commission, scheduled castes and backward castes form a list of 2,399 communities, out of which 913 alone account for a population of about 11.51 crores. Such a report points to the general backwardness of the whole country, but also by its lists creates privilege lobbies based on religious sub-castes.[24]

As noted in Part II, Chapter II, dealing with principles and policies, the most important affirmative action provision is India's Article 46. It reads as follows:

> Promotion of educational and economic interest of Scheduled Castes, Scheduled Tribes and other weaker sections.

24. Chari, V.K. Thiruvenkata: "The Courts and the Constitution in India." In R.N. Spann, editor, *Constitutionalism in Asia,* Asia Publishers, New York, 1965, p. 44.

The State shall promote with special care the educational and economic interests of the weaker sections of the people, and, in particular, of the Scheduled Castes and the Scheduled Tribes, and shall protect them from social injustice and all forms of exploitations.

But because it was enacted as a matter of principle and policy, it may not be enforced directly by the courts. This is the major criticism of this and similar articles which are set forth in similar policy sections of, for example, the constitutions of Pakistan and Bangladesh. For despite Article 17 on the abolition of Untouchability, the situation still exists. Article 46 should have been a part of the "Fundamental Rights" part of the constitution and an amendment to that effect should have been promulgated. The leadership of the untouchables argues that the preferences inherent in Article 46 should be used to encourage integration rather than to protect and preserve group rights. Dr. B.J. Borale argues, for example, not only for the compulsory admission of members of Scheduled Castes and Scheduled Tribes to student bodies, but also quotas to insure representation of such individuals on faculties.[25]

Most of the affirmative action provisions in the world's constitutions deal with special rights for women, but many go much further.

Here, for example, under Fundamental Rights, is Article 28, Sections 1 and 4 of the 1972 Constitution of Bangladesh: "(1) The state shall not discriminate against any citizen on grounds only of religion, race, caste, sex or place of birth. (4) Nothing in this article shall prevent the State from making special provision in favour of women or children or for the advancement of any backward section

25. For background material on Dr. P.T. Borale's position, together with his general discussion on advancing the cause of the Scheduled Castes and Scheduled Tribes, see his major work, *Segregation and Desegregation in India,* Bombay, Manaktalas, 1968. This work also seeks to demonstrate a relationship between the problems of the Untouchable in India with the problems of the Black man in America.

of citizens.'' And this must be supplemented by Article 29, which is also included among the Fundamental Rights. It reads as follows:

> 29. (1) There shall be equality of opportunity for all citizens in respect of employment or office in the service of the Republic.
>
> (2) No citizen shall, on grounds only of religion, race, caste, sex or place of birth, be ineligible for, or discriminated against in respect of, any employment or office in the service of the Republic.
>
> (3) Nothing in this article shall prevent the State from -
>
> (a) making special provision in favour of any backward section of citizens for the purpose of securing their adequate representation in the service of the Republic;
>
> (b) giving effect to any law which makes provision for reserving appointments relating to any religious or denominational institution to persons of that religion or denomination;
>
> (c) reserving members of one sex any class of employment or office on the ground that it is considered by its nature to be unsuited to members of the opposite sex.

See also Article 23 which was promulgated as one of the Fundamental Principles of State Policy.

> 23. The state shall adopt measures to conserve the cultural traditions and heritage of the people, and so to foster and improve the national language, literature and the arts that all sections of the people are afforded the opportunity to contribute towards and to participate in the enrichment of the national culture.

Pakistan has many similar provisions in its current 1973 Constitution, but most of these are set forth under its Principles of Policy. Particularly interesting examples include Articles 33, 36, and 37a and 37e.

33. The State shall discourage parochial, racial, tribal, sectarian and provincial prejudices among the citizens.

36. The State shall safeguard the legitimate rights and interests of minorities, including their due representation in the Federal and Provincial services.

37. The State shall -

(a) promote with special care, the educational and economic interests of backward classes or areas;

(e) make provision for securing just and humane conditions of work, ensuring that children and women are not employed in vocations unsuited to their age or sex, and for maternity benefits for women in employment;

In Pakistan's Fundamental Rights Section, the most important affirmative action provision is Article 22 (4) which is part of the article providing safeguards as to educational institutions in respect of religion. It reads: ''Nothing in this Article shall prevent any public authority from making provision for the advancement of any socially or educationally backward class of citizens.''

Here are affirmative action provisions from two more constitutions -- the 1975 Constitution of Papua New Guinea and the 1972 Constitution of the Philippines.

Papua New Guinea

55. Equality of Citizens

(1) Subject to this Constitution, all citizens have the same rights, privileges, obligations and duties irrespective of race, tribe, place of origin, political opinion, colour, creed, religion or sex.

(2) Subsection (1) does not prevent the making of laws for the special benefit, welfare, protection or advancement of females, children and young persons, members of underprivileged or less advanced groups or residents of less advanced areas.

Philippines

> Article XV, Sec. 11
>
> The State shall consider the customs, traditions, beliefs, and interests of the National cultural communities in the formulation and implementation of state policies.

Malaysia has one affirmative action provision which would apparently make it a crime to thwart affirmative action. It reads:

> 149. Legislation against subversion:
>
> > (1) If an Act of Parliament recites that action has been taken or threatened by any substantial body of persons, whether inside or outside the Federation ...
> >
> > > (c) to promote feelings of ill-will and hostility between different races or other classes of the population likely to cause violence; . . .

Whatever the Philippines' objectives, in practise affirmative action programmes in the U.S.A., no matter how well intended, became manisfestations of racism. Specifically their object was to provide special advantages to workers, students, etc., for two reasons: (a) because they were members of minorities and (b) because they were black. Such reasons cannot be scientifically defended in the name of redressing wrongs that were imposed by state laws 50 or 200 years ago. It has led to the bogus notion that minority, notably black, students have a civil right to higher education at public expense and that black workers have a civil right to employment (and to promotion above others) because they are a minority. This is the principle reason why the U.S. Commission on Civil Rights early in 1984 denounced affirmative action quotas and said: "Such racial preferences merely constitute another form of racial discrimination. . . create a new class of victims and . . . offend the constitutional principles of equal protection of the law for all citizens."

CHAPTER VI

SLAVERY

Slavery is not explicitly mentioned in most national constitutions, yet the subject of slavery is fundamental to the consideration of human or group rights. Unless members of a group can be considered as full human beings rather than objects of commerce there can be little genuine human liberty. Any society which condones slavery implicitly denies the value of some human lives. Of course, the silence of most constitutions on the subject of slavery does not mean that slavery is approved as a practice. All the same it is troubling that no Communist country (save Cuba) and few Arab states have consitutional provisions regarding slavery, although both kinds of states have been accused of subjugating human beings.

For the record, slavery is explicitly condemned and abolished in the constitutions of the following nations: Argentina; Bahamas; Bolivia; Columbia; Costa Rica; Cuba; Cyprus; Ecuador; El Salvador; Ghana; Grenada; Guatemala; Guyana; India; Jamaica; Liberia; Malaysia; Mauritius; Mexico; Nigeria; Papua New Guinea; Rhodesia; Rwanda; Seychelles; Sierra Leone; Somali Democratic Republic; Trinidad and Tobago; Uganda; United Arab Emirates; United States of America; Western Samoa; Yemen Arab Republic; Zaire; Zambia.

The story of slavery and constitutions really begins with the Argentine and the United States of America.

The 1853 Argentine Constitution preceded the American in abolishing slavery. That document also provided for indemnification of slaveholders. Slaves from any other country were freed "by the mere act of setting foot in the territory of the Republic" (Article 15).

The American Constitution of 1789 contains several references to slavery in its original language. Slavery was much discussed at the constitutional convention of 1787. The American founding fathers were inclined to treat the question of slavery as primarily an economic and political matter, especially in light of the fact that American southerners were strong defenders of slavery. As a result, the American Constitution nowhere mentions or approves of slavery explicitly. Instead, the Constitution refers to "persons" whom the states shall think it proper to import, or "persons" bound to service or labor. But it must be recalled that the world's first single documentary constitution defended and protected the institution of slavery, in spite of the American's official committment to doctrines of individual liberty and freedom.

Article I, Section 1 of the 1789 Constitution is the infamous three-fifths clause which allowed "all other persons" (meaning Blacks) to be counted at three-fifths the value of a freedman or indentured servant for the purposes of representation and taxation. Article I, Section 9 of the Constitution prohibited "the migration or importation of such persons as any of the states now existing shall think proper to admit" until *at least* 1808, after which Congress might prohibit slave importation. Incidentally, the careful phrasing of this provision reveals a delicate sensitivity about even mentioning slavery. Article IV, Section 2, Clause 3 of the 1789 Constitution requires the rendition of escaped slaves, while Article IV, Section 2, Clause 1 mentions privileges and immunities extended to citizens of the United States, which some have taken to mean the right of slaveowners to keep their slaves as property when travelling to another state which did not condone slavery.

All these provisions have been wiped off the American constitutional slate. The Thirteenth Amendment, adopted in 1865, ratified the results of the American Civil War when it prohibited slavery and involuntary servitude. The Fourteenth Amendment, ratified in 1868, made all persons born or naturalized in the United States citizens of the United States and the states wherein they resided, thus giving freed Blacks full citizenship. The second section of this Amendment repealed the three-fifths clause. The right of freedmen to vote was guaranteed by the Fifteenth Amendment (1870). All three post Civil War Amendments give Congress power to enforce appropriate legislation, which has been done to some extent. The most important aspect of these changes in the Constitution insofar as slavery is concerned is the language of the Fourteenth Amendment, Section I, which prohibits any state from denying "to any person within its jurisdiction the equal protection of the laws." Not only was slavery constitutionally prohibited in America, but the states of the Union were also prohibited from discriminating against former slaves. This action became a model for later constitutional thinking.

Many other Latin American nations have specifically abolished slavery by constitutional provision. Most follow the Argentine model, as in Colombia. In all Spanish America the Mexican constitution of 1917 has the most comprehensive anti-slavery provisions. The Mexican Constitution forbids slavery but also exempts military duty, jury service and elective duties from its coverage. Monastic orders are forbidden because of their compulsory sacrifice of labor (Article 5). Another unique provision of the Mexican constitution states that "professional services of a social character shall be compulsory and paid according to the provisions of law" (Article 5), a rarely invoked clause.

The 1960 Western Samoan constitution provides the most thoughtful modern approach to slavery. Article 8 prohibits forced or compulsory labor. However, certain activities are excluded from the definition of forced or compulsory labor. Work required as a consequence of a judicial sentence is excluded. So is "any serviced extracted in case of an emergency or calamity threatening the life or well-being of the community" and "any work or service which is required by Samoan custom or which forms part of normal civic obligations." Military service is excluded, as is alternative service for conscientious objectors.

The Arab constitutions are generally silent on the subject of slavery. Three are not. Somali Democratic Republic; United Arab Emirates and Yemen Arab Republic. The Yemen Arab Republic has the most interesting provision, asserting that "no forced labor shall be imposed upon anyone except in cases in the public interest prescribed by law and with appropriate wages." The provision seems self-contradictory and may be read as condoning slavery under certain conditions prescribed by the State. Slavery still seems to be practiced in many of the Arab states, although its actual incidence is unknown. [26]

Most African constitutions prohibit slavery. Nonetheless reports of African slavery leak out from time to time. In 1978 stories about slavery in Communist Mozambique came to public attention. Most of the reports came from expatriates and may be entirely reliable. Nonetheless, forced labor seems to be a feature of Communist regimes -- a treatment reserved for political prisoners and agricultural workers pressed to meet food production quotas, as in Cambodia.

African states which have played an active role in the human rights field at the United Nations have often been the last to outlaw slavery in their own backyards. Mauritania is a good example and it was only in July 1980 that the Mauritanian government formally abolished slavery, although Blacks and Haratines continue to be employed almost exclusively in menial jobs.

---

26. Cf. United Nations: *Report on Slavery,* U.N., New York, E/4/168/Rev. 1., 1966· Glaser and Possony, op. cit., pp. 461-462.

The *practice* of slavery has not been eliminated. There are many subtle modern varieties of slavery as well as unsubtle means of ownership by human beings or other human beings. In the past 5,000 years of recorded history, probably more men and women have lived under the yoke of slavery than have been free. So wrote Robert Buron, president of the *Union Federalist Mondiale,* in an occasional paper (undated) distributed by the Society. He believes that the West freed itself from slavery thanks to the invention of the rudder and the horse collar and bridle. For these inventions rendered navigation under sail more profitable than movement at sea with galley slaves, and established the superiority of the horse over the man to transport heavy loads. But it was not until 1865 that slavery ended in the United States, not until 1895 that it was officially abolished in Brazil, and not until 1962 that it was officially abolished in Saudi Arabia. The word "officially" is important because slavery still exists in Brazil and Saudi Arabia and at least forty more countries.[27] The Anti-Slavery Society estimates the number of people suffering the discrimination of slavery is more than one percent of the world's total population. This is a figure approaching 50 million people. But that figure is predicated upon the modern definition of slavery and emphasizes racial, religious and sex discrimination.

The Forms of Slavery

Slavery persists today in five forms, as defined in the United Nations Supplementary Convention on Slavery, the Slavery Trade and Similar Institutions and Practices, adopted in 1956. These five are: (1) chattel slavery, (2) serfdom, (3) debt bondage, (4) pseudo-adoption and (5) service forms of marriage. And these are so widespread, that most of those who practice the discriminations involved in slavery do not even see anything wrong with such activities.[28]

27. Glaser and Possony: op. cit., pp. 461-462.

28. Report of Colonel Patrick Montgomery, Secretary, Anti-Slavery Society, 1970. Summarized in the *Daily Telegraph,* London, August 18, 1970.

Chattel Slavery

This is the traditional slavery of history and literature which has survived in modern times principally in the Sahara and in the Arabian peninsula. While it is now illegal in every nation of the world, it still persists in at least Algeria, Chad, Libya, Mali, Mauritania, Morocco, Niger, Pakistan, Philippines, Saudi Arabia and Senegal.

Much of the existing chattel slavery is based on race, and represents discrimination against Blacks, and recently, those who are racially defined as Asian Indians. There is a long history of the enslavement of black African Moslems making the pilgrimage to Mecca. Sometimes blacks are seized and forced into slavery; more often these Africans sell their children as slaves to pay for the return journey. Now, as a result of increased purchasing power in the oil regions of the Middle East, Asian Indians are being recruited to work in Arab nations and have reportedly been forced into chattel slavery. Yet, this type of "ownership" between employer and employee, as in the pre-Civil War American soldier, is minor compared to other types of slavery.

Serfdom

The second type of slavery, serfdom, exists primarily in Afghanistan, Bolivia, Ecuador, Ethiopia and Peru. There the "slave" is tied to the land. And such serfdom is generally based on racial characteristics. People of American Indian stock are the serfs of Latin America. In 1976, however, a combination of chattel slavery and serfdom was imposed upon 20,000 Fang tribesmen who were rounded up under the orders of the president of Equatorial Guinea to work in the cocoa fields. Cocoa is the principal crop of the Island of Macias Neguema (formerly Fernando Po) and labor in the past had been recruited from Liberia and Nigeria. Following the repatriation of Nigerian laborers, after many of them were killed for demanding back wages, the Fang were forced into slavery on the cocoa plantations.

In many parts of the world agricultural workers have no real opportunity to own the land, but serve as tenant farmers to large landholders. In Ethiopia, prior to the revolution, genuine feudal conditions of serfdom existed, with hereditary nobility virtually "owning" the agricultural workers. Tenant farmers are not feudal serfs in Latin America, but the large "latifundia" plantations near serfdom in many places. Land reform has become a radical cause in many nations. Drawing distinctions between penury and peonage may be nearly impossible in many nations.

Debt Bondage

Debt Bondage, the third form of slavery, is described by the United Nations in its 1956 report as:

> "the status or condition arising from a pledge by a debtor of his personal services of those of a person under his control as security for debt, if the value of those services as reasonably assessed is not applied towards the liquidation of the debt or the length and nature of those services are not respectively limited and defined."[29]

It still exists in Burma and India, although it has been officially outlawed in the latter.

Psuedo-Adoption

Sham adoption and exploitation of children is the fourth type of slavery. This practice is widespread in West Africa, Southeast Asia, Syria, Turkey, and most of the Pan-American nations. Sometimes it is a matter of children being kidnapped to work for private factories or to work as servants. More often, it is a matter of poor people encouraging the adoption and exploitation of their own children in order that they be somehow housed and fed.

Servile Forms of Marriage

29. The United Nations Supplementary Convention on the Abolition of Slavery, the Slave Trade and Institutions and Practices similar to Slavery, 1956.

Perhaps the most prevalent form of slavery today is in servile forms of marriage, coupled with forced prostitution. This is common throughout the Islamic world. And because it does involve primarily the 40 Islamic countries, it is a matter of religious as well as sex discrimination and classification.

In India, as well, poor husbands have been known to sell their wives into prostitution in order to pay off debts owed to money lenders. Sometimes the wives have their freedom bought back by their husbands. Sometimes the wives remain enslaved. This traffic in Indian women seems to persist in remote rural areas.

Slavery in Practice

Specific examples of modern slavery are so numerous that they also go beyond the scope of this study. And the problem is certainly not solved by the numerous constitutional provisions outlawing the existence of slavery -- not even the elaborate provision in the 1971 Constitution of the Yemen Arab Republic.

> Article 36: Every citizen has the right to undertake work chosen by him and in accordance with the law. No forced labor shall be imposed upon anyone except in cases in the public interest prescribed by law and with appropriate wages.

The point is that it is probably easier to identify the existence of traditional racial slavery in the Yemen Arabic Republic than in any place in the world. Along the Red Sea Coast live tribes which can only be classified as African enclaves amidst the Arabs. The largest group, numbering more than 60,000, are the Akhdam, generally Black with thick lips and other so-called Negro features, who are reputed to be the descendants of an invading Ethiopian army back in the 6th century A.D. Both religious and tribal leaders sanction their menial status, denying them the right to own land and property or to intermarry.

While the Yemeni Government has give the title of "worker" to the Akhdam who are in government service, their status is that of the street sweepers. "As late as 1962, when street cleaners were needed in Sana (the capital), the army sent a detachment of soldiers to the area of Zabid, rounded up 100 Akhdam and gave them to the Municipality of Sana where today, as workers, they are sweeping the streets." [30]

But the circumstances of slavery are not limited to the Arab world or to less developed Third World peoples. Nor are they merely isolated examples of slavery in the enlightened West where there appeared to be no need to have constitutional prohibitions against the institution of slavery.

Take West Germany, for example, one of the five richest and most educated nations in the world. "Take home an angel from the City of Angels," is one of the advertisements which appears in German newspapers. So reports the Bangkok correspondent of London's *Economist* in an article on "Packaged Brides" in the issue of July 25, 1977. For about 1,000 pounds sterling, the German can buy a package tour that includes a round-trip ticket to Thailand, marriage to a Thai girl, and a return ticket for the bride. "The first week is devoted to sampling the goods. If a Thai girl does not appeal, there are Chinese, Laotians or Burmese."

But traditional marriage is not the result and many known that prostitution awaits them. A Thai public welfare official estimates that more than 1,000 Thai girls are working as prostitutes in West Germany and many more in Britain, France, Sweden, Japan and Hong Kong. And there does no appear to be any end or any solution to such practices.

India abolished bonded labor by statute in 1976, [31] every bonded laborer in India was supposedly freed by the act, the obligations of bonded laborers to repay bonded debts were extinguished. Property taken from bonded laborers by force was to

30. James Horgen, "Adhdam Tribe Inservitude," *Geographical Magazine*, Washington, June 1976, p. 533, p. 538.

31. The Bonded Labour System (Abolition) Act, 1976, No. 19 of 1976.

be restored to them. Newly freed bonded laborers may not be evicted from their homesteads. Implementation of the stringent provisions of this act is specifically the responsibility of the District Magistrate (or his subordinate) who has the assigned duty to inquire into the existence of bonded labor or any other form of coerced labor within his jurisdiction, and to eradicate it. In addition, the act empowers state governments to constitute "vigilance committees" to advise the District Magistrate and to provide economic and social assistance to freed bonded laborers. These vigilance committees may also defend bonded laborers against suits brought by the former employers. Severe fines and even imprisonment for up to three years are the sanctions to be applied to those who coerce others to work for them or impose conditions of bonded labor.[32] No more strict or detailed law can be found in other nations. However, some observers feel that the practice still exists in subtle forms.[33]

The most modern constitutional statement regarding slavery is to be found in the 1976 Seychelles constitution. This document provides that "no person shall be held in slavery or servitude." Forced labor is also prohibited. However, the constitution excludes labor required of a member of a disciplined force " in pursuance of his duties" or alternate service required of conscientious objectors. Probably, future constitutions will be even more detailed in their treatment of slavery and bonded labor and the turn examples of India and the Seychelles should be consulted by drafters who wish to effectively abolish slavery and involuntary servitude.

---

32. Article 15.

33. No one knows the extent of bonded labor in India, but there are names for it in many parts of the country, and it is believed especially prevalent among scheduled castes and scheduled tribes in Orissa, Bihar, Gujarat, Karnataak, Rajasthan and Uhar Pradesh. Reported in the Shara, Law and Bonded Labour System, Mimeo, University of Delhi, 1976.

CHAPTER VII

INDIGENOUS PEOPLE

Descendants from members of a native population subsequently submerged by later inhabitants, settlers or "invaders," often are victims of various forms of discrimination. This kind of discrimination need not be racial in its foundation, but the notions of the inferiority of the old native stock may resemble classic racism in its classification and implicit condemnation of an entire group. The term "aborigine" is also used, even in statutes, to define the status of a member of such a group. Thus, in the Australian state of Queensland legislation defines an "aborigine" as a person who is a descendant of an indigenous inhabitant of the commonwealth of Australia.

Euphemisms abound in referring to indigenous populations. In Brazil an Indian or Forest Dweller is defined as "Any individual of pre-Columbian origin or ascent" (Act No. 6001 of 19 December 1973, Art. 2, I). In Norway and Sweden persons are considered Lapps if either one of his parents or grandparents normally speaks Lapp. In New Zealand, where indigenous Maoris have separate electoral rolls from the Europeans, persons who declare themselves Maoris may vote on the Maori rolls, although subjective identification of Maori status seems to presume no proof.

Cultural differences are frequently used to distinguish

indigenous populations from the rest of society. Chilean law defines indigenous persons in terms of the different way of life, customs and religions of certain groups in Guyana. Indigenous culture means "living the life of an Amerindian," according to the Amerindian Ordinance. Ainu culture in Japan seems to be the criterion for identification of members of that indigenous group. Cultural identification seems critical in the Philippines, Panama, Sri Lanka, and Venezuela for their indigenous populations.[34]

Many groups may be considered indigenous merely because they are isolated or marginal, living apart from the bulk of the population. So it is in Ethiopia and the Philippines, as examples, where groups still live who have never suffered conquest or colonization. Their cultural isolation, however, sets them apart, even if formally they are supposed to live under the same state structures as others. Often members of culturally isolated groups are unaware of the existence or meaning of the national state.

State policies towards indigenous populations vary enormously. There are 5.5 million descendants of the once powerful Mayat living in Guatemala. They provide a cheap labor source for sugar, cotton, and coffee plantations, when they can find work at all. Their annual per capita income is officially listed at $200 and their life expectancy is under 50 years. Their culture remains quite lively, and relatively free of dominant culture. They retain 23 languages and 100 dialects, but because there are so many of them living as subsistence farmers, many are reduced to starvation or migrant farmer status.[35] The Guatemalan government barely notices them. Although there is a National Indian Institute assigned to represent the majority of these Indians, the operating budget of the agency is a mere $8,000.

---

34. See U.N. Economic and Social Council, Commission of Human Rights: *Study of the Problem of Discrimination Against Indigenous Populations* E/CN 4/Sub 2/L.622 July 17, 1975.

35. See account in *New York Times,* March 27, 1978, p. 5.

Australia, on the other hand, has taken a great interest in its 150,000 Aborigines, one of the world's most primitive peoples. As a result of a 1967 referendum full citizenship was bestowed upon them. Hundreds of millions of dollars have been poured into the education of Aborigines and into improving their living conditions. A government Aboriginal study grant program pays many students a weekly stipend to attend classes through university levels. However, one of the effects of this heightened government concern has been injury to the traditional cultural structure. Tribal structure has almost collapsed; the crime rate and alcoholism have both increased. Cultural disintegration may be the price of Australian efforts towards equality of opportunity.[36]

Another familiar policy towards indigenous peoples is genocide, mass slaughter or deliberate destruction through neglect and oppression.[37] The Guarani Indians of Paraguay seem to have suffered a fate of slow starvation similar to that of other Indians in North and South America. In Paraguay Indians have been massacred, herded into concentration camps and enslaved, and the process is still continuing. Protests have been made by the International League for the Rights of Man and by the Inter-American Association for Democracy. The genocide committed by the Khmer Rouge regime in Cambodia cost the lives of 1,2 million people. This was clinically set out in John Barron's book *Murder of a Gentle Land,* published by Reader's Digest Press in 1977.

Recently, the Eritrean Liberation Front has accused the Ethiopian government (with Russian and Cuban allies) of genocide in Eritrea.

The constitutional status of indigenous people was first treated in the United States Constitution. The Constitution gives the American Congress the power to "regulate commerce with foreign nations, and among the several states, and with the Indian

---

36. See account in *New York Times,* June 3, 1977, p. 8.

37. The near extermination of Brazilian forest and jungle peoples is described in John Heming, *Red Gold,* Harvard University Press, Cambridge, 1978.

tribes.''[38] Thus, the American Indians were placed in the position of being a separate entity, apart from the rest of the population and somewhat like a foreign people. Indians were seen as external to the rest of society and a policy of virtual isolation was begun. Relations with Indians became the subject of the treaties, which were sometimes broken. The effect of this constitutional perception of Indians was to continue well into the twentieth century until today the American Indians are small, scattered and dependent groups, only recently asserting their claims upon the society.

Modern constitutions seem to aim either at some kind of assimilation of indigenous peoples or to preserve their cultural identity. An example of the first is the Venezuelan Constitution of 1961. This constitution, although it gives special privileges to Indian communities, expresses the hope that these will result in ''their progressive incorporation into the life of the nation.''[39] Indonesia is the best example of constitutional regard for cultural differences. The Indonesian constitution provides that ''the ancient and indigenous cultures which are to be found as cultural heights in all the regions throughout Indonesia are part of the nation's culture'' which ''raise the height of humanity of the Indonesian nation.''[40] The division of Indonesian territory into administrative units must, constitutionally, ''be in accord with the principle of consultation and the traditional rights of particular territories.''[41]

Some constitutions effectively bar indigenous populations from citizenship, from voting and from office-holding. Latin-American constitutions often contain such provisions. In Brazil those ''who do not know how to express themselves in the national language'' are regarded as illiterates, unable to vote,[42] barring most (not all) Indians. Yet Brazil also makes the lands held by

38. Article I, Section 8.

39. Article 77.

40. Article 31.

41. Article 36.

42. Constitution of Brazil, Article 147, Paragraph 3.

"forest-dwelling aborigines" inalienable.[43] Since the Brazilian constitution requires elementary education to be offered only in Portuguese,[44] Indians must learn the language in order to vote or hold office. Ecuador gives citizenship only to those who know how to read and write,[45] effectively excluding most Indians, although the constitution does permit indigenous languages to be used in schools in addition to Spanish.[46] Many other Latin-American constitutions are silent on the subject, in spite of their large Indian populations. Policies of discrimination or neglect towards Indians are frequently justified by the requirement of knowing Spanish to participate in governmental affairs.

African states present difficulties for the conditions of indigenous people which are rarely expressed in their constitutions. Nigeria has still failed to come to grips with its tribal differences, although a draft constitution, referred to later, appears to at least make some attempts. In Africa it is sometimes difficult to decide who the indigenous people are because of the paucity of historical sources and because of the fact that national boundaries do not parallel tribal boundaries. Then, too, some tribes are quite sophisticated and leaders are well educated, while others, such as the Noens and some pygmy groups are not far from their stone age ancestors in terms of development.

In Africa only South Africans have minority white control of political, social and economic life. (White capitalist control in Rhodesia ended mid-December 1979, and was replaced by the Marxism of Robert Mugabe).The majority Black groups are, in various ways, economically and politically disadvantaged, although far reaching steps are now being taken to remedy the economic situation. For the Asians and Coloureds (mixed-bloods), political power sharing becomes a reality with the new constitution of 1984. Whether these measures will enable whites, blacks,

43. Article 198.

44. Article 176, Paragraph 3.

45. Article 15, Constitution of Ecuador.

46. Article 143.

Asians and Coloureds to live side by side in one state is a test of ingenuity, good will and power. In South Africa historical homeland territories of the Black peoples may, under the constitution be declared self-governing and eventually request and be granted independence.[47] This provision is the basis for the creation of such independent states as Transkei, Ciskei and Bophuthatswana. The policy of carving up South African territory into independent homelands for the distinctly different black peoples, although historically and politically well founded, and not without precedent in the world[48] has been attacked by other nations as an inadequate substitute for black majority rule in South Africa. However, if some of these homelands can be consolidated into one area, enlarged and sustain themselves economically and politically, the homeland approach might enjoy more sympathy. At the moment vast international pressures are being placed on South Africa to abandon its homeland policy and in South Africa itself the government of Mr. P.W. Botha seems to be bending to this pressure. South Africa retains English and Afrikaans, two Indo-Germanic languages, as the only official languages[49] although the majority of the people has a Nguni or Sotho language as their mother tongue.

Rhodesia, once the other white-dominated African state, has suffered protracted guerilla conflict in the name of black majority rule. The 1969 Rhodesian constitution of Mr. Ian Smith gave African chiefs ten representatives in the Senate.[50] Parliamentary debates could be conducted in Chishona and Sindebele, as well as in English.[51] But only English could be used as a

---

47. Bantu Homelands Constitution Act of 1971.

48. Many prominent American scholars have advocated a homeland for the Palestinians on the West Bank of the Jordan. The Muslims in the Philippines are fighting for their own homeland. The Red Indian in the U.S.A. are living in so called reservations which are, in reality, homelands. For the South African point of view, see *Official Yearbook*, Pretoria, pp. 203-224.

49. Article 108 (1).

50. Article 13, Rhodesian Constitution of 1969.

51. Article 36.

language in the High Court [52] and only English was the official language in Rhodesia [53] although the vast majority of the population spoke other languages.

In 1979 the Rhodesian constitution was "rewritten" at Lancaster House in London to permit effective black majority rule, but with some safeguards and guarantees for the white minority group, several which have been cast overboard by the new black Marxist government. Clearly, South Africa will soon have to face the problem of finding a workable political structure between Zulus and Whites. The Zulu are numerically the largest Black nation with their own language and culture, but if this problem is posed as a black versus white question, instead of the Zulu nation vs. the White nation, then the issue of race becomes the bone of contention, not the rights of indigenous peoples. Unlike the other Black groups, such as the Xhosa in the Transkei and the Ciskei the 7 million Zulus (whites, about 5 million) have refused to request independence in their own homeland, but see themselves as individuals of a greater South Africa and believe that only a one-man one-vote system in a unitary state will work.

The Constitution of India appears to give the most thorough treatment to the rights of indigenous peoples. The constitution declares that "the state shall promote with special care the educational and economic interests of the weaker sections of the people, and in particular, of the Scheduled Castes and the scheduled tribes, and shall protect them from social injustice and all forms of exploitation. [54] Seats are reserved in the upper house of the Indian legislature for most of the Scheduled Tribes in proportion to their population. [55] Seats are also reserved for scheduled tribes in the legislative assemblies of the states. [56] Assam, a state with a large indigenous population, must reserve

52. Article 65.

53. Article 81.

54. Article 46, Constitution of India.

55. Article 330.

56. Article 332.

an autonomous district in its legislative assembly.[57] The reservation of seats for indigenous groups is constitutionally required to terminate before the turn of the century.[58] Civil service appointments must take under consideration the claims of members of the scheduled tribes.[59] The constitution creates a special officer to investigate the status of rights of members of the scheduled tribes[60] and permits the president to establish a commission which could recommend intervention in a state on behalf of the scheduled tribes.[61]

The scheduled tribes of India, also known as aboriginals, are those elements of the Indian population who still live in their tribal ways and observe their peculiar customs and cultures. These people are found in three sections of the country. They tend to be nomadic and to live in fairly primitive conditions. They number about 25 million and constitute nearly 6.8 percent of the country's total population. They also constitute one of the world's largest concentration of indigenous people.

The Indian government aims to improve their socio-economic condition, but not at such a rapid pace as to do violence to their way of living. The gradual adaptation of the tribal population and their slow integration into the general life of the country are policies embodied in the constitution and statutes of India. The Indian state legislatures are constitutionally empowered to protect the scheduled tribes against exploitation by the more advanced elements of the population.[62] Movement of people into the tribal areas is restricted by legislation. The transfer of tribal land to non-tribals is prohibited, and a system of permits controls access to tribal lands. The constitution also calls for special educational institutions and government services.[63]

57. Article 332(4) and (5).

58. Article 334.

59. Article 335.

60. Article 338.

61. Articles 339, 340, 341 and 342.

62. Articles 19(1) (d), 19(1) (e) and 19(1) (f) in particular.

63. Articles 15(4) and 16(4).

The Indian constitution does not specify the tribes which may be designated as protected. The president of India has the power to list and notify these tribes with respect to each Indian state and territory. [64] Thus, the lists of scheduled tribes may vary from state to state and territory to territory. State governors must be consulted by the president before listing a tribe. The constitution specifically provides that there shall be a minister for tribal welfare in the states of Bihar, Madhya Pradesh, and Orissa. [65] Provision was also made in Assam for the formation of two new states, Nagaland and Meghalaya which are closely concerned with the protection of tribal life and customs.

64. Articles 366(24) and 341 and Article 366(25). Read with Article 342.

65. Article 164(1) Proviso.

CHAPTER VIII

RELIGION

While most of the world's constitutions make some sort of provision for freedom *of* religion or freedom *from* religion, a considerable number proclaim a religious base.

This is particularly prevalent in regard to the 40 Muslim states. Examples are legion. Other states, however, have religious foundations -- either stated in constitutions or statutes. And these religious provisions take many forms.

In analyzing the position of religion in the constitutional framework, it is necessary to organize and classify the following:

1) Constitutional provisions guaranteeing the separation of church and state;

2) Constitutional provisions guaranteeing state protection of religious freedom and practices;

3) Constitutional provisions setting forth the basic religious character of the state;

4) Constitutional provisions proscribing religious limitations, and,

5) Statutory provisions supplementing constitutional pronouncements.

1] Freedom of Church and State

By far the most important constitutional statement on the subject appears in Article I (or Amendment I) of the Constitution of the United States. Ratified in 1791, it is the international model for provisions of this type. It reads: "Congress shall make no law respecting an establishment of religion, or prohibiting the free exercise thereof; . . ."

Few other constitutions seek to achieve similar ends. The 1919 Weimar German Constitution went even further than the American Constitution by asserting, in Article 136, that "no one shall be bound to disclose his religious convictions," and denying the government "the right to inquire into a person's membership of a religious body." Another provision explicitly forbade the compulsory performance of any religious act or ceremony.

The current West German constitution is unique in that it has a specific constitutional provision protecting conscientious objectors (Article 4 (3)).

All Communist constitutions proclaim the separation of church and state and certain guarantees of freedom of anti-religious propaganda (which is financed by the state). But religions are tolerated within these states, usually quite grudgingly. Some newer Communist constitutions actually permit state aid to religion. The wall of separation was broken down by the Yugoslav Constitution of 1961 (Article 46) which even gave religious communities the right "to ownership of real estate within the limits determined by the federal law," an astonishing concession in a Communist state, committed to atheism.

The status of religions in Communist countries varies considerably. Evidence of deliberate anti-semitic policies directed by officials in Soviet Russia, Poland and elsewhere in Eastern Europe is abundant. Jews have special difficulties in employment, travel and in the exercise of their religion. Many Russian Jews are no longer actively practicing their religion, partly because of official pressure against the practice of Judaism. All this, of course, is in spite of the provisions of the Soviet Constitution.

Anti-Semitism has been a historic policy in Russian and Eastern Europe. Under the Communist dispensation, Christian communities sometimes suffer persecution, too. This seems much less true in heavily Catholic Poland than in the Soviet Union, with its state dominated Orthodox Church. Baptists, Mennonites, Evangelicals and other Protestant Christian groupings exist in the Soviet Union, but are vulnerable to changes in government policy. Under Premier Krushchev, from 1959-64, there was an extensive persecution of Protestant groups, as the government turned militantly atheist. Even today, Bible smuggling is a kind of offense. In some areas government agents take religious censuses in order to keep tabs on believers. Baptists and some other Protestants in the Soviet Union are often barred from access to higher education.

The most meaningful aspect of Communist constitutions insofar as religion is concerned is the "Freedom of anti-religious propaganda." This provision may be the springboard of periodic campaigns to spread atheism and to discourage religious practices. The Soviet state has virtually established atheism as the state non-religion. The state has created secular versions of baptism, marriage, funerals, First Communions, and Christmas in order to supplant religious ceremonies and holidays. Atheist's clubs, films, plays, magazines and books are promoted by the Russian government. Periodically atheists attend church meetings and services in order to "monitor" them. Since atheism is taught as a subject in the schools, children from religious families are often discouraged from or actively pressured to abandon their religions.

2] State Guarantees of Religious Freedoms

Religious freedom in the United States and in the many nations which have followed the American pattern is a very much watered-down freedom. These provisions are subject to what is loosely described as public policy.

That public policy (in the case of the United States) has been formulated and developed in case law. And this is true in other nations as well. Still other nations have placed "public policy" provisions in their constitutions. Here are some examples:

The Sudanese Constitution, while declaring Islam the religion, also says that the society shall be guided by Islamic values. But since there are Christians, too, in the Sudan "the state shall endeavor to express its values" (Article 16).

The Yemen Arab Republic bases its economy upon "the principles of Islamic social justice" (Article 10). Its guarantees of private and public freedoms are grounded upon the Shari'ah (Article 8). Such provisions, found in most Islamic constitutions, mean that non-Muslims are subject to Islamic Law and even to decisions of Islamic religious leaders.

Malta, more expressly than most countries, makes religious teaching a fundamental right, but, curiously, does not make its fundamental rights enforceable in courts (Article 22). Apparently, religious rights are morally, not legally, obligatory in Malta.

Hinduism, the religion of the Indian majority, enjoys constitutional protection. Article 48 of the Indian constitution prohibits "the slaughter of cows and calves and other milk and draught cattle," a provision which may be offensive to India's 50 million beef eating Muslims. Pork-slaughter is not constitutionally prohibited.

Trying to strike the balance between public policy and the guarantee of religious freedom is the subject of world-wide litigation. Perhaps the most interesting is the existing litigation brought by Israeli Muslims in the State of Israel demanding the right to practice state-proscribed bigamy so that they may give full affect to their adherence to the Koranic tradition.

In Bangladesh, a 1977 change in the constitution was decreed ordering an end to constitutional secularism. In its place Islam was made a fundamental principle and source of public policy.

Much more meaningful in terms of state guarantees are provisions such as found in Articles 26 through 28 of the Indian constitution. In examining these provisions, note their detail, including the two explanations which follow Section 25. These are as follows:

> Explanation I: The wearing and carrying of *kirpans* shall be deemed to be included in the profession of the Sikh religion.
>
> Explanation II: In sub-clause (b) of clause (2), the reference to Hindus shall be construed as including a reference to persons professing the Sikh, Jaina or Buddhist religion, and the reference to Hindu religious institutions shall be construed accordingly.

Under provisions such as these, the Parsees of Bombay dispose of their dead in accordance with their age-old tradition. Those who have passed away are placed near their temple (right in the City of Bombay) where the bodies are picked clean by vultures and the bones are washed into the sea. Certainly such practices would not be permitted in a Western nation.

3] Basic Religious Character of the State

Muslim orthodoxy is on the increase. Even Egypt, the most cosmopolitan of all the Arab countries, has recently passed a new law imposing the death penalty on any Muslim-Egyptian who renounces his religion. The Comoro Island's new constitution of October 1, 1978 provides for a federal Islamic state.

In constitutional terms, some of the Arab states are so bound by religious faith that their official constitutions are the Quran itself. This is true in regard to Saudi Arabia and Oman. The Bangladesh Constitution of 1972 (Article 8 (1)) emphasizes Muslim secularism. A constitutional amendment passed by Egypt on April

30, 1980 approved by a referendum on 22 May 1980 made the Islamic legal code (Shari'a) the principle source of law.

Other states with established "religions" are Israel (Judaism), Shri-Lanka, Laos and Malaysia (Buddhism), Denmark (Lutheranism), Iceland (Evangelical Lutheran) and the Catholic religion, apostolic and Roman, in Monaco.

The 1956 Pakistan Constitution not only described the country as an Islamic republic, but provided that all laws were to be brought into conformity with Islam -- e.g., to provide facilities to make the teaching of the Quran compulsory for Muslims.

The Afghan constitution of 1933 declares Islam the official religion and the Hanafi version is proclaimed official. Other religions, such as Hinduism and Judaism, are permitted, provided "they do not infringe the ordinary rules of conduct and propriety" (General Principles). Non-Muslim private education is forbidden (Articles 21 and 22). The modernised constitution of 1977 was abolished following the military coup of April 27, 1978 and the new military power announced it would rule by decree until a new constitution, also based on the promotion of Islam, had been adopted. On April 14, 1980, the Revolutionary Council ratified a provisional constitution entitled The Basic Principles of the Republic of Afghanistan "assuring" equal rights for all tribes, nationalities and ethnic groups.

Greece is openly committed to the promotion of its prevailing religion, the Eastern Orthodox Church. Its constitution protects church property against expropriation. Moreover, the religious community on Mount Athos retains, under Article 105, "its ancient privileged status" and is a "self-governed part of the Greek state" with its sovereignty preserved intact. Other religions are "subject to the same supervision by the state" as is "the prevailing religion," but other religions do not enjoy special privileged status.

Israel was declared at its birth in 1948 to be the birthplace of the

Jewish people. The declaration of the establishment of the state of Israel proclaims the area as the ancient homeland of the Jewish people. The document encourages the world's Jews to regard Israel as their home. While Israel is not exactly a religious state in the same sense, say, as Iran, there is little doubt that the Jewish religion is paramount. Arabs in Israel cannot practice their age-old Quranic belief in multiple wives. The Quran permits Muslims to have up to four wives. Israeli law bans polygamy. Oddly, the law also permits a Jew to legally marry a second wife if "100 rabbis permit." Arab tradition and religious practices in Israel are restricted by the religious doctrines and legal doctrines of Jews in Israel.

Italy, of course, recognizes a special privileged status for the Catholic church. Article 7 of the Italian constitution says that "the state and the Catholic Church are, each within its own ambit, independent and sovereign." Italy recognizes the Lateran Pacts which give autonomy to the papacy in Vatican City. No changes may be made in the Lateran Pacts unilaterally by Italy without a constitutional alteration.

The Cyprus constitution recognizes two established religions, that of the Greek-Orthodox for the Greek community, and Islam for the Turkish community. By virtue of Article 2 of the Cyprus constitution, all citizens must belong to one or the other religious group. Movement from one religious group to the other requires a written, signed declaration submitted to an appropriate officer of the republic. Married women belong to the group to which their husbands adhere (Article 7). Children under the age of 21 belong to the religious group of their parents, effectively of the father. Only after reaching the age of 16 may a child choose on his own to adhere to a particular religion. Religious groups are represented directly in the communal chamber of the localities (Article 109). The law of marriage, divorce, separation and family relations for members of the Greek Orthodox Church in Cyprus is governed by the law of that church and its tribunals (Article III). Article 18 of the Cyprus constitution seems to protect other religions besides the two established religions when it states "all religions whose doctrines or rites are not secret are free," but the net effect of the Cyprus constitution is to discourage the practice of other religions by denying them representative status within the Greek and Turkish communities, except as they are acceptable to Muslims or to the Greek Orthodox Church.

Denmark is typical of the established churches in Scandinavia. The Danish constitution requires the constitution of the established Lutheran church to be laid down by statute. Furthermore, part VII of the Danish constitution requires that rules for religious bodies dissenting from the established church be laid down by statute. Nonetheless, religious discrimination is discouraged by other provisions. Certainly, the Danish protection of their Jewish population during World War II gives evidence that the rights of non-established religions are secure in Denmark.

El Salvador, typical of other Central and Latin American nations, recognizes the "juridical personality of the Catholic church." Guatemala (Article 67) also recognizes the juridical personality of other religions. The Guatemalan constitution gives the Catholic Church deeds of ownership in real property (Article 67) in sharp contrast to Mexico, which stripped the church of much of its property and justified this condition in its constitution. The established status of the Catholic Church in Latin America is under attack. The constitutions reveal the slow decline of the privileged status of the Catholic Church in Central and Latin America. The Brazilian constitution of 1967 expressly forbids (Article 9) the establishment of a church or sect. The prohibition extends to the national, state and local governments. There may well be a developing trend in Central and Latin America toward church-state separation, following the Mexican example.

Probably the most unique provision regarding established religions may be found in Iceland. Article 64 of the Icelandic constitution requires all those who are not members of the state church nor of other religious groups to pay to the University of Iceland or to "a designated scholarship fund of that university dues otherwise payable to the church." So much for the rights of atheists, agnostics or non-joiners in Iceland.

4] Religious Limitations

Many constitutions, while otherwise professing religious freedom, make specific requirements as to the religion of the head of state. These include Argentina, Denmark, Greece, Iran, Norway, Paraguay, Spain, Sweden, Thailand, and the United Kingdom, as well as the Muslim nations.

In Morocco, under the current constitution, the King is the Defender of the Faith. At the same time he is responsible for the rights and liberties of all the citizens, communities and social groups (Article 19). This seems to mean that all the people of the Book (The Old Testament), Muslims and Jews, enjoy his protection.

Another form of religious limitations is the prohibition placed upon political activity by religious groups. The most extreme example is Burma. Article 178 of the Burmese constitution denies to members of religious orders both the right to vote and the right to stand for election. Article 156 prohibits political activity by religious groups. The Colombian Constitution, like some other Latin-American constitutions, prohibits (Article 54) priests from holding public office. In Cuba it is "illegal and punishable by law to oppose one's faith or religious belief to the Revolution" (Article 54), meaning, one supposes, that religious groups cannot be active politically. Similarly, Article 20 of the constitution of Kampuchea forbids "reactionary religion which is detrimental to Democratic Cambodia."

5] Statutory Provision

While the constitutions are silent on the subject, such nations as

Lebanon and Iran have made special statutory provisions of great significance in the study of religious classification.

One of the great compromises involved in the achievement of Lebanese independence in 1944 made that country an independent Arab State -- but one where the Christians promised that they would not seek Western protection and the Muslims pledged that they would not try to make Lebanon part of the larger Arab Islamic state. In the civil wars of 1983, the U.S.A., Israel, Iran, Libya, and Syria were all directly involved.

"Among the checks and balances worked out in the system were provisions that the president of Lebanon would be a Maronite, a Roman Catholic sect whose members make up about half of the Christian population of the country. The prime minister would be a Moslem of the Sunni sect, the largest and most economically influential Moslem group in Lebanon."

The above quote appears in the *New York Times* of March 16, 1978, in an article headed, "Once-Prosperous Lebanon Is A Battleground Again" -- when once again issues concerning the organization of Lebanese sovereignty is a matter of world-wide concern.

Note that Lebanon has Armenian, Christian, Jewish and Zoroastrian representatives in parliament. This situation was detailed in the section dealing with institutional arrangements.

Statutory limitations upon religious freedoms are numerous, and, in a way, beyond the scope of research. Yet some striking examples should be mentioned. In Israel a 1978 statute imposes heavy fines for offering "material inducements" to get another to change his religion. A 1978 Argentinian decree requires all religions other than Roman Catholicism to register with the state or be banned (See *New York Times,* February 15, 1978). Jehovah's Witnesses and two other groups have been banned from religious activity in Argentina.

No detailed world-wide survey of religious persecution exists.

Doubtless, many religions are as threatened as the Christian Copts in Egypt. In 1972 alone, there were 11 anti-Coptic riots. [66] In Egypt the Muslim Ministry of Religion has, in the past, led efforts to restrict the practice of Christianity and published books and articles attacking Christianity. The Egyptian constitution was no source of protection against militant Muslim policies, no more than in many other Muslim Nations, or, for that matter, Communist countries. Only in a handful of nations are religious rights enhanced by constitutional protections.

De facto religious discrimination as opposed to outright persecution and constitutional discrimination is still widespread in Ulster, Zaire, the majority of the Arab states, Israel, Thailand, Malaysia, Indonesia, Nigeria, Kenya, Ghana, Ethiopia, Zambia, Turkey, Northern Ireland and many other states. [67] Persecution takes place in the Sudan (against Christians), in Iraq and Syria (against Christians and Jews), in the Philippines (against Muslims), but nowhere with such militancy as in the Soviet Union. Since 1964 the penal code has been strengthened to root out religious practices. The USSR which in 1962 adopted a UN Convention guaranteeing the right of parents to rear their children in their own religion, has expressly denied this right in its own domestic legislation. "Communist ideology is irreconcilable with that of religion . . . (it is the duty of every Soviet teacher) to do everything possible to make atheist education a constitutional part of Communist education . . . to bring up every school child as a militant atheist." [68]

Islam, the main religion in the Soviet Unions Turkic Central Asia is as badly persecuted as Christianity. Some 40 percent of all children in the Soviet Union in 1980 were Muslim. Some scholars have pointed out that Communism considers Islam as more

66. *Newsweek*, December 4, 1972, p. 47. Cf. Wakin, Edward: *A Lonely Minority: The Modern Story of the Egyptian Copts*, William Morrow Publishers, New York.

67. Glaser, K. and Possony, S.: *Victims of Politics*, pp. 306-313. Also *Veenhoven*, Vol. II, pp. 110-113, 168-169.

68. *Uchitelskaia Gazeta* (Teachers Gazette), Moscow, November 13, 1971.

dangerous and objectionable than Christianity.[69] To convince the Arabs of Soviet friendship for Islam while continuing to exterminate their religion in the USSR requires impressive ideological acrobatics. The Roman Catholic Church has also suffered persecution.[70]

6] Need for Further Research

Few subjects cry out more for further research than religious discrimination, be it by constitutional dictate, by state or provincial law or by custom. An in-depth-study, which is at once comparative in approach, international in character, comprehensive in research and critical in work product will make a fundamental contribution to world knowledge. Up until mid-1980 there were no such studies available and it is my conclusion that there is no religious entity or scholarly foundation geared to undertake such an effort. My preliminary conclusion in 1980 was also that the directors of international religious organizations vastly overrate what the UN has done or is capable of doing. The best study under UN auspices, ''Discrimination in the Matter of Religious Rights and Practices,'' by Arcot Krishnaswami was completed in 1960 and this is hopelessly outdated. The UN is again looking at a draft declaration on elimination of all forms of intolerance and discrimination based on religion and belief, but one must also realistically assume that the Communist and fundamental Islamic countries will stall the declaration to death and will not permit research on this subject within their territories.

Generally speaking, there is therefore an absence of organized source data. Most of the materials are also old and all of the available data seems to be one-dimensional. Most studies are concerned with discrimination against one religious group in one particular state. Much of the data provided at international level is

69. Wheeler, A.: *Racial Problems in Soviet Muslim Asia*, Oxford University Press, London, 1974.

70. Cf. Gerstenmaier, Cornelia: *The Voices of the Silent*, trans. Susan Hecker, Hart Publications, N.Y., 1972.

also suspect. What Muslims say about their treatment of Hindus is bound to be subjective in much the same way as what Protestants say about Catholics in Ireland, or what Copts say about the Muslim majority in Egypt. The first real research topic should therefore be as factual as possible and should be on the *legal environment* of religion since one must be concerned with freedom from as well as freedom of religion. There is also the legal position of the clergy and the legal position on religion and family planning.

The label "discrimination" itself should be very carefully handled. One must recognize the right of the Hindu religion and a Hindu nation to authorize its Muslim minority to practice polygamy. There are laws in Iran which permit Jews to inherib property under Jewish law. There must also be an examination of civil codes, marriage and divorce laws and judicial decisions in so far as they are prescribed by religion. Care must be taken to separate the laws of the state on matters of religion from the laws of religious groups affecting their congregants.

One dimensional source materials are always a problem. There exists a report on discrimination in education against Armenian Christians in Turkey. Should we now seek data on educational discrimination against other Christians in Turkey? Or other kinds of discrimination against Armenian Christians in Turkey? Or educational discrimination faced by Armenian Christians in other nations? The linkage between race and religion, caste and religion and indigenous people and religion must be examined for religious discrimination does not leap off the pages of legal texts.

The focus of research should be on the most important countries such as the United States and India since they have the most developed and mature legal policies towards religion. American constitutional case law is a rich mine of legal policy toward religion which, while unique, still is more well-developed than that of any other nation. Indian constitutional provisions and case law concerning religion are also rewarding sources of insight into deliberate policymaking in the area of religion.

One will have to concentrate, as well, on the Arab Muslim states. Because of the close connection between Islam and the government in those nations there is extensive legislation over many matters of public and private life. Incorporation of the Holy Quran and the various injunctions of Islam into the law of these Muslim states provide striking examples of state-church relationships.

To a lesser extent Iran provides valuable lessons, especially in its extensive efforts at legislative protection of religious minorities. The Scandinavian countries reveal important trends toward secularization, in spite of the existence of state churches. In Mexico and Latin America, further efforts to reduce state contact with religion bears close examination. The treatment of Jews in Arab countries, in the Soviet Union and in other nations has been the subject of significant legislation and administrative rulemaking. Contrariwise, the treatment of Muslims and other religious groups in Israel is an important source of policy statements. Certain failures of religious accomodation, as in Burma, Egypt, the Soviet Union, Ulster, Cyprus and Lebanon, are also worthy of special study.

Each religious group so far seems to have taken care of its own struggles for recognition. International pronouncements are generally useless. Collective international activity on behalf of religious groups is virtually unknown. The study of religious freedom is a composite, consisting of the story of the Copts in Egypt, Jehovah's Witnesses in Malawi, Jews in the Soviet Union, Protestants in Spain, etc.

The following organizations appear to be good sources of information: African-American Institute; American Jewish Committee; American Jewish Congress; Americans United for Separation of Church and State; Anti-Defamation League of B'nai B'rith; Center for the Study of Religion and Communism, Kent, England; Church of the Latter Day Saints, Salt Lake City, Utah; Conscience et Liberte, Berne, Switzerland; General Conference of

Seventh Day Adventists; Human Rights Commission -- Liason Office in the U.N.; Irani Academy of Philosophy; International League for Human Rights; Institute for the Study of Ethnic and Religious Groups, Rab Illan University, Israel; International Religious Peace Colloquium, Washington, D.C.; Islamic Center, Washington, D.C.; Jehovah's Witnesses; National Council of Churches; National Council of Churches of Christ; Office of International Justice and Peace, African Affairs, U.S. Catholic Conference, Washington; Permanent Observer of the Holy See to the U.N.; United Nations Library; UNESCO -- Geneva; World Conference on Religion and Peace; World Jewish Congress, Geneva, Paris and World Organization of Jews from Arab Countries.

Written sources are few and far between, particularly those written after 1970 and even the primary UN documentation dates from the sixties. There are not more than a dozen works which can be recommended as a good starting point. [71]

---

71. Bailey, S.C. "Religious Freedom and the United Nations." *Christian Century*, Chicago, 77:508-510, 27 April 1960; Jack, Homer, "Elaborating a Declaration Against Religious Discrimination: Opportunities and Frustrations in the U.N. System," W.C.P.R. Report, New York, 1978; Pfeffer, Leo. *God, Caesar and the Court: The Court as a Referee of Church-State Confrontation.* Boston, Beacon Press, 1975; United Nations: Badouin, Ibrahim (Egypt). *Elimination of All Forms of Religious Intolerance*, Report of the Third Committee, 19 December, 1976; Blahaslav, S. Hubrig, ed. *Religion in Communist Dominated Areas,* Volume XV, Research Center for Religion and Human Rights in Closed Societies, New York, 1978; "Chronical of the Catholic Church in Lithuania -- A Translation of Authentic Reports from Soviet Occupied Lithuania" Lithuanian Roman Catholic Priests League of America, New York, 1978. First World Congress on Religious Liberty, Amsterdam, March 21-23, 1977, International Religious Liberty Association, Washington, D.C., 1978; Jack, Homer, ed. International Inter-Religion Symposium on Peace, *World Religion and World Peace*, Boston: Beacon Press, 1968; *Soviet Persecution of Religion in Ukraine*, World Congress of Free Ukrainians, Toronto, Canada, 1978; United Nations: Cossessers, Autrium, United Nations Economic and Social Council, Commission on Human Rights, Sub-Commission on Prevention of Discrimination and Protection of Minorities on its 13th Session "Study on the Rights of Persons Belonging to Ethnic, Religious and Linguistic Minorities. 2 September 1977 E/CN.4/Sub.2/384/Add. 1-7 Geneva; United Nations. *Report of the Sub-Commission on Prevention of Discrimination and Protection of Minorities.* 2 September 1977.

CHAPTER IX

THE LEGAL ENVIRONMENT OF WOMEN

There are few constitutions in the world in which distinctions between men and women are clearly drawn or which contain prescriptions either discriminating against women or protecting the other sex. United Nations pronouncements generally decry the existence of any disabilities against the female of the species. On another level (not the subject of this study) are measures which governments have promulgated, enacted and decreed as law and which do discriminate against women. Thirdly, there are the laws passed by autonomous regions within a federal structure enabling one state to pass discriminatory measures not existing in the state next door or in federal legislation. Finally, there is the vast field of *de facto* discrimination.

Despite what governments may say at the United Nations, despite the principles entrenched in constitutions of countries, despite laws passed by provinces, federal states and national governments to outlaw discrimination between the sexes or against the female of the species, *dejure* and *de facto* discrimination against women almost everywhere exists on a significant scale.

In African states tribal customs which often enjoy the same status as a law of Parliament allows for appalling discrimination against women. The Muslim religion automatically spawns negative discrimination. Of course, discrimination, like beauty and objectivity, is in the eyes of the beholder. To the African tribesman or Muslim clergymen, it may not appear to be discriminatory or to be wrong at all. To a resident of New York City, it is discriminatory and abhorent. On October 2, 1983 a wire service report from Islamabad, Pakistan read as follows: "A widow (sic) accused of adultery cried out as she was flogged 15 times before 5,000 onlookers . . . many of those watching were women who broke into sobs." [72] In New York City the average Christian would consider this a barbaric act, but in Pakistan the community was merely imposing Islamic (religious) penal law.

There are 300 million women in the Muslim world whose status are regulated by Muslim religious laws derived from the Koran. Many are subject to marriages and adoptions against their will. The modern definition of slavery includes such matters as forced marriage, pseudo-adoptions, both of which are violations of women's rights -- in our eyes -- but not in the eyes of the Muslim world.

* * *

Once again, there is a lack of reliable source material which proves how women are legally discriminated against -- using discrimination in its Western context and for comparative purposes.

The literature on women's rights are mostly one-dimensional. There are no overall studies covering statutes or covering cases, no comparative analysis of voting rights or restrictive inheritance practises around the world, with the exception of population studies which covers the world's family planning and abortion laws. To the novice researcher in the U.S.A. or Europe, there is an

72. *The Atlanta Constitution.* The flogging took place in the town of Liagapur. The widow was 35 years old. Normally 100 lashes are applied.

embarras de richesse and material on women's rights abounds. But of comparative analysis, particularly in the strictly legal field or in the field of constitutional law, there are few if any really good ones.

One of the best books on the rights of women was written by Susan Ross of the Civil Rights Division of the US Department of Justice and by Ann Barcher, an attorney, of New York, but the book (*The Rights of Women*) deals exclusively with women's rights in the U.S. under existing U.S. laws. [73] If a similar book existed on the rights of women in Pakistan then we can begin with a comparative analysis.

An extremely well written work, but not as strictly legal as the Ross-Barcher work, is that on women in the Soviet Union by Gail Lapidus. [74]

Third World literature on the same subject is more often than not too politicised to be useful. The same with the Communist states. It is simply untrue, as left wing propaganda would have it, that Communist nations, particularly the Soviet Union, effectively guarantee the equality of the sexes and that discrimination against women is the fault of capitalism. The Lapidus book proves this beyond doubt.

There is a vast literature from the International Women's Year of 1975 and since we are in the midst of the United Nations Decade for Women, more and better publications of the nature of Ms. Lapidus can be expected. The major defect with existing materials is that they are one-dimensional. The study of the human rights of women seems to have no unified basis.

In this chapter there will be references to constitutional discrimination and differentiation in so far as it affects women as well as some data on the existence of discrimination despite the legal environment. Thus, a definition of sex discrimination is now necessary. The best seems that of Constantina Safilios-Rothschild:

---

73. Bantam Books, New York, 1983. An earlier excellent book is Coote, Anna: *Women's Rights,* Penquin Books, 1974.

74. Lapidus, G.W.: *Women in Soviet Society,* University of California Press, 1978.

"Sex discrimination refers to the differential treatment of women and men on the basis of their categorical membership, that is, on the basis of their gender, and without consideration of individual differences, in terms of ability, competence, inclination and committment." [75]

With the foregoing definition in mind, let us now look at the constitutional and legal situation in the Muslim world.

To any Christian, the Islamic laws as they apply to women are discriminatory in principle and in practice. The Koran, the holy Bible of the Muslim world, is the constitution in many of the world's 40 Muslim states. It contains discrimination against women which would be unconstitutional in the U.S.A. and illegal in dozens of other countries of the world. A Western woman in Saudi Arabia could be contravening the Moslem laws in ways which appear to us, as Christians and Westerners, to be even absurd! She may not drive a car; she may not appear in public in anything less than a floor length dress with arms covered to the wrist; it is illegal for women to work openly; women who do work face the constant threat of discovery by the religious police who may confiscate their passports and, if they are not Saudi citizens, impose heavy fines or deport them. In her own home, she has to occupy separate quarters. [76]

In Pakistan in 1983 there were massive riots with police in Lahore having to use tear gas and batons to break up a women's demonstration against proposed legal changes such as making the testimony of one man equal to that of two women. [77] The previous year there were demonstrations when the men-only Pakistani contingent flew out to the Asian Games, the Asian

75. "Sex Discrimination: Theory and Research" in *Case Studies on Human Rights,* Vol. V., p. 140.

76. Lewis, Jane: "A Western Woman in Saudi Arabia" in *International Living,* Baltimore, U.S.A., Vol. 3, No. 4, 1983, p. 1. Cf. Coulson, N.J.: "The State and the Individual in Islamic Law," *International and Comparative Law Quarterly,* 6/49, 1957 and "Arab Women," Minority Rights Group Reports, Benjamin Franklin House, London, No. 27.

77. Reuters, *International Herald Tribune,* February 22, 1983.

equivalent of the Olympic Games. If ever there was a field in which the effort of the individual should be above discrimination on the basis of race, religion, politics and sex, it is sports, particularly at international level such as the Olympic and Asian Games. Yet Pakistan could not send a women's hockey or basketball team since men are forbidden to watch teams of women play. The demonstration casts an interesting sidelight on the morality of the International Olympic Games (IOC) which prohibits South African athletes from participating in the Olympic Games, not because the teams are racially segregated, on the contrary, South African athletic teams are all multi-racial (so are the selection committees and the audiences who watch them play), but because the South African political system discriminates against Blacks. The Pakistani action clearly calls for a similar boycott against Pakistani teams by the IOC but it is not to be. Though there may be no discrimination against athletes on grounds of race, religion or sex, clearly discrimination on grounds of race is considered to be a greater evil in the eyes of the IOC. (This is known as selective indignation.) The counter argument is also that if South Africa is to change its entire political structure to satisfy the IOC (and the United Nations) then Pakistan should change its Islamic legal structure, which it cannot do because the legal structure is derived from their Bible, the Koran.

Islam is to a high degree simply a male oriented doctrine. The constitutions of most Arab states, for example, fail to provide a realistic picture of discrimination against women. In the Islamic law of succession, a woman's portion is equal to half the portion of a man; the daughter of a testator receives under the law only half the share of the brother. This is exemplified in the civil code of Morocco, Articles 237-244 and the civil code of Syria, Articles 277/2. Article 65 of the constitution of Pakistan specifies that there shall be 15 seats in the assembly set aside only for women.

The pattern of discrimination is set by the Koran. "Men should be favoured above women . . . because they (men) are responsible for them (women).''[78] Here are further examples: Children remain under the father's authority even after a divorce or after ''banishment'' of the mother. In the case of the father's death, his authority is transferred to his closest male relative. A Moslem woman may not be married to a man of a different faith, neither Jew nor Christian.[79] The right of banishment of a woman from her home is entirely the man's prerogative.[80] On principle he can dissolve the marriage at any time. If a woman dies childless, half of what the woman leaves belongs to the husband. If the husband dies first in a childless family, the wife receives only one fourth (the rest goes to the father or mother of the deceased or to the community) and if the man dies, leaving children, the woman's part is further reduced and she receives only one-eighth of the man's estate.[81]

Sexism is deeply rooted in the religious and cultural norms of Islam. According to the Koran feminine names should not be used for Angels.[82] Other basic texts of Islamic law show clearly that women do not enjoy the same status and prestige as men. Nor can they claim the same rights.

In Egypt men often divorce their wives if they do not give birth to boys. ''No alimony is due to a woman in case she is imprisoned, even unjustly, or arrested, or raped, or left her husband's house. . . or she was in any condition which rendered her useless as a wife.''[83] It should always be kept in mind that Muslim law is an echo of Mosaic law in which women were property.[84] In the less modernised Muslim societies women have to contend with a form of quasi-slavery including servile marriage. The Anti-Slavery Society has also directed considerable attention to female

78. The Koran: 4S., 35V.

79. Ameluxen, Clement: ''Marriage and Women in Islamic Countries in *Case Studies on Human Rights,* Vol. II, pp. 94-95.

80. The Koran: 2,228-237; 5,288 and 65, 1-6.

81. Ibid., 4,12-13.

82. Sura, 53 V 29.

83. Egyptian Marriage Law, Article 67. Cf. O'Kane, Joseph P.: ''Islam in the New Egyptian Constitution,'' *Middle East Journal,* 26/137, 1972.

84. *Encyclopedia Biblica,* Vol. III, p. 2942.

circumcision which accompanies servile marriage.[85]

From time to time one is struck by oddities in Islamic Law and in customs which seem to contradict the discriminatory pattern. Article 75 of the 1973 Constitution of Sudan dictates that a pregnant woman may not be executed, but this is not because of the woman, but for the sake of the unborn child. The execution takes place after birth. In Saudi Arabia the recent opening of a bank for women is seen in the same context as the first all-women bank in New York. Yet there is a world of difference. In Riyadh, where the particular bank is situated behind the National Commercial Banks' Nassiriah Street branch, the women's bank is conspicuous for the fact that an armed guard sits in the foyer to prevent any male from entering. The windows are closed and draped so that no man can see the female clerks at work.[86] This is merely a further response of Islam's restriction on co-mingling between men and women.

Elsewhere in the Muslim world the situation is much the same. The Bengali women in Bangladesh, both rural and urban, traditional and modern, live in a social system that sanctifies an unequal and inferior status for women. "There has been no serious movement to modify the legal system to give women equal rights of inheritance, guardianship, or marriage and divorce."[87] Several researchers have referred to the fact than in Islam a woman who has been raped is rejected by society. Of an estimated 200,000 cases of rape in Bangladesh one year only 22,500 were reported because the family wanted to keep the rape secret.[88]

A most interesting statistical analysis by Marielouise Jannsen-Jurrei in her book *Sexism* (originally published in German under the title: *Seximus: Uber Die Abtreibung der Frauenfrage*) shows that whereas in Western society the proportion of women in the population is higher than that of men, by the year 1985 the

85. Glaser and Possony, op. cit., pp. 458-9.

86. Alford, Jane in *The Atlanta Journal and Constitution,* November 6, 1983, p. 37-A.

87. Jahan, Rounaq: "Women in Bangladesh" in *Case Studies On Human Rights,* Vol. V, p. 558.

88. Jannsen-Jurreit, Marielouise: *Sexism,* McGraw Hill, 1982, p. 237.

proportion of women is projected to drop to 49.78 percent. In Arab and Islamic countries, however, the decrease is more significant and highly visible. In Libya it is already 48 percent, in Iran 46.92, in Kuwait 43.19 and in the United Arab Emirates the figure is down to 38.14 percent. "Either the women are regarded as so insignificant that any census of their numbers is inadequate, or they are consciously decimated by negligent hygiene." [89]

Women and Communism

Most recently some excellent studies have shown that it is simply untrue that the status of women in a Communist society such as the Soviet Union is better than that of women in the West (a) because of the Soviet constitution and (b) because discrimination against women is said to be the fault of capitalism. One such study is that by Gail Lapidus *Women in Soviet Society.* Her conclusion was that despite a deliberate expansion of female political and economical participation in the Soviet society the past decade "the terms on which it occurred both sustained and reinforced a pervasive assymmetry of male and female roles. This . . . was not merely a consequence of cultural lag, but reflected, rather, a coherent, mutually reinforcing and systematic pattern of official perceptions, priorities, and institutional arrangements that impinged on every dimension of social structure." Ms. Lapidus presents a strong case , based on Soviet official sources and Soviet documents that: "The utilization of women as a major political and economic force . . . could not help but transform the very meaning of equality, ultimately draining it of libertarian and humanitarian underpinnings and infusing it with instrumental and utilitarian concerns . . . sexual equality ultimately came to mean an equal liability to mobilise." She pointed out that Soviet patterns of political authority precluded the emergence of a genuine civic culture that would permit the political participation of men and women alike as citizens rather than as subjects. "The very

80. Jannsen-Jurreit, op. cit., pp. 264-265.

recognition accorded women as a collectivity is itself a reflection of a subject political culture in which no outonomous group activity is permitted.'' [90] According to Ms. Lapidus both classical Marxist theory and Soviet revolutionary ideology were insensitive to the deeper psychological roots of family patterns and sex roles. ''By assimilating sexual relationships into Marxist models of stratification, Soviet ideology obscured the ways in which patterns of sexual inequality derived from irrational and indeed unconscious psychological processes . . . Soviet ideology thus concentrated on the more superficial economic aspects of women's roles . . . [91] Ms. Lapidus' views of Marxism and women is shared by that of the German researcher Marielouise Jannsen-Jureit who observed that in the few instances where Marx makes special mention of women, it is always to say that the cheaper women's and children's work supplant that of a man. [92] In the Soviet Union there is a critical distinction between mobilization and liberation. ''The fact that women were perceived as a major economic and political resource was compatible with an extreme degree of exploitation.'' [93] The Soviet version of affirmative action was protective labor legislation, public child care institutions, expansion of educational opportunities -- all aimed at providing more and educated labour units. Entry to schools and technical institutions were carefully regulated. There was no question of really opening Soviet economic society to women because they deserved it as fellow Soviet citizens, but in order to regulate the supply of labour. Gail Lapidus quotes Soviet figures that of 607 students attending a special school for maths and physics in Novosibirsk only 67 were girls. She found that even during the seventies there was substantial evidence that discriminatory admissions policies persist. [94] It was the same in the political field. Women are largely absent from the upper reaches of power. In some areas women's participation in politics even declined between 1944 and

90. Op. cit., pp. 335-340.

91. Ibid., p. 7.

92. Op. cit., p. 109.

93. Lapidus, G.: Op. cit., 338.

94. Ibid., pp. 147-151.

1974. Ms. Lapidus quotes official Soviet statistics to show that in Tadzhikistan women formed 30 percent of the party membership in 1944 and only 18.9 percent in 1974. In primary Communist Party organizations women formed only one third of the total. Women formed less than 4 percent of all urban and district Party secretaries in the USSR in 1973. In March 1976 the Central Committee of the Party had 426 members, but of the total only 3.3 percent were women. Despite the new Soviet Constitution and its liberal phraseology, the fact is that since 1928 the proportion of women in the Central Committee never exceeded 4.3 percent.[95]

Women in the Western World

Given the massive apparatus available to women in the United States to promote their cause in the field of constitutional rights, the press, television, organized women's movements, women in Congress, in government and the high values which American society accord to freedom and democracy, it seems almost strange that by 1984 American women (or men) had not yet succeeded in obtaining a specific constitutional guarantee of equality of the sexes while such an equal rights clause has been enshrined in the French constitution since 1946: "The law guarantees to women, in all fields, rights equal to those of men." In addition female employees are formally guaranteed equality of rights by virtue of French membership of the European Common Market. Article 119 of the Treaty of Rome requires equal pay for equal work in all Common Market countries. Consequently career women in France enjoy an acceptance and status that professional women of other countries envy, helped along by the fact that the most recent polls, conducted in the seventies, indicate that French men overwhelmingly have no objection to women working, obtaining better jobs or holding more important positions than they do. Almost 70 percent voted that they would accept a woman for a boss.[96] France has a

95. Op. Cit., pp. 213-217.

96. Steiner, Shari: *The Female Factor: Women in West Europe*, Intercultural Press, Chicago, 1977, p. 182.

higher percentage of women lawyers and engineers than any other Western country. The situation has changed much since the twenties when France was the only country in Europe where women did not even have the right to vote in municipal elections. The French Napoleonic Code served to restrict women's energies to backstage intrigue for over a hundred years. World War II and particularly the Presidency of Valerie Giscaird d'Estaing changed all of this.[97] There is still a gap between what the law states and what happens in practice, but that gap is less than what it is, for example, in the United States. In 1972 average wages for women in France was 93.3 of men's.[98] In the United States in 1972 it was 58 percent and even by 1982 it was still only 59 percent.[99] But in certain industries, banking, insurance, commerce and the textile industry, the women's percentage in France compared to men dropped sharply to about 60 percent. Also in top command positions at universities, the civil service, politics or business the French society still do not see women in true posts of influence.

In the rest of Europe the progress towards constitutional protection and legal assistance to address the imbalance in women's rights had an equally late start. It was only in 1970 that the British Parliament passed a simple law requiring equal pay for equal work and even this only became effective in December 1975 and was hastened by the Treaty of Rome after Britain joined the ECC. But the act does not provide for equality of opportunity, leaving room for manipulation of the law.[100] It was only at the end of 1974 that the Wilson government launched a Women's Rights Law.

Constitutionally, it would not appear on the surface that there should or could be discrimination in Britain against women but it is

---

97. Steiner, Shari: Op. Cit., p. 134.

98. *Le Nouvelle Observateur,* Paris, January 28, 1983.

99. Data supplied by U.S. Departments of Commerce and Labor, Equal Employment Commission and graphically set out in *U.S. News and World Report,* November 29, 1982, p. 55.

100. Cf. Chester, L. and Boston, S.: "Secret Memos Aims to Stop Equal Pay for Women," *The Sunday Times,* London, February 11, 1973.

very much the case. In certain areas, such as medical practitioners, women have made incredible strides, elsewhere she still finds herself in the traditional areas of employment of twenty years ago and wage and legal discrimination remain. The average English woman cannot enter into contract unless she has her husband's signature, even if this is to make a contract with the gas or electric company. Legally, she has no right to see her husband's tax returns, although he is required to sign hers. English law is adamant that man is the breadwinner and owns the home. If a woman does not contribute regularly to the joint account, it is considered to be entirely the husband's. For a loan to start a business, even if she finances and staffs the venture on her own, the woman must obtain her husband's signature on the application form. [101]

British laws on divorce were long among the most discriminatory in the world when it comes to the rights of women, but in a protective sense. A woman divorced in her twenties can expect to receive money from her ex-husband for the rest of her life. There is absolutely no need, no provision, no incentive, or discipline in the law that divorced women should make an effort to become financially independent. By 1983 the climate appears to have changed in the British Parliament based on the recommendations of the British Law Commission on the subject. The new laws proposed is that there should be a clean break between couples and in some cases, end the so-called meal-ticket-for-life maintenance payments. The Law Commission recommended maintenance to be given only for the time it takes the spouse to adjust to his or her situation and to find a job, with priority given to the needs of children. For women, the compensation is that the courts will have far greater power and discretion to divide the property of spouses.

Generally speaking, the past five years have seen women make great strides towards obtaining both equal rights and treatment as well as equal opportunity in England but equality in practice is

101. Steiner, Shari: Op. cit., p. 41.

vitiated by the segmentation of the labour market, by level, by sector and by skill categories. Female labour is still treated as being supplementary while opportunities for upward mobility are limited by lower continuity of employment and indirect, if not outright, discrimination. In political life men and women are educated equally for citizenship and afforded equal rights of participation though no special effort is made to encourage the exercise of such rights. Despite the image presented by Mrs. Margaret Thatcher, Prime Minister of Britain, few women play an active role in politics at national level. [102]

Switzerland is the only exception among the so-called Germanic countries when it comes to legislative support for the women, particularly the female work force. The others, Austria, East and West Germany all have equality clauses in their constitutions and paid pregnancy leaves in their laws. The West German Basic Law or constitution also states: "Men and women shall have equal rights."[103]

West German women have made an impressive mark in the political and legal profession. In December 1972 West Germany's Bundestag elected Annemarie Renger as President of the Bundestag, the third highest offices in the German state after the Federal President and the Chancellor. Wiltraut von Brunneck became only the fourth woman in the world to become a Supreme Court Judge. The other three were all in Scandinavia. (In 1982 she was followed by the fifth, Ms. Sandra O'Connor, of the United States.)

Women play a far more important role in the labour union movements in Germany than in the United States. One of the three-menber ruling committee members of Germany's Amalgamated Workers' Union (the second largest federated union, in membership, in the world, after England's Trade Union Congress)

102. Cf. Blake, Judith: "The Changing Status of Women in Developed Countries," *Scientific American,* 231 (1974) pp. 137-147.

103. Section I, Basic Rights, Article 3, par. 2.

was a woman, Maria Weber. But as Shari Steiner observed: ''Once one looks past the outstanding examples the picture of women takes on a decidedly less optimistic cast.'' She pointed out that second rate status is reflected in wages and that equal pay for equal work remains a major objective for women in West Germany.[104] Thus the Treaty of Rome seems to have had little practical legal impact on Germany.

On the vexing question of abortion the situation remains fluid at the end of the seventies. Sterilization was legalized in West Germany in 1973 and in Austria in 1975 and in Swiss law varies from canton to canton. Abortion on demand was legal in East Germany, but is illegal in Switzerland. Abortion on demand was legalized in West Germany and Austria in 1974 but the German Constitutional Court later declared the law unconstitutional. Abortion is now available only for health reasons.

There remains a vast area in which discrimination against women are prevalent and for which a constitutional solution seems difficult to achieve. The fact that it took 100 years for the Berlin Philharmonic Orchestra to admit a woman to membership and that this only took place in 1983 is a good example, as was the strike threatened by the orchestra when the Director, Herbert von Karajan wanted to bring in a second female.

Since World War II the legal status of women in Italy, long the most neglected group in Europe together with women in Greece and Spain, has undergone enormous changes. June 1946 marked the first election with women's suffrage. The 1948 constitution stated explicitly that women are fully equal with men: ''All citizens have equal social dignity and are equal before the law, regardless of sex, race, language, religion, political opinions or personal and social conditions.''[105] Subsequent governments have passed

---

104. Op. cit., pp. 213-214 and cf. Kuhrig, Herta: *Equal Rights for Women in the German Democratic Republic,* Publication of the GDR Committee for Human Rights, 1973.

105. Article III of the 1948 Constitution.

equal employment and equal opportunity laws, as well as equal eligibility for public office.

Italian women are covered by special protective statutes as an employee e.g. she cannot do heavy or dangerous work and cannot be fired for marriage or pregnancy. During the sixties the law that made adultery only a crime for the wife was invalidated by the Italian Supreme Court. The seventies saw legalization of divorce and birth control and even abortion became legal when the court ruled in 1975 that it is legal for women whose physical or mental health was endangered by her pregnancy. In fact, it can be said that progress in Italy was quite incredible considering the Italian women's lack of support in the media as compared to the United States and the low level of organization of women's rights movements.

In April 1975 there were further revisions by Parliament in the family laws of Italy. The wife obtained equal say in where the family lives and how the children should be educated. Unlike Britain, she may sign the family's electric, gas and telephone contracts, using her maiden name. She may keep her own bank account. Compared to Britain, Italian women are legally and constitutionally in very good shape but although it looks impressively solid, authorities rarely fulfill the promise and the rights held out by legislation. Nonetheless, Italian women have made impressive strides in education and in business. It is only in politics where Italian women have fared less well. During the seventies, no-one made it to the Cabinet. Women have never been considered serious candidates for the post of mayor of any major Italian city. Their strength has been in business and the arts. [106]

The dynamics of equality has worked best in Scandinavia, although the suicide rate among women is highest in this part of the world than anywhere else in Europe, with Denmark the highest. The price women have to pay in Scandinavia for achieving an equal status both in terms of the law and in practice, appears to

106. Steiner, Shari: Op. cit., p. 126.

be high. Today Finland and Sweden lead the West in their efforts to make the working mother and wife a practical reality. Legal systems have been revamped for this purpose in all Scandinavian countries. Taxes no longer penalize a two career family as they do in so many countries. The Scandinavian commitment to sexual equality is clear cut. The abortion laws are ''liberal'' and is available to residents until the nineteenth week of pregnancy.

Career wise the Scandinavian women have done well and up until the end of the seventies the highest post held by a woman in the United Nations was that occupied by the Finn, Helvi Sipila. Women totally controlled the city councils of Norway's largest cities. The President of the Norwegian senate during the seventies was a woman. The Vice President of the Swedish Parliament is a woman. Women are Supreme Court Judges in both Norway and Demmark. All four Scandinavian countries have women in the cabinet. Finland and Denmark had the largest female proportion in their work forces of any country outside the Eastern bloc during 1976. [107]

One area in which Scandinavian women have not made the progress they had hoped for is in business and female candidates for the post of Prime Minister are taken less seriously than in France and England. But as Shari Steiner quite rightly observed after her study of Scandinavian women: ''For the moment Swedish women have the most freedom to develop their individuality of any women on earth.'' [108]

Africa and Israel

The fate of women elsewhere in the world, in Latin America, Israel and Africa is one of great concern, not so much because of

---

107. Steiner, Shari: Op. Cit., p. 296.

108. Ibid., p. 300. Cf. Schreiber, Anna P.: ''The Status of Women in the United States and Scandinavian Countries'' in Richard Claude (ed.), *Comparative Human Rights*, Johns Hopkins University Press, Baltimore, 1976 and Thalman-Antenen, Helene: ''Equal Pay: The Position in Switzerland,'' *International Law Review*, 104/275, 1971.

lack of constitutional protection, but because of the huge gap which exists between policy and practice, between what the law and the constitution states and what practice proves.

It is not only in the Muslim states that women are discriminated against because of religious prescriptions. This is also true of society in Israel. The woman is certainly the principal victim of theocratic legislation. In archaic Jewish (as well as Islamic law) she is considered not only as an unequal, but to be the property of her husband. [109] In Israel it is explicitly laid down that the Law of Equality of Women (1953) does not apply to marriage and divorce. Israeli women cannot obtain divorce without their husband's consent. A man may remarry if his wife is declared insane, but the wife remains forever chained to an insane husband. The offspring of adulterous relations of a married woman will be barred for ten generations to marry pure Jews but the offspring of a married man with an unmarried female are pure Jews. [110]

In Africa there is so much discrimination against black women that a few general observations will suffice. Most African states have introduced concepts of liberty, equality, freedom and democracy in their constitutions based on race, religion and sex. But African tribal law is frequently given legal recognition, even in the most industrially developed African states, such as South Africa. Tribal law, tribal customs, subject most black women to social and legal disabilities. Among the Bantu-speaking nations of East and Southern Africa a women does not inherit her husband's property when he dies. The inheritance goes to a male descendent. A widowed African woman is always subjected to a man's guardianship. If she wishes to travel overseas, she may have to ask written permission from her own sons. [111]

There are a number of classless societies in Africa in which

109. Tamarain, G.R.: "Israel Society: Authoritarian Traditionalism vs Pluralist Democracy" in *Case Studies on Human Rights,* Vol. II, p. 119. Cf. Berinson Svi: "Freedom of Religion and Conscience in the State of Israel," *Israel Yearbook of Human Rights,* 3/223 (1973) and Lahav, Pnina: "The Status of Women in Israel: Myth and Reality," *American Journal of Comparative Law,* 22/107, 1974.

110. Cf. Tamarin, G.R., *The Israeli Dilemma,* Rotterdam Univ. Press, 1973, pp. 33-34.

111. Glaser and Possony, op. cit., 270.

women not only bring up the children and do all the housework but are also responsible for almost the total production of society, such as the Somali in East Africa. The Somali once regarded their female children as capital and sold them as slaves in time of famine.[112] Among the Masai of East Africa it is common for the wife to be thrashed and the courts are reluctant to act against tribal custom and law. For many years the same custom could be found among the Zulu, Xhosa and Sotho in South Africa and where the accused has the right to be heard according to tribal law.[113]

Black women in white ruled South Africa are the victims of triple discrimination. They are discriminated against (i) because they are Black, (ii) because they are women and (iii) because they are Black women. About 99 percent of all Black women in South Africa during the early eighties were still legal minors. Whether they are married under civil law or under tribal law their husbands have marital power over them and are their legal guardians. Thus Black women may buy houses from the Department of Community Development but at the same time they are not eligible for building society loans. Marital power which gives a husband rights over his wife's estate and denies her contractual capacity is not enforced in any other western state, but it was still the case in South Africa in 1983 -- for both Black and White women. Thus a married woman, married in community of property, has less legal status than her unmarried 18 year old daughter.

A Law Commission has been appointed to look at the plethora of discriminatory legislation against women in South Africa and made several recommendations to Parliament during 1983 to try and rectify the situation. One of the Commissions' proposals are

---

112. Sanday, Peggy: "Towards a Theory on the Status of Women," *American Anthropologist,* Vol. 76, 1973, p. 1696.

113. *Official Yearbook,* Department of Information, 1977, pp. 305-306. Cf. Jannsen-Jurreit, Marielouse: Op. cit., pp. 224-225; cf. Mbilinyi, M.J.: "The State of Women in Tanzania," *Canadian Journal of African Studies,* 6/371, 1972 and Dryden, P.K.: "Annotated Bibliography of Political Rights of African Women," *African Law Studies,* 7/27, 1972.

that marital power should be abolished -- but only for future marriages which means that a whole generation of women now married will have to die before marital power in South Africa ends. The proposals were not enthusiastically endorsed by everyone. Some newspapers suggested editorially that it is doubtful that the Commissions recommendations are the real answer to the problems faced by women.[114] Others considered it a giant step and that a women's charter has now become a matter of urgency.[115] In 1977 a study group on women in employment was set up in South Africa to investigate the working conditions and legal status of women and to make recommendations to a government commission of inquiry into labour legislation. The group found that women represent 32 percent of the working force in South Africa and that they are subject to various forms of discrimination in employment: (a) traditional discrimination by employers (b) lack of mobility and (c) through education and training. Job advertisements are often worded to deter women from applying. The group also believed that the danger of the rate for the job without fair employment legislation could lead to the retrenchment and discharge of many women. "Only legislative sanctions against discrimination could avoid malpractice." Female agricultural workers are in particularly bad circumstances. They are covered by the Workmen's Compensation Act but have no standards of pay, working conditions or housing laid down for them. Black pregnant women almost invariably lose their jobs (unlike most western states). Maternity benefits are only 45 percent of the worker's salary compared to full pay in Australia and 90 percent of salary in Great Britain.[116]

In general women are paid much less than men in South Africa, the professional division in the public service being a major

114. *Die Vaderland*, Johannesburg, May 10, 1983.

115. *The Star*, Johannesburg and *The Pretoria News*, May 10, 1983.

116. Women's Legal Status Committee: "Memorandum to the Commission of Inquiry into Labour Legislation," Johannesburg, September 1978. For an interesting comparison see Polson, Y.E.: "Rights of Working Women," *Virginia International Law Review*, 15/729, 1974.

exception. The South African Wage and Industrial Conciliation Acts make no explicit provision for the abolishment of discrimination based on sex. Childless professional women, married career women and highly qualified married women with children who are employed are the subjects of massive tax discrimination. The government's argument that their income are jointly taxed with that of their husbands' because they are only working to supplement the family income is belied by the tens of thousands of married career women in South Africa whose husbands make more than enough for the entire family. Joint taxation militates not only against well-qualified and professional high-salaried women but also against their husbands. When both husband and wife are highly qualified, for example, lawyers or medical practitioners, the women in fact are working for the state -- for no net income.

There are many other examples of discrimination against women in South Africa, both Black and White. Women have to work more years than men before qualifying for entry into a pension scheme. A woman's pension also dies with her but not that of the man. Educational loans are often denied to women employees but are freely available to men. Women in public service have almost no hope ever to become head of a government department. No woman has ever served in the South African cabinet. No woman has ever been appointed as a South African Ambassador abroad. In general, women in South Africa also find themselves in the so-called women's ghetto when it comes to categories of employment. The overwhelming majority end up as typists, secretaries, shop assistants, clerks, factory workers, cashiers, teachers, and civil servants.

The United States

The Constitution of the United States contains no clause which discriminates against women. But there are laws passed by the various states which make up the Union which are discriminatory. There are also federal statutes that contain gender differences. In 1983 there were still 113 such federal statutes -- 44 to do with the armed forces, 20 with Social Security benefits and ten dealing with Indian tribal law, e.g. that a white man may not acquire right to Indian tribal property by marrying an Indian woman. A number of American states still have community property laws and in all the community states, except Texas and Washington, the husband has power of attorney over the community property. There are also discrepancies in criminal law. Several states, such as New Mexico, have statutes which exonerate a husband who kills his wife's lover *in flagrante delicto* but leaves punishable a similar crime committed by a wife against her husband's mistress.[117]

There is a foolish notion that the passing of an equal rights amendment to the United States Constitution would bring a speedy end to discrimination against women, but that would only be symbolic. Let us look first at some of the non-legal forms of discrimination which existed in the United States during the seventies and early eighties.

Women professors in the State of Georgia, on the average, earn about $5,000 less per annum than their male colleagues at the same universities and far fewer gain tenure. Similar disparities exist at all other college faculty ranks according to a 1983 report by the United State's Department of Education's National Centre for Education Statistics. The report showed that only 38.3 percent of Georgia's faculty members had tenure or were working with job security compared to 61.7 percent of men. Full time male faculty members outnumber women by three to one despite passage of Title VII of the 1964 Civil Rights Act and Title IX of the Higher Education Act -- both which outlaw sex discrimination.

A Cox newspaper survey in 1983 discovered the following situation in the citadel of freedom and equality, the U.S. Senate: Of all employees of Senate staff the average male salary was

117. Glaser and Possony, op. cit., p. 333.

approximately 30 percent higher for males than for females in the post of secretary. When comparable positions are taken such as press secretary, the average male still earns about 18 percent more than female. In the higher paid ranks of committee staffers in Congress, 77 percent are men. At the other (lower) end of the scale women make up for 79 percent of the staff. In both the House and Senate, regardless of party affiliation, eight of the nine lowest paying job categories contained more women than men.[118]

In 1982 only 19 of the 435 members of the U.S. House of Representatives were female, i.e. roughly 4.3 percent. In the Senate it is one percent.

So sexually segregated is the American job market in 1982 that 60 percent of all working women would have to move across occupational categories in order to equalize the distribution of the sexes by job. Two researchers of the University of California, working with data collected by the U.S. Department of Labour and the Bureau of Census between 1968 and 1979 found that this pattern has changed very little since 1900. "Economic discrimination against women is not just unequal pay for equal work," the two researchers concluded, "It's rather an issue of not having equal access." So pervasive is sexual segregation in the working place, they added, that even women's rights groups seems largely unaware of the economic and professional handicap it places upon female workers. Women are accorded fewer training opportunities, narrower advancement possibilities and lower salaries.[119]

Only five percent of the top executives of the 50 biggest U.S. companies are women. On management level the situation is no better. In 1980 the median salary for managers and administrators was $12,936 for women and $23,558 for their male counterparts. According to a special survey made by *Time*, following the

118. Checco, L. and Alexander, A.: "Congress Still Biased," *The Atlanta Journal and Constitution,* August 21, 1983, 6-A.

119. Bielby, W.T. and Baron, J.N.: *Women's Place Is With Other Women; Sex Segregation in the Workplace,* University of California, 1983, study sponsored by the National Academy of Sciences.

defeat of the Equal Rights Amendment Act.[120] weekly medians for earnings by occupation in other areas during 1981 revealed the ratio of men's pay compared to that of women to be the following: clerical workers 3.2 to 2.2; computer specialists 4.8 to 3.5; engineers 5.4 to 3.7; lawyers 5.7 to 4.0; physicians 4.95 to 4.0; sales workers 3.6 to 1.9; teachers 3.7 to 3.1; waiters 2.0 to 1.4 and among the moral conscience of the nation, the press, 3.8 to 3.2.

Today there are 47 million women in the labor force in the U.S.A. Despite massive publicity concerning discrimination against women in the U.S.A., change, in a broader sense, has been at snails pace. In 1962, women formed some 38 percent of the labour force, in 1972 almost 44 percent and in 1982 almost 53 percent. How did the median earnings of full time wage and salary workers change? Women's pay as share of men's were only 56 percent in 1962, only 58 percent in 1972 and only 59 percent in 1982. Basically, the discrimination and the lower median income is directly related to what sociologists call the "women's ghetto" in the employment world. Women formed more than 90 percent of all bookkeepers, nurses, therapists, telephone operators, bank tellers, receptionists, secretaries and typists, more than 80 percent of all librarians, archivists and cashiers and more than 70 percent of all non-college trained teachers, sales clerks and health technicians.[121]

The foregoing examples are to show that discrimination against women in the U.S. is not only widespread and severe in the economic field but that change has been painfully slow.

Returning now to the notion that an Equal Rights Amendment Act to the U.S. Constitution would bring a rapid change to all of this, it must be pointed out that, realistically, it will not be the case. There are basically three reasons. One is that existing laws

---

120. *Time Magazine,* July 12, 1982, p. 23.

121. Basic data: U.S. Departments of Commerce and Labor, Equal Employment Opportunity Commission and graphically illustrated in *U.S. News and World Report,* November 29, 1982, p. 55.

outlawing discrimination and which have been on the law books for 20 years continue to be violated. In July 1983 the U.S. Supreme Court banned employers from offering retirement plans that provide men and women with unequal benefits, but the law on which the court based its decision was passed in 1964 some twenty years ago and is known as Title VII of the Civil Rights Act which forbids employers to discriminate on the basis of sex, race, religion or ethnic origin. (The court ruled by a narrow majority of one.) It will therefore take a decade of massive litigation before the existing laws are implemented by the vast majority of American companies. In December 1983 a Federal Court ruled that the state of Washington had violated the same act by paying less for jobs traditionally performed by women than it paid for jobs done mostly by men. The state of Washington itself documented chapter and verse the discrimination between men and women employees and devised a comparable worth system that compared the value of job performed mostly by women with jobs performed mostly by men. The immediate pay rises which the court ordered totalled $838 million. [122]

When states of the American Union still continue such open discriminatory practices, clearly illegal, then the amount of discrimination in private companies must still be immense. But even if the law were to be vigorously applied, there is a subtle discrimination against women that would take much longer to eradicate and which no ERA would be able to assist. It is the sort of discrimination which states that women may not become members of prestigious private clubs. In this and other respects the attitude of the average American male is not within decades of that of the average Frenchman towards women. That is the second reason why the ERA will not bring massive change within a year, or even within ten years. The third reason is that in looking at the ERA care must be taken not to equate sex with race. If the idea is that there must be no law or no rules that establish disparate treatment

122. *The Atlanta Journal Week-end,* December 3, 1983, 8-A.

for men and women and that any differentiation would be a violation of the Constitution, then organizations catering to both men and women (and widely supported by both sexes) would be seriously jeopardized, e.g. the Boy and Girl Scout movement; it would require the integration of all single sex private schools and colleges receiving federal aid in any form; school policies will have to be sex-neutral, e.g. on the length of hair; Catholic seminaries would lose their tax exempt status unless they admit women for training to the priesthood, so would Jewish universities and seminaries which maintain separate seating for men and women according to their religious beliefs. Separate toilet facilities and separate showers for men and women in the U.S. Armed Forces could be successfully challenged -- by men. It is therefore a foolish argument that sexual equality in the work place, in schools, universities, in training, in wages and in social intercourse can be fought with the same constitutional language as race.

Perhaps the best book on the rights of women to be published in the U.S. the past decade is that of Susan Ross and Ann Barcher who adopted the approach that women do have rights not limited to marital status and that their interests are similar to men. Their book tells women how to cope with discrimination by using existing laws. Instead of merely bewailing the defeat of the ERA the authors state that women should realize that in the same decade that the ERA was defeated, sex discrimination law in the U.S. was transformed. Under pressure of the women's movement, the U.S. Supreme Court changed its interpretation of the Constitution and ruled that many of the existing sex discriminatory laws of states were in fact unconstitutional. They maintain that the constitutional doctrine which can be effectively used to get rid of sex discrimination is derived from the 14th amendment to the Constitution. The key language provides: No state shall . . . deny to any person within its jurisdiction the equal protection of the laws. This clause can be used to combat both discriminatory laws and practices. Their argument is that technically the equal protection clause prohibits discrimination, i.e. a state legislature may not treat its citizens differently.[123]

Ross and Barcher maintain furthermore that apart from the constitution there are four major federal laws and a myriad of state and city laws which also forbid discrimination in the important field of employment. The Civil Rights Act of 1964 (Title VII), The Equal Pay Act, The Pregnancy Discrimination Act of 1978 and the Age Discrimination Act of 1967. Of all Title VII of the 1964 Civil Rights Act is the most far reaching and most important law. Teachers have additional relief under the Education Amendment Act of 1972 but in 1982 the Supreme Court also ruled that Title IX prohibits sex-based discrimination against students and employees in federally funded education programs.

It may be that women in the United States are closer to the goal of equality in terms of the Constitution, the laws of Congress and the laws of the states than even informed members of the women's rights movement realize and that the major problem in the United States may be less of a constitutional one, less the correct wording of a potentially successful Equal Rights Amendment Act and more that of the attitude of men towards women in general. As Caroline Bird wrote in her 1983 preface to *Feminism and Philosophy:* "It is still necessary to identify and re-identify the problems facing women in today's world."[124] The education of the American male is apparently the most important task facing U.S. feminists movements and it is a much more daunting task than getting the U.S. Congress to pass an ERA.

* * * * * *

Women in general nonetheless look to increasing interest in the legal possibilities of easing their plight and of assuring their rights. Some important conferences have already been held, and

---

123. *The Rights of Women,* pp. 1-4. Cf. Brown, Freedman, Katz and Price: *Women's Rights and the Law,* Frederic Praeger, Inc., New York, 1977, which contains a comprehensive survey of sex discriminatory state laws and Picker, J.M.: "Laws and the Status of Women in the United States, "*Human Rights Law Review,* 8/1139, 1977.

124. Edited by Mary Vetterling-Braggin, Frederic Eliston and Jane English, Littlefield Adams and Co., 1977.

important studies launched and published, dealing with this particular approach.[125]

This chapter does not pretend to have covered the global scene, even in broad outlines, such an outline alone would have to run into fifty pages while a comparative analysis of the legal environment of women is a volume on its own. The writer is currently busy with research in the preparation of such a volume which will be published in 1984. What has been presented will, hopefully, stimulate research by others in the same field. It may well be that a thesis is developed to prove that in some countries discrimination against women as a group is worse than discrimination on grounds of race. According to World Bank statistics there are more illiterates among blacks in the world than among any other race, but 75 percent of all illiterate people in the world are women. In the so-called Third World (overwhelmingly non-white) the number of women unable to read and write actually increased by 65 million between 1960-1980 compared to only 12 million illiterate men. Small wonder that in Kenya, one of Africa's more developed black states, women still constitute more than 50 percent of the road workers. And in the Soviet Union, the most vociferous oponent of racial discrimination, women make up 88 percent of the ditch diggers at any typical hydro-electric project while constituting less than one percent of the Soviet Academy of Science.

---

125. Bae, Lyung Sook: *Women and the Law in Korea,* League of Women Voters, Seoul, Korea, 1973; Cortes, Irene R.: "Women's Rights Under the 1973 Philippine Constitution," *Philippine Law Journal,* 50/1, 1975; Curtin, Katie: *Women in China,* Pathfinder Press, New York, 1975; McDougall, M.S.; Laswell, H.D. and Lung-Chu Chen: "Human Rights for Women and World Public Order: The Outlawing of Sex Based Discrimination," *American Journal of International Law,* 69/497, 1975; Tandon, M.P.: "Constitutionality of the Hindu Marriage Act," *Allahabad Law Review,* 5/75, 1973; United Nations. "Law and the Status of Women: International Symposium," *Human Rights Law Review,* 8/1, 1977 and cf. Cordell, Magda and McHale, John: *Women in World Terms, Facts and Trends,* Center for Integrative Studies, State University of New York, 1975.

PART III

NATIONAL PATTERNS

NATIONAL PATTERNS

Classification of constitutional provisions under such headings as "race," "sex," "religion," and "other ethnic" are undoubtedly of great value. This is the *sine qua non* of any comparative study of these subjects. How else would one compare and contrast the different ways that different states have made classifications based on these factors! How else could one develop and evaluate "patterns"?

But a study based solely upon comparisons and analyses of each of these subject areas -- each separately evaluated -- does not go far enough. Such treatment leaves lacunae. For in order to understand how the different nations have responded constitutionally to the special demands of their different racial, religious, and ethnic groups, there must also be studies along the lines of *national* as well as subject patterns.

For it is also essential to see the interrelationships of the several (and varied) responses of each country. The *total* Yugoslav "package," for example, must be compared with the *total* of what has been done in Malaysia. Even more important, there must be studies of Yugoslavia and Malaysia separately in order to compare and contrast the way these nations have handled the entire spectrum of differences among their peoples.

Just as it is impossible to delineate and expound on all of the varied, generalized "patterns" resulting from this study, so is it impossible to do a study on each separate country.

And thus this part of the study is likewise *selected*. Only certain countries will be considered -- the most important and a few of the more interesting by way of illustration. What these selected analyses do is to provide an understanding of what has been done in those nations which have tried to meet the problems of group rights in a forthright and comprehensive constitutional response. And, at the same time, these analyses pave the way for further and more detailed expositions.

The major studies here are based on the total constitutional patterns of nine significant nations. Other nations whose constitutional responses have been analyzed are treated in less detail elsewhere.

CHAPTER X

KINGDOM OF BELGIUM

Belgium, with its 9 million inhabitants and its 11,700 square miles is one of the most densely populated countries of Europe. Belgium has three distinct linguistic groups within its small territory: a French-speaking group, a Dutch-speaking group, and a German-speaking group. There is also a sort of natural linguistic distribution of these elements, rather like the Swiss situation, but the Belgian constitutional approach to ethnic, linguistic, cultural, and religious differences is even more thorough than the Swiss.

The Northern Belgian provinces of West-Vlaanderen, Oost-Vlaanderen, Antwerpen, and Limberg are predominantly settled by Flemish Dutch speakers who also tend to be Protestants. Catholics tend to be concentrated in the Southern Belgian provinces of Hainaut, Namur, Luxembourg, and the western portion of Liege. A German-speaking majority occupies the eastern portion of Liege. Brussels, the capitol, is bilingual and the Province of Brabant is divided between the Flemings (Dutch-speaking) and the Walloons (French-speaking). These differences have always been reflected in the politics of Belgium, with a powerful Catholic party often dominant. [1]

The political and social life of Belgium has been much more

1. Veenhoven: Volume II, pp. 4-5.

violent and intense than Switzerland's street demonstrations. Riots and bitter political strife have marked much of Belgian history. This tension has resulted in the promulgation of several constitutions and many changes in the electoral laws in an attempt to bring peace, particularly to the Flemings and the Walloons.[2] The composition of the legislature, the nature of the monarch, the rights of minorities, and many other fundamental issues have divided Belgian from Belgian.

The origins of Belgian discontent can be traced to the artificial union of its composite parts. In 1815 the great powers of Europe decided, at the Congress of Vienna, to unite seventeen Belgian provinces with Holland to form a kingdom of the Netherlands, under the Dutch king. A series of constitutional manipulations by the Dutch king forced acceptance of the 1815 Fundamental Law of the United Provinces.

A rebellion against Dutch rule broke out in 1830 and a provisional government proclaimed the existence of a state of Belgium. A Belgian Constitution of 1831 was produced by the National Congress. This remarkable document launched the rich, complex and strife-torn constitutional history of Belgium.

The 1831 Constitution ignored the existence of the linguistic and cultural regions.[3] Prince Leopold of Saxe-Coburg, a Lutheran, accepted the throne as king of the Belgians in 1831, but after his 1832 marriage to Princess Louise, agreed that all children of the marriage would be brought up in the Catholic faith. In general, Catholic dominance of the nation prevailed in the period prior to World War I.[4]

In 1861 the Flemish party demanded official use of the Flemish language. Because of its similarity to Dutch, the Flemish remained politically inactive for fear of reviving memories of the Dutch rule.

---

2. Articles 6(a) and 59(a) of the amended constitution of 18 July 1971 is a good example.

3. See J.J. Thomssen: *La Constitution Belge Annotee,* Brussels, 1879.

4. Henri Pirenne: *Histoire de la Belgigue,* Tome III, (Brussels, 1926).

The Flemish-speaking population, although forming 55 percent of the Belgian population, had been relegated to an inferior political and cultural status. Although Flemish could be used in Flemish judicial proceedings (1873) and in administration of Flemish provinces (1878), these statutory concessions were insufficient to remove the perception of French domination of Belgian life.

In 1893, a number of major constitutional amendments were made, most notably a new Article 47 which provided for nearly universal male suffrage. However, the same Article also provided for double voting for heads of families paying 5 francs habitation taxes and an additional vote for those who had a university degree. This system particularly aided the Catholic party.

Equal voting rights for all were resisted by the Catholics, leading to a general strike of a revolutionary type just prior to World War I. The constitutional and legal authorities ceased to exist after the German invasion. Interestingly, the German occupiers favored the Flemish language at the expense of the French in 1916.

After the war, a system of pure and simple universal suffrage was gradually introduced. Proportional representation was inserted into the constitution. Other related important amendments were made in 1920. [5]

Universal male suffrage was finally placed on a constitutional plane by the new Article 47 of the constitution, promulgated in 1921. At the same time, the Senate was reformed to make it more representative.

Belgium remained a state of two divided nations throughout the interwar period. When the German invasion of 1940 again overran Belgium, a split occurred between the king who remained in Belgium and a Belgian government-in-exile composed of most of the king's former ministers. Pro and anti-Leopold forces struggled

5. Most notably Articles 48, 50, and 52.

to redefine the constitutional position of the monarchy and when, in 1950, a vote was held on the question, "Are you of the opinion that King Leopold III should resume the exercise of his constitutional powers?", the voting was polarized into Flanders (72 percent pro-Leopold) and Walloonia factions. The return of the king revived the animosity between Flemings and Walloons.

In 1962 a new law was passed fixing the linguistic boundaries by dividing Belgium into four regions: a Dutch-speaking region; a German-speaking region; the bilingual region of Brussels; and a French-speaking region. The constitution was to be revised to express these new conceptions. Drastic revision of the constitution was in order, but it took many years to reach agreement on the necessary changes.

Finally, in 1970 and 1973 major changes were made in the constitution recognizing the special rights of the cultural communities of Belgium. At the same time, the representational system was altered to provide some legislative power for two language groups, Flemish and French, over their own regions.

The constitution stated that Belgium comprised four linguistic regions: the French, the Dutch, the German and the bilingual region of Brussels.[6] Three cultural communities were recognized, each having certain powers vested in it by the constitution.[7] The constitution also guaranteed the rights and liberties of ideological and philosophical minorities.[8]

A linguistic group could make a motion to delay the passage and consideration of a proposed bill which, in the view of three-fourths of its members, was of such a nature as to have a serious effect on the relations between communities.[9] The power was in addition to the additional powers of linguistic groups within the parliament to legislate for their linguistic region.

---

6. Constitution of Belgium, Blaustein, Heading I, Article 3b.

7. *Id.*, Heading Ib, Article 3c.

8. *Id.*, Heading II, Article 6b.

9. *Id.*, Heading III, Chapter I, Article 38.

One of the most important parts of the constitution provided that "for those cases prescribed in the constitution, the elected members of each house are divided into a French-language group and a Dutch-language group."[10] A cultural council was created for the French cultural community "made up of members of the French linguistic group of both houses"[11] of the legislature. A bill passed on a majority vote within each linguistic group must also have two-thirds of both linguistic groups in order to conduct most of the parliamentary business. But each cultural council was limited in the sphere of its activities to that kind of legislation which deals with cultural matters, education, the use of languages and similar matters.[12] There was also a cultural council for the German cultural community, although its composition was unspecified.[13] The cultural councils exercised their competence by decrees which had the force of law in the respective linguistic regions to which they apply. Unfortunately, no special provision was made for the bilingual Brussels region.

This representational arrangement of linguistic groups was a novel solution to an historic problem. The political arrangement was more than just federal and has been denoted a "consociation" by some scholars.[14] The linguistic and cultural cleavages of Belgium were made constitutionally permanent. Yet the significance of these cultural councils remained shrouded in doubt and ambiguity. The Brussels situation was especially ambiguous.[15]

The Cabinet must, "with the possible exception of the Prime Minister," be comprised of an equal number of French and Dutch-speaking members.[16] Since budget bills are also subject to the

10. Constitution of Belgium, Blaustein, Chapter I, Article 32b.

11. *Id.*, Chapter I, Section III, Article 59b.

12. *Id.*, Chapter I, Section III, Article 59b, Section 2.

13. *Id.*, Chapter I, Section III, Article 59c.

14. Arend Lijphart, "Consociational Democracy," *World Politics*, Volume 20 (January, 1969), pp. 207-225.

15. It is difficult to understand the meaning of the relevant section: Constitution of Belgium (B & F), Chapter I, Section III, Article 59b, Section 4.

16. *Id.*, Chapter II, Section II, Article 86b.

potential power of linguistic groups, it is difficult to see how any major policies can be adopted by a government without the tacit consent of the two largest language groups, the Flemish and the Walloons.

In 1971 an Act was passed refining the powers and structure of the linguistic groups. The Act contains elaborate provisions for bilingual areas, especially Brussels. It provides formal voting procedures and even the form of main motions. Perhaps the most important portion of the Act defines more clearly the cultural matters which fall under the jurisdiction of the linguistic groups. These are, among others: protection of the language, the arts, the national heritage, radio and television broadcasting, youth policy, education, and leisure facilities, and travel.[17] Nowhere else are group rights so specifically delineated, and incorporated within the constitution. In February 1978 the government approved the abandonment of the provincial structure described in favour of a much clearer ethnic linguistic division and a series of constitutional reforms in mid-1980 provided that Flanders and Wallonia could by 1982 arrange for direct election of regional legislative assemblies.

The Belgian Constitution is not noteworthy because of its treatment of women, races, or religious groups. Its claim on our attention rests upon the explicit recognition of group rights of a linguistic-ethnic-cultural nature. Belgium is still experimenting with this advanced version of group rights, but it is an experiment well worth watching.[18] Should it fail a strict federalism or even the break-up of the state into two independent states is possible. The political strife of 1982-1983 referred to in the general introduction to this work is particularly painful to political scientists, constitutionalists and political liberals who have frequently advocated that goodwill and co-operation between different peoples can be overcome by the right constitutional

17. Act of July 3, 1971 (B & F, Appendix 2), Chapter II, Article 2.

18. Cf. Glaser and Possony: *Victims of Politics*, pp. 299-300.

paperwork, for example, in the case of South Africa, Zimbabwe, Namibia and other multi-national states in Africa. The Zimbabwean effort has already failed, South Africa's new National Party government of Mr. P.W. Botha launched a new constitutional provision in 1984 which bears many similarities to the Belgian arrangement in so far as Whites, Indians and Coloureds are concerned. The Namibian constitution is yet to be drawn up.

The Belgian example has also been followed by Spain, for example, in trying to satisfy the nationalism of the Catalans in Catalonia. (Capital city -- Barcelona). King Juan Carlos of Spain in 1979 approved of the rebirth of Catalonia as an autonomous region within the Spanish democracy. As in the case of the Flemish, language was the catalyst and the one factor which held the Catalonians together ever since they were deprived of their autonomy by Philip V of Spain in 1714. Under the new dispensation of 1979 the Catalans, like the French in Quebec, Canada, were given the right to use their own language as the official language of the region. Their 800 year old governing body, the *Generalitat* were given powers to rule in regional matters of trade, primary education, industry and housing. In *National Geographic* (January 1984) Randall Peffer accurately describes the revolutionary fever among the young in Catalonia, the expressions of nationhood and nationalism, an indication that, like the Flemish in Belgium, the present state of affairs may be only the end of the first round in a battle for statehood and even greater autonomy from Madrid.

CHAPTER XI

CANADA

Canada was and remains a nation ripe for constitutional change. Its multi-ethnic, multi-linguistic character, which was evident from the earliest years of the nation's independent history, has never been truly reflected in its basic constitutional document, the British North America Act of 1867. The tensions between the French and English speaking populations has increased over the last few decades, taking the form of open physical attacks at times. Whether a more suitable constitutional arrangement would have relieved some of these tensions is not certain, but, clearly, it would not have endangered the Canadian state if it had constitutionally recognized the concept of group rights for French-speakers and perhaps some other minorities as well.[19]

Quebec and "French Canada" are not the same entities. There are over six million French Canadians, but twenty percent of them do not live in Quebec. Also, twenty percent of the residents of Quebec are not French Canadians, in the sense that their first language is not French. Yet, because of the French Canadian majority in one province, and a feeling of neglect and discrimination suffered by the French Canadians, the problem of

19. There is no group rights notion in Canadian constitutional law. See Government of Quebec: *Report of the Commission of Inquiry on the Position of the French Language and on Language Rights in Quebec,* Book II, Language Rights, Montreal, 1972, p. 20.

the continued union of Canada is, in many respects, a question of the role of Quebec in a bicultural society two-thirds English and one-third French. [20]

Quebec separatism is a large and important movement. French Canadian scholars and politicians have begun to make their case for independence. The right to the self-determination of peoples, so frequently asserted in Europe, Africa, Asia and Oceania (often for less than 200,000 people) has now been claimed for six million people in North America. [21]

The formation of the Canadian federal union occurred during the American Civil War. That fratricidal conflict cast a shadow over the Canadian deliberations. There was general agreement that exaggerated news of states rights were to be avoided. Hence, the Canadian federalism consciously was adapted to create a stronger national government. The basic federal arrangement gave the provincial government power over the local matters, reserving residual powers to the central government, [22] reversing the American constitutional arrangement. [23]

The framers of the Canadian federation thought of submitting their handiwork as a draft constitution subject to popular approval. Britain preferred ratification by the provincial legislatures, but this, too, seemed impossible to obtain. The British parliament passed the British North America Act in 1867, giving scant attention to the matter. William Lyon MacKenzie, one of the leaders in the establishment of the Canadian federal system asserted before the passage of the British North America Act that "we have, in a great measure, avoided in this system which we propose for the adaption of the people of Canada, the defects which time and events have shown to exist in the American

---

20. Dale C. Thomson, "Quebec and the Bicultural Dimension," *Academy of Political Science. Proceedings*, Vol. 32, No. 2, (1976), pp. 27-39.

21. For a detailed presentation see Jacques Brossard, L'accession ala L'Universite de Montreal, 1976.

22. Section 91, B.N.A. Act.

23. Tenth Amendment to the Constitution.

Constitution.''[24] But the people of Canada did not themselves agree to the Act, and the confederation consisted of four provinces, one of which, Nova Scotia, attempted immediately to secede from the new union.

The British North America Act is a most peculiar document. It is not a native constitution, but a piece of British legislation. It contains no bill of rights. No amending process is laid down. Changes are a matter for legislation by the British Parliament. Some changes have been made in this fashion, but most of these legislative amendments have dealt with the composition of the two houses of the Canadian legislature or with the admission of new provinces. For a modern multinational state, the British North America Act seems a most inappropriate expression of the dualistic character of the nation.

Although the Act consisted of 147 clauses in eleven sections, there are no provisions regarding sex in the British North America Act and only a few minor considerations touching upon religion. Little mention is made of Eskimos or Indians or other groups in Canada. The right or privilege to have access to demonstrational schools is provided specifically,[25] as is the right to separate Catholic and Protestant schools in Quebec.[26]

The federal nature of the union is created by the combined effects of sections 91 and 92 of the British North America Act. Section 91 assigns to the central government power ''to make laws for the peace, good order, and good government of Canada, in relation to all matters not coming within the class of subjects . . . assigned exclusively to the legislatures of the provinces.'' Section 92 sets forth the largely local and private subjects over which the provincial legislatures have exclusive authority, these include ''property and civil rights in the province.''[27] Immigration into

24. Quoted in Edgar McInnis, *Canada*, Holt, Rinehart, and Winston, New York, 1969, p. 300.

25. Section 93, 1.

26. Section 93, 2.

27. Section 92, 13.

the provinces may, by virtue of another provision, be a shared responsibility between the national and provincial governments, with the national government's laws supreme in case of conflict.[28]

The linguistic and cultural differences among the provinces are touched upon very lightly. The English and French languages are made official in both houses of the Canadian parliament and in the houses of the legislature of Quebec.[29] Acts of the Canadian parliament and of the Quebec parliament must be printed and published in both English and French. Both languages may be used in Canadian courts. Otherwise, the British North America Act is silent upon this important issue.

There is a so-called Canadian Bill of Rights, although it did not form a part of the Canadian constitution until 1982. The Canadian Bill of Rights is merely an act of the Canadian parliament. It was not a constitutionally entrenched bill of rights because it was never directly incorporated into the British North America Act. As a statutory bill of rights, it was subject to amendment or repeal by the federal parliament, just as with ordinary legislation. Nonetheless, the Canadian Bill of Rights of 1960 has been given some significance by the federal judiciary.[30]

This Bill of Rights had no application or legal control over the provinces, but was strictly an example of federal law making. In introducing the Bill into the Canadian parliament the Prime Minister stated that it would be impossible to pass an amendment to the B.N.A. Act which would be binding both on the provinces and on the Dominion, because the provinces were too jealous of their jurisdiction to support an amendment applicable to themselves.[31] For our purposes the Bill of Rights in Canada seems mild and unremarkable, prohibiting "discrimination by

28. Section 95.

29. Section 133.

30. See Walter Surma Tarnopolsky: *The Canadian Bill of Rights,* McClelland and Steward, Limited, Toronto, 1975.

31. Ibid., p. 89.

reason of race, national origin, colour, religion or sex."[32]

The problems of creating a bill of rights for Canada were intertwined with the difficulties of amending the British North America Act. The redrawing of a fundamental charter of government may be necessary to preserve the Canadian union, but few politicians seem ready to grapple with this fact. Constitutional conferences were held in 1968, 1969, 1970, 1972 and 1981. Prime Minister L.B. Pearson declared at the first constitutional Constitution that "rights of the individual -- human and linguistic -- are so fundamental to the will of the nation to survive, that the Government of Canada suggests as the first step in reviewing Canada's constitution the guarantee of these rights in the fundamental law."[33] Until 1981, little had been accomplished to carry out this pledge. Up till then there was not even any agreement on the proper method for amending the Canadian constitution.[34] There is reason to be gloomy as the country seems to be "engaged in a process of partial disintegration" because "a great number of its citizens lack a common national consciousness and because the Que'beco's no longer accept the leadership of the English speaking majority."[35]

Canada needs a new constitution recognizing group rights. Time is running out. A law passed on August 26, 1977 by the Quebec government (based on a White Paper of 1 April 1977) limited English-medium instruction in schools and all newcomers to Quebec, English speakers included, must send their children to French-medium schools. This polarisation is becoming indelible.

Following the re-writing of the constitution in 1981 Quebec Premier Rene Levesque remained angry and bitter at what he called "betrayal" by English Canada and remained convinced that

---

32. Sec. 1, *The Canadian Bill of Rights,* 8-9 Elizabeth II.

33. See *Federalism for the Future: A Statement of Policy by the Government of Canada,* Ottawa, 1968, p. 18.

34. See Edwin R. Black: *Divided Loyalties,* McGill Queen's University Press, Montreal, 1975, pp. 228-234.

35. Michael Brunet, "Continentalism and Quebec Nationalism," *Queen's Quarterly,* Vol. 76, 1970, p. 511.

independence for Quebec was the answer. His plan for diluted independence called ''sovereignty-association'' was rejected by a 60-40 margin in a referendum in May 1980, but this has not changed his point of view. Many people in Quebec were worried by the fact that the constitutional agreement of November 1981 has left their state standing alone. Of the nine premiers of the states of Canada who agreed to the changes Quebecs' Levesque was the only one to reject the agreement which enabled Canada to ask Britain to insert the charter of rights as an amending formula into the 1867 British North America Act. Levesque believed the rights charter would dilute Quebec's authority over legislation crucial to his view that Quebec is a French island in North America. These include laws on language of primary education and a province's right to favour its own people during periods of unemployment.

Not only Quebec and its Prime Minister, but also native Indians and Eskimos were bitter because provisions that would have guaranteed their aboriginal rights were cut from the rights charter at the insistence of other provincial premiers. Women's groups were upset because provinces will be able to veto rights charter clauses on equality between the sexes.

On 17 April 1982 Britain by order of Queen Elizabeth II finally sent the British North America Act to Canada giving Canada sole right to the Act and to any changes which the Canadian federation may wish to bring about. The Constitution Act of 1982 thus achieved the longstanding goal of ending the formality of British control over amendments to Canada's constitution. Now any seven Canadian provinces, with at least 50 percent of the nation's population, can approve of such amendments.

CHAPTER XI

REPUBLIC OF INDIA

India is a crazy quilt, and has a constitution to match. Constitution-making on the subcontinent of India has consumed more time and effort (and more paperwork) than in any other part of the world. And the result is failure.

No one can be sure, however, whether the failure (perhaps, more accurately, one should say failures) can or should be blamed upon the constitution-makers. Perhaps the blame should be directed at those charged with implementation and interpretation: the administrators and legislators, as well as the judiciary. Perhaps the fault lies in the failure of government to enforce the constitutional mandates. Perhaps the problems which India faces are just too great and too complicated for constitutional solution.

But are there any other alternatives?

India has produced not only the world's longest constitution, but the most intricate. And the constitutional process is still going on -- deliberately, painstakingly, and painfully. More than a year after the downfall of the first Indira Gandhi government, the Lok Sabha (Parliament) had not as yet produced the constitution's amendment 43, designed to overturn constitutional formulae in the amendments of Mrs. Gandhi's regime. (In January 1980 Mrs. Gandhi was returned to power.)

But before one can discuss either constitutional alternatives or alternatives to constitutionalism, a few words must be said as a background to India and as a background to the Indian constitution. This last statement calls for editorial comment: -- emphasis must be placed upon the phrase "a few words." For the literature on the Indian constitution is endless, and it would be the height of futility to attempt a comprehensive summary.[36] Further, it is questionable whether a comprehensive survey is necessary to provide insights as to what is wrong with the Indian constitution, or whether some of India's problems can be better solved through extra-legal action.

The Indian Subcontinent

As a prologue to any discussion of the Indian constitution comes the hackneyed truism that India is not a country but a continent. Its population of 750 million exceeds that of Europe. It has 24 languages, each of which is spoken by a million or more persons, plus at least 200 other active languages and dialects.

In addition to its major ethnic and religious groupings (Indo-Aryan and Dravidian; Hindu, Muslim, Christian, Sikh, etc.), there are more than 450 distinct tribal minority groups in the country. The population of these tribal people was estimated at 38 million in India's 1971 census, when the total population was given as 548 million. This particular seven percent of the population is reported to be located in 285 "subdivisions," i.e., administrative units of the nation.[37]

Added to this is the particular (and peculiar) situation concerning the nation's Anglo-Indians, a small but universally

---

36. To supplement the many commentaries on the constitution and articles on specific aspects of the constitution, one is directed to the five volume work on *The Framing of India's Constitution,* published in New Delhi by the Indian Institute of Public Administration in 1967-1968. Four of the volumes consist of "Select Documents," including all of the various preliminary drafts, conference reports, and debates. The fifth volume is designated "A Study," providing commentary on the constitution's development. The project committee was chaired by B. Shiva Rao, whose name is on the spines of the five volumes.

37. See D.H. Mathur, "India's Tribal Minorities: Bringing Them into the Mainstream of National Life." 5 *Plural Societies* No. 2 (Summer, 1974), p. 25.

recognized separate entity.[38]

To make matters even more complicated than might be expected in a nation with so many ethnic groups, religions, languages, and tribes, India has the additional problem of caste. At the very bottom of the caste ladder is an identifiable group, referred to constitutionally as the "Scheduled Castes," and referred to in earlier constitutional laws and documents as the "Depressed Classes." Mahatma Gandhi called them the Harijans, or "Children of God." They are better known as the "Untouchables."

The horrible fact is that India's Harijan population, now estimated at 93 million, is greater than the total population of all but seven of the world's countries.[39]

Finally, adding to all of these complications, are the twin facts that India is a federal republic, and that the boundaries of her 22 states and nine Union Territories are drawn along linguistic lines. The configurations of India's component states have been re-shaped and renamed because of the pressures of various linguistic groups.[40] During the early years following independence in 1947, the Congress Party leadership resisted fragile federation. Nehru reluctantly conceded to demands for the separation of Andhra from Madras in 1953, and then approved the States Reorganization Act, 1956, which resulted in a comprehensive reorganization of state boundaries on linguistic lines. Bilingual Bombay State was divided into two unilingual states in 1960; the Punjab was divided in 1966.

What makes this type of linguistic division still more complicated is the fact that people do not necessarily arrange their places of residence to meet nationally prescribed linguistic boundaries.

38. See W.T. Roy, "Hostages to Fortune, a Socio-Political Study of the Anglo-Indian Remnant in India." 5 *Plural Societies* No. 2 (Summer, 1974), p. 55.

39. The seven are China, India, the U.S.S.R., the United States, Indonesia, Brazil and Japan.

40. See S. R. Mohan Das: "Discrimination in India" in *Veenhoven:* Part II, pp. 167-168. Also Kodesia, K.: *The Problems of Linguistic States in India,* 1969, Sterling Publishers, Delhi.

The States Reorganization Commission, charged with revising state political boundaries, concluded that there would be at least some linguistic minorities within even the most linguistically homogeneous state. How could it be otherwise when only fifteen languages (four added by amendments) are recognized in the constitution's English schedule? As one Dutch commentator put it, "Every federal state is a reduced reflection of India itself, for besides these 14 official languages, there are about 200 mutually unintelligible idioms."[41]

The Indian Constitution -- An Overview

Reading the Indian Constitution, without knowing its history and background, leaves the impression that the document is overly concerned with the protection and preservation of group rights. This, the world's longest constitution, certainly has a lot to say on the subject. It is filled with institutional arrangements on behalf of its various groupings, to adjust the political balance among them and to protect the lowly. But it was always so in India. As a matter of fact, the present constitution, as adopted in 1948, reflected a trend in the opposite direction.

Institutional arrangements providing safeguards for the various communal minorities of India were a part of British law for the century preceding the transfer of power in 1947. And such safeguards have been part of all Indian constitution-making, going back to the Swaraj Bill of 1895. The then-Aga Khan, in 1906, as leader of Muslim elements, succeeded in obtaining the creation of separate electorates based on religious distinctions. England pursued this approach with its approval of the 1917 Montagu-Chelmsford Report, in which the authors visualized India as

> a sisterhood of States, self-governing in all matters of purely local or provincial interest, in some cases corres-

41. J. Prins: "The World's Plural Societies: An Introduction," *Plural Societies*, The Hague, Holland, Vol. I, (1970) p. 3.

ponding to existing provinces, in others perhaps modified in area according to the character and economic interests of their people. Over this congeries of States would preside a central government, increasingly representative of and responsible to the people of all of them; dealing with matters, both internal and external, of common interest to the whole of India; acting as arbiter in inter-State relations, and representing the interests of all India on equal terms with the self-governing units of the British Empire.[42]

By the time of the most important of all of the pre-independence constitutions, the Government of India Act, 1935, it was agreed that representation through separate electorates would be given to Muslims, Europeans, Sikhs, Indian Christians and Anglo-Indians.

> Seats were also reserved for the Marathas in selected general constituencies in Bombay. The depressed classes were given seats to be filled by election from special constituencies in which they alone could vote, though they were also entitled to vote in the general constituencies. Special seats were also allotted to women, labour, commerce and industry, mining and planting, and landholders.[43]

In the face of 1946 Resolutions to divide the country and to create two constitution-making bodies, one for Hindustan and one for Pakistan, the government under the 1935 Act expressed opposition:

> The Congress was totally opposed to the division of the country. It was, however, prepared for the maximum amount of local autonomy consistent with the maintenance of the unity of the country. Accordingly, it suggested

42. B. Shiva Rao: *The Framing of India's Constitution: A Study*. New Delhi, Indian Institute of Public Administration, 1967-1968, p. 5.

43. Rao, *op. cit.*, p. 742.

> that the future framework of the country's Constitution be based on a federal structure with a limited number of compulsory central subjects such as defence, communications and foreign affairs; the federation would consist of autonomous Provinces in which would vest the residuary subjects. The Congress also suggested that there should be a list of "optional subjects" in respect of which any Province or group of Provinces would be free to accept federal executive and legislative jurisdiction. It was proposed that on the completion of the constitution-making process a Province could elect to stand out of the Constitution altogether, or federate on the essential as well as the optional subjects. [44]

Group rights safeguard for soon-to-be independent India were hotly debated during the 28 months of constitutional draftsmanship which began in the summer of 1946.[45] It is still not over. There have been changes giving still more protections to India's minorities in the course of the 42 amendments promulgated to date.

---

44. Rao, *op. cit.*, p. 65.

45. During the course of debate, the Sub-Committee on Minorities drafted a questionnaire in the following language:

> (1) What should be the nature and scope of the safeguards for a minority in the new Constitution?
>
> (2) What should be the political safeguards for a minority:
>
> (a) in the Centre;
>
> (b) in the Provinces?
>
> (3) What should be the economic safeguards for a minority?
>
> (a) in the Centre;
>
> (b); in the Provinces
>
> (4) What should be the religious, educational and cultural safeguards for a minority?
>
> (5) What machinery should be set up to ensure that the safeguards are effective?
>
> (6) How is it proposed that the safeguards should be eliminated, in what time and under what circumstances?
>
> Rao, *op. cit.*, p. 748.

There are those who claim that the problem of constitutional safeguards for minorities was purely a British creation, "developed from a non-existent issue."[46] Whether or not this is true, group divisions were encouraged by Britain in its efforts to maintain control over the Subcontinent.

> Each step in the direction of the establishment of popular government and representative institutions was accompanied by a corresponding emphasis on the obligation of the British Government to ensure that the minorities were protected from oppression and exploitation at the hands of the majority. More and more minorities came to be recognized as being in need of protection, through separate representation in the Legislatures, reserved quotas in the public services, and in various other ways. In course of time, the Sikhs, the Anglo-Indians, the Indian Christians, the depressed classes (the name then given to the "untouchable" section of the Hindu community -- now generally known as the "Scheduled Castes") -- all these communities were treated as minorities in need of such protection. In fact, the concept of minorities was so expanded as to include even the prosperous European commercial and mercantile community in India as needing separate representation in the Legislatures.[47]

Britain's policy of divide and rule in India has a parallel in the history of Southern Africa where she proclaimed the protectorates of Bechuanaland, Swaziland and Lesotho within what was then known as "British South Africa" thereby creating a geo-political nightmare with Lesotho (later) becoming a sovereign independent state surrounded by the equally sovereign Republic of South Africa.

---

46. Ralph H. Retzlaff, "The Problem of Communal Minorities in the Drafting of the Indian Constitution." In: R.N. Spann, ed., *Constitutionalism in Asia.* Bombay, Asia Publishing House, 1964, p. 56.

47. Rao, *op. cit.*, pp. 741-742.

With an appreciation of this background, one can understand the comments of Professor Galanter on the constitutional scope of the "preference" policy in India:

> The constitution of independent India drastically restricts the use of such arrangements. They are discarded as a general principle of governmental operation and may be used only for the purpose of promoting equality. Communal preferences and quotas for the purpose of political accommodation are outlawed. The protective (or compensatory) discrimination authorized by the constitution is envisaged as an exceptional and temporary measure to be used only for the purpose of mitigating inequalities; it is designed to disappear along with these inequalities. The constitution-maker did not intend it as a device to consolidate and protect the separate integrity of communal groups. But while the preferential principle is thus confined in the purposes for which it may be used, it has been expanded in scope and extent to embrace a wide array of governmental schemes and programs. (footnotes omitted) [48]

Further, as Professor Galanter points out, "the exceptional character of compensatory discrimination has frequently been emphasized by the courts." [49]

Professor Galanter's overview observations, pointing out the Indian constitution's emphasis upon equality and non-discrimination, are consistent with the views of the chairman of the Draft Constitution. It is the view that minorities must be protected and group rights recognized during the early states of nationhood, so that at some time in the future the minorities will vanish and merge with the majority into one. This is of importance because the chairman was Dr. B.R. Ambedkar, acknowledged leader of the

48. Marc Galanter: *Competing Equalities: The Indian Experiment with Compensatory Discrimination.* Chapter 2 (manuscript).

49. *Id.*

untouchable community. Presenting the Draft Constitution to the Assembly, Ambedkar, referring to the articles on safeguards for minorities, observed:

> The Draft Constitution is also criticized because of the safeguards it provides for minorities. In this, the drafting Committee has no responsibility. It follows the decisions of the Constituent Assembly. Speaking for myself, I have no doubt that the Constituent Assembly has done wisely in providing such safeguards for minorities as it has done. In this country, both the minorities and the majorities have followed a wrong path. It is wrong for the majority to deny the existence of minorities. It is equally wrong for the minorities to perpetuate themselves. A solution must be found which will serve a double purpose. It must recognize the existence of the minorities to start with. It must also be such that it will enable majorities and minorities to merge some day into one. The solution proposed by the Constituent Assembly is to be welcomed because it is a solution which serves this two-fold purpose. To die-hards who have developed a kind of fanaticism against minority protection, I would like to say two things. One is that minorities are an explosive force which, if it erupts, can blow up the whole fabric of the State. The history of Europe bears ample and appalling testimony to this fact. The other is that the minorities in India have agreed to place their existence in the hands of the majority. In the history of negotiations for preventing the partition of Ireland, Redmond said to Carson, "Ask for any safeguard you like for the Protestant minority but let us have a united Ireland." Carson's reply was, "Damn your safeguards, we don't want to be ruled by you." No minority in India has taken this stand. They have loyally accepted the rule of the majority which is basically a communal majority and not a political majority. It is for the majority to realize its

> duty not to discriminate against minorities. Whether the minorities will continue or will vanish must depend upon this habit of the majority. The moment the majority loses the habit of discriminating against the minority, the minorities can have no ground to exist. They will vanish.[50]

It should be pointed out, however, that certain constitutional amendments have re-emphasized group rights. The best example is Article 15 (4), added by the First Amendment in 1951. It must be compared with both Article 15 (1) and Article 29 (2). These read as follows:

> 15(4) Nothing in this article or in clause (2) of Article 29 shall prevent the State from making any special provision for the advancement of any socially and educationally backward classes of citizens or for the Scheduled Castes and the Scheduled Tribes.
>
> 15(1) The State shall not discriminate against any citizen on grounds only of religion, race, caste, sex, place of birth or any of them.
>
> 29(2) No citizen shall be denied admission into any educational institution maintained by the State or receiving aid out of State funds on grounds only of religion, race, caste, language or any of them.

It is interesting to note that during the constitutional debates, the Constituent Assembly rejected the inclusion of a provision similar to 15(4).

Article 15(4) reflects the same spirit as Article 16(4), which reads:

> Nothing in this article shall prevent the State from making any provision for the reservation of appointments or posts in favor of any backward class of citizens which, in the

50. Rao, *op. cit.*, pp. 766-767.

> opinion of the State, is not adequately represented in the services under the State.

Note, however, that 16(4) should be read in connection with 16(1), which provides that "There shall be quality of opportunity for all citizens in matters relating to employment or appointment to any office under the State."

The equality principle -- in economic terms -- is stated in Article 39(a) and (d):

". . . that the citizens, men and women equally, have the right to an adequate means to livelihood;" and ". . . that there is equal pay for equal work for both men and women."

However, as noted at several points in this study, there is also the important and basic principle of state policy set forth in Article 46:

> The State shall promote with special care the educational and economic interests of the weaker sections of the people; and, in particular, of the Scheduled Castes and the Scheduled Tribes, and shall protect them from social injustice and all forms of exploitation.

The Indian Constitution -- Conflict and Complications

When a constitution preaches equality on one hand and special group rights protections on the other, the conflict is obvious. And it is a real conflict. It does not disappear because Christian Ambedkar envisions the day that protected minorities will merge with the majority. There is a fundamental conflict between Articles 15(1) and 15(4), and between 16(1) and 16(4).

Nor are the provisions on equality before the law consistent with all of the "Special Provisions Relating to Certain Classes," encompassing Articles 330 through 432. These provide that legislative seats in the House of the People shall be reserved for the

Scheduled Castes and Scheduled Tribes. Despite the language of Article 81, which bases legislative representation on population, Aticle 331 gives the President the power to nominate not more than two members of the Anglo-Indian community if he is of the opinion that such community is not adequately represented. This reservation of seats and special representation was to be in effect for 20 years, but it was extended to 30 years by the Twenty-Third Amendment in 1969.

The Conclusions of Professor Galanter are valuable in understanding this conflict in the Indian setting. Here is his position:

> The constitutional embrace of the antagonistic principles of equal treatment and compensatory discrimination, individual rights and group rights, confronts both government and courts with the problem of reconciling them in specific settings. The sweeping language of Articles 15(4) and 16(4) indicates that their framers relied primarily on the discretion of the politicians and administrators of the future, rather than on the courts, to effect such a reconciliation. But while these provisions give the executive and the legislatures broad discretion in their application, judicial review is not entirely excluded. The leverage for judicial intervention is the placement of these provisions as exceptions to the judicially enforceable Fundamental Rights. These rights can only be vindicated to the extent that the courts scrutinize the government's designation of backward classes to see that only the backward are included, that the extent or method of operation does not prejudice others unduly, that the schemes are designed and administered to work in favor of the intended beneficiaries and not to their detriment. Such review is necessary not only to vindicate individual rights but to effectuate the policy of these provisions -- by preventing unwarranted

> dilution of benefits (for the more unrestrained the inclusion of beneficiaries, the less the assistance the intended beneficiaries will receive) and abuses that undermine public support for these measures.
>
> Overseeing the administration of preferences brings out the delicate tensions involved in the process of judicial review -- the courts must steer between the requirements of boldness and caution. They must be ready to intervene to prevent abuses while avoiding usurpation of the political role of making the complex choices of policy which are involved in designing and implementing in schemes of preference. For while the courts may keep the use of preferences within constitutional boundaries, the main problem of the use, extent, method, duration and administration of preferences lie with other agencies. If there is much that the courts can contribute to their working, the most important determinants of the success of compensatory discrimination lie beyond the power of the judiciary.[51]

So much for the conflict. As to the complications, two quotes illustrate the point. One is a discussion of Article 16(4); the other is a philosophic analysis of the situation.

Professor M.P. Jain, in his article on "Safeguards to Minorities: Constitutional Principles, Policy, and Framework," says this:

> Article 16(4) does not envisage any reservation in services on grounds other than backwardness. No reservation is thus envisaged on a caste basis. Accordingly, reservation by the Madras Government of Munsiffs' posts in favour of various castes and communities like harijans, backward Hindus, Muslims, Brahmins, non-Brahmin Hindus, Christians, has been held to be inconsistent with article 16(1) and (2)

---

51. Galanter, *op. cit.*, Chapter 2 (manuscript).

and not protected by article 16(4). Similarly, the policy adopted by the Government of Jammu & Kashmir of recruiting government servants on the basis of Hindus and Muslims has been held to be invalid. The Court has emphasized that the expression 'backward class'' in article 16(4) is not synonymous with 'backward caste' or 'backward community.' To determine whether a section forms a class or not for purposes of article 16(4), a test based solely on caste, community, race, religion, sex, descent, place of birth or residence cannot be adopted as it would directly offend the Constitution. (Footnotes omitted) [52]

Here is the philosophical approach of M.N. Srinivas and R.D. Sanwal:

> India has always been heterogeneous in terms of race, language, religion and culture. The essence of Indian unity lies in this diversity, and any attempt towards unity to succeed must be within the framework of this cultural, religious and ethnic pluralism. Even the institution of caste which has nearly an all-India spread and provides a common cultural idiom for the national majority unites by dividing people. India provides one of the most extreme expressions of cultural pluralism and the only hope for the emergence of a feeling of nationhood in India lies in working towards emotional integration and not towards assimilation. [53]

The Harijans and the Law

To understand the legal position of India's 93 million Harijans, one starts with Article 17 of the constitution. It reads:

> 'Untouchability' is abolished and its practice in any form is

---

52. In: Iman, *Minorities and the Law*. Bombay, Tripathi, 1972, p. 8.

53. M.N. Srinivas and R.D. Sanwal. "Some Aspects of Political Development in the North-Eastern Hill Areas of India." In: K. Suresh Singh, ed. *Tribal Situation in India*. Simla: IAAS, 1972. p. 126 as quoted in Mathur, op. cit., p. 35.

> forbidden. The enforcement of any disability arising out of 'Untouchability' shall be an offence punishable in accordance with law.

That would appear to take care of the problem.

Relevant also are such cases as *Moosa v. State of Kerala.* [54] . This held that a government order requisitioning land for the construction of a colony of Harijans, previously held discriminatory under Article 15(1), was now valid under Article 15(4).

There is also a law, first enacted in 1955 and then amended in 1976, giving the untouchables the legal right to enter any temple, draw water from any well or tap, or use any public restaurant.

What does this mean in practice? While the origins of untouchability in India are obscure, there is reference to a caste system existing since 1500 B.C. It is not a separateness based upon religion, since untouchables are also Hindus. It has been a separateness based on heredity and group descent manifested by restrictions on political and occupational activities. And it persists. While it is true that some Harijans have become lawyers and doctors, it is also true that all of the sweepers in the city of Bombay are untouchables.

The caste system in India evolved over more than 2500 years. Aryan (Persian) speaking groups that conquered Indian used it to perpetuate their domination over the non-Aryan natives. The names of the four classic or main castes appear for the first time in the late Vedic hymns: Kshatriyas, Brahmins, Vaishyas and Sudras. They corresponded roughly to aristocratic warriors, priests, commoners and slaves. Eventually the Brahmins rose to the top, the Vaishyas became the traders, and the Sudras the servants and agricultural workers. Skilled workers were later absorbed by the Sudra caste. The Harijans became the fifth component but not the fifth caste. They were literally the outcasts, traditionally treated as a pariah group. It is also interesting to note that in the ancient Sanskrit the word caste apparently refers to

54. A.I.R. 1960, J.E.R. 355.

colour. It is a fact that the top caste, the Brahmins, are far more fair skinned than the lowest class, who are more often as black as West Africans.

Whether the origin of untouchability was or was not based upon ethnic or racial differences more than three millenia ago is a moot question. What persists is the distinctiveness of a given group within a society whose members have been forced to associate and mate with each other for this extended period of time.

Both the constitution and the laws ending discrimination against Harijans are widely disregarded.

> The defeat of Indira Gandhi and her Congress Party, which had instituted a "20-point program" pressing for distribution of land to untouchables, minimum wages for them, and abolition of bonded labor (which has some 7 million in virtual lifetime slavery), has turned back the clock. Landlords in many areas are reported to have grabbed back the land formerly distributed to the Harijans, and harassment is rising.[55]

There are many reports of the shooting of poor untouchables, and likewise reports that the killing of wealthy landlords by untouchables "has become almost a regular feature in recent times in several backward areas in India."[56] One study argues that new laws and regulations have actually worsened the Harijan position and they not only live as virtual serfs, but are severely punished for failure to obey their masters. "As an example, all the accused in connection with a massacre in which 42 Harijans, including women and children, who were burned alive in a village near Madras in South India, were acquitted for lack of

55. "India's 93 Million Harijans: Country Within a Country." *Intercom* (a publication of the Population Reference Bureau, Inc.), No. 1 (January, 1978). Mrs. Gandhi was re-elected Prime Minister in January 1980.

56. D. Wickramanayake. "Harijan Terror in India." *Plural Societies,* No. 3 (Autumn, 1975), p. 17.

evidence."[57].

Thus, conflict. High-caste landlords take Harijan women as mistresses, and police rape Harijan women. According to district officials, it is reported, the landlords who have been killed are those who had kept Harijan women as mistresses.

There can be no better example than this of the inadequacies of constitutional safeguards in trying to solve the peculiar problems of discrimination against the particular ethnic or cultural group.

Constitutional Safeguards and Their Alternatives in India

As complicated as India's multi-racial society is today, it was even more complicated in the period prior to independence. At that time, the principal group rights problem was the ever-present conflict between Hindu and Muslim. This was, of course, primarily a religious problem. It was also a language problem. Mahatma Gandhi had argued for the adoption of Hindustani as the language of the entire sub-continent -- a language which would combine both Hindi and Urdu.

But Britain's Empire of India was not to become a separate, independent state. What is now a subcontinent of more than 850 million was first broken up to create an India and a Pakistan. Then Pakistan was divided once again to create the new nation of Bangladesh and to constitute the separate nation of Pakistan.

The first separation was based on religious differences: Pakistan was established as a Muslim nation. The second separation was based upon ethnic and cultural differences -- the Bengali Muslims of East Pakistan (who speak Bengali) differing in physiognomy, culture, and language from the people of West Pakistan (who speak Urdu).

The division of British India into two separate nation-states in 1947 resulted in the greatest human migration in history. Millions of Muslims left what was to become the Republic of India to go to

57. *Id.*, pp. 18-19.

Pakistan; and millions of non-Muslims migrated in the opposite direction. (But even after all of the migrations were over, there are today at least 10 million Hindus in Pakistan and Bangladesh, and 60 million Muslims in India.) Would it have been possible to have avoided such separation and transfer of population with any kind of constitutional language? Would it have been better? The answers to these questions must be in the negative.

And it remains to be seen whether the constitutional safeguards preserving group rights will preserve the unity of today's India or lead to its further division. The violence and massacres in India's state of Assam in 1983 serves to underline the problem. The strife killed more than 3,600 people, mostly Bengalis and 230,000 became refugees. At the roots of the strife, the worst since India's independence in 1947, is the yawning religious and economic gulf between the largely Hindu Assamese and mostly Moslem Bengalis who came from Bangladesh. A split, if it comes, may occur over the question of language rights. The insistence of many northern Indians for the adoption of Hindi as the nation's sole official language is bitterly opposed by the South and has led to separatist threats.

But whatever occurs, the Indian experience must be studied and re-studied, for it is here that group rights problems are most severe and it is here where the greatest efforts have been made to solve them in a legal context.

CHAPTER XIII

MALAYSIA

Malaysia -- its past, present and future -- provides enough source materials on the subject of race relations to fill a library of scholarly works. "It is strange to observe life in Kuala Lumpur and talk with members of the two very distinct communities." So writes Thomas Molnar in his "Observations in a Bi-racial Society."[58] But Dr. Molnar has only scratched the surface.

"Malaysia," according to Nancy L. Snider, "represents one of the most complex and intriguing examples of this (multi-ethnic) phenomenon. Malaysia's polyglot peoples tend to be lumped by outsiders into four basic ethnic groups -- Malays, Chinese, Indians, and indigenous peoples. Malaysians themselves also tend to accept consciously and subconsciously these categories and to use them on many levels in different aspects of their lives. These communal groups often are seen as mutually antagonistic due to differing and strongly held 'primordial attachments' . . . Members struggle against the members of other groups."[59]

And similar comments in French have come from the pen of George Fischer in a major section of a lengthy article on "Les Etats Multi-raciaux" in the Human Rights Journal.[60] But perhaps H.S.

58. Thomas Molnar, "Malaysia: Observations in a Bi-Racial Society." *Plural Societies,* No. 1, p. 41 (1970).

59. Nancy L. Snider, "Malaysian Noncommunal Political Parties." In John A. Lent, ed. *Cultural Pluralism in Malaysia: Policy Military, Mass Media, Education, Religion and Social Class.* The Center for Southeast Asian Studies, Northern Illinois University, DeKalb, 1977, p. 1.

60. H.S. Leng, "Ethnic Politics in Malaysia," in *Veenhoven,* Volume III, p. 1, 3.

Leng said it best when he summarily characterized Malaysia as "inherently unstable because of its multi-ethnicity." [61]

He continues: "The fact that the new nation of Malaysia is a plural society is nothing extraordinary. What is unusual is that it is a plural society of minority communities. In numerical terms no ethnic community commands a majority . . ." [62] All of this is true to such an extent that it is remarkable that there exists any Malaysia at all.

Yet, (again Dr. Leng), "until 1969, Malaysia was widely seen to be a model Third World country." [63] It is not important to agree or disagree with Dr. Leng's choice of 1969 as some sort of watershed in Malaysian development. The remarkable thing is that it continues to survive as a single nation.

One method -- at least a partial method -- of alleviating and reconciling racial conflict is by means of constitutional provisions. Thus, it is not surprising that the most multi-ethnic nation in the world -- India -- has by far the longest constitution in the world. Whether Malaysia or Yugoslavia is the second largest is difficult to determine without counting the actual number of words. For while Malaysia has only 181 articles as compared to 406 in the Yugoslav constitution, the Malaysian document is filled with so many more sub-sections, together with thirteen "Schedules" and special constitutional acts.

Part of the problem is the simple fact that so many different peoples were just there when the British Colonial Office decided to put them together in one way or another to form conveniently administered "federations." And then the British complicated the matter still further in Malaysia as they, in Molnar's words, "imported considerable numbers of Indians and Chinese." [64] To this must be added religious complications. Most of the Malays are

---

61. H.S Leng: "Ethnic Politics in Malaysia," Veenhoven, Vol. III, pp. 1-3.

62. Leng, id., pp. 4-5.

63. Leng, id., p. 3.

64. Molnar, supra note 58, p. 41.

Muslims and are much affected by the potential leadership of the world's largest Muslim nation, Indonesia. Will the situation become even more complicated by the possible creation of "Maphilindo" -- a new nation made up of Malaysia, the Philippines and Indonesia? That step has been suggested.

Today's Malaysia came into being on Sept. 16, 1963. It consists of the Peninsula Malaysia, which includes 11 states of the former Federation of Malaysia, plus East Malaysia, which includes two former colonies of North Borneo (renamed Sabah) and Sarawak.

This former Federation of Malaysia constitutes what was the independent Malaysian State when British colonialism came to an end in the area on August 31, 1957. This is still known as Merdeka or Freedom Day. Between 1957 and 1965 Singapore became part of the Federation and later separated from it. (Singapore became an independent state within the British Commonwealth on August 9, 1965.) Of the total 12,500,000 people of Malaysia, 50 percent are Malay, 35 percent are Chinese and 10 percent are Indian.[65] More than half of the people in Sabah and Sarawak consist of indigenous tribesmen. The Malays are nearly all Muslims, the Chinese are predominantly Buddhists and the Indians are predominantly Hindu. Nor do they speak the same language. Malay is now the official language on the Peninsula, but there is also English, Tamil and Chinese dialects, plus numerous tribal languages in Sabah and Sarawak.

And, while Singapore (and its 80 percent Chinese population) is no longer a part of Malaysia, these continuous states complement each other economically as well as geographically.

Or, to restate the problem-situation in other words:

> Both in the original Federation of Malaya established in 1948 and the wider Federation of Malaysia created in 1963,

65. See statistics in United States Central Intelligence Agency: *National Basic Intelligence Factbook,* Washington, D.C., July, 1977: For an understanding of the nature of the Indian population, see also N.J. Colletta, "Malaysia's Forgotten People," in *Veenhoven,* Vol. V., p. 101.

the most significant political feature was the communal character of the population. Since the language, religion and related social customs of the Malay, Chinese, Indian and indigenous Bornean communities within Malaysia are sharply distinct and often incompatible, not surprisingly communal tension has coloured the entire political scene. In the federations of Malaya and Malaysia each of the states itself contained a variety of races. But there were significant regional variations in the relative strengths of the different communities and these gave the states their distinctiveness. The cultural contrasts were perhaps sharpest between the Malay-dominated and conservative states of peninsular Malaya and the overwhelmingly Chinese population of Singapore with its more radical outlook to politics. This accounted for the exclusion of Singapore from the federation established in 1948. When it later became apparent that, unless Singapore was taken under the protective custody of the federation it might become a base for subverting the federation, the Malays agreed to its accession. At the same time, however, the British Borneo territories were added in order to offset Malay fears of Chinese preponderence within the federation. Singapore itself, because of its distinctive character and interests, was given substantially greater autonomy than other states within the federation, but this experiment of an "associated state" lasted only two years before mounting political tension led to its separation again from the federation.[66]

How can any constitution, or the laws passed pursuant thereto, order the relationships of so complicated a society? "Democratic equality is taken for granted by the Malaysian constitution . . . yet no equality exists in fact between Malays and Chinese," in the

66. Ronald L. Watts, "Asian Multicultural Federations." In Jean-Guy Savard and Richard Vigneault, eds., *Les Etats Multilingues, Problems et Solutions,* Quebec Information Center for Research on Bilingualism, Publication A 9, p. 561, 562-563.

view of Dr. Molnar.[67] And he quite properly points out that the Chinese argue that they have no future . . . in an increasingly nationalistic (Malay) and religiously (Moslem) oriented Malaysia.[68]

Further, the constitution which exists has an inevitable Western orientation which is part of the heritage of British colonialism. Britain's Federal Council of the Federated Malay States was established in 1909. Britain's Malaysian Union was created in 1946. Then the Federation of Malaya replaced the Malaysian Union in 1948. During the year prior to independence in 1957, the Federation of Malaya Constitutional Conference met in London, working on a new constitution with a newly-appointed Commonwealth Constitutional Commission. All of this resulted in a British-oriented Independence Constitution. And then there were more consultations and conferences with Britain. The present Federation of Malaysia was technically established, effective September 16, 1963, by the "Agreement Between the United Kingdom, the Federation of Malaya, North Borneo, Sarawak and Singapore Concerning the Establishment of the Federation of Malaysia." [69]

The fact that Malaysia has a Western-oriented constitution, based on Western concepts of democracy, has further complicated the multi-ethnic situation. On this subject Dr. Molnar again has a pertinent comment. "Each of the races now formally integrated in the new community . . . becomes apprehensive lest its specific religious, cultural and social profile might be blurred in the resulting am- gam. Add to this fear, the ideologies spread among these peop s which promise them instant paradise, and then you are ready o appreciate the concise statement by Mircea Eliade that 'the political independence and the cultural freedom proclaimed by the millenialist (ideological) movements among the colonial peoples are conceived as the recovery of an original state of bliss' In other words, each race or creed or tribe expects to be

67. Molnar, supra note 58, p. 43.

68. Id. at p. 47.

69. See constitutional development in chronology section of pamphlet on Malaysia in *Blaustein.*

alone exalted and alone to recover its legendary privileges guaranteed by the ancestors and robbed briefly by the colonial powers.'' [70]

Adopting the basic precepts of Western constitutionalism, Article 8(1) embodies the principle Malaysian version: ''All persons are equal before the law and entitled to the equal protection of the law.'' This, of course, resembles the language of the third of the key phrases of Section 1 of the 14th Amendment of the U.S. Constitution (ratified in 1868) which provides that no state shall ''deny to any person within its jurisdiction the equal protection of the laws.'' [71]

But recognition of the racial and economic contrasts between the Malaysian Peninsula, Singapore and the Borneo States has resulted in a constitution with many provisions contradicting the concept of legal equality. The constitution is overburdened with special clauses made for special classes of people, based on racial, religious and ethnic grounds. Before examining specific provisions, however, the following from Article 8 must be examined carefully:

> (2) Except as expressly authorised by this Constitution, there shall be no discrimination against citizens on the ground only of religion, race, descent or place of birth in any law or in the appointment to any office or employment under a public authority or in the administration of any law relating to the acquisition, holding or disposition of property or the establishing or carrying on of any trade, business, profession, vocation or employment.
>
> (3) There shall be no discrimination in favour of any

70. Molnar, supra note 58, pp. 49-50.

71. Article 6(1) of the Malaysian Constitution provides that ''no person shall be held in slavery.'' It, of course, is a typical provision of so many modern constitutions, but one which can hardly be classified as ''Western.'' Slavery was not prohibited in the United States, for example, until the addition of the 13th Amendment to its Constitution in 1865.

> person on the ground that he is a subject of the Ruler of any State.

Note particularly the word "against" in Article 8(2) and the word "favour" in Article 8(3).

And there is still one more part of Article 8 which serves as an introduction to this problem. Article 8(5)c reads:

> (5) This Article does not invalidate or prohibit . . .
> (c) Any provision for the protection, well-being or advancement of the aboriginal peoples of the Malay Peninsula (including the reservation of the land) or the reservation to aborigines of a reasonable proportion of suitable positions in the public service;

One of the ways in which Article 8(5)c is carried into effect is by the second paragraph of Article 45 dealing with the composition of the Senate. Article 45(2) has this language:

> The members to be appointed by the Yang di-Pertuan Agong (Supreme Head of the Federation) shall be persons who in his opinion have rendered distinguished public service or have achieved distinction in the professions, commerce, industry, agriculture, cultural activities or social service or are representative of racial minorities or are capable of representing the interest of aborigines.

As noted by Watts, "the Malayan Constitution of 1957 contained explicit arrangements on behalf of the Malays, who were more backward educationally and economically concerning reservation of land, quotas for permits, and quotas for employment in the public services with the states. (Footnote omitted.) Similar protections were also extended in the Malaysian Federation to 'natives' in the Borneo states, together with additional safeguards concerning the continued use of native languages and the protection of the Muslim religion and education." [72]

72. Watts, supra note 66, p. 575. See articles 89, 90 and 153 (10) of Malaysian Constitution; see articles 161, 161A, 161C, 161D of present constitution.

The "additional protections for Borneo States," set forth in Part XIIA of the Constitutions, are extremely lengthy. In sum, they grant a considerable degree of autonomy to the two Borneo states of Sabah and Sarawak as part of Malaysian recognition of the racial and linguistic distinctiveness of their indigenous peoples. The various subdivisions of Article 161 are in Part XIIA. Article 161 itself deals with language rights -- a matter treated in many portions of the constitution. Of more interest here is Article 161A which deals with special provisions (quotas) for public service -- another special subject in the analysis of the Malaysian Constitution.

Especially interesting subsections of Article 161A are those which define the word "native" and list the races of indigenous peoples who are to classified as "native." Articles 161C and D deal with religious rights, exempting the Borneo states from certain provisions which, under Article 3, proclaim Islam as the religion of the Federation.[73]

Observations by Dr. Watts summarize the complicated language situation of Malaysia:

> In Malaya and Malaysia, too, official language policy has been one of the issues on which the most extreme positions have been taken. The Malays have insisted upon Malay as the official federal language since it is indigenous to the peninsula, and they have opposed the recognition of English because it would favour the immigrant races.

73. See also The Ninth Schedule, Article 95B(1) (a) which develops language in Articles 74 and 77. It reads in part:

> List IIa -- Supplement to State List for Borneo States
>
> 13. Native law and custom, including the personal law relating to marriage, divorce, guardianship, maintenance, adoption, legitimacy, family law, gifts or succession testate or intestate; registration of adoptions under native law or custom; the determination of matters of native law or custom; the constitution, organization, and procedure of native courts (including the right of audience in such courts), and the jurisdiction and powers of such courts, which shall extend only to the matters included in this paragraph and shall not include jurisdiction in respect of offences except in so far as conferred by federal law.

> Many of the Chinese and Indian citizens of the federation, on the other hand, have had little opportunity to learn to speak Malay fluently, and therefore would clearly be handicapped if Malay were to become the sole federal language. The 1957 Constitution incorporated a compromise whereby in addition to Malay as a "national language," English would continue to be used for an interim period of ten years. Following independence the governing Alliance party continued to reiterate its determination to make Malay the country's sole official language by 1967, the first occasion on which this would be permitted by the Constitution. When the federation was widened into Malaysia in 1963 a concession was made to the newly acceding states, guaranteeing that in these states, English would continue to be used for a period of at least ten years after they joined the federation. In 1967 Malay was made the sole official language in West Malaysia (Malaya) although provision for the continued use of English for certain purposes was made. The extent to which the insistence of the Alliance Party upon recognition of Malay as the sole official language had alienated Indian and particularly Chinese support became apparent in the 1969 general elections which were followed by violent communal rioting and the proclamation of a state of emergency.[72]

Article 52 provides that the national language shall be the Malay language, but this is followed by a large number of provisos. For example, no one is prohibited or prevented from using other languages "otherwise than for official purposes." And, as Dr. Watts pointed out, there was at least a ten-year interim period to permit the use of English. Article 152 (4) indicates that "all proceedings in the Federal Court or a High Court shall be in the English language" under specified circumstances.

The right to the use of the English language and of native

74. Watts, supra, note 66, pp. 581-582.

languages in the Borneo States is set forth at length in Article 161 and Borneo language rights are also protected by Article 16A(d). This latter section deals with the question of citizenship, requiring that an applicant has a sufficient knowledge of either Malay or English. For those in Sarawak, however, "any language in current use" there will be accepted as a substitute.

Long a matter of racial conflict (with significant overtones of linguistic conflict) are the exceptions and qualifications to Article 36. It reads as follows:

> 136. Impartial treatment of federal employees.
>
> All persons of whatever race in the same grade in the service of the Federation shall, subject to the terms and conditions of their employment, be treated impartially.

That article should be read in conjunction with the following statement by Dr. Watts: "Malays have resented the dominance of commerce by the energic Chinese, while the Chinese in turn have resented the constitutionally guaranteed dominance of the Malays in the civil services."[75]

The correctness of this conclusion must be based upon an analysis of Article 153 and 161A.

While 153(5) states that "this Article does not derogate from the provisions of Article 136," it is difficult to reconcile this with the specific language of other parts of Article 153. For example, here is the exact wording of the first two subdivisions of Article 153:

> (1) It shall be the responsibility of the Yang di-Pertuan Agong (Supreme Head of the Federation) to safeguard the special position of the Malays and the legitimate interests of other communities in accordance with the provisions of this Article.
>
> (2) Notwithstanding anything in this Constitution, but sub-

75. Id., p. 569.

ject to the provisions of Article 40 and of this Article, the Yand di-Pertuan Agong shall exercise his functions under this Constitution and federal law in such manner as may be necessary to safeguard the special position of the Malays and to ensure the reservation for Malays of such proportion as he may deem reasonable of positions in the public service (other than the public service of a State) and of scholarships, exhibitions, and other similar educational or training privileges or special facilities given or accorded by the Federal Government and, when any permit or licence for the operation of any trade or business is required by federal law, then subject to the provisions of that law and this Article, of such permits and licences.

And here is the first subsection of Article 161A.

> (1) Subject to Clause (2), the provisions of Clauses (2) to (5) of Article 153, so far as they relate to the reservation of positions in the public service, shall apply in relation to natives of any of the Borneo States as they apply in relation to Malays.

All of the above -- meaning all of the problems, all of the ambiguities and all of the contradictions -- illustrate the difficulties of ordering the details of multi-racial, religious and ethnic peoples by means of a long, complicated constitution. Certainly, clearer draftsmanship would help. But so would brevity.

Nonetheless, the ever-growing importance of group rights must have constitutional recognition even at the expense of the kinds of analytical problems encountered in the Malaysian model.

CHAPTER XIV

REPUBLIC OF NIGERIA

The West African state of Nigeria is one of the most complex multi-national states in all of Africa. Nigeria is Africa's most populous state with major tribal divisions consisting of the semi-nomadic Northern Hausas, the urbanized Western Yorubas and the Ibos of the east. The three regions, together with Lagos, the administrative center, were long part of a single vast British colonial possession. By a policy of juggling one group against another Britain kept Nigeria together from 1900 until 1960. The unity of Nigeria was a colonial invention, maintained from British economic advantage, but it continued even after independence.

Nigeria became independent on October 1, 1960. In 1961 the Northern portion of the trusteeship of the Cameroons voted to join Nigeria. Its first constitution provided for four regions with local autonomy permitted to a limited extent.

In 1966 there were two military coups. In the first coup of January 15, 1966 the Prime Minister and some other ministers were killed by a group of officers. In two days the head of the army suppressed the revolt and himself assumed power. The army head, General Ironsi, suspended the constitution and set up a supreme military council to rule the country. General Ironsi was overthrown on July 29, 1966 by a group which accepted

Lieutenant-Colonel Yakubu Gowon as its leader.

On May 30, 1967 the Eastern Region of Nigeria seceded, proclaiming itself the Republic of Biafra. A Civil War ensued resulting in massive casualties on both sides. The Biafrans (mostly Ibos) lost as many as a million lives, many by starvation. By 1970 the Biafran rebellion had collapsed and General Gowon took power over all Nigeria.

In 1975 General Gowon was overthrown, to be replaced by General Murtala Ramat Mohammed. General Mohammed was killed in a coup in 1976. The present head of state is Lieutenant General Owsegun Obasanjo. (Retired in 1979.)

English is the official and business language of Nigeria. However 250 languages and dialects are spoken in Nigeria. Sizeable minorities speak Hausa, Fulani, Ijaw, Ibibio, Kanuri, and TW. Of the 250 or so tribal groups the dominant ones are the Yoruba (13 million), the Ibo (7.8 million) and the Hausa (6.8 million), one million Ibibio live in the East. There are 5 million Fulani and 2.9 million Kanuri in a nation of about 60 million people.

Northern Nigeria is largely Moslem and the remainder Christian, but these figures are only crude estimates.

Nigeria is entirely in the tropics but has a very varied topography. In the extreme north it is desert. A mangrove swamp forest lies along the entire coast. The country is divided by many major rivers and rises to a 5,000 to 6,000 feet plateau in the east. In this geographic setting the difficulty of maintaining a unified nation of such diverse elements should be obvious. This tropical multi-national state is a leading example of the need to describe group rights clearly, and to provide institutional guarantees for those rights.

In October, 1975, General Murtala Ramat Muhammed appointed a 50 man constitution drafting committee to prepare a constitutional text for the consideration of the government and people of Nigeria. The committee issued its report in September, 1976. The document and the observations of the members of the drafting committee are important examples of constitutional thinking in multi-national states.

Section 9 of the draft constitution recognizes the problem of promoting national loyalty in a multi-ethnic, multi-national society. It states that "national integration shall be actively encouraged whilst discrimination on the grounds of place of origin, religion, sex, status, ethnic or linguistic association or ties shall be prohibited." Interestingly, a number of specific policies are described in the draft constitution. The State shall "encourage intermarriage among persons from different places of origin, or of different religions, ethnic or linguistic associations or ties." [76] The national government should, in other ways, "promote or encourage the formation of associations that cut across ethnic, linguistic, religious or other sectional barriers." [77] As the draft committee pointed out, loyalty to one's own community ought not to detract from national loyalty. [78]

The drafters were more concerned with the domination of public affairs by certain regions and ethnic groups. Heated debate upon the best method to safeguard the interests of groups previously neglected appears to have taken place. The best method of securing minority rights may be to systematically ensure group participation in government, but the draft constitution itself stopped short of such a guarantee. The language adopted states that:

> The composition of the Federal Government or any of its agencies and the conduct of their affairs shall be carried out in such manner as to recognize the federal character of Nigeria and the need to promote national unity and to

76. Draft Constitution of the Federal Republic of Nigeria, Section 9 (c) in *Report of the Constitution Drafting Committee,* Vol. I, Lagos, 1976, p. 11.

77. Draft Constitution, Section 9(d).

78. *Report of the Constitution Drafting Committee,* Vol. I, p. VIII.

> command national loyalty. Accordingly, the predominance in that Government or its agencies of persons from a few states, or from a few ethnic or other sectional groups shall be avoided.[79]

This provision may reassure the Ibos, the Hausas, and the Ibibios that the Yoribas will be less dominant in a future Nigeria under the proposed constitution.

The "federal character of Nigeria" was also defined in such a way as to stress the promotion of national unity, "notwithstanding the diversities of ethnic origin, culture, language or religion which may exist."[80] Few details about the structure of the federation were provided by the text of the draft constitution. The allocation of powers between the states and federal government are referred to in the sections describing the legislature. Broad national powers over public safety,[81] taxation,[82] film censorship,[83] and elections[84] were also included.

The draft constitution was considerably more centralist than would be expected in such a diverse multinational state, but the fragile character of the federation since independence probably created a drive for greater centralization in order to resist further disintegration. However, the constitution does provide for the existence of nineteen states,[85] and makes the creation of new states or the alteration of the boundaries of the nineteen states very difficult.[86] A two-thirds vote of the national legislature and a two-thirds vote of the state legislatures is required.[87] The constitution itself may be amended, ordinarily, by a simple act of the national legislature, but these federal boundary guarantees

79. Draft Constitution, Section 8 (2).
80. Draft Constitution Section 210 (1).
81. Draft Constitution, Section 101.
82. Draft Constitution, Section 103.
83. Draft Constitution, Section 105.
84. Draft Constitution, Section 107.
85. Draft Constitution, Section 3.
86. Draft Constitution, Section 100 (6) (7).
87. Draft Constitution, Section 100 (8).

may not be amended without a four-fifths vote of both houses of the national legislature and a two-thirds majority of all the states. Yet this Federal guarantee of the territorial integrity of the states is not unamendable and a state may see its territory changed without its consent.

The upper house of the national legislature is called the Senate. Seats in the Senate are based on constituencies carved out of the states, each state comprising five senatorial districts. Although population quotas are factors in the formation of Senate election districts, other factors include "geographical peculiarities" and "the distribution of different communities" within the state. [88] Equality of the states within the Senate is assumed. [89]

Political parties are also subject to federalizing features. No association can function as a political party unless "its membership is open to every Nigerian citizen irrespective of his place of origin, religion, ethnic grouping or sex." [90] The rules of each political party must provide an arrangement ensuring that the "members of the executive committee or other governing body reflect the federal character of Nigeria, [91] which means that its membership must belong to different states comprising not less than two-thirds of the states in the federation. [92] This restriction on regional parties is one of the most stringent features of the constitution. Although it does not absolutely ban such parties, such a prohibition is legally possible.

The anti-discrimination provisions of the constitution display group right concepts. Nigerian citizens of particular communities, ethnic groups, or adherents of any religion may not be subjected to disabilities or restrictions to which citizens of Nigeria of "other communities, ethnic groups, places of origin, religions or political

---

88. Draft Constitution, Section 100 (10).
89. Draft Constitution, Section 68.
90. Draft Constitution, Section 172 (6).
91. Draft Constitution, Section 173 (6).
92. Draft Constitution, Section 35(a).

opinion'' [93] are not subject. The other provisions found in the fundamental rights portion of the draft constitution are conventional expressions of individual rights.

The most troubled multi-national state has tried to construct greater national unity through a tighter federation with stronger national powers. A few constitutional guarantees have been accorded to the states, but the chief means chosen for protecting group rights is to be found in the fundamental rights section. Whether this formula will prove sufficient to hold the federation together is doubtful. Without institutional guarantees to the diverse groups beyond representation in the Senate, it is hard to believe that the groups in Nigeria can be drawn together.

Following elections during mid-1979 Dr. A.S. Shagari was elected President of Nigeria and the draft constitution of 1975 became law. After 13 years of military government the civilians were back in power with a constitution establishing a U.S. type federal system with the powers divided among three federal branches, the executive, legislature and judiciary. The constitution also confirmed the increase of the number of states from 12 to 19. Though the increased occurred during 1975 it was done by military decree by the previous President, General Abasanjo. The centrifugal tendencies in Nigeria were resisted by a strong military dictatorship. A civilian regime under a centralist constitution may be insufficient.

---

93. Draft Constitution, Section 35(6).

CHAPTER XV

REPUBLIC OF THE PHILIPPINES

Unlike the constitutions of Belgium, India and Yugoslavia, the constitution of the multi-ethnic Philippines does not go into detail on issues of race, religion and ethnicity. The national charter of 1972 sums up state responsibility in the single sentence which comprises Article XV, Section II -- a provision which demands comparison with the Famous Article 46 of the Indian Constitution of 1949.

Philippines **Article XV, Sec. 11**	**India** **Article 46**
The State shall consider the customs, traditions, beliefs, and interests of national cultural communities in the formulation and implementation of state policies.	The State shall promote with special care, the educational and economic interests of the weaker sections of the people, and, in particular, of the Scheduled Castes and the Scheduled Tribes, and shall protect from social injustice and all forms of exploitation.

Under the umbrella of Article XV, Section 11, the government has passed laws, issued decrees, etc., which have recognized local holidays, authorized particular religious practices, approved classroom instruction in local dialects for grades 1 through 7, etc.

Much of what the government has done in carrying out this mandate has been channeled through the efforts of the Panamin Foundation. This group has led the campaign to bring doctors, lawyers, technicians, etc., to the aid of minority groups and has sponsored governmental action in their behalf. Panamin was started by Manuel Elizalde, Jr., in 1968, when he was serving as Presidential Advisor on National Minorities. He was named on December 17, 1968 as Presidential Assistant on National Minorities, with cabinet rank.

The Panamin administrative structure is unique. It was established in large measure to lessen the financial burden of the government in taking care of minority problems. Pursuant to a Presidential Proclamation in 1969, it is authorized to raise funds within the private sector.

A good example of the protection of cultural minorities through this combined governmental-private activity is in the preservation of the primitive Tasaday peoples. The Tasaday leads a life completely dependent upon their forest environment and any disruption of forest ecology would destroy their sources of food. Panamin reported the construction of three roads by loggers near the Tasaday area in early 1972, and President Ferdinand E. Marcos responded with Proclamation No. 995 on April 6, 1972. This proclamation sets aside 19,247 hectares (46,299) acres "withdrawn from entry, sale, lease exploitation or other disposition" . . . "reserving for settlement purposes of the national cultural minorities, known as the Manubo Blit and Tasaday, a certain parcel of land of the public domain situated in the municipalities of Surallah and Kiamba, province of South Sotabato, Island of Mindanao, under Panamin management."

Some idea of the cultural-ethnic problem of the Philippines is illustrated by the following:

> The population of the Philippines, whether belonging to the majority or the minority, belong basically to the Southern Mongoloid racial group and speak languages and dialects that belong to the Malayo-Polynesian family of languages. There are 87 ethno-linguistic groups, of which some 60 are classified as belonging to the Minorities -- totalling 4 million persons out of a national population of 37 million.

There are two additional sections of Article XV dealing with ethnic matters. Under Section 3, the National Assembly was directed to "take steps towards the development and formal adoption of a common national language to be known as Filipino." Section 8(8) gives parents the option of having religion taught to their children in public elementary and high schools "without cost to them and the Government."

The fact that the Philippine constitution does not deal specifically with religious freedom or religious discrimination has abetted those who led the Christian and Muslim communities whose struggle has separatist characteristics. The Muslims want to make their traditional homeland in the south an independent state. Their arguments as to differences in culture and background from the northern Christians are much the same as advanced by the proponents of a Palistinian homeland on the West Bank of the Jordan in Israel and for the homelands policy in South Africa. By the end of 1974 the religious cleavage in the Philippines assumed the form of Civil war. The Philippines remains a classic example of a government which found reason in group conflict to suspend the constitution and to continue a policy of discrimination against the Chinese (who are only 2 percent of the population), despite the fact that they have lived in the islands for more than 5000 years.[94] The Chinese, Hunt and Walker found, were viewed by the Filipinos as cohesive and clanish and "as a self-perpetuating foreign irritant in the body politic." If there is an

94. Glaser and Possony: *Victims of Politics*, p. 194, 288 and Cf. *Newsweek*, 28 May 1973 and *International Herald Tribune*, Paris, 25 March 1974.

effort towards assimilation it is on the part of the Chinese and "it is the exclusionist policies of Filipinos which enable the Chinese to survive as a distinct and separate group.[95]

Despite statistics of increasing intermarriage the Filipino's group consciousness remains very strong and according to the Philippine Law on Citizenship even a Filipino mother did not constitute automatic grounds for establishing Philippine ancestry.[96] Constitutional provisions after 1948 excluded the Chinese from owing land or operating public utilities. Supreme Court decisions during the fifties expanded the constitutional provision against the Chinese ownership of agricultural or mineral land to include also urban land. Later, legislation was passed to drive the Chinese out of the rice and corn trade and by 1965 they were excluded from many professions and in a very broadly defined retail trade. The prospects of group conflict between the Chinese and Filipinos in the Philippines is therefore a very real one.

---

95. Ethnic Dynamics, op. cit., pp. 100-110.

96. Peck, Cornelius: "Nationalism, Race and Developments in the Philippine Law of Citizenship," *Journal of Asian and African Studies,* Vol. II, January-April, 1967, pp. 128-143.

CHAPTER XVI

SWISS CONFEDERATION

Switzerland is a leading example of a constitutional design intended to cope with linguistic-cultural-religious diversity. Protestants and Catholics who once struggled against each other have found a formula for a friendly relationship. Switzerland had four major linguistic groups, but these seem to have been accommodated. In fact, the Swiss Constitution is the centerpiece of Swiss social life. Doubtless, there are deeper explanations for the stability of the Swiss federal government, but the ingenuity of its constitutional arrangements partly accounts for the success of the Swiss system.

There is an important geographic non-coincidence of language, religions and cultural boundaries. Cultural co-existence as well as religious co-existence is reinforced by the distinctly separate location of groups which pursue their own ways of life. Only a series of maps portraying these regions can heighten our awareness of this fortuitous condition. Nonetheless, the Constitution provides a sufficient amount of unity to contain this diversity and to perfect minorities in regions where other majorities prevail.

The Constitution of 1848, which is still the Swiss Constitution of today, was essentially the creation of a twenty-three man committee of the Swiss Diet. Most were the chiefs of their cantonal governments. In spite of the fervent opposition of the small Catholic cantons the constitution was approved on September 12, 1848. The six and a half cantons which opposed the new constitution included three cantons, Uri, Schwyz, and Unterwalden, the originators of the Swiss confederation. [97]

To achieve a stable federal state the 1848 Constitution adopted a bicameral legislature in order to avoid the centralizing tendency of a single house popularly elected legislature. Although the Swiss reluctantly adopted this American-style compromise, they also invented the unique system of a collegiate seven-man executive serving on a rotating leadership basis. This plural executive was intended to further weaken the tendency toward centralization and the combination of a single group or canton.

The religious settlement is one of the main bases of Swiss federalism. Article 49 of the Swiss Constitution puts the central government in the position of actively defending groups and individuals against religious oppression. The old Swiss regime made Roman Catholicism unlawful in Protestant territories and vice-versa. But Article 49 declares that "freedom of conscience and belief is inviolable" and also brings delicate religious matters directly under the law of the state. Primary education, marriage, holidays, oaths, even church jurisdiction are all defined by law under the constitution. The territorial principle is rejected in favor of a national solution to the problem of religious tolerance.

Article 50 of the constitution guarantees the free exercise of religion, compatible with public order and decency and Article 49 prohibits compulsion to join a religious body or to pay taxes to a religious group of which he is not a member. Yet the cantons are free to create a single state church. Most cantons have recognized state churches (called National Churches) and the cantonal governments support them by granting them subsidies, special tax funds or other privileges. In order for taxes to support state

---

97. W.E. Rappard: *La Constitution Federale de la Suisse,* Editions de la Baconniere, Neuchatel, 1948.

churches to conform to Article 49 of the Constitution, provisions are made for individuals to be relieved of these taxes by publicly and formally denying that they adhere to the state religion of the canton. Separation of church and state prevails in Geneva and Basle while several Catholic cantons, on the other hand, operate under a "concordat system," negotiating arrangements between Civil authorities and the Pope and Bishops. This enormous diversity is all consistent with the Swiss Constitution.[98]

Many of the former practices of the Catholic religion are curbed by specific constitutional provisions. Civil ceremonies of marriage are made the exclusive means of legal marriage by Article 54, inserted in the Constitution in 1874. Similarly, cemeteries are placed in the care of civil authorities. No new Catholic bishopries may be set up on Swiss territory without the consent of the federal authorities. Until 1973 the Constitution contained articles (Article 54, 1874 Amendments, in particular) which expressly banned Jesuits and the foundation or resurrection of monasteries. This anti-Catholic measure has been removed, although the provision concerning bishopries remains.

Religious neutrality is not a prevailing principle of Swiss constitutionalism. Article 50 states that the cantons and the national government may take the measures necessary to maintain public order and peace between members of different religious communities, and to prevent the encroachments by ecclesiastical authorities upon the rights of citizens and of the state. The same article permits disputes arising out of schisms in existing religious groups to be brought before "competent federal authorities," presumably the courts. Ecclesiastical courts are abolished by Article 4.

The provisions of the Swiss Constitution regarding religion reveal generally anti-clerical attitudes based upon the experience of the 1848 drafters following periodic religious conflicts. The

98. See George Codding: *Federal Government of Switzerland,* Houghton Mifflin Co., Boston, 1961, p. 53.

increase in anti-clerical provisions by the revisions of 1874 were based on similar attitudes. Nonetheless, the decentralized structure of the federation combined with the diversity of the religious distribution of the population permit a great deal of local variation in the practical implementation of religious freedom.

Equality before the law is declared by Article 4 of the Federal Constitution. This formal equality is extended to the cantons by Article 60 which says "every canton is obliged to accord citizens of other confederate states the same treatment it accords to its own citizens, as regards legislation and all that concerns judicial discrimination." These provisions ensure that members of different religions, cultural or linguistic groups will not be the victims of discrimination within a canton dominated by members of another group.

The Swiss Constitution specifically provides (Article 116) that German, French, Italian and Romanche are national languages, and makes all but Romanche official languages. The three official languages are supposed to be represented in the Federal Tribunal (Article 107). This cold language established a freedom of languages which has been given unusual prominence in Swiss constitutional practice. In reality Switzerland is treated as though the map of the country were divided into French, German and Italian areas. Although Swiss citizens are entitled to speak their own languages, the territorial principle is regarded as superior to the personal principle. The language sovereignty of each canton is called *Sprachenhoheit,* and this extra constitutional concept fits in with the decentralization of the Swiss Federation by giving the canton the power to choose the language of school instruction and similar sensitive questions. The federal government, for its part, attempts to maintain equitable representation of linguistic groups through legislation in support of the constitutional principle of freedom of languages.[99]

99. On this and on many other basic issues of Swiss laws in support of the Constitution, see *Recuiel Systematique des Lois et Ordonnances,* published by the Federal Chancery of Berne. Swiss constitutional law is most accessible through Jean-Francois Aubert: *Traite de Droit Constitutionnel Suisse,* Editions de la Baconniere, Neuchatel, 1967.

The position of Romansch speakers in Switzerland is interesting. Only .9 percent of the population -- approximately 50,000 of 5.35 million speak Romansch. But in 1938 the Constitution was amended by referendum [100] to recognize Romansch as a national language. The petition was made by the executive of the Canton of Grisons and the amendment received the support of 92 percent of the voters. This is a vivid example of Swiss public policy toward weaker language groups. [101]

In general, the Swiss constitution provides that "the Cantons are sovereign insofar as their sovereignty is not limited by the Federal Constitution, and, as such, they exercise all rights which are not transferred to the federal power." [102] This provision is reinforced, as to language rights, by the fact that the seven-man Federal Council always provides some representation for each of the three language groups.[103] The Constitution also permits federal subsidies for education [104] which amounts to linguistic generosity to support instruction in cantonally dominant languages.

The latest change made to the cantonal arrangement was on 24th September 1978 when Swiss voters approved cantonal status for the Roman Catholic French speaking area of Jura, making it the 23rd canton and the first increase in the number of cantons since 1815.

---

100. Required by Article 121.

101. See K.D. MacRae, Switzerland: *Examples of Cultural Co-Existence,* Canadian Institute of International Affairs, Toronto, 1964.

102. Article 3.

103. MacRae, *op. cit.,* p. 26.

104. Article 27.

CHAPTER XVII

UNION OF SOVIET SOCIALIST REPUBLICS

Soviet Russia is one of the most interesting and important multinational nations. Not only is there extreme diversity of cultures, languages and ethnic groups, but even religion is displayed in numerous different ways in a state which is generally indifferent, if not opposed to religion. The treatment of women, too, is distinctive and important. Even if these considerations were not enough to merit our consideration, there is the further significance of the Soviet constitutional examples for large numbers of nations in the world, even those which do not consider themselves Communist or Socialist.

The dominant nationality group, the Great Russians, comprise about 53 percent of the population of the Soviet Union. This third largest nation in the world, with its population of 258 million is populated by more than a hundred different nationalities.[105] The Ukranians, the second largest ethnic group, number 40.7 millions, 17 percent of the population. There are 9 million Byelorussians. Estonians, Latvians, and Lithuanians also are linguistic, cultural groups of the Soviet Union, and each group enjoyed an independent history between the two world wars. The Georgians, with a population just under 5 million, speak their own language

105. Figures from: *U.S.S.R. '77 Sixty Soviet Years,* Novosh Press Agency Publishing House, Moscow, 1977, pp. 15-22.

and have an ancient culture and religion. Jews, Tatar, Moldavians, and Mordvins are to be found in European Russia; Armenians, Azerbhaidzhanis, Kazakhs, Kirghis, Turkmens, Uzbeks, and Tadzhiks live in central and southern Asia. Turans, Buryats, Yakuts, Chunchi, Evenks and Chuvash dwell in northern and eastern Asia. Yet the Soviet Union is a unitary state, a self-avowed dictatorship, dominated by a single party. There is no doubt, in spite of all appearances that the Soviet Union is faced with a definite nationality problem.[106]

Religion, too, is a problem for the Soviet State. The Russian Orthodox Church remains as the largest and most widespread Christian confession in the U.S.S.R., with a membership between 30 and 50 million adherents. There are, in addition, smaller groupings of schismatic communities drawn from factions split off from the Russian Orthodox Church, some of which are not legally recognized.[107]

Roman Catholics were never numerous in old Russia, being associated in Russian History with Polish imperialism. But in the Baltic states of Lithuania and Latvia, once independent nations, there are sizeable Roman-Catholic congregations. Protestantism is still rather small, with the largest officially recognized group the Evangelical Christian-Baptists. Many of the central Asian minorities are Moslems and much of east Asian Russia is Moslem. Armenians have their own Christian church, with its world center in Soviet Armenia.

The Jews of Russia settled in Eastern Europe even before the birth of Christ. The Czars were openly anti-Jewish. Massive programs instituted by royal officials in 1881, 1884, and 1903 forced many Jews to flee Russia, but many remained, and some were among the leaders of the Bolshevik Revolution. No one knows

106. See Richard Pipes: "Introduction: The Nationality Problem," *Handbook of Major Soviet Nationalities*, Zer Katz, Rosemarie Rogers, Frederic Harned, eds., The Free Press, New York, 1975.

107. Edward Rozea, "The Problems of National Minorities in the Soviet Union," *Veenhoven*, Vol. IV, p. 461.

how many Jews there are in the Soviet Union, but there may be between two and three million. Although many Jews have assimilated to Soviet culture, the existence of the state of Israel stirred a widespread demand for Jewish emigration.

One of the earliest Soviet decrees was personally prepared by Lenin in 1918 to provide for the separation of church and state.[108] Ever since the proclamation of the first Soviet Constitution (July, 1918) the religious question has been of great concern, in a state committed to a political doctrine resting upon atheist principles. The first Soviet Constitution gave a right to religious and anti-religious propaganda, but subsequent constitutions whittled away religious rights and religious communities became subordinated to the state (officially and unofficially) as the atheists gained dominance. The Stalin Constitution of 1936 made a fundamental change permitting "freedom of religious worship and freedom of anti-religious propaganda,"[109] but eliminating the former freedom of religious propaganda.

The so-called Stalin constitution was not written in style that enabled the Communist government to sing happily along in choir either with the Third World in the General Assembly of the United Nations or with the intellectual left in Europe and the U.S.A. On Nikita Kruschev's personal instructions, a commission began work in 1962 to overhaul the Stalin constitution and to phrase it in more acceptable terminology. From 1964 onwards, the commission was chaired by Leonid Brezhnev who later succeeded Kruschev. The commission's work was completed and approved by the Supreme Soviet on October 7, 1977. Essentially, it did not depart from its predecessor -- just as Kruschev had instructed. But in structure as well as in limited particulars (as well as in terminology) the 1977 constitution is indeed new. It contained a total of 69 articles compared to only 27 in the 1936 model, delineating a wide range of principles, rights, liberties and obligations in the political,

108. See Richard H. Marshall, ed., *Aspects of Religion in the Soviet Union*, University of Chicago Press, Chicago, 1971, pp. 437-438.

109. Article 124, 1936 Constitution.

economic and social sphere; however, most of these clauses merely serve to make more explicit select components of prevailing Communist ideology. As the authors of McGraw Hill's *Political Handbook of the Year* (1981) observed: "The new constitution, in sum, exhibits both restrictive and liberalising language while offering no indication of basic change . . ."

The new Constitution of 1977 does make some interesting and perhaps significant changes in the freedom of religion. The new provision speaks of "the right to profess any religion and perform religious rites" and it says that "incitement of hostility and hatred on religious grounds shall be prohibited." [110] These two new phrases suggest a broader amount of official protection of religion against atheistic repression. It also suggests that anti-semitism and other forms of religious persecution will be officially discouraged. In constitutional language, at least, this new constitution represents a return to original Leninist principles.

Soviet constitutions have pioneered in the expression and recognition of women's rights. They have set a model for much of the rest of the world, socialist and non-socialist, in this regard. The 1977 constitution continues the trend. To a considerable extent this seems to have been a genuine ideal of the Soviet state, which has attempted in the most far-reaching ways to improve the status of women. The constitution declares that "in the USSR, women shall have equal rights with men." [111] It goes on to guarantee equal opportunities for education and professional training, for employment, remuneration and promotion. It permits protective legislation for women, including paid leaves for mothers and state aid to unmarried mothers. The family is placed under the protection of the state and the constitution explicitly recognizes the need for child-care institutions, family allowances, and maternity benefits. [112]

---

110. Article 52, 1977 Constitution.

111. Article 35, 1977 Constitution.

112. Article 53, 1977 Constitution.

However, of all the unresolved internal problems of the Soviet Union the nationalities problem appears most serious. As a result, it draws the most extensive constitutional treatment of all rights issues. Indeed, the Soviet Union is at least a paper example of a society constitutionally committed to group rights. The preamble to the 1977 Constitution speaks of the "juridical and actual equality of all nations and nationalities of the Soviet Union." The very first article speaks of a socialist state composed of the working class, the peasantry and the intelligentsia,"of all the nations and nationalities in the country." The unity of the nation and the single party state is a constant Soviet theme, but the many group rights provisions for nationalities, ethnic and linguistic groups suggests the need to at least superficially accommodate the very numerous groups which make up the Soviet state.

A comparison between the group rights provisions of the 1936 and the 1977 Soviet constitutions reveals a growing concern with these rights.

The provisions of Article 1 of the 1977 Constitution, mentioned above, represent an added category for the nations and nationalities, a significant addition to the ideologically correct recognition of the status of workers, peasants and intelligentsia. Article 19 of the new constitution also adds new language, as it commits the Soviet state to "developing and drawing together all the nations and nationalities of the USSR." [113] Another new provision says that "the state shall show concern for protecting and multiplying society's cultural values. [114]

Some changes in old articles are especially revealing. Old Article 123 which guaranteed equality of rights made no mention of language, while the new provision does. [115] The most interesting change is the addition of a new article specifically conferring equal rights upon Soviet citizens of different

113. Article 9, 1977 Constitution.

114. Article 27, Constitution of 1977.

115. Article 34, Constitution of 1977.

nationalities and races.[116] However, the same article also speaks ambiguously of "the policy of all-around development and drawing together of all nations and nationalities of the USSR" and of "education of citizens in the spirit of Soviet patriotism and socialist internationalism." Apparently the Soviet recognition of group rights is half-hearted and, perhaps a cause of deep concern to the party leaders who drafted the constitution. Nonetheless, the same article extends "the opportunity for using the mother tongue and the languages of the other peoples of the USSR." Finally, compounding the ambiguity, the same article prohibits, on the one hand, restriction of the rights of citizens on the grounds of race and nationality, and on the other, prohibits "any advocacy of racial or national exclusivity."

The right to educate in the mother tongue is retained from the 1936 Constitution in the current constitution.[117] A new duty of citizenship is created by the 1977 Constitution. Now it is the duty of every citizen "to respect the national dignity of other citizens" in order to "fortify the friendship of the nations and nationalities of the Soviet multi-national state."[118] This is the first constitutional reference to the multi-national character of the Soviet Union.

The state structure of the Soviet Union remains essentially unchanged. The federal system is virtually identical to the system of 1936. The Soviet regime has not followed the Yugoslav example of modifications in the structure of government to accommodate its nations and nationalities. Yet, the new provision defining the structure of the state refers to "an integral federal multi-national state formed on the basis of the free self-determination of nations."[119] This second reference to a multi-national state is conditioned by the language of a succeeding paragraph which speaks of "the state unity of the Soviet people" and the bringing of "all the nations and nationalities together for the joint building

116. Article 36, Constitution of 1977.

117. Article 45, Constitution of 1977.

118. Article 64, Constitution of 1977.

119. Article 69, Constitution of 1977.

of communism.'' None of this language appears in the 1936 constitution.

There is an odd omission from the 1977 Constitution which deserves attention. Omitted as a power of a Union Republic is maintenance of its own military formations.

The intentions of the drafters of the 1977 Soviet constitution are unknown to us. The document, as with past Soviet constitutions, is intended principally as a propaganda instrument for internal and external use. But even if group rights in the Soviet Union are on an uncertain basis, there is a new heightened sense of their importance. The 1977 constitution gives clear expression of the recognition, albeit a tentative one, of the separate needs of the various linguistic, ethnic, racial and national entities of which the Soviet Union is composed. If in this model of a Communist centralized dictatorship the centrifugal forces of group rights can gain recognition then, indeed, group rights may flourish almost anywhere.

CHAPTER XVIII

SOCIALIST FEDERAL REPUBLIC OF YUGOSLAVIA

The Yugoslavian Constitution is important to a sound understanding of group rights as they concern ethnic, linguistic and cultural groups. The current constitution, promulgated in 1974, is the tenth Yugoslavian constitution. Each document has had to deal with the tensions among the various groups of Yugoslavia. The 1974 constitution presents some unique answers to these tensions by providing a large number of institutional arrangements designed to preserve these group rights. While there may not be a direct application of these constitutional arrangements to any other nation, they suggest a series of fresh approaches to group rights in multi-cultural societies.

The current Yugoslav constitution is deserving of careful, detailed consideration. In its attention to ethnic, linguistic and cultural rights it is more specific and detailed than any other nation. Building on a brief history marred by conflict among groups in the nation, the Yugoslav Communist leaders have attempted to create a multi-ethic, multi -cultural federal state which can be stable, while allowing for great diversity among the regions of the state. The Yugoslav experience is highly relevant for those concerned with group rights and ideological issues ought not get in the way of a sound examination of the constitutional arrangements painstakingly developed by the Yugoslav government in recent years.

Yugoslavia came into existence at the end of the First World War. At first it was called the Kingdom of Serbs, Croats, and Slovenes, in recognition of its principal constituent ethnic groups. Each of those groups had its own historical cultural and political development. In fact, there were several other ethnic groups which were not recognized at the time.

Woodrow Wilson's Fourteen Points dealt with the aspirations of the people of the region. Point X states that "the peoples of Austria-Hungary, whose place among the nations we wish to see safeguarded and assured, should be accorded to the freest opportunity of autonomous development." [120] Point XI assumed that relations of Balkan states would be "along historically established lines of allegiance and nationality." This Yugoslavia was a succession state carved out of the old Hapsburg Empire. Effectively, it was a union between pre-war Serbia and the south Slav territories of the Hapsburgs. The leading Serbian politicians sought to construct a unitary kingdom in which they would dominate.

Squabbling between Serbians and other groups came to the surface in 1920 when six different constitutions were being considered. In 1921 a first constitution was established, lasting only five years, when a constitutional revision was effected. A third, authoritarian, constitution was enacted in 1931. Serb and Croat antagonism increased up until World War II when, under Axis occupation, the state of Yugoslavia was dismembered. Croatia was declared an independent state. Slovenia was divided between Germany and Italy, and Macedonia was chopped up into bits.

---

120. Woodrow Wilson, *War and Peace: Presidential Messages, Addresses and Public Papers*, eds.: R.S. Baker and W.E. Dodd, Harper, New York, 1927, Vol. 1, pp. 160-161.

An independent Yugoslavia was reestablished on March 5, 1945. In 1946 a new constitution was enacted, patterned after the Soviet Constitution of 1936. However, the 1946 Yugoslav Constitution recognized six member republics: Serbia, Croatia, Slovenia, Bosnia, Hercegovina, Macedonia and Montenegro. Article 10 of this constitution declared that "any act directed against the sovereignty, equality and national freedom of the peoples of Yugoslavia and their people's republics is contrary to the constitution."

In June, 1948 Mashal Tito broke with Stalin, the Russian dictator. Yugoslavia was determined to define its own type of state socialism. This resulted in a 1953 constitution which lasted ten years, to be replaced by the strikingly novel constitution of 1963. Yugoslavia was transformed into a "Socialist Democratic Federal State," an experiment in greater decentralization than had hitherto been known under Communism.

The 1963 constitution recognized the multi-ethnic and multi-cultural character of the nation. Special provisions for representation of ethnic and cultural groups were made. The introductory part of the 1963 Constitution dealt with fundamental principles and explicitly referred to "the peoples" of Yugoslavia and the right of every people to self-determination. [121] The constitution speaks of free and equal peoples and nationalities (Narodnosti).

The implementation of this fundamental principle was aided by later amendments. The Seventh Amendment made mention of two socialist autonomous provinces, in addition to the six socialist federal republics. Vojrodina and Kosord, though part of other republics, were given greater cultural autonomy than under any previous constitution. Amendment nineteen further extended the powers of communes of which had already been defined as "the basic socio-political community in which citizens shall . . . exercise

121. Edvard Kardelj, the Chairman of the Constitutional Commission, wrote an introductory statement to the original version. (Yugoslavia-Constitution). *Ustav Socijaliticke Federativne Republick Jugoslavije.* Izanje Sluzbenog Lista SFRF, Beograd, 1964.

social self-government as directly as possible.''[122] Other constitutional amendments gave legislative powers to the Chamber of Nationalities, a deliberately multi-ethnic, multi-cultural body in such a way that virtually all ethnic and religious groups were represented.[123]

Article 43 of the 1963 Constitution assured all citizens of the freedom ''to express their nationality and culture.'' The article refers directly to national minorities, stating that ''every nationality -- national minority -- shall have the right to use its language freely, to develop its culture, and to set up organizations to this end, and shall enjoy other rights laid down by the Constitution.'' This intent was reinforced by the passage of the Nineteenth Amendment.[124]

The latest Yugoslavian constitution was promulgated on February 21, 1974 superceding the constitution of 1963.[125] The new constitution represents the fruits of years of constitutional experimentation. It is highly original and most unlike the constitutions of other Communist nations. Intended in part to exemplify the advances in Marxism during the Yugoslav experience, the constitution also is the most distinctive constitution in the world, in its detailed attention to questions of ethnicity and cultural rights and, to a lesser extent, to sex. The 1974 constitution is the conscious product of party theoreticians, especially President Tito and Edward Kandelj. It embraces the principle of federalism and carries it to greater lengths than ever before.[126]

The 1974 constitution attempts to provide a new kind of federalism which enhances the rights of groups and especially, of

---

122. Article 96, 1963 Constitution of Yugoslavia.

123. Especially Amendment Nine, paragraph 7, 1963 Constitution of Yugoslavia.

124. Paragraphs 2 and 3.

125. For an excellent study of Yugoslav constitutions from 1945-1963, see Jovan Djordjeni: *Novi Ustavini Sistem.*

126. See K. Joncic, *The Yugoslav Constitution and Relations Between the Nationalities*, Editor, Medjunarodna: Stampa-Interpress, Belgrade, 1967.

ethnic, linguistic and national minorities. It has been said that the Federation is not a separate superstructure but rather an embodiment of the community of nations and nationalities.[127] Mijalko Todoroni, President of the Federal Assembly, who played a leading role in the preparation of the 1974 constitution claims that it creates "a new kind of federalism" which has eliminated "all possibility of the engineering of majorities among the nations and nationalities, the republics and provinces."[128] Compared with the 1963 constitution, the current document has many more articles dealing with ethnic, linguistic, national and other group rights, but the 1963 constitution also made notable contributions to the development of the special Yugoslav version of federalism.

The Introductory Part of the 1974 Constitution sets forth basic principles of interest to those concerned with group rights. The first sentence describes Yugoslavia as composed of "nations" which "proceeding from the right of every nation to self-determination, including the right to secession" have "united in a federal republic of free and equal nations and nationalities" which perfect "the interests of each nation and nationality separately and of all of them together."[129] Thus the United States of America and Yogoslavia follow contrasting patterns in both governmental organization and divergent approaches toward ethnicity. The U.S.A. was formed on the basis of territorial convenience, rather than on the ethnic background of the inhabitants, while Yugoslavia developed into a federation based on cultural differences of its peoples.

Lest it be understood that Yugoslavia is a decentralized federation with highly autonomous national groups, the fact still remains that the league of Communists of Yugoslavia is not decen-

127. Mijalko Todorovic "Yugoslavia's New Constitution," *Review of International Affairs,* Vol. XXV (March, 1974), pp. 7-10.

128. Alexsandar Fira, "Federalism Under the New Constitution of the SFRY," *Review of International Affairs,* Vol. XXV (March, 1974), pp. 4-6.

129. This quotation and all other quotations from the Constitution of 1974 are from the official Yugoslav government translation as found in Albert P. Blaustein and Gisbert H. Flanz, *Constitutions of the Countries of the World,* Oceana Publications, Inc., Dobbs Ferry, N.Y., 1974.

tralized or organized along ethnic, linguistic or national lines. Communist ideology still requires a centralized unitary party. Consequently, although the Yugoslavian constitution represents a dramatic expansion of the Federal principle on behalf of groups and minorities, it is important to remember that the single state party is still all powerful. Perhaps the federal structure of government will modify the centralizing effects of single party rule, but at the moment the 1974 constitution, in spite of its striking features, is still somewhat influenced by the thinking inherent in the 1936 Soviet constitution which also extended some recognition of group, ethnic and linguistic rights. The explicit recognition of the multinational character of the Russian State was a feature of the thought of both Lenin and Stalin. Many of the Communists states have a multi-national basis, but the party still prevails.[130] It remains to be seen whether the principles of Yugoslav Federalism represent a genuine breakthrough for group rights, but it is possible, that having extended so many new rights to national groups the Communist party itself will be decentralized and federalized in Yugoslavia.

The introduction to the constitution also sets as a goal of the Yugoslavian state "the brotherhood and unity of the nations and nationalities," calling for "the rapprochement of the nations and nationalities." All the major officers of the state, including the President of the Republic must make a declaration (the equivalent of an oath) that they shall "strive for the achievement of brotherhood and unity and for the equality of the nations and nationalities."[131] Thus, Yugoslavia poses as the champion of ethnic and national rights, a position far in advance of other Communist nations. Incidentally, the word "nationality" is given a special usage in the constitution and is defined as "a term used for members of nations whose native countries border on

130. See Bernard Touret: *L'amenagement Constitutionnel des etats de Peuplement Composite*, Les Presses de L'Universite Laval, Quebec, 1973, pp. 89-92.

131. Article 397.

Yugoslavia.''[132] The term "nation," it seems, refers to the people of the six socialist republics and of the two socialist autonomous provinces.[133]

The Yugoslav Constitution treats people in their status as members of their national groups. The introduction speaks of "the working people and citizens, nations and nationalities of Yugoslavia.[134] It is dedicated to "respect for the rights of national minorities, including the rights of members of Yugoslav nations living in other countries as national minorities.[135] The six socialist republics are then, nations. These are the Socialist Republics of Bosnia-Herzegovina, of Croatia, of Macedonia, of Montenegro, and of Serbia. The Socialist Autonomous Provinces of Vojvodina and of Kosoro are also regarded, as are their citizens, as "nations." Rarely have group rights ideas been presented so directly.

The constitution also recognizes other group entities such as "socio-political communities," "self-managing communities of interest" and "associations of citizens." Each, it seems, though non-governmental is assigned certain decision making responsibilities. Yet the key groupings appear to be those denoted "socio-political organizations," which include the League of Communists of Yugoslavia, the Socialist Alliance of the Working People of Yugoslavia and the Federation of Trade Unions. The constitution says little about their function, although they seem to occupy roles much more significant than the other groupings. The lynchpin appears to be Article 71 which states that the "social plans of the socio-political communities, shall be adopted on the basis of agreements on the common interests and aims of economic and social development in the Communes, municipal or regional communities, Autonomous Provinces, Republics and the Federa-

132. Found in explanation section following Part Six of the Constitution, at page 259 of the translation.

133. Constitution, Articles 1 and 2.

135. Translation, p. 21.

135. Translation, p. 24.

tion." Taken literally, this would mean that the Yugoslav Communist party would bargain with the various Yugoslav nations and other groupings to arrive at national plans. Other articles also suggest that investments as well as planning policies are to be decentralized among various groups and labor organizations. [136] In general, the constitutional language so mingles the "socio-political communities" (including the Communist Party) with other groupings of workers and nations that it is sometimes hard to discern what the relationship between the nations, groups and parties is supposed to be.

Chapter II of the constitution is entitled "The Foundations of the Socio-Political System." This seems to refer to the Communist Party and its relations with other groups. Since it is stated that "the functions of power and management of other social affairs in the socio-political communities shall be discharged by their assemblies and by agencies responsible to them," [137] each segment of the community seems to be responsible chiefly to its own organs.

The constitution refers to the common interest and functions of power and management" to be shared by "the working people, nation and nationalities." [138] The socio-political community is sharply distinguished from the socio-political organizations. This means that the structure of the political organizations is supposedly not dominated by the Communist party. When Article 143 declares that "an assembly shall, within the scope of the rights and duties of its socio-political community formulate policy and decide on the basic questions of significance for political, economic, welfare and cultural life" we should remember that the term "socio-political community" embraces virtually all territorial grouping in Yugoslavia separate from the "socio-political organizations" [139] of which the League of Communists is the most outstanding.

---

136. See Article 72.

137. Article 92.

138. Article 91.

139. Articles 132 and 133 do make vague references to delegations and assemblies of "the socio-political communities and of agencies responsible to them."

Yugoslavs like to call their system of government "delegational" and they look upon it as a novel improvement upon federalism and democracy. The delegate system supposedly transcends the traditional electoral system and abolished "the separation of the deputies and the representative body from the social base." [140] The delegational system is "the groundwork upon which assemblies (communal, provincial, republican and federal) are constituted." [141] The system, it is said, "ensures the direct presence of working people in the assemblies" and it "makes impossible political outvoting of one category of the population by another." [142] The Yugoslavs believe that they have, in the constitution, woven divergent national groups, minorities and the Communist party into one coherent self-managing entity.

The constitution contains elaborate provisions for the election of delegates from the lowest to the highest levels of government, drawing from a base at the most local level. The delegates are, in some sense, bound to take stands on questions in assemblies in conformity with the guidelines of the groups, communities and organizations which select them. [143] Some independence in delegate voting is permitted, but the delegates remain responsible to the groups which chose them. Referenda may be called for to endorse statutes, regulations and other enactments and these referenda are binding. [144]

At the federal level the nations and nationalities of the Socialist Federal Republic of Yugoslavia are given equal rights. [145] The nationalities retain their "sovereign rights" in all levels of government, [146] but federal statutes must be enforced by

140. Pavle Nikoki, "Basic Characteristics of the System of Delegates," *Review of International Affairs,* Vol. XXV (April, 1974), pp. 3-7.

141. Translation, p. 256, definition section.

142. Translation, p. 257, definition section.

143. See Article 141.

144. Article 146.

145. Article 245.

146. Article 248.

republican and provincial agencies "when so specified by federal statute." [147]

To safeguard these rights of the nations and nationalities the constitution provides, in the legislative branch of the federal government, an application of the delegation system which provides representation for constituent national groups. The Chamber of Republics and Provinces (the second house of the legislature) is "composed of twelve delegates of each Republican Assembly and eight delegates of each Provincial Assembly," [148] elected by their respective Chambers and subject to their recall. These delegates, once chosen, retain their seats in the assemblies from which they have been chosen. These delegates in taking their stands in the Chamber of Republics and Provinces must represent the stands of their respective assemblies. [149] This, the delegation system, is combined with the legislative structure in such a way as to enhance the rights of the nations and nationalities. Even after the Chamber of Republics and Provinces has adopted a bill, it must refer it to the assemblies of the republics and of the autonomous provinces for endorsement, [150] failing which the Presidency may temporarily adopt the measure. [151] These provisions seem to further magnify the power of the national groups.

The two parts of the national legislature are the Federal Chamber and the Chamber of Republics and Provinces. Although the Federal Chamber appears to be much more powerful, certain powers are assigned to the second chamber. The power to decide on the formulation of certain regulatory Federal Statutes to the Chamber of Republics and Provinces, [152] together with a few minor powers. But the main task of the second chamber is to "ensure the adjustment of stands" of the republic and provincial

147. Article 274.
148. Article 292.
149. Article 296.
150. Article 300.
151. Article 301.
152. Article 286.

assemblies with federal statutes, apparently a legitimatizing role.

Both houses together elect the President and the members of the Federal Executive Council.[153] The President of the Republic is President of the Presidency. The Presidency is a plural executive consisting of a member from each republic and autonomous province.[154] This plural presidency is the capstone of the federal concept in Yugoslavia, but it is unlike the plural presidency of Switzerland in that the members are subordinate to the separately elected President of the Republic. The purpose of the plural presidency is "to realize the equality of the nations and nationalities[155] and ostensibly, it is the plural presidency which proposes legislation and sets foreign policy for Yugoslavia.[156] Appointments of judges, planning national defense, even granting pardons are all functions assigned to the plural executive.[157] However, the President of the Presidency convenes the meetings of the Presidency, is in charge of the armed forces, represents Yugoslavia abroad, and "ensures the implementation of acts and conclusions of the S.F.R.Y. Presidency.[158]

As though to further complicate matters there is also a federal Executive Council which is the executive body of the Yugoslav legislature.[159] This cabinet-like executive is also assigned some traditional executive functions, including proposals for budgeting and expenditures. This Federal Executive Council also rests upon the principle of equal representation of the republics and autonomous provinces.[160] This Council, too, has its President so that there are a number of individuals designated as presidents, but only one President of the Republic. The chief functions of this

---

153. Article 288.
154. Article 321.
155. Article 313.
156. Article 314.
157. Article 315; Article 316.
158. Article 328.
159. Article 346.
160. Article 348.

cabinet-like Council seem to be the introduction of legislation[161] and the adoption of regulations concerning the enforcement of statutes falling within the competence of the Chamber of Republics and Provinces.[162] The smoothing over of differences between the national government and the various republican and provincial agencies also is assigned to the Federal Executive Council.[163]

The judiciary, too, is based upon the Federalized, pluralistic principle. Members of the Constitutional Court of Yugoslavia are elected two from each republic and one from each autonomous province.[164] These fourteen judges, then, are drawn from the "nations" of Yugoslavia, and each nation is guaranteed representation of the high court. This principle makes more palatable the power of the court to decide disputes between the "nations"[165] and to declare republican or provincial statutes unconstitutional.[166]

In general, all Yugoslav citizens are constitutionally equal in their "rights and duties" regardless of nationality, race, sex, language, or religion.[167] All citizens have the right to the free use of their language and alphabet, and no citizens can be obliged to state to which nation or nationality he belongs.[168] Members of nationalities and nations have the right to be educated in their own language.[169] Every person has the right to use his own language before the courts or other state agencies.[170] There is an equality of languages and alphabets of the nations and nationalities in the armed forces, which may even extend, with

161. Article 354.
162. Article 355.
163. Article 357.
164. Article 381.
165. Article 375.
166. Article 384.
167. Article 154.
168. Article 170.
169. Article 171.
170. Article 214.

limitations, to matters of command and military training.[171] The languages of the nations of Yugoslavia are to be used in treaties with other nations.[172] Finally, as though to seal the principle of equality of nations and nationalities, the constitution may not be amended without the approval of each of the assemblies of the republics and the autonomous provinces.[173]

As for other group rights, little is said, other than about religion. Religious communities are separate from the state. Religious affairs may be freely conducted, except that parochial schools are not permitted.[174] Religious communities have a limited right to own real property. There is little mention of women's rights except in their capacity as mothers[175] and parents.[176]

The most remarkable feature of the Yugoslav Constitution is, of course, its detailed attention to the rights of linguistic and nationality groups. Representation schemes of the most elaborate kind have been provided, making it difficult to pursue national policies which are repellent to any of those constituent groups. The recognition of group ethnic and linguistic rights has never before been so elaborately described in any constitution. Whether these provisions are a mere facade behind which a centralized Communist party still pursues its own goals and purposes remains to be seen. It must be said that the Yugoslav Communist party has considered respect for national differences important ever since its accession to power after World Warr II.[177]

Communist ideology seems to require a unified, centralized party. Yet, Yugoslavia has attempted to blend together these

---

171. Article 243.
172. Article 271.
173. Article 402.
174. Article 174.
175. Article 188.
176. Article 190.
177. See Paul Shoup: *Communism and the Yugoslav National Question*, Random House, New York, 1968, p. 142.

contradictory tendencies. The frequency of constitutional changes in Yugoslavia is evidence of the tensions of centralism and localism. Perhaps the 1974 constitution, by making extensive concessions to sentiments of ethnic and linguistic feeling will succeed where earlier constitutional arrangements have failed, and perhaps Yugoslav Communism can adjust to it.

PART IV

CONCLUSION[S]

CHAPTER XIX

CONCLUSION OF CONCLUSIONS

Group Rights and Freedom

Group rights are fundamental and, in the words of the American Declaration of Independence, "inalienable." And it is in recognition of this fundamental conclusion that constitutions, laws passed pursuant thereto, and practices consistent with these constitutions and laws ought to be a keystone and touchstone of governmental policy. Where laws and practices can and do preserve the existence and interplay of group rights, the result is a successful plural society. Where group rights are denied, it is proper to consider the restructuring of society and rethink the meaning of nationhood.

The fact that mankind is diverse rests upon the existence of ethnic differences. This diversity is one of mankind's greatest assets and has been a major factor in mankind's progress. [1] It will not, as some scholars alledged 10-20 years ago, go away, rather, as Harold Isaacs said: "Our tribal separatenesses are here to stay." Ethnic differences demand recognition and protection. As Glazer and Moynihan observed: "The hope of doing without ethnicity in a society . . . may be as utopian and as questionable an enterprise as the hope of doing without social classes in a society." [2] That is what group rights are all about. Where

---

1. Isaacs, Harold: "Idols of the Tribe: Group Identity and Political Change," Harper and Rowe, N.Y., 1975, p. 216. Cf. Possony, S..: "Nationalism and the Ethnic Factor," *Orbis,* Foreign Policy Institute, University of Pennsylvania, March, 1967 and Said, A.A. and Simmons, L.R.: op. cit.

2. *Ethnicity: Theory and Experience,* p. 3.

nations can develop institutional arrangements to reconcile and handle the conflicting group rights in a multi-ethnic society, a plural society can survive as a national entity. [3] Sometimes arrangements for autonomy and minority treaties, as well as constitutional and legal formulations, preserve that identity. Where they fail, group rights may have to be preserved, protected, and implemented by such stringent steps as separation, partition, population exchanges or population removal.

Only the free society can and will nurture a plural system which preserves group rights. "Minorities have no place in the totalitarian regime, where everything exists for the state and minorities have to submerge themselves . . . In a democratic society, however, minorities are to be given due expression of their freedom of action without at the same time disturbing the fabric of national unity." [4]

Semantics may confuse the issue. The most democratic of all nations, the United States of America, is a nation which until recently espoused the concept of the "melting pot," and is now busily altering its legal structure toward the achievement of "integration." However, those in the forefront of the integration struggle are often among the leaders in fostering the keen, cultural identity which is at the heart of the group rights demands of Hispanics, Blacks, Puerto Ricans, Chicanos, and, to a lesser degree, Jews and Polish, Italian and Greek "ethnics." [5] The

---

3. Arend Lijphart in *Democracy in Plural Societies,* showed how the political experiences in Austria, Belgium, the Netherlands and Switzerland exemplify the use of consociational methods in achieving and maintaining stable democracies in the face of deep religious, ideological, linguistic, cultural and ethnic cleavages.

4. *Minorities and the Law,* Mohammed Inman, ed., Tripathi Publishers, Bombay, 1972, preface. (Papers presented at the Seminar on Law and Minorities, India Law Institute, New Delhi, 1971.)

5. Fort, E.: "Some Educational Imperatives Regarding the Peaceful Pursuit of Intergroup Accommodation in a Plural Society," in Rhoodie, Nic, op. cit., pp. 202-204. Cf. also Glaser and Possony: op. cit., p. 315 and de la Garza, R.O. and Arcieniega, T.A., eds.,: *Chicanos and Native Americans -- The Territorial Minorities,* Prentice Hall, New Jersey, 1973, pp. 97-98.

melting pot and integration in the American scheme, however, do not deny group rights. The two are coexistent tendencies.

Freedom must not be confused with equality. It is difficult to avoid that confusion for the concept of equal treatment, equal protection, etc., lies at the heart of all constitutions which profess a free society. But one cannot achieve a recognition of group rights by treating everyone equally. Primitive peoples need special protection lest their cultures be destroyed; small minorities, like the Parsees of India, need special recognition lest laws designed for the vast majority swallow up the differences which exist; Christians in Moslem nations need special treatment so that adherence to their faith may be permitted, etc.

Totalitarianism, on the other hand, denies racial, religious and ethnic identities. Under totalitarianism, there is ideological imperialism and cultural genocide. Cambodia is a good example. Nazism destroyed a half million gypsies as well as six million Jews and was prepared to destroy the cultural identity of Slavs and other designated *untermenchen.* The Soviet Union has consistently denied political group rights, forcing adherence to a central totalitarian pattern. The latest manifestation of this was the constitutional activity following the adoption of the new Soviet Constitution on October 7, 1977. This event was followed by plans for new constitutions for all of the Soviet Republics. Three draft constitutions have been published already -- for Georgia, Armenia and Azerbaijan, all of which had dropped articles providing for the protection of local languages and the official status of such language use. Local pressures in these Republics, however, forced the retention of existing linguistic rights.

But is it always true that freedom and democracy are on the side of cultural rights? The right-wing Rhodesian Action Party, which opposed the 1979 internal settlement in soon-to-be Zimbabwe, developed its own constitutional ideas for the preservation of group rights. The party "proposed arrangements under which each race group would have been substantially self-governing, running its own residential areas, hospitals and schools. At the top would have been a multi-racial body controlled indefinitely by the country's 'most responsible' elements, by which it meant the Whites.'' [6]. Because such advocacy of group rights was forthcoming from a right-wing group, it confused the issue of the basic linkage between group rights and freedom. The linkage, however, was there. The important thing was to distinguish between the consent and meaning of the two sentences which summed up the program of the Rhodesian Action Party. Substantial group rights, buttressed by constitutional safeguards guaranteeing autonomy, are not necessarily synonymous with a policy of white supremacy.

Group Rights and Nationalism

Nationalism -- meaning the creation and maintenance of nation-states -- involves the merging and accommodating of diverse groups into one nation. The oldest (beginning in 1291) highly successful example of such nationalism is Switzerland, where the will to live together as a multi-ethnic nation is accompanied by numerous constitutional safeguards to preserve group rights. But it must be emphasized that in the Switzerland situation both the merger and the guarantees of group rights were voluntary arrangements, not the result of conquest or coercion of other groups. There was a tradition of accommodation. [7] There was also no racial groups to contend with.

Unusual in Africa is the ordering of group rights relationships which occurred in Tanzania, where there are more than 100 tribal groups with different languages and dialects.

But between 1921 and the formation of Tanzania in 1964 there have been innumerable failures as well as innumerable successes

---

6. "Rhodesian Rightists Denouce Smith as a Traitor for Pact with Blacks," *New York Times,* March 25, 1978.

7. Lijphart, A.: *Democracy in Plural Societies,* op. cit., pp. 100-101.

in accommodating group rights in order to maintain successful plural societies. Group rights caused Holland to separate from Spain and group rights, language and religion in particular, caused Belgium and Holland to separate in 1830.[8] Religious demands caused the partition of British India into the Hindu State of India and the Islamic State of Pakistan, and then language and other ethnic differences caused the further division of Pakistan as East Pakistan became Bangladesh. A half a million people died in the process.[9]

Treaties among the colonial powers toward the end of the last century, culminating with the Berlin Conference of 1884-85, divided Africa along artificial lines which disregard tribal identities, language, cultural preferences and all of the other manifestations of group rights. Yet it became a cardinal principle at the time of African independence to maintain the borders created under colonialism. The alternative would be continuous conflict.

Yet, institutional arrangements in the former colonies have generally not been able to solve group rights problems. Most of the new constitutions are authoritarian in character and have incorporated one-party systems. What has resulted has been an intensification of ethnic conflict rather than an accommodation recognizing minority and group rights. In Africa, ethnic particularism far from fading is on the rise.[10]

When in June 1978 the Mauritanian constitution was revised it was to enable the government to change the legal code according to the precepts of Islam. Black protests against Arabic as sole language in instruction in schools won a respite which terminates in June 1984. A conflict on mother tongue education seems inevitable.

---

8. Rabushka, A. and Shepsle, K.: *Politics in Plural Societies,* op. cit., p. 108.
9. Glaser and Possony: op. cit., p. 162.
10. Lefever, E.: "Limits of Government in the Third World," in Rhoodie, Nic., op. cit., p. 16.

Contrasted with the moderate success in Tanzania was the trauma of the Biafran War which avoided the dismemberment of Nigeria, Africa's largest and most important nation next to South Africa and Egypt. Ruanda-Burundi was divided into the nations of Rwanda and Burundi. The northern part of what was once the British Cameroons is now a part of Nigeria, while the southern part is now incorporated into the United Republic of Cameroon. Zaire has been, and still is, threatened by the possible separation of its richest province, Katanga. Ethnic Somalis in both Ethiopia and Kenya are seeking separation of their lands from those states. And the Ethiopian Province of Eritrea is fighting to dissolve the union forced upon it by Ethiopia's Haile Selassie.

Population exchanges are another manifestation of the failure to develop internal arrangements to preserve group rights. The greatest population exchange in history was that between India and Pakistan on the eve of their independence in 1949 and 1950 respectively, when the West Pakistan army struck against the Bengalis' 8 million fled to India.[11] So, too, have there been population movements and exchanges resulting from the creation of Israel. Uganda's expulsion of its Indian population and the expulsion of ethnic Germans from Czechoslovakia and Poland are other examples. In the early sixties Burma expelled some 500,000 Indians during Prime Minister Ne Wins' drive to Burmese socialism.[12]

Less dramatic are the situations in regard to the many minority groups whose rights are not recognized and whose strength is too limited to achieve any kind of recognition. This can be said to a certain extent about the Amerindians in the Americas, the Romany in Europe, the Kurds in Iran and Iraq, etc. And still greater potential problems exist in attempting to reconcile group rights conflicts in Zimbabwe and South Africa.[13]

---

11. Glaser and Possony; op. cit., p. 162.
12. Cf. *Time,* July 17, 1964 and April 9, 1965.
13. Cf. Benyon, J.A. op. cit., and Rhoodie, Nic: op. cit.

The list is almost endless. The inevitable conclusion is that failure to work out a constitutional system recognizing and preserving group rights inevitably leads to conflict.

Absence of a Uniform Solution

While group rights are fundamental and "unalienable" (and can only be enjoyed in a free society), and while group rights must be recognized and preserved in order to maintain nation-states (avoiding partition, separation and population movements), there is no single or simple formula which can be offered as a solution. No one has all of the answers or even pretends to have such answers. Virtually all "solutions" remain open to question.[14]

One of the important United Nations efforts in this area was the famous Seminar on the Multi-National Society held in June, 1965, in Yugoslavia. The objectives of the seminar, as set forth in its agenda, were to prepare:

1. Measures which should be taken to ensure the realization of human rights and fundamental freedoms of all without discrimination.
2. Measures which should be taken to ensure the realization by ethnic, religious, linguistic or national groups, of the special rights necessary to enable them to preserve their traditions, characteristics, or national consciousness.[15]

While there was much conference talk about the recognition of group rights and platitudes as to state responsibility, no real conclusions were reached. (Additional conference formulations are discussed under some of the other conclusions here.)

But could there possibly be any one particular conclusion or solution to group rights recognition within the unified national

14. Rabushka, A. and Shepsle, K.: op. cit., p. 213.

15. United Nations: *Seminar on the Multi-National Society,* 1965, ST/TAO/HR/23.

state? The answer must be "No." For it must be concluded that constitutional safeguards will vary from country to country, depending upon the particular situation in each country. There is no problem in the homogeneous nation of Norway. South Africa, on the other hand, argued for 30 years that the differences between the population groups was so great that the present state must be broken up into ten separate nations. That was the grand concept of separate political development of the white and black peoples in 1966 (mistakenly called *apartheid*] but stymied in 1979 when the most important group, the Zulus, refused to accept independent statehood. Moreover, the fatal flaw in South African policy was that even after independence, eg. the Transkei, Ciskei and Bobhuthatswana, citizens of those states travelling to white South Africa remained subject to petty *apartheid*, i.e. they were treated differently than, say, visiting Swedes.

Perhaps the greatest past experiment in the accommodation of group rights demands -- was the Hapsburg Empire. This ill-starred experiment failed -- or collapsed -- after World War I. The diverse ethnic groups which comprised the Hapsburg Empire claimed constitutional status for their languages, cultures or religion. The problem was how to accomplish that task without disrupting the fragile union. The problem was compounded by the fact that some ethnic communities inhabited clearly delineated territories while others did not.

In 1867 a "dual system" was established which provided separate policies for Hungary and Austria. In Hungary a policy of integration, called "Magyarization," was pursued. But in Austria separate development was encouraged. However, Hungary, too, permitted some autonomy for Croatia and Slavonia.

In 1899 the Social Democratic Party of Austria proposed the novel and constructive idea of a democratic confederation of nationalities, giving each ethnically uniform group effective self-government within districts where they were dominant. This solution has never been fully implemented in Austria or elsewhere. The Habsburg Empire collapsed under the strain of World War I. In its wake new nation-states emerged. But the vexatious problem of ethnic minorities remained to the current day.[16]

Yugoslavia is a prime example of a continual constitutional experiment within a multi-ethnic society, but authoritariasm and Communist party politics threaten to wreck the experiment.[17]

Undoubtedly the most ambitious effort to create a unified nation and still recognize group rights came in the formulation of the Constitution of India. Constitutional expert M.P. Main expresses that position in the following language:

> . . . along with various safeguards extended to various minority groups, the (Indian) Constitution keeps in view the over-all aim of integrating the minorities politically in one main stream of national life and to keep within check the divisive forces which the existence of so many minority groups may release. The Constitution thus seeks to weld and integrate the diverse elements into one national and political stream.[18]

What resulted is the world's longest and most complicated constitution. It must be studied to determine if, how, and to what extent it has helped to solve the problem in India. More important, it must be studied to determine whether there are any lessons to be learned which may be relevant to group rights problems in other environments, under other conditions, in other countries of the world.

---

16. Cf. Prinz, Friedrich: "A Model of a Multi-National Society as Developed in Austria-Hungary Before 1918," in Rhoodie, Nic: op. cit., pp. 44-52.

17. Cf. Bridge, Susan: "Some Causes of Political Change in Modern Yugoslavia," in Esman, M.J.: op. cit., pp. 343-370.

18. M.P. Jain, "Safeguards to Minorities: Constitutional Principals, Policies and Framework," in supra note 4 at p. 23.

CHAPTER XX

NEED FOR MORE EFFORTS -- AND EXPENDITURES

More research is required in the study of group rights and constitutional prescriptions. For there are follow-up efforts required to study what has been accomplished in the constitutional process. In terms of practical politics soul-searching, together with agonizing reappraisals are demanded to chart or possibly re-chart the scope of institutional arrangements to solve the problems of religious discrimination, racism, sexism and conflict predicated upon ethnic diversity.

Public Information and Public Relations

Discriminations and the problems of ethnic diversity are minimal in certain areas of the world. What does the citizenry of homogeneous Norway know of such problems? And are not the people of India so concerned with the problems of caste and the people of Nigeria so concerned with the problems of tribalism that they are indifferent to the plight of World Jewry [19] and the near genocide of the Ache Indians of Paraguay? [20] In addition, while America, the land of the "melting pot," is well aware of the fact

---

19. See, for example, Maurice M. Roumani, "The Case of the Jews from Arab Countries: A Neglected Issue," *Veenhoven*, Volume Five, p. 69. See also, Joseph Dunner, "Anti-Jewish Discrimination Since the End of World War II," in *Veenhoven*, Volume One, p. 65. See also Costa Luca, "Discrimination in the Arab Middle East," in *Veenhoven*, Volume One, p. 211.

20. See for example, Mark Munzel: "The Manhunts, Ache Indians in Paraguay" in *Veenhoven*, Vol. IV, p. 351.

that it has minorities and ever growing problems of ethnicity, Americans are dismally unaware of their own situation, let alone the situation of others. America is, after all, the second largest black country in the world. In 1978 it was the fifth largest Spanish-speaking country in the world and it will probably be the third largest Spanish-speaking nation (after Mexico and Spain) by century's end.

> Until very recently, Americans have (only) thought of discrimination as anything which inhibited the efforts of minorities to acculturate fully: . . . The hope of civil rights movements . . . was that discrimination . . . could be eliminated; instead the victimization has merely been shifted to other sectors of the population. The resultant marshaling of ethnic blocks, whether to achieve new victories or to defend the traditional norms of justice, suggest a new pattern for American society. [21]

The United States is far from being the only country which is unaware of the scope of its own ethnic problems. Quick (none are quicker) to condemn possible racism and ethnic discrimination outside of their own borders, the Swedes have a way of ignoring these problems at home. They do not discriminate overtly against the Yugoslav "guest" workers in their midst. They just provide them with housing in their "own" neighborhoods and manage somehow to avoid contact with them. They are similarly impervious and immune to the problems of their own "aborigine" indigenous peoples, the Lapps. [22]

Even near-homogeneous West Germany still retains various types of ethnic discrimination which it painfully pretends no longer exists -- a problem which cries for a public information

21. See *National Review,* N.R., January 20, 1978, p. 94. Cf. Isaacs, Harold, op. cit., pp. 19-23.

22. See, for example, Eric Brodin, "The Lapps of Sweden," in *Veenhoven,* Volume Four, p. 29.

program.[23]

But the awareness of a nation's own ethnic problems -- an awareness which is an essential prerequisite to constitutional and other action to do something about it -- is only one part of the awareness to be achieved by public information and public relations programs. There must be an awareness of the problem outside of one's own borders.

Here are the words of two scholars who have thought about this problem as it relates to ignorance and on the part of Americans:

> Systems of caste and class unheard of in New York and the nation are still the basis of ruthless discrimination in scores of countries around the globe. The Tamil minority in Ceylon, the Aborigines of Australia, the Indians of East Africa, the Untouchables of India and the Hindus of Pakistan -- these are but some of the groups that suffer oppression and obloquy as a "normal" part of their lives around the world. Even in liberal multi-racial Brazil there is a wide if subtle color prejudice that keeps the darker-complected Indians and Negroes near the bottom of the social and economic ladder; the preference for the European physical type reveals itself in the prevailing belief that Negroes and Indians will eventually disappear as distinct groups through intermarriage or "bleaching."[24]

And again:

> To WASP-ish Americans bemused for many decades by the ethnic melting pot myth, the slowly dawning realization that communal and ethnic groupings within their own society are intensely solid and durable comes as a shock. Many Third World multi-ethnic societies have attempted

---

23. See, for example, Katharina Otzen, "Discrimination and Preferment in the Federal Republic of Germnay," in *Veenhoven*, Volume Two, p. 31; and Clemens Ameluxen, "Foreign Workers in West Germany," in *Veenhoven*, Volume One, p. 113.

24. Marrow: *Changing Patterns of Prejudice*, Chilton, Philadelphia, 1962, p. 15.

> to structure themselves as independent nation-states in the period since World War II. A similar phenomenon -- the solidity and stolidity of mutually abrasive communal groups within their boundaries -- has proved the greatest stumbling block to creating relatively stable and durable governments. This circumstance also often has brought imposition of severe limitations on political party formation and operation, and on freedom of speech and assembly, to prevent continual civil chaos stemming from communal group frictions.[25]

Note that this not only calls for a recognition of existing ethnic diversity problems throughout the world, but also calls for an understanding of the difficulties which other societies face in coping with such problems.

The third public information and public relations objective is to create a recognition of "*Comparative*" discrimination, and note that I have emphasized this word "comparative" to the best of my typographical capabilities. For comparative understandings are a necessary prerequisite to intelligent action or inaction.

The Western World is guilty of "selective outrage" in its reactions to the existence and nature of discrimination. Its press is selectively objective in its reporting and critiques. And politicians do not differentiate between discrimination as reflected in a constitution, or in laws, or in practices. Compassion is also influenced by fashion. The West condemned the institutional arrangements of separate voting patterns in the Rhodesian constitution,[26] but revealed understanding "of why this must be done in the constitution of Fiji."[27] The West decry the preferred

25. Nancy L. Snider, "Malaysian Noncommunal Political Parties," in Johan A. Lent, ed.,: *Cultural Pluralism in Malaysia: Polity, Military, Mass Media, Education, Religion and Social Class,* (DeKalb, Illinois: Northern Illinois University Center for Southeast Asian Studies, 1977), p. 1.

26. See, for example, Marshall W. Murphee and Donald G. Baker, "Racial Discrimination in Rhodesia," *Veenhoven,* Volume Five, p. 375.

27. See, for example, R.K. Vasil, "Ethnic Discrimination in Fiji: An Indian View: in *Veenhoven,* Volume Two, p. 191.

position of whites guaranteed by the constitution of South Africa and either ignore or ''understand'' Articles 13 and 21 of the Sierra Leone constitution which restrict citizenship, voting rights, or governmental office to those who may qualify as ''persons of negro African descent.''

The West show proper outrage when blacks and East Indians suffer discrimination in London [28] or a handful of Irish suffer police brutality at the hands of British troops. [29] But we ignore the extensive discrimination against East Indians practiced throughout the African continent. [30] The United States even acquiesced in the genocidal acts of Iraq and Iran against ethnic Kurds, [31] and Americans actually ''tilted'' toward Pakistan in its war against what is now Bangladesh where the death toll reached three million. [32] There is somehow compassion for West Bank Arabs who have higher educational health standards and greater civil rights than Arabs in the Arab world. But the West are somehow unconcerned with the plight of Arabs killed by Jordan's King Hussein. And not only Arabs. How great the sympathy for the handful of Jews murdered in Munich or kidnapped to Entebbe. Why then the almost complete disregard for the plight of those Jews still in Iraq and Syria, living lives of terror and still forbidden to emigrate. [33]

Of course, South African apartheid circa 1948-1958 is

---

28. See, for example, Winifred Crum Ewing, "Discrimination in Great Britain, in *Veenhoven,* Volume Two, p. 191. See also Chris Mullard, "Racism in Britain: Management Concepts, 1948-1975," in *Veenhoven,* Volume Five, p. 197.

29. See, for example, David E. Schmitt, "Discrimination and Conflict in Northern Ireland," in *Veenhoven,* Volume Five, p. 1.

30. See for example, Pierre Naudin: "The Violation of Human Rights in Uganda," in *Veenhoven,* Vol. V, p. 415.

31. See, for example, L.M. Von Taubinger, "Suffering and Struggle of the Kurds," in *Veenhoven,* Volume One, p. 241. And Emmanuel Sivan, "The Kurds: Another Perspective," in *Veenhoven,* Volume Two, p. 137.

32. See, for example, Anthony Mascarenhas, "Bangladesh: A Profile of Twentieth Century Genocide, in *Veenhoven*, Volume Five, p. 239.

33. See note 19 op. cit.

socio-politically unacceptable and there is much of separate development of the 1958-78 period that can be condemned, but nothing that has ever taken place in South Africa (or could take place) matches the brutality of Sudanese Arabs toward their own black citizenry,[34] or matches what different black tribes did to each other in Rwanda and Burundi.[35]

In fact, if the shoe had been on the other foot in South Africa, had Mr. Vorster or Mr. Botha been black, and had they planned and executed exactly the same policy towards whites as they did in the case of the present black population, they would probably both have ended up as Presidents of the Organization of African States, if not of the General Assembly of the UN. It is not what they did which was important but the fact that they were white. This reverse discrimination, manifesting itself in journalistic racism when newspapers report on events in South Africa under headlines while relegating similar events to the music page if it happened in an independent black state, bedevils a realistic appraisal of developments and problems in South Africa more than anything else.

Of course, it is fruitless to prepare a comparative analysis of whether Hitler was worse than Stalin, etc. But a comparative analysis which provides both policymakers and their constituents with a realistic appraisal of these problems is a prerequisite to the kinds of constitutional and other legal responses which must be forthcoming. This applies to the great nations like the United States with power to take action, but it likewise applies to nations like Norway where acknowledged high moral and ethical standards should provide an important moral force in such international fori as the United Nations.

---

34. See, for example, Arye Oded, "The Southern Sudan Civil War," in *Veenhoven*, Volume Four, p. 227.

35. See, for example, Jeremy Greenland, "Ethnic Discrimination in Rwanda and Burundi," in *Veenhoven*, Volume Four, p. 95. See, also, Stanley Meisler, "Holocause in Burundi, 1972," in *Veenhoven*, Volume Five, p. 225.

Additional Research and Scholarship

This study of constitutional responses to the problems of race, religion, sexism and ethnicity very rapidly revealed its own innate limitations. Even assuming that the problems could be studied and resolved through the medium of the law, constitutions constitute only one legal mechanism. It was soon concluded that this constitutional study must necessarily be followed by studies of applicable statutes and cases. And such studies must in turn be followed by research in the international field.

Here are some illustrations of constitutional "inadequacy": The constitutions of the Arab States, for example, fail to provide a realistic picture, or perhaps, any picture at all, of discrimination against women. In the law of succession, a woman's portion is equal to half the portion of a man; the daughter of a testator receives under the law only half the share of a brother. This is examplified in the civil code of Morocco, articles 237-244, and the civil code of Syria, articles 277/2.

Even where the constitution speaks to a subject, supplemental information and explanation must be forthcoming in the statutory law. Liberia provides an excellent example. Section 14 of Article V of the constitution reads:

> "The purchase of any land by any citizen or citizens from the Aborigines of this country for his or their own use, or for the benefit of others, or estates in fee simple, shall be considered null and void to all intents and purposes."[36]

Yet to understand this constitutional provision one must examine Liberia's Aborigines Law. Here are two sections:

> Paragraph 270: Each tribe is entitled to the use of as much of the public land in the area inhabited by it as required for farming and other enterprises essential to tribal necessities.
>
> Paragraph 273: A person who enters the territory of a tribe

36. Liberia. Constitution, 1955.

> of which he is not a member for the purpose of farming, shall observe the following procedure: (a) obtain permission of the Tribal Authority prior to commencing his activities; (b) agree to pay some token . . .; (c) pay taxes . . . In case of his failure to comply with any of the foregoing requirements, the Tribal Authority may cancel the permission granted and confiscate the crops. [37]

These explanations merely scratch the surface of the problem, but they are useful in pointing out the need for further research and analysis. So, too, the necessity of case studies, discussed in greater detail in the introductory materials of this report.

And, of course, all of this must be supplemented by work in the field of international human rights law. To begin with, this involves a study of what has been done by the United Nations. One could not complete a comprehensive study of discrimination, for example, without examining these two items:

(1) United Nations. Protection of Minorities; Special Protective Measures of an International Character for Ethnic, Religious or Linguistic Groups. United Nations, New York, 1967.

(2) Unesco, *Cultural Rights As Human Rights;* Unesco, Paris, 1970.

And there are, of course, numerous other United Nations publications, reflecting both international action and compiling responses of individual nations to United Nations inquiries. (Some of the most important of these have been noted and annotated in the bibliography.) And there are numerous United Nations organizations, agencies, and sub-agencies whose work must be explored.

Yet, research into United Nations activities is only a beginning in the sense that United Nations efforts must be followed by similar research in the work of the European Community, the Organization of American States, the Organization of African

37. Aborigines Law, Liberian Code of Laws of 1956, as amended, Vol. I.

Unity and other regional groups, the work of the League of Nations, the part played by treaties in general and the post-World War I minority treaties in particular, etc.

Research into the activities of the United Nations and its sister organizations and progeny is only a starting point in another sense. For I have come away from this study with ample documentation and the conclusion that United Nations material is suspect. Perhaps I already knew this (and should have known this) before I began my study; perhaps this is a simple, elementary fact of which we can all take judicial notice. Any organization which equates Zionism with racism must necessarily be dominated by either knaves or fools. Yet I resolved from the very beginning that my study would be objective and that I would approach the constitutions and commentaries with utmost objectivity. I assert that the conclusions are the results of induction. And so the conclusion that United Nations material is weighted, slanted, and not completely trustworthy is based upon my research -- even though the conclusion may be obvious.

To provide one simple illustration: women's groups in the more advanced countries have sought to take action against genital mutilation which literally affects the lives of millions of African and Middle Eastern women. Yet, adherence to both the clitoridectomy and infibulation in the Third World has precluded not only United Nations action but even United Nations discussion.[38]

Nor is it possible to compile and use the data furnished by and through the United Nations without realizing its special bias against South Africa,[39] its special bias for the Palestine Liberation Organization, and other familiar predilections.

In terms of sheer numbers, there is probably more racial, religious, sex, ethnic and cultural oppression and persecution in

38. Hosken, Fran P., *Genital Mutilation of Women in Africa,* Pasadena, California Institute of Technology, Munger Africana Library Notes, 1976.

39. Cf. "The UN Crusade Against South Africa is a Disgrace," *Barons,* New York, 28 December, 1964; Dehint, A.: *The United Nations and South Africa,* Tjeenk Willink, Zwolle, Netherlands, 1976; Rhoodie, E.M.: *The Paper Curtain,* Voortrekkeipers, Johannesburg, 1969, pp. 82-112.

Black Africa and Communist China than in any other place in the world. Even more than in the Soviet Union. It is obviously not an easy task to assemble the documentation, but the need for such documentation is one of the inevitable conclusions of the present study.

This need for further efforts was also emphasized in the *Seminar On The Multi-National Society*. One of the major operational conclusions was that much more research was needed on ethnic, religious, linguistic and international problems. [40]

And when all of the data are compiled and all of these studies are completed and when everyone becomes cognizant of the importance of public information and public relations, there still remains the final task of dissemination. For this one needs the computer.

The biggest problem is that there is no scanning mechanism which can enable a computer to read and store the printed pages containing all of the constitutions. Materials to be stored in a computer's memory bank must be fed by hand, a letter at a time, via the computer's own typewriter mechanism. It is, of course, possible to code and classify special categories of constitutional information in advance, and then have research associates search through the constitutions themselves to extract the desired material which can then be fed into the computer. But if all of the coding/classification has to be done in advance, the benefits from the computer will be minimal, except for the advantages of a quick retrieval for future research.

As indicated in Part I, Chapter II, two scholars at Erasmus University in Rotterdam have extracted sections from the world's constitutions on a predetermined basis and have fed them into a computer. [41] The effort proved valuable.

---

40. Supra, note 15, particularly pars. 58 and 87.

41. Professors Henc van Maaseveen and G.F.M. van der Tang.

State Responsibility

Perhaps the principle conclusion of the Seminar on the Multi-National Society reads as follows:

> There was general agreement that all governments should promote and protect the rights of ethnic, religious, linguistic, or national groups, not only through the adoption of constitutional and legislative provisions, but also through the promotion of all forms of activities consistent with the political, economic and social conditions of the State or country concerned. [42]

Whether, how, and to what extent constitutional and legislative provisions can provide solutions to such problems raises questions and doubts to be discussed *infra* in Chapter IV "Group Rights and the Need for Constitutional Safeguards."

But I can conclude, without any question, that governments should do more in this area, and that "more" must go beyond research and studies. Experimentation is also demanded. Research and analysis must be followed by constitutional and legislative provisions, designed to solve these problems. This, in turn, must be followed by empirical studies of the effects of the provisions on target groups. This brings me back to the computer. In the process of making decisions about appropriate constitutional and legislative provisions, governments must possess the knowledge of what has been tried and done elsewhere. Extracting all of such data goes far beyond the wording of the items compiled for the annexes here.

Ideally, every word of every constitution should be pre-fed into the computer, making it possible for applicable material to be extracted through a key word in context system. The solution to a racial problem, for example, might be found not in a constitutional guarantee of racial equality, but in a constitutional provision restricting the amending process. For one need to know (study,

---

42. Supra, note 15, par. 144a.

analyze, experiment, verify) which kinds of provisions are most effective in addressing the needs of ethnic, linguistic, religious or national groups. Only careful empirical analysis can reveal what kinds of provisions are effective. Such studies are still in their infancy, but a constitutional survey is certainly the appropriate beginning towards a fuller understanding of group rights in action. A country such as the United States could do not better than to provide state funds to put the entire contents of the Blaustein set [43] into a computer, and then to announce that it will provide any nation, or any group or entity with references to those constitutional provisions which might serve their needs. The United Nations is an international agency which ought to consider such a project as a priority if it could only get its priorities in order. It is currently spending several million dollars a year to discredit *apartheid* in South Africa, a policy which is already universally discredited and whose own masters are now rapidly restructuring the social fabric of South Africa along more liberal, internationally acceptable lines. The United Nations could be contributing to change in South Africa by using one year's anti-apartheid budget to provide the new government in South Africa with the knowledge of how group rights are handled elsewhere.

---

43. *Constitutions of the Countries of the World*, 15 Volumes.

CHAPTER XXI

GROUP RIGHTS AND THE NEED FOR CONSTITUTIONAL SAFEGUARDS

Constitutional safeguards are not necessarily the answer to the problems of group rights. Certainly, they are not *always* the answer; certainly, they are not the *only* answer; certainly, they are not the *complete* answer; and perhaps they are not even the *best* answer.

This is one of the principal conclusions which flows from the study of all of the constitutional provisions designed both (1) to prevent discrimination against various groups; and (2) to protect and maintain the identity of such groups.

And the doubts and questions concerning the value of constitutional provisions on these subjects likewise applies to legislation, treaties, and the entire panoply of the legal order.

In saying this, one challenges at the same time axioms, theorems, and shibboleths which most of the world has taken for granted. One challenges whether, indeed,

> All governments should promote and protect the rights of ethnic, religious, linguistic, or national groups, not only through the adoption of constitutional and legislative provisions but also through the promotion of all forms of activities consistent with the political, economic and social conditions of the State or country concerned. [44]

But I hasten to point out that this conclusion/challenge has a

44. Supra Note 15, par. 144a.

caveat. For one cannot yet be sure. My appeal now is for more research and study to determine the validity of the common wisdom which proclaims the importance of constitutional safeguards. I would urge more experimentation so that what are now regarded as axioms may be tested further. But, based on my present studies, I doubt that the solutions to group rights issues lie solely in constitutional or statutory draftsmanship, certainly not in the resolutions of the United Nations. In addition, my studies have even raised doubts about whether bills of rights or lists of fundamental rights belong in a constitution.

My challenge to the conventional wisdom of constitutional safeguards is in two parts: first, I question whether the world community should be dedicated and committed to the preservation of nation-states which contain diverse (and oft-times conflicting) racial, religious, and other ethnic entities which might demand or otherwise be entitled to manifestations of group rights which might be inconsistent with "national" policies or interests. Second, I question whether group rights demands should be institutionalized into a constitution without an accompanying restructuring of the socio-political system.

What is wrong with pursuing a general policy of separatism -- by race, tribe, religion, etc? Is this really wrong? Or has the West come to think of it as wrong because it is the policy advocated by white people in South Africa to protect their own identity and the accompanying privileged political position? Why is it not wrong for the Scandinavian peoples to be divided among five separate countries? The people of Denmark, Finland, Iceland, Norway and Sweden are relatively homogeneous in race, religion, language, and culture. Yet the forces of history and their own present desires see them as five distinct nations. The world community sees nothing wrong with this. But why doesn't the world community look upon this as a possible model and guide to group rights problems throughout the world? One could also refer to the two Koreas and the two Germanys.

Would there have been anything wrong in the creation and maintenance of Israel as a state exclusively for the Jewish people? Would it not be advantageous to redivide Lebanon geographically to meet the original objective of creating a separate state in the Middle East for Maronite Christians? Wouldn't the peoples of Estonia, Latvia, and Lithuania be happier if they were able to maintain their own separate states rather than be subject to Russian domination? (They certainly think so.)[45] Why is there no Armenia? Why is there no Kurdistan? Why is it right for every second group of islands in the Caribbean basin, some with a population of less than 100,000 souls to be declared "independent nations," while the Xhosa in South Africa's Transkei, numbering millions, and who elected independence by secret ballot are denied recognition? The independent state of Antiqua-Barbuda has only 70,000 people, Kiribati only 58,000.

One cannot attend any gathering in Milan without hearing sighs about Garibaldi and his efforts which brought about the final unification in Italy in 1870. And this is a nation where the people are all of the white race, speak the same language, and, with few exceptions, attend the same church. Yet the main topic of conversation is always the economic burden which the south imposes upon the north and the wistful dream of a separate northern Italy.[46]

Where is there evidence that Canada would not be a happier place if Quebec became a separate nation? Or Biafra? Or Katanga? Or Kwa-Zulu? Or Eritrea? Why are these entities different from

---

45. Glaser and Possony: op. cit., pp. 133-135.

46. See for example, Anthony Haden-Guest: "The King of Fiat: Living with Terrorism." *New York Magazine,* May 1, 1978, at pp. 40, 41, 42:

> 'The Piedmontese,' he told me, 'are sober, quiet, industrious. Italy's laboratory.' Turin is the capital of Piedmont.It gave Italy not just its first industrial revolution, but its royal family. Now it is 50 percent Southerner. 'This,' he said, 'was like . . . Biafrans coming to Sweden. Turin used to be a quiet Catholic town, controlled by one family. It is now the most Communist city in Western Europe.'

Bangladesh? Why is it right to plan for a Palestinian homeland on the West Bank, but wrong for South Africa to plan a homeland for the Zulus who speak their own language and have their own King?

On the other hand, where the forces of history have brought diverse groups together under some nationalistic umbrella, what is wrong with the old philosophy of the melting pot? Why does modern conventional wisdom insist upon the preservation of group rights through constitutional safeguards? Why not integration? Why not assimilation? Is it possible that Brazil provides the ultimate model? -- a state in which there is a maximum of interracial marriage, a "bleaching" of the population? The intellectual fashion of our time is to praise diversity and to extol its role in national development. It is the popular view that the majority or dominant element of each nation should encourage and preserve the cultural heritage of its minorities. It is even popular to espouse the proposition that the state offer incentives to help develop and maintain group characteristics and traditions. But why?

What has been accomplished thus far in the legal order has not solved the problems of group rights. There is much to be said against joining identifiably separate groups into a pluralistic state. Separatism and resettlement are still solutions worthy of re-examination, as are the completely opposite solutions of integration and assimilation.

But, as noted above, the more important conclusion is that we must first attempt to find solutions to group rights problems through constitutional and legal *means*. The problem now is to decide how constitutions should be used in the process.

Homogeneous Societies

It is axiomatic that the homogeneous society needs no legal safeguards (in the constitution or any other document) for group or minority rights. If there are no religious, racial, ethnic, or cultural minorities, there is no need for laws to protect them from discrimination or laws to protect and foster their existence as separate entities. Further, there is much to be said in favor of creating and/or maintaining the homogeneous state. Much of the United States' flag-waving, proclaiming that America's greatness is due to its diversity, is pure politics. Racial strife has been prevalent in America since its founding, and has diverted energies which should have been used for the uplifting of the total population. And there has been much unhappiness in the process. Certainly, life is easier in the homogeneous states of Scandinavia; certainly, Britain was a happier place before the influx in recent years of both West Indians and East Indians. It was only after this influx that Britain introduced its Race Relations Act of 1965 and 1968. [47]

Having said this, however, there are two further issues. Is it possible to create a nation-state in a given area which is homogeneous? Is it advantageous (in terms of human costs) to take steps to achieve homogeneity? Today's America, for example, could never be a homogeneous society. The nation is more than 25 percent Catholic, and nearly three percent Jewish; it has a black population of 12 percent and a Hispanic population which is nearly ten percent. American history reflects numerous efforts to return blacks to the African continent. The American Colonization Society [48] led efforts to bring blacks to Africa, culminating in the establishment of Liberia. The fact that the slaves returned to the area which became Liberia were far more educated and sophisticated than natives, and that this led to a new type of conquest, new classes, etc., is another matter. The idea of repatriation persisted right up to the Civil War, and was advocated by Abraham Lincoln in the famous Lincoln-Douglas debates of 1858. [49]

47. Nanda, V.P.: "Racial Discrimination and the Law -- Recent Legislation in Great Britain, Canada and the U.S.A.," in Claude, R.P.: *Comparative Human Rights*, Johns Hopkins University Press, Baltimore, 2nd printing, 1977, pp. 218-227.

48. American Colonization Society: A Memorial to the United States Congress. Annals of Congress, 16th Congr., 1st. Sess. (February 3, 1820), pp. 1047-1051.

49. Lincoln-Douglas Debates. Lincoln at Freeport, August 27, 1858.

Nor would it be possible (to say nothing of practical) to carve separate homogeneous states out of today's India. And while Zaire, with scores of tribal groups and dozens of languages, has more cultural diversity than the nation seems to be able to endure, it would be economically impossible to divide the country to achieve the benefits of homogeneity.

This is not universally so. Israel is a good example of the advantages of trying to create a homogeneous society.[50] And the situation would be even better if the transfer-of-population principle were carried to its logical conclusion and Arabs in that area were settled among the 21 Arab countries which comprise their self-proclaimed "Arab Nation." The major source of intergroup conflict in the entire Middle East has been this Arab conception of Islamic uniformity.[51] More than 700,000 Jews, living in the perpetual status of second-class citizenry in the Arab world, have emigrated to Israel. Reverse emigration would undoubtedly be the best solution.[52]

World War I was the breaking up of both the Hapsburg and Ottoman Empires -- a breakup into states which, to a greater or lesser extent, provided a better life for their citizenry because they were homogeneous. One must, however, contrast the creation of a separate homogeneous Hungary with the plural society of Czechoslovakia which followed the end of the Hapsburg Empire. Again, contrast the homogeneous Greece and multinational Yugoslavia which resulted when Ottoman rule came to an end. The establishment (or reestablishment) of states like Hungary and Greece are preferable to the Hapsburg or Ottoman monstrosities.

---

50. Lijphart, A.: op. cit., pp. 129-134.

51. Ma'oz Moshe: "Islamic-Arabism versus Pluralism; the Failure of Intergroup Accommodation in the Middle East," in Rhoodie, Nic: op. cit., pp. 137-138.

52. While Israel has a complicated set of laws, regulations, union rules, etc., to prohibit discrimination against its Arab citizens, the fact of unequal treatment still exists. There are, for example, segregated schools. Further, in their desire to advance their religious and ethnic identity, Arabs have recently brought a legal action challenging Israel's bigamy laws as being discriminatory to those of the Muslim faith.

Entities like Yugoslavia (discussed in detail in the previous section) might or might not be better off after a division into more homogeneous cultural units. Many Croats and other minority elements think so. [53] Certainly it is a very complicated legal machinery, indeed, which is utilized to keep the nation together, while respecting group rights.

Population transfer (resettlement) was a principal means of solving group rights and minority problems both after World War I and during the Hitler period, from 1939 to 1945. It is true that some argument could be made against some of the transfers. But it was the best approach, *as far as Germans were concerned.* Those who identified as European Germans (unlike those of German nationality who came to the Americas) remained culturally German regardless of the nation within whose borders they were confined. The European German outside of Germany was ever the irredentist, even more than the Italians who created the name a century earlier. No constitutional or statutory scheme could ever solve the group rights, discrimination, or identification demands of Germans, and efforts to achieve homogeneity by resettlement were, where Germans were concerned, advantageous.

Resettlement is still a practical solution today, in many areas of the world. It is unofficially going on in a great many parts of the world. Whites are leaving Zimbabwe; Hindus have been leaving Bangladesh. Indians have left Burma. Jews who are fortunate enough to be able to do so are leaving the Soviet Union and the Arab world. In fact, humanitarian efforts are directed toward programs which will enable Jews to leave such countries as Syria and Iraq.

World support should now be given to aid in the resettlement of Muslim refugees from Burma to Bangladesh.No solution to the Muslim problem can be found in the current legal structure of Burma, or for the 250,000 stateless Indians since Burma's

53. Bridge, Susan: op. cit., pp. 361-364.

constitution does not recognize the Indians, not even as a minority. [54]

What has been said above about the advantages of homogeneity over constitutional safeguards (where it is possible to achieve them), cannot, of course, be used to justify genocide or to advocate population movements which may result in human suffering. It must be remembered that Hitler also spoke in favor of achieving a homogeneous population. Nevertheless, this does not mean that the solution to the German "Jewish problem" could be found in laws prohibiting discrimination. Had an Israel existed at that time, population transfer would have been possible. Would that the Armenians and Kurds, both second class citizens spread out among the Soviet Union, Turkey, Iran, and Iraq, had their own state, to which they might be transferred!

And the world must be increasingly aware of the dangers inherent in forced population transfers by conquest. This is specifically prohibited by Article 49 of the Geneva Convention Relative to the Protection of Civilian Persons in Time of War, August 12, 1949. The applicable provisions are:

> Individual or mass forcible transfers, as well as deportations of protected persons from occupied territory to the territory of the Occupying Power or to that of any other country, occupied or not, are prohibited, regardless of their motive.
>
> * * *
>
> The Occupying Power shall not deport or transfer parts of its own civilian population into the territory it occupies.

Israel has been accused of violating this provision by the creation of settlements in the so-called West Bank. But the principal manifestation of such undesirable settlement is in

---

54. Chakravarti, N.R.: *The Indian Minority in Burma*, Oxford University Press, London, 1971, p. 178. During the sixties, Burma expelled 500,000 Indians, stripping them of all property and personal valuables.

Indochina, where the Vietnamese, with a population of more than 50 million, are gradually moving into large areas of Democratic Kampuchea, which has fewer than 6 million people, and Laos, with a population of about 3 million.

The Integrated Society

The achievement of an "integrated society" is out of fashion today. It has been honored and respected in its American manifestation. *E pluribus unum* was ever the American motto, and the melting pot represented the ideal. And nations such as Canada and Australia and the Latin American countries were quick to follow the model.

But this is no longer the model or goal -- even in America. Group rights are "in," it is now trendy to advocate all sorts of laws and regulations to foster and preserve differences among people. Spanish is on its way to become the unofficial second language. In advocating a society likened to the salad bowl, where each distinct vegetable contributes its part to the totality of the salad, I see ever more effort towards diversity. This is true in regard to negritude ("black is beautiful") and other racial distinctions. It is true in American encouragement (often by law) of religious differences. A Seventh-Day Adventist does not lose unemployment benefits by refusing to take employment which might require Saturday labour.[55] The United States Supreme Court has even gone so far as to require the schools to provide bilingual instruction, in order to accommodate those members of ethnic groups with insufficient knowledge of the English language.[56] And this, despite the fact that this has delayed or actually prevented the acquisition of sufficient competency in English to compete in the job market. Encouragement of ethnic dining does indeed improve a nation's cuisine. But why have compulsory bilingual training?

Contrast the modern American approach to ethnic and language

55. *Sherbert v. Verner,* 374 U.S. 398 (1963).

56. *Lau v. Nichols,* 404 U.S. 563 (1974).

rights with the position taken by Eleanor Roosevelt, while chairman of the Committee responsible for drafting the Universal Declaration of Human Rights. Throughout the debate she prevailed in her position against any provision relating to the protection of minority or group rights. She simply maintained that the problem of minorities did not exist on the American continent. It was her position that the aim of states was to assimilate and absorb large foreign groups, and make them a part of the nation. As summarized by Urmilia Haksar in her excellent book on *Minority Protection and The International Bill of Human Rights* [57], Mrs. Roosevelt made the following argument on the matter of language:

> Unless all citizens of a given country could speak the same language, there was the danger that public order might be disrupted by persons who might not understand their duties as citizens of the country in which they were a minority.

Australia agreed that the principle of assimilation of all groups was in a nation's best interests, but differed from Mrs. Roosevelt by saying that special groups in some countries might be entitled to special protections. The French argued on the side of Mrs. Roosevelt that the development of France into a homogeneous state had resulted from the application of universal human rights to the entire population. In the French view, it would have been disadvantageous to have a statement on the rights of minority groups, since that might hinder their integration within a state. [58]

But all of this happened in 1947, which was the heyday of American prestige and respect, both in world opinion and the opinion of its own citizenry. As Ms. Haksar summarizes the events of the time: "There was a general expectation that the bill on Human Rights would contain provisions relating to the protection of minorities. Yet, when (it) was finally adopted, it made no

---

57. *Bombay and other Indian Cities,* Allied Publishers, 1974, p. 47.

58. Doc. E/CN. 4/5R. 73, p. 7.

reference to the problem of minorities.'' [59] The drafting committee had proposed the following as Article 46:

> In states inhabited by a substantial number of persons of a race, language or religion other than those of the majority of the population, persons belonging to such ethnic, linguistic or religious minorities shall have the right as far as compatible with public order to establish and maintain their schools and cultural and religious institutions and to use their own language in the press, in public assembly and before the courts and other authorities of the state.'' [60]

The provision was hotly debated and several times revised, coming before the Commission in final form as Article 31 of the Geneva text in 1948. [61] The Universal Declaration of Human Rights, in its final form, ended with Article 30. Those who advocated United Nations recognition of group rights dominated the Sub-Commission on Prevention of Discrimination and Protection of Minorities. By 1950, the following resolution had been formulated:

> **Recognizing** that there are among the nationals of many states, distinctive population groups possessing ethnic, religious or linguistic traditions or characteristics different from those of the rest of the population, usually known as minorities, and that among these are groups that need to be protected by special measures, national or international, so that they can preserve and develop the traditions or characteristics in question, **Recognizing**, however, that not all such groups pose this problem of protection, which is not required:
>
> (a) when the group in question, though numerically inferior to the rest of the population, is the

59. Urmilia Haksar; op. cit., pp. 47-48.

60. Ibid, p. 47.

61. Doc. E/CN. 4/21, Annex F, Article 36, p. 81.

dominant group therein, and

(b) when the group in question seeks complete identity of treatment with the rest of the population, in which case its problems are covered by those articles of the Charter of the United Nations, the Universal Declaration of Human Rights and the Draft International Covenant on Human Rights that are directed towards the prevention of discrimination.

Recognizing, at the same time that any definition of minorities that is made with a view to their protection by the United Nations must take into account complex situations such as:

(a) the undesirability of imposing unwanted distinctions upon individuals belonging to a group who, while possessing the distinctive characteristics described above, do not wish to be treated differently from the rest of the population,

(b) the undesirability of interfering with the spontaneous developments which take place when impacts such as that of a new environment or that of a modern means of communication, produce a state of rapid racial, social, cultural or linguistic evolution,

(c) the risk of taking measures that might lend themselves to misuse amongst a minority whose members' spontaneous desire for a tranquil life as tented citizens of a state disturbed by parties interested in fomenting amongst them a disloyalty to that State,

(d) the undesirability of affording protection to practices which are inconsistent with human rights as proclaimed in the Universal Declaration of Human Rights,

(e) difficulties raised by claims to the status of a minority by groups so small that special treatment would, for instance, place a disproportionate burden upon the resources of the state,

Resolves that from the standpoint of such measure of minorities as the United Nations may wish to take, and in the light of the exceptions and complexities set out above;

(a) The term minority includes only those non-cominant groups in a population which possess and wish to preserve stable ethnic, religious or linguistic traditions or characteristics markedly different from those of the rest of the population: such minorities should properly include a number of persons sufficient by themselves to develop such characteristics;

(c) the members of such minorities must be loyal to the State of which they are nationals. [62]

Group rights were finally given United Nations recognition in Article 27 of the International Covenant on Civil and Political Rights, which became effective on March 23, 1976. It reads:

> In those States in which ethnic, religious or linguistic minorities exist, persons belonging to such minorities shall not be denied the right, in community with the other members of their group, to enjoy their own culture, to profess and practice their own religion, or to use their own language. [63]

Constitutionally, achievement of the integrationist position comes through the application of what Oscar Schachter calls the "universalistic approach." This, he says, is the role of public authority in "the removal of barriers to the equal enjoyment of

62. Doc. E/800, Appendix, p. 25.

63. Doc. E/CN. 4/Sub. 2/117, pp. 15-17.

rights by all. irrespective of race, colour, descent or ethnic affiliation.'' [64]

As an advocate of the "universalist-integrationist" philosophy, he does, however, recognize that legal recognition of group rights may be:

> . . . justified on the ground that integration and a universalist, non-discriminatory system has not been achieved and it is contended that only through separatism (or considerable autonomy) can the disadvantaged groups overcome the effects of discrimination and in particular, attain economic and political power. Parallel to this is the belief that racial groups, like many ethnic groups, have a distinctive culture, way of life and system of values that can best be fostered by autonomous communities based on the "separate but equal" principle. [65]

In the same vein -- and here he reflects my viewpoint:

> No matter how strongly one is committed to the values of universalism and the elimination of distinctions on racial lines, it would be unrealistic to disregard those historical situations in which integration is not a common value and where equality may more effectively be achieved through a system of co-existence of separate groups within the national society. [66]

Legal vs. Extra-legal Safeguards

My primary research concerns have been directed toward those societies which are not and cannot be homogeneous or integrationist. The focus is on the Belgiums and Indias and South Africas and Yugoslavias and similar nation-states of this world.

---

64. Oscar Schachter. "How Effective Are Measures Against Racial Discrimination?" 4 *Revue des Droits de l'Homme* 293 (1971) at p. 299.

65. Id., at p. 306.

66. Id., at pp. 309-310.

And the question now is whether the protections and support accorded to each of the diverse groups making up those societies should also be spelled out in the law. Conventional wisdom responds in the affirmative -- an overwhelming affirmative. And certainly this is the way it has been done, going back to Magna Carta in 1215, when the barons were guaranteed rights as barons. But the fact that constitutional and other legal safeguards for group rights have so long been an accepted practice does not mean that the practice is correct, or that they are the best way to handle group rights problems.

There are two issues here. First, whether the protection of group rights should be a matter of law; and, two, whether the law relative to group rights should be a part of the constitution.

The first question can be answered with a yes. This is because of the overwhelming evidence that laws change behavior and behavior changes attitudes. The famous American case of *Brown vs. Board of Education* [67] was instrumental in changing the school segregation laws which then existed in 17 states and the District of Columbia. It had a ripple effect. The Court order striking down segregation laws resulted in gradual compulsory integration which brought black and white into contact previously unknown. This was followed by attitude changes and so forth. Further, the Supreme Court imposition of a legal proscription against discrimination affected those who could not be swayed by any other means. [68]

The existence of laws protecting a group gives members of that group confidence and a feeling of security. Some laws also give an opportunity to be heard, since stated rights often provide judicial remedies for their infraction. Finally, there is still a great deal of

---

67. 347 U.S. 483 (1954).

68. See, for example J. Harding and A. Hogrefe. "Attitudes of White Department Store Employees Towards Negro Co-Workers." 8 *Journal of Social Issues,* pp. 8-18, 1952, discussed in the Schachter article (at p. 298) cited at notes 64-66 *supra* and analyzed in accompanying text.

respect in this world for the written word, and the fact that something is emblazoned in the law of the land is enough to make it right to a large segment of the population.

On the other hand, there are numerous counter-arguments. One does not have to be a student of the law to know of the substantial difference between law on the books and law in action. It would be fatuous to argue that the law (despite its vastness) has ended racial discrimination in America. Law has helped change attitudes, but it cannot always do so if strong resistance to change exists or if the agents of change are not diligent in enforcing the law.

No nation in the world devoted so much effort to finding legal solutions to group and minority rights problems as did India. And yet the discrimination problems there are so far from a solution. The evils of untouchability, affecting nearly 100 million members of the Indian population, are still prevalent. One of the generally acknowledged leaders of the Harijan community in India, P.T. Borale, former mayor of Bombay and former dean of the faculty of law at the University of Bombay has proved beyond any doubt the continued existence of the caste system. [69]

Much of what Dr. Borale says is summed up in a paper read at the world religious conference held in Moscow on June 5, 1977. After discussing a 1972 case in which the leader of the untouchables tried to assert the right to draw water from a public tank, he says this: "Even after 50 years or half a century, this (untouchable problem) is still existing and cannot be solved by our country alone without the help of international bodies even though our rulers are sympathetic."

Yet Dr. Borale remains optimistic about the efficacy of the law. It is his principal contention that Article 46 of the Indian Constitution should be moved from "Part IV -- Directive Principles of State Policy" to "Part III -- Fundamental Rights," so that it may be in the category enforceable by the courts. Said Article 46 reads:

---

69. Also author of *Segregation and Desegregation in India.* Bombay, Manaktalas, 1968, discussed elsewhere in this study.

> The State shall promote with special care the educational and economic interests of the weaker sections of the people, and, in particular, of the Scheduled Castes and the Scheduled Tribes, and shall protect them from social injustice and all forms of exploitation.

And then there are such huge, comprehensive efforts as the series of minority treaties after World War I -- which were followed by a library of volumes which tried to analyze why the treaties failed. One student, Jacob Robinson, questions "whether minorities problems are by their nature capable of solution by legal means." [70] That is still a question which cannot be answered with certainty. Thus, in addition to the counter-argument that laws will not solve the problem because of inevitable non-compliance, there is the additional counter-argument that laws by their very nature cannot do so.

An interesting analysis of this theme -- one with which I am not in agreement -- is given by S.C. Thanvi, Dean of the Faculty of Law and the University of Jodhpur, in India:

> Democracies in their constitutions provide safeguards for minorities which are meant for the uplift, progress and full development of the members of the minority communities in all fields of human activity -- social, political, cultural, economic, etc. Notwithstanding these safeguards, the minorities in all democracies present problems which have baffled solutions. These problems arise mostly on account of the psychology of the minorities. The minority mind is the most dis-satisfied mind in the world today. Protestants in Spain and South America, Jews throughout the world except in their home country, Negroes in the U.S.A., Muslims in India, remain dissatisfied with the majority and often come into conflict with the majority . . .

---

70. Jacob Robinson: *Were the Minorities Treaties a Failure?* New York, 1943, p. 331. Cf. Isaacs, Harold: op. cit.

> The typical minority mind feels insecure and if not properly understood and suitably treated, it may give rise to a national catastrophe and make national life full of tensions. In its abnormal condition, the minority feels suspicious and has imaginary fears and these cause a high level of anxiety and a consequent aggressiveness. As a reaction against this, the majority become suspicious of the minority and there is a chain reaction resulting in fear and anger on both sides. Consequently, the national goals and human values are lost sight of and people become guided by a communal and religious feeling. They are haunted by a sense of conspiracy. As a further reaction to this, a sense of heroism is developed and people become ready to even suffer martyrdom in the hope of attaining immortality. This is purely a pathological condition and if a timely cure is missed, it may bring disaster to the community. In monolithic countries the dictator solves the problem of minorities by their persecution and liquidation. But in democratic countries law has to ensure smooth human relationships between the majority and the minority. [71]

There is one final argument against the protection of group rights through legal process. It is a good argument and it is sustained by the obvious facts in such diverse places as the United States and the United Kingdom on one hand and India and Malaysia on the other. Group rights protections are inevitably perceived as preferential treatment, and this in turn results in increasing majority hostility and resentment, leading in turn to still more discrimination.

Notwithstanding all of these counter-arguments, however, I have concluded that, on balance, legal solutions should be sought for group rights problems -- at least in those societies where homogeneity cannot possibly be achieved and where integration is

71. "Indian Minorities -- Legal and Social Factors of National Integration" in: Mohamed Iman, op. cit., pp. 79-80.

not possible. Now the question is whether the legal solution should be incorporated into the constitutional structure of a nation or whether it should be manifested in other laws.

Choosing Between Constitutional and Other Legal Safeguards

Regardless of whether it is better to create constitutional safeguards for human rights (including group rights) or whether it is better to achieve such protections through other legal formulations, today's constitutional draftsmen will inevitably draft such provisions. As a matter of fact, the process has been going on for a long time -- so long that it is taken for granted that this is an inherent part of every constitution. Whether the formulation is based on the American Bill of Rights or the French Declaration of the Rights of Man or the UN's Universal Declaration of Human Rights or the listing of Economic Rights in the Soviet constitution, a section setting forth such rights is taken for granted. Perhaps history has made it inevitable.

Perhaps the real question is how rights should be protected through statutes, regulations, and caselaw *in addition to* the constitutional mandate.

This is a particularly interesting question to a nation which does not have a constitution. Israel provides an excellent example. While many Israeli legal scholars argue that rights are adequately defended by legislation and the protections accorded by its Supreme Court, others argue even more forcefully that a constitution would advance the cause of both individual human rights and group rights. Hebrew University Law Professor Pnina Lahav has spoken of the "very luxurious legal system where Americans do have a Constitution and judicial review and the luxury of a framework of legal principles within which they can develop and improve political and civil rights." She continues: "The situation in Israel, where we don't have a constitution or judicial review, is undesirable." [72]

72. See remarks in "The Rights of the Individual Under American, Israeli, and Halakhic Law," *Congress Monthly,* Vol. 45, No. 3, March/April 1978, p. 24.

The fact that human rights provisions are taken for granted is found in much of the literature surrounding the preparation of the Indian constitution. Professor Joseph Minattur states it this way:

> Most of the framers of the Indian Constitution were born in or about the year in which Dicey's *Introduction to the Study of the Constitution* was published. In their undergraduate days or at their law schools, they imbibed Dicey's ideas of the rule of law. During their public life they came in contact with Fabian socialism which was something of a rage during the interwar years. When they set about drafting a Constitution for India they applied their minds to the Diceyan concept of the rule of law, but gave it a veneer with their own notions of Fabian socialism. So they put down in the Constitution a general rule that "The state shall not deny to any person equality before the law or the equal protection of the laws within the territory of India," taking their cue from constitutions of countries where certain sections of citizens are not, in fact, considerably less equal than other sections.[73]

It has been so for a long time. Three major provisions of the United States Constitution of 1787 are concerned with slavery; diverse religious guarantees are set forth in the Swiss Constitution of 1798; linguistic differences and rights arising out of those differences constitute a feature of the Belgian Constitution of 1831, etc. And note that these are group rights and not the more generalized "Rights of Men." And remember that even the Magna Carta was the result of action by feudal barons to secure their own group position against the king, rather than a declaration of the rights of all men.

Yet after this lengthy study of what all of the constitutions have done toward the protection of group rights, I am not sure that the answer lies only in constitutional formulations. Constitutional

---

73. Joseph Minattur: "Protective Discrimination and the Rule of Law," in: Mohamed Iman, op. cit., p. 226.

formulations of rights can be criticized on two grounds. The first involves the question of rights *from whom*. Where the people as individuals or the people as selected groups are seeking rights as against the authority of a king, certainly they are properly spelled out in constitutional directives. On the other hand, where all of the power resides in the people from the very beginning, it need not be spelled out. All of the rights and freedoms are already there. All that the constitution then does is to delegate some of those rights to the executive, legislature, and judiciary whom the people themselves choose.

The second argument against constitutional safeguards was best summed up by Alexander Hamilton in his opposition to a Bill of Rights:

> The argument most used by proponents of the Constitution was that inasmuch as Congress was delegated no power to do those things which a bill of rights would proscribe no bill of rights was necessary and that it might be dangerous because it would contain exceptions to powers not granted and might therefore afford a basis for claiming more than was granted. [74]

These are still valid arguments.

Also valid is the history of what has gone wrong with constitutional arrangements designed to protect group rights. Nowhere is this more true than with the British experience in Nigeria. This is a long and complicated history. To summarize: in their various Nigerian constitutions, [75] the British made Nigeria into a federation, creating three separate regions which corresponded with the three major tribes in the area. While this recognition of special tribal rights appeared to be the best solution to maintaining Nigeria as one country, it resulted in regional politics dominated

---

74. *The Federalist,* No. 84, Modern Library ed., 1937, pp. 555-567.

75. See, for example, the Lugard Constitution of 1914, the Richards Constitution of 1946, the Lyttleton Constitution of 1954, and the Independence Constitution of 1960.

by tribal loyalties and eventually led to the unsuccessful Biafrian War of Secession. [76] Today's Nigeria is held together as a single country via the military. But regional and tribal loyalties are still far stronger than adherence to nationhood. Other English constitutional failures (although, to be fair, they were not all based upon recognition of group rights) were the East Africa Federation, the West Indies Federation, the Central Africa Federation and the Malayan Federation.

There is also the important point that some group rights are more efficiently protected through legislation (and the flexibility it entails) than in constitutions (with their rigidity). In the pre-Ayatollah Khomeini period the election laws of Iran, for example, provided representation in Parliament for three minority groups whose numbers were so small that representatives could not possibly be elected on a one-man, one-vote basis. [77]

Nor is the constitution the best instrument to handle such matters as school discrimination or the maintenance of separate schools by separate racial, religious, or ethnic entities. And it is frequently more desirable to have decisions made on particular matters by a court of law than to prescribe human rights in constitutional generalities.

Finally, the sad situation is that group rights and protection for individuals are today lacking throughout the world, notably Africa, despite the plethora of constitutionalism. [78] Speaking of the Third World in general, Professor Ernest Lefever said: "This evidence suggests the validity of my central thesis: that Western style democracy has failed to take root in the Third World. . ." [79] And the United Nations has been of little help in advancing group

---

76. Cf. Lijphart, A.: op. cit., pp. 161-164.

77. Representatives were selected by Zoroastrian, Jewish, and Armenian Christian communities.

78. Cf. Breytenbach, W.: "The Protection of Minority Rights in Africa," in Rhoodie, Nic: op. cit., pp. 285-297.

79. "Limits of Government in the Third World," in Rhoodie, Nic: op. cit., p. 21.

rights. One of the conclusions which follows this study is that one should re-examine the 1919 Minorities Treaties which followed the end of World War I. [80]

The Polish Treaty which follows served as a model for all of the other Minorities Treaties.

Article I

Poland undertakes that the stipulation contained in Articles 2 to 8 of this Chapter shall be recognized as fundamental laws, and that no law, regulation or official action shall conflict or interfere with these stipulations, nor shall any law, regulation or official action prevail over them.

Article II

Poland undertakes to assume full and complete protection of life and liberty to all inhabitants of Poland without distinction of birth, nationality, language, race or religion.

All inhabitants of Poland shall be entitled to the free exercise, whether public or private, or any creed, religion or belief, whose practices are not inconsistent with public order or public morals.

Article III

Poland admits and declares to be Polish nationals *ipso facto* and without the requirement of any formality German, Austrian, Hungarian or Russian nationals habitually residents at the date of the coming into force of the present Treaty in territory which is or may be recognized as forming part of Poland, but subject to any provision in the Treaties of Peace with Germany or Austria respectively relating to persons who became resident in such territory after a specified date.

80. The Minority Protection Treaties were administered by the Council of the League of Nations.

Nevertheless, the persons referred to above who are over 18 years of age will be entitled under the conditions contained in the said Treaties to opt for any other nationality which may be open to them. Option by a husband will cover his wife and option by parents will cover their children under 18 years of age.

Persons who have exercised the above right to opt must, except where it is otherwise provided in the Treaty of Peace with Germany, transfer within the succeeding 12 months their place of residence to the state for which they have opted. They will be entitled to retain their immovable property in Polish territory. They may carry with them their movable property of every description. No export duties may be imposed upon them in connection with the removal of such property.

Article IV

Poland admits and declares to be Polish, *ipso facto,* and without the requirement of any formality, persons of German, Austrian, Hungarian or Russian nationality who were born in the said territory of parents habitually resident there, even if at the date of the coming into force of the present Treaty, they are not themselves habitually resident there.

Nevertheless, within two years after the coming into force of the present Treaty these persons may make a declaration before the competent Polish authorities in the country in which they are resident, stating that they abandon Polish nationality, and they will then cease to be considered as Polish nationals. In this connection, a declaration by a husband will cover his wife, and a declaration by parents will cover their children under 18 years of age.

Article V

Poland undertakes to put no hindrance in the way of the exercise of the right which the persons concerned have, under the Treaties concluded or to be concluded by the Allied and Associated Powers with Germany, Austria, Hungary or Russia to choose whether or not they will acquire Polish nationality.

Article VI

All persons born in Polish territory who are not born nationals of another state shall *ipso facto* become Polish nationals.

Article VII

All Polish nationals shall be equal before the law and shall enjoy the same civil and political rights without distinction as to race, language or religion.

Differences of religion, creed or confession shall not prejudice any Polish national in matters relating to the enjoyment of civil or political rights, as for instance, admission to public employments, functions and honours or the exercise of professions and industries.

No restriction shall be imposed on the free use by any Polish national or any language in private intercourse, in commerce, in religion, in the press or in publications of any kind, or at public meetings.

Notwithstanding any establishment by the Polish Government of an official language, adequate facilities shall be given to Polish nationals of non-Polish speech for the use of their language, either orally or in writing, before the Courts.

Article VIII

Polish nationals who belong to racial, religious or linguistic minorities shall enjoy the same treatment and security in law and in fact as the other Polish nationals. In particular, they shall have an equal right to establish, manage and control, at their own expense charitable, religious and social institutions, schools and other educational establishments with the right to use their own language and to exercise their religion freely therein.

Article IX

Poland will provide in the public educational system in towns and districts in which a considerable proportion of Polish nationals of other than Polish speech are residents, adequate facilities for ensuring that, in the primary schools the instruction shall be given to the children of such Polish nationals through the medium of their own language. This provision shall not prevent the Polish Government from making the teaching of the Polish language obligatory in the said schools.

In towns and districts where there is a considerable proportion of Polish nationals belonging to racial, religious or linguistic minorities, these minorities shall be assured an equitable share in the enjoyment and application of the sums which may be provided out of public funds under the State, municipal or other budget for educational, religious or charitable purposes.

The provisions of this Article shall apply to Polish citizens of German speech only in that part of Poland which was German territory on August 1, 1914.

Article X

Educational Committees appointed locally by the Jewish Communities of Poland will, subject to the general control of the state, provide for the distribution of the proportional share of public funds allocated to Jewish schools in accordance with Article 2, and for the organisation and management of these schools.

The provisions of Article 9 concerning the use of languages in schools shall apply to these schools.

Article XI

Jews shall not be compelled to perform any act which constitutes a violation of their Sabbath, nor shall be placed under any disability by reason of their refusal to attend courts of law or to perform any legal business on their Sabbath. This provision, however, shall not exempt Jews from such obligations as shall be imposed upon all other Polish citizens for the necessary purposes of military service, national defence or the preservation of public order.

Poland declares her intention to refrain from ordering or permitting elections, whether general or local, to be held on a Saturday, nor will registration for electoral or other purposes be compelled to be performed on a Saturday.

Article XII

Poland agrees that the stipulations in the foregoing Articles, so far as they affect persons belonging to racial, religious or linguistic minorities, constitute obligations of international concern and shall be placed under the guarantee of the League of Nations. They shall not be modified without the assent of a majority of the Council of the League of Nations. The United States, the British Empire, France, Italy and Japan hereby agree not to withhold their assent from any modification in these Articles which is in due form assented by a majority of the Council of the League of Nations.

Poland agrees that any Member of the Council of the League of Nations shall have the right to bring to the attention of the Council any infraction, or any danger of infraction, of any of these obligations, and that the Council may thereupon take such action and give such direction as it may deem proper and effective in the circumstances.

Poland further agrees that any difference of opinion as to questions of law or fact arising out of these Articles between the Polish Government and any of the Principal Allied and Associated Powers or any other Power, a Member of the Council of the League of Nations, shall be held to be a dispute of international character under Article 14 of the Covenant of the League of Nations. The Polish Government hereby consents that any such dispute shall, if the other party thereto demands, be referred to the Permanent Court of International Justice. The decision of the Permanent Court shall be final and shall have the same effect as an award under Article 13 of the Covenant.[81]

The minority treaties were, of course, also imperfect. They were also in many respects ineffective.[82] But they did represent something tangible and have no real counterpart today. The Paris Peace Treaties of 1919 redrew the map of Europe in the name of "self-determination." The considerations which prevail today are not concerned solely with self-determination.[83] Nonetheless, the relationship between increased ethnicity and the ideal of self-determination is there for everyone to see and several respectable

---

81. Treaty of Peace between the United States of America, the British Empire, France, Italy, Japan and Poland, Treaty Series, 1919, No. 8, cm. 223. This treaty came into force on January 10, 1920. All other Minorities Treaties were framed on the pattern of the Polish Treaty only with minor changes necessitated by local differences.

82. Jaksch, W.: *Europa's Weg Nach Potsdam,* Verlag Wissenschaft und Politik, Cologne, 1967, devotes an entire chapter to their ineffectiveness.

83. Gastil, R.D.: "The Right to Self-Determination: Definition, Reality and Ideal Policy," in Rhoodie, Nic: op. cit., pp. 84-108.

scholars have noted that there has been an energetic reaffirmation of the populist right of self-determination.[84]

There is little doubt in the mind of Western observers that had the Minority Treaty survived in Poland, history would never have heard of such organisations as Solidarity or of people such as Lech Walesa, the 1983 Nobel Peace Prize winner. The counterpoint is that not even the bare substance of the various clauses could survive in a Communist state. Such provisions as Poland agreed to in 1919 can only be applied in a democracy.

84. Esman, Milton J.: op. cit., p. 12 and Lijphart, A.: "Political Theories and the Explanation of Ethnic Conflict in the Western World: Falsified Predictions and Plausible Postdictions," in Esman, Milton, J.: op. cit., p. 63.

CHAPTER XXII

GROUP RIGHTS AND INDIVIDUAL RIGHTS

It is necessary to compare and contrast group rights and individual rights. One must determine whether they are consistent with each other or inherently contradictory. One must consider (or at least analyze the question) whether one is more important than the other. And somehow, in this process, one must take into account the concept of equality. Is there a fundamental right to be treated as an equal? Is there a fundamental right to equal treatment? And how do the responses to these questions relate to either or both group rights and individual rights?

These questions and variants of these issues have concerned constitutional scholars going back to the formulation of the Philadelphia Constitution of 1787. They are still in dispute.[85] They were the subject matter of the numerous debates in the preparation of the Universal Declaration of Human Rights. And, then, because of discontent with the Universal Declaration, these issues were basic during twenty years of laborious drafting of the International Covenant on Economic Cultural and Social Rights and the International Covenant on Civil and Political Rights. The contradictions within these Covenants and the Universal Declaration reflect the difficulty in understanding the relationships between group rights and individual rights.

---

85. Cf. Duchacek, I.D.: *Rights and Liberties in the World Today: Constitutional Promise and Reality,* University of California Press, Santa Barbara, 1973.

The Dominant Importance of Group Rights

Group rights are more important than individual rights when it comes to preventing (or causing) human conflict and are more important in the settling of ideological or political disputes, be it international, national, or regional. This is one of the most important conclusions reached as a result of this study. I am not sure whether this comes solely from the study of the constitutional provisions on the subject or whether it is a conclusion developed by conferences and discussions on constitutional literature. But I am convinced that group rights and individual rights will often come into conflict (a point to be developed later) and that group rights are, politically speaking, more important.

This is not consistent with prior observations about the advantages of an integrated society -- *in certain instances*. For there is much to be said on behalf of the achievement of the American melting pot. But the American who studies group rights problems must stop thinking exclusively like an American. For it is primarily in America (and Canada to a lesser degree) that there has been any major support for the integrationist, melting pot philosophy. And, as everybody knows, that philosophy is a thing of the past. Canada is in the throes of its greatest constitutional crisis as its roughly 20 percent French-speaking population makes formal its refusal to "melt." According to observers their cultural nationalism "may well give way to general demands for secession." [86] In the United States, the modern trend of the sociologist-philosophers is to question whether there was indeed ever a melting pot, or whether it was merely a stated, unreachable ideal -- the ideal of a concept whose time has passed.

Nor did any of the other countries of the New World really accept the integrationalist or universalist philosophy. As has been noted, the greatest degree of interracial mixing occurred in Brazil. In this nation of more than 110 million, fully 50 percent of the

---

86. Brazeau, J. and Cloutier, E.: "Interethnic Relations and the Language Issue in Contemporary Canada," in Esman, M.J.: op. cit., p. 227.

population could be classified as mulattoes. One might envision the day when every native of the country would be racially mixed and in that event group rights would lose their significance. But that is not to be. In Brazil, as in so much of the rest of the world, the darker the skin the lower the status and the job. Interracial breeding has neither been an objective nor a solution. Brazilians have more than twenty different expressions for variations in skin tone between the extremes of black and white.

None of the other New World countries has even given lip service to the melting pot philosophy espoused in the literature of the United States and Canada. Because Argentina was settled by Spanish and Italians, there are special constitutional provisions requiring that officials, etc., be of the Catholic faith. On the other hand, no such constitutional mandate has been promulgated in Chile where the Spanish immigration was mixed with that of German Lutherans. And similar observations might be made in varying forms about the situation throughout the Western Hemisphere -- the only part of the world where integration was ever seriously considered as a policy.

When one stops thinking like an American, one realizes that the ideal throughout most of the world is for the homogeneous society, or if that is not possible, for the society in which adequate safeguards are provided to preserve, protect and foster group rights.

In saying that group rights are more important than individual rights, one is tempted to philosophize along these lines: Granted that such individual rights as habeas corpus are important, and granted that when one needs habeas corpus he needs it badly, there are still very few times in the lives of very few persons where habeas corpus is needed at all. But the right to practice one's religious customs and the right to speak one's own language, are group rights which exist on a daily basis.

It is very important (and this too many Americans do not know) that a Croat demands continual identification as a Croat, even though he is a citizen of the nation-state called Yugoslavia. The Ibo will not permit one to confuse him with a Yoruba; it is less important that they are both Nigerians. Political scientists have long asserted that, as a rule, loyalty in the plural society is *communal,* not *national.* [87] And this is the way of the world. It has been part of the American philosophy to think that Jews, for example, are unique in being ''unmeltable'' ethnics who uniquely preserve a group identity and who uniquely assert group rights. But throughout most of the world the ''unmeltable'' is more the rule than the exception. And even in America, in addition to Blacks, Puerto Ricans, Chicanos, Amerinds, etc., there has been an increase in certain years of the asserted group rights of what is crudely called the PIGS: Poles, Italians, Greeks and Slovaks.

But then, if group rights are more important than individual rights, the next question is why the latter has been so dominant in constitutional and legal philosophy.

The Individual Rights Philosophy -- And Its Decline

The American Constitution, the first of them all, is still nearly a decade away from its 200th anniversary. Constitutional philosophy is not that much older. It was not until the mid-1700's that lawyers achieved a measure of prominence and importance in England, France and the United States. [88] It took another hundred years for them to play an important role in the rest of the continent and India. (They have yet to achieve significant status in the Communist World, and they have no position at all among the 23 percent of the world's population which inhabits the People's Republic of China). And the world's first copyright statute was enacted in England in 1710.

These are the reasons, I believe, that the literature on human rights has been dominated by concern for individual rights rather

87. Rabushka, A. and Shepsle, K.A.: op. cit., p. 80.
88. Claude, Richard, P.: op. cit., p. 19.

than group rights. Locke, Rousseau, and Jefferson (and their intellectual heirs) have been progenitors of the philosophy of individual rights. This has been the universal theme from Tom Paine's *The Rights of Man* to the 1948 Universal Declaration of Human Rights.

Significantly, there was substantial dissatisfaction with the Universal Declaration both during and after its promulgation. This dissatisfaction has subsequently resulted in a new United Nations literature emphasizing the importance of group rights. This is also reflected in post-World War II constitutions. But this does not reflect conventional wisdom on human rights.

Conventional wisdom teaches that the emergence of human rights parallels the development of individualism. We are told that this has been a three-stage process. The eighteenth century witnessed the first serious recognition of individual claims against the state. This was followed in the nineteenth century by the granting of voting rights and the recognition of the right of the individual to participate in the governance of the state. And the twentieth century saw the acceptance of positive rights bestowed upon the individual by the state -- the development of economic and social human rights to enhance the development of the individual and to fulfill the idea of individual rights. [89]

Thus it is that scholars have not appreciated the significance of group rights development -- either in the formative period of constitution writing from 1787 to World War I, in the breakup of Austria-Hungary and the Ottoman Empire and the minorities provisions of the Czechoslovakia and Yugoslavia constitutions between the great wars, or in the Third World constitutions and the various documents of the United Nations following World War II.

There are also a number of personal, perhaps Freudian reasons why constitutional scholars have parroted individual rights dogma.

---

89. Ibid., pp. 6-39.

The fact is that these scholars -- with scant exception -- have been well-educated, free-thinking, white men and usually lawyers and writers by trade. (For lawyers began to dominate government in the eighteenth century, and with the advent of the copyright laws came the growth of the trade of authorship.) And in the beginning these tasks were performed only by men, and white men at that. Thus, the disregard for group rights which might have been advanced by women, or blacks, or other minority leaders, and thus the lawyer-emphasis on due process and *habeas corpus* and the writer-emphasis on freedom of speech and press. The work of clerics for religious rights is the sole exception.

In our collective egotism, we of the West who have studied the philosophies underlying the American Constitution and the French Declaration of the Rights of Man have accepted their philosophy on individual rights as immutable. This has been a Western philosophy and a Western literature and we embellished it and told the entire world to accept it. It had its last flowering as Mrs. Roosevelt dominated the discussions leading to the final formulation of the Universal Declaration of Human Rights. [90]

Today we know better. This is true both in space and in time. Locke, Rousseau and Jefferson were fine for England, France and America. But the constitutions embellishing their philosophies which were forced upon the Third World have proved unsuccessful. They were not meant for tribal societies; they were not meant for multi-ethnic societies; they were not meant for that vast majority of the world where group rights are more important than individual rights.

---

90. Following adoption of the Universal Declaration of Human Rights in 1948, the United Nations prepared these Covenants to transform Universal Declaration principles into treaty provisions to establish legal obligations on the part of the ratifying nation-states. The United Nations Assembly adopted the International Covenants on December 16, 1966. They were not to come into force, however, until they were ratified by thirty-five countries. The International Covenant on Economic Cultural and Social Rights came into force on January 3, 1966; the International Covenant on Civil and Political Rights became effective on March 23, 1976.

Nor have their philosophies met the test of time. The death of six million Jews and the creation of Israel is given by some as the turning point. Or perhaps it was the breakup of British India in 1947. It certainly is a post-World War II phenomenon. While it has not made Locke, Rousseau, and Jefferson obsolete, it has focused one's direction toward a growing realization of the importance of group rights in the developed world.

This is manifested in the multi-dimensional documents of the United Nations on colonialism, race, genocide, and so forth -- documents which are the modern guideposts for the new constitutions of the world, supplanting the American model.

Individual and Human Rights -- The Inherent Contradictions

There is an inherent contradiction between group rights and individual rights. This has disturbed everyone who has worked with these problems. A constitutional provision relating exclusively to minorities is necessarily discriminatory for it signals out one group for special treatment. A bill of rights or statement of fundamental rights should be applicable to minorities as well as *majorities.* As Ben Whitaker, Director of the London based *Minority Rights Group,* has said: "Some minorities are far from faultless . . . people do not become virtuous merely by reason of their predicament; and, of course, *majorities,* too, have their rights as well as their responsibilities." [91] Thus the formulation of such a document, in its emphasis upon freedom for all and an absence of any discrimination, necessarily avoids the granting of any special rights and privileges to any group.

It follows that any such document is thus devoted to individual rights. For if it gives cognizance to the rights of any particular group, be it women or Catholics or English-speaking members of the society, then there is no longer an absence of discrimination.

---

91. In *The Fourth World: Victims of Group Oppression,* London, 1972, Sidgwick and Jackson, pp. 10-11.

Differential Treatment is Discriminatory

This also involves the concept of equality. In one sense, equality means absolute identical treatment for members of minorities and groups and the members making up the majority population. The argument is then made that equality in law results in inequality in fact. Yet the goal may be the creation of an equality among peoples which has nothing to do with equality or equal treatment in law. It may be that the achievement of equality in fact may involve the necessity of unequal treatment. Such unequal treatment is advocated by many if its objective is equality, even if it involves racial or religious classifications. [92]

The movement from individual rights to group rights is reflected in America in changed attitudes towards constitutional phraseology. Where Americans preached the dictum that the constitution is colorblind, they now argue that the equal protection of the laws required them to be color-conscious.

A final thought: While I have taken the position that in problems of politics, nationalism, ethnicity, etc., group rights are more important than individual rights (and that the legal mechanisms of our society must recognize individual demands to act as members of groups) I do recognize the danger involved. Group rights recognition is by its very nature divisive. The giving of special rights and privileges to an enclave of the larger society emphasizes differences and fosters discrimination. It is often the case that the creation of separate religious or ethnic barriers may, in the long run, have a negative impact upon the group. The fact remains, however, that if individual rights continue to dominate in a plural society, stricken by group problems, the long term effect may be even more negative and harmful than under a policy where group rights dominate.

---

92. This position is treated excellently in depth in Ronald Dworkin: *Taking Rights Seriously,* Cambridge, Harvard University Press, 1978.

The Inherent Contradictions in International Practice

Numerous constitutions -- particularly those discussed in detail in Part III, "*National Patterns,*" -- attempt to guarantee both individual rights and group rights. On one hand, they proscribe discrimination; on the other hand, they grant certain group rights.

The only way one can argue that this is not contradictory is by taking the position that the Constitution only prohibits an *invidious* classification (by race, religion, language, ethnic culture, etc.) and recognizes and authorizes classifications which are designed to benefit minority groups within the society. That such benefit may be invidious to the majority is of no importance.

This is best illustrated by comparing and contrasting certain provisions of the Universal Declaration of Human Rights (1948) with the International Covenant on Civil and Political Rights (1976). Theoretically, these documents seek the same universal aim of the benefit of mankind and should be consistent.

The ultimate statements on individual rights are in Articles 1, 2, and 7 of the Universal Declaration. Because of their importance as statements of rights and because they are repeated in so many constitutions, they should be set forth in full at this point:

> Article 1. All human beings are born free and equal in dignity and rights. They are endowed with reason and conscience and should act towards one another in a spirit of brotherhood.
>
> Article 2. Everyone is entitled to all the rights and freedoms set forth in this Declaration, without distinction of any kind, such as race, colour, sex, language, religion, political or other opinion, national or social origin, property, birth or other status.
>
> Furthermore, no distinction shall be made on the basis of the political, jurisdictional or international status of the country or territory to which a person belongs, whether it be independent, trust, non-self-governing or under any

> other limitation of sovereignty.
>
> Article 7. All are equal before the law and are entitled without any discrimination to equal protection of the law. All are entitled to equal protection against any discrimination in violation of this Declaration and against any incitement to such discrimination.

This is repeated in similar words in Article 26 of the International Covenant:

> Article 26. All persons are equal before the law and are entitled without any discrimination to the equal protection of the law. In this respect, the law shall prohibit any discrimination and guarantee to all persons equal and effective protection against discrimination on any ground such as race, colour, sex, language, religion, political or other opinion, national or social origin, property, birth or other status.

But all of this is contradictory to Article 27 of the International Covenant which has become the basic statement for the protection of group rights. This reads:

> Article 27. In those States in which ethnic, religious or linguistic minorities exist, persons belonging to such minorities shall not be denied the right, in community with the other members of their group, to enjoy their own culture, to profess and practice their own religion, or to use their own language.

It is not enough to attempt to reconcile Article 27 with Article 26, and Articles 1, 2, and 7 of the Universal Declaration. There is also the problem of dealing with three other articles which, on their face, provide opportunity for still more contradictions.

Article 15(1) of the Universal Declaration provides that "Everyone has the right to a nationality." Is this the acknowledgement of a group right? And who is to recognize such right?

See also Article 1(1) of the International Covenant. This speaks in terms of "peoples" rather than "individuals." It provides: "All peoples have the right of self-determination. By virtue of that right they freely determine their political status and freely pursue their economic, social, and cultural development." In real world terms, this is nonsense. Tell that to the Kurds. Tell that to the Armenians. Ask the Estonians about what this paragraph means. And why does the world then react in horror when white South Africans, as much an African people as the whites in Australia are an Australian people, put this principle into practice? And is it consistent or does it have anything to do with Article 15(1) of the Universal Declaration granting everyone the right to a nationality?

If everyone has a right to a nationality, and if a group of "everyones" constitute a "people" who may freely determine their political status, where does that place the population of the black Republic of Transkei? A majority of the Xhosa people voted in secret ballot for their own nationhood in the Transkei, a Belgium-size area in South Africa which their forefathers settled 400 years ago and where their descendents have lived ever since. Should not this be encouraged by the world community? The answer appears to be no. The United Nations has denied recognition to the Transkei as a separate nation, based on the argument that it is merely another manifestation of South Africa's *apartheid* policy. Without having to take sides in this matter, it is clearly a situation which can be cited to point up a gross contradiction or evidence of anti-white racism on the part of the UN.

The specific contradiction and the possible manipulation of group rights in order to deny individual rights appears in the new UNESCO draft declaration on race and racial prejudice. [93] Article 5(1) is an amplification of Article 27 of the International Covenant encouraging group rights. But because it is so broad, it is immediately followed by sections qualifying these group rights in order to avert the possibility that group rights might have

93. SS-77/CONF. 201/1. Paris, August 18, 1977.

"invidious" results. Article 5 reads as follows:

Article 5

(1) Culture, as the production of all human beings and the common heritage of mankind, and education in its broadest sense, offer men and women increasingly effective means of adaptation, enabling them to affirm not only that they are born equal in dignity and in rights, but also that they must live on a footing of equality, fully recognizing the right of all groups to their own cultural identity and the development of their distinctive cultural life within the national and international context, it being understood that it rests with each group to decide in complete freedom on the maintenance and, if appropriate, the adaptation or enrichment of the values which it regards as essential to its identity.

(2) Governments, as well as all competent authorities and the teaching profession, must see that the educational resources of all countries are used to combat racialism, more especially by ensuring that curricula, textbooks and courses include scientific considerations concerning human unity and diversity and that no invidious distinctions are made with regard to particular peoples; by training teachers to achieve these ends; by making the resources of the educational system available to all groups of the population without restriction or discrimination; and by taking appropriate steps to remedy the handicaps from which certain groups suffer as regards their level of education and standard of living, and in particular, to prevent such handicaps from being passed on to children.

(3) The mass media and those who serve them should promote understanding, tolerance and friendship among individuals and groups and should contribute to the eradication of racialism, discrimination and racial prejudice, in particular by refraining from presenting a stereotyped,

partial, unilateral or tendentious picture of individuals and of various human groups. Communication between human groups must be a reciprocal process, enabling all groups to express themselves and to be fully heard without let or hindrance.

Further, to make sure that the promotion of group rights is not invidious, the Draft Declaration pointedly declares that "apartheid as practised in southern Arica, is a crime against humanity and constitutes a serious threat to international peace and security." This same approach, in more precise language, was taken by the International Commission of Jurists in its Statement of Principles concerning minority rights. [94]

The Commission agreed to the following statement of principles concerning minority rights:

> In this statement of principles the term "rights of minorities" refers to the rights of non-dominant groups. The gross violation of human rights involved in the domination of a people by a minority group, such as occurs in South Africa, Zimbabwe/Southern Rhodesia and Burundi has no place in the subject of minority rights.
>
> 1. The right of an ethnic minority to enjoy its own culture, of a religious minority to profess and practise its religion, and of a linguistic minority to use its language is now recognised in international law under Article 27 of the International Covenant of Civil and Political Rights. Serious or persistent violations of these rights are, therefore, a proper matter of international concern.
>
> 2. While the problems of minorities have certain common elements, the analysis of and solution to any particular minority issue must take into account the political, economic, geographical, social and historical context in which it arises.

---

94. *Journal of the International Commission of Jurists,* Vol. 18, June 1977.

3. Preservation of minority cultures is important to the happiness and well-being of the individuals who belong to the minorities and may contribute to the enrichment of the life of the nation as a whole.

4. Cultural diversity and the freedom of the individual are inter-related. Opportunities for free expression of minority languages, religions and cultures may contribute to the freedom of the individual.

5. The elimination of all forms of discrimination against minorities promotes social stability and economic development of the whole community.

6. An ethnic minority within a state has a right to a feasible opportunity to pursue its economic, social, and cultural development, subject to the interests of the whole community.

7. Any claim of a minority to autonomy within or secession from a state should be advanced by peaceful means, considered, and dealt with in accordance with the principles of international law.

8. Members of minorities who are citizens should enjoy the same rights and be subject to the same duties as other citizens without prejudice, however, to any special rights provided for their protection. Members of minorities who are residents but not citizens, including migrant workers, should as far as possible have the same rights and duties as citizens.

9. Lawyers have a responsibility to promote and implement measures which guarantee the equality of status and other rights of minorities.

10. Parallel to constitutional and legislative measures, there must be appropriate administrative action, especially in the field of education as indicated in the UNESCO Convention on Discrimination in Education of 1960, to make effective the enjoyment of minority rights.

11. As a general principle, minorities should benefit equitably from national expenditures for economic, social and cultural development. In some circumstances, they may require special programmes to promote their economic, social, and cultural development.

12. When disagreements arise out of a minority's economic, social and cultural claims and the interests of the whole state community, such conflicts should whenever possible, be settled by negotiation with the representatives of the minority.

13. Where minorities live or move across national boundaries, such as nomads, stateless persons, and refugees, the international co-ordination of policies towards them by the states concerned is desirable.

14. In a case where a public authority seriously or persistently violates a minority's rights, some international protection should be developed through existing or strengthened UN human rights machinery or otherwise. It is recommended that in such cases minorities should be given the opportunity to present their grievances before an impartial international forum, and that such a forum should be able where necessary, to investigate and to make recommendations.

The other provision of importance in this connection is Article 20(2) of the International Covenant. This states that "Any advocacy of national, racial, or religious hatred that constitutes incitement to discrimination, hostility or violence shall be prohibited by law." A dangerous provision in this! This makes it possible to condemn advocacy of group rights. For who is to say that such advocacy is or is not discriminatory, which may or may not result in hostility?

All of which brings one back to the role of constitutional safeguards in the protection and preservation of group rights. For I see it as a major objective of society to protect group rights. And my studies of constitutional dictates toward that goal have pointed up inadequacies of language and both the difficulties and dangers in attempting to solve such major problems with tools as weak as constitutional formulations.

CHAPTER XXIII

CONFILIATION OR CONDOMINIUM AS A STRUCTURE OF GOVERNMENT FOR A PLURAL SOCIETY AND THE INTEGRATION MODEL

I end the series of conclusions by stating that there are two types of societal arrangements which could afford maximum recognition of group rights, protect individual freedom and still maintain the unity and identity of the plural society in which those group and individual rights are recognized. One can be called *confiliation.* This is the brain child of Professors Albert Blaustein and J. Singler of the Law School at Rutgers University in the U.S.A.

The other is the principle of *condominium* and I would like to think of this as my own idea, based on current research but leaning heavily on certain principles of law and politics advanced by Professors Vernon van Dyke and Walker Connor, both of the U.S.A.

CONFILIATION:

A summary of Blaustein's concept of **confiliation** follows. [95]

Ethnic consciousness and ethnic identification are on the increase throughout the world. So is ethnic-oriented aggressiveness and aggression. And so is the determination (South Africa excepted) to oppose Balkanization -- to resist the break-up of existing nationalistic sovereignty to meet the demands of ethnicity.

If ethnic rights are to be recognized (and satisfied) within the boundaries of today's internationally recognized state entities,

95. Based on a memorandum submitted by Blaustein and Singler to the Prime Ministers of Israel and South Africa in 1977.

there must be compromise. And it must be in the form of a new type of governmental structure. A *confiliation.*

Under a confiliation, each ethnic "child" (Filiation is the fact of being a child of a certain parent) pursues its own cultural rights, with that "parent" (i.e., the central authority of the state) responsible for rights common to all. Each ethnic entity, for example, might choose to follow certain religious practices, or speak a particular language, or operate its own schools, or maintain customary courts, etc. The parent would be charged with national security, foreign affairs, etc.

A confiliation is not merely a federation on a geographic foundation. It is a new constitutional form which recognizes the human dimension of government by preserving the rights of groups to be different while remaining part of the common union.

Other scholars, groping for adequate terms to explain constitutional forms designed to preserve group rights, have added a variety of new words and phrases to law and political science lexicons. Such terms as "segmented pluralism," "consociational democracy" and "subcultural segmentation" have now been invented. But none of these really explain either the form or process of recognizing the rights or accommodating the demands of divergent groups within a particular society.

Ethnic rights are group rights. For the most part they are also minority rights. They are rights based on race, religion, language and culture. And to the people concerned with such rights they are far more pervasive and more important than the rights to a public trial or even freedom of the press, according to Blaustein. They are rights too fundamental (and too precious) to be determined by majority rule. Language and religion cannot be subject to majoritarian determination.

"The right of everyone . . . to take part in cultural life" is guaranteed by Article 15 of the International Covenant on Economic, Social and Cultural Rights.

This is largely foreign to American thought, history and practices. "Ours," Blaustein argued, "is a *federal* system (meaning the U.S.A.) based both on geographical and historical accidents, and upon the failures of the governmental structure predicated on Articles of Confederation." And during the great schism of 1861-65, the seceding states organized as the Confederate States of America.

The important fact about the American federation, however, is that it was **not** based on ethnic divisions. The original boundaries of the thirteen states were primarily historical (only slightly cultural) and not lines of demarcation between ethnic entities. True, Maryland was unique in being settled by Catholics, but the borders of that state were not decided on a religious basis or on religious bias.

Of course, the U.S. has some recognition of ethnicity. For example, there is the First Amendment, providing that "Congress shall make no law respecting an establishment of religion or prohibiting the free exercise thereof." (What a watered-down right that is -- according to the thinking of religious entities in most nations! The First Amendment does not permit the American Moslem husband to have more than one wife; it does not authorize rabbinical courts to divorce Jewish couples; it does not give separate religious (or non-religious) entities authority to make their own rules on abortion; it does not permit each group to run its own schools without government interference.)

Where the ethnic entity occupies a specific geographical area, Blaustein argued, it is not difficult to devise a governmental structure to accommodate ethnic rights. Belgium is an excellent example. Article 3b of its constitution provides that "Belgium comprises four linguistic regions" and Article 3c provides that Belgium comprises three cultural communities. Appendix 1 of the constitution calls for splitting the members of the Lower House into a French linguistic group and a Dutch linguistic group, each with legislative powers over its own group. Its constitution also provides for equal representation of the two language groups in the cabinet.

For this type of union -- of virtual co-equal, area-identified ethnic entities -- Netherlands political scientist Professor Arend Lijphart has coined the term *consociation.* But this implies a granting of powers from each consociation member to the central authority, rather than a granting (or permitting) of ethnic rights from the parent to the children of the confiliation.

Article 27 of the International Covenant on Civil and Political Rights emphasizes the importance of ethnic rights. "In those states in which ethnic, religious or linguistic minorities exist, persons belonging to such minorities shall not be denied the right, in community with the other members of their group, to enjoy their own culture, to profess and practice their own religion, or to use their own language."

But to give effect to such a manifesto requires the recognition and establishment of more confiliations.

According to Blaustein, one can apply the confiliation concept to the rights of Palestinian Arabs, to the rights of Jews in the Egyptian Sinai, to the white minority in Zimbabwe, to South African blacks both in and out of the so-called Homelands, to French-speaking Canadians who do not live in Quebec, to the Kurds in Iraq, to the Asian Indians in Guyana and Fiji, to the ethnic Chinese in Thailand and Vietnam, to all the diverse peoples of Indonesia, to Moslems in the two-dozen countries where they constitute a substantial minority, to Jews in the Soviet Union, to Armenians, Estonians, Latvians, Lithuanians, etc., etc., in the Soviet Union, to gypsies, and to the rights of every other ethnic minority every place.

This type of institutional arrangement, of course, is not applicable in the separate homogeneous society. Nor does it serve the melting pot or integrationist state. It is applicable to multi-ethnic plural states, particularly those which can no longer be geographically divided on the basis of group rights, e.g. South Africa, Zimbabwe, Namibia, Israel. It is an institutional arrangement consistent with and in the spirit of Article 27 of the International Covenant.

Those who would argue against Blaustein's confiliation might find words of criticism phrased in terms of neo-colonialism, extra-territorality, or settlers' rights. This would be unfair. Consistent with the principles of individual rights and consistent with a sense of international morality, this confiliation plan is designed to afford maximum accommodation between and among the various groups comprising any type of plural society.

CONDOMINIUM:

The *concept of Condominium,* which I advocate for multi-national, multi-racial, multi-ethnic i.e. plural societies is based on the principle that racial groups, communities, ethnic groups, which find themselves within one state boundary, not from own choice, but becaue of the forces of history, i.e. war, colonialism, conquest, the re-drawing of international boundaries, have a irreducible right to exist as a unit and that this unit, or group, have both moral and legal rights to a future existence. By employing constitutional *and* legal powers a state, already independent, can build a condominium for its various groups or units which would neutralise the forces of nationalism while promoting ethnic and national cohesion.

By condominium I am not referring to the principle of Roman i.e. common ownership by two or more persons holding undivided fractional shares in the same property and having the right to alienate their shares resembling tenancy in common in Anglo American Law rather than joint tenancy with its rights of survivorship, but the principle of individual ownership of a unit in a multi-unit structure. If this principle is applied as a concept of political science it can be translated to read as follows: the country is the structure. It is composed (constructed) of various blocs or units i.e.

races, ethnic communities or other groups. Each unit has a moral and legal right to continued existence. Each unit "owns" such rights as the use of their own language, educational and legal system, religion, local and provincial government, etc.

In the condominium structure, comparable to a large apartment block, each tenant (group) enjoys ownership of his unit and can do what he wants inside this unit. Outside the unit he shares the elevators, the gardens, the sports amenities, the services available in the basement such as washing and drying, communal parking, the telephone system, the nightwatchmen and doormen. Each tenant i.e. unit, contributes financially to the upkeep of the structure and joint services and amenities proportionally to the size of his unit and the number of inhabitants.

The structure is rigid, as a rigid constitution, so that the majority of the tenants (units) cannot deprive the individual unit (group) of any of his fundamental rights, e.g. the right to do and say what he wants in his own unit, including the right of association and friendship and the right to refuse any other tenant admission to his territory (unit) for whatever reason. However, *outside* his apartment (unit), in the *common areas* of the condominium, the parking areas, the elevators, the basement, the lounge and surrounding parks, he shares on an equal basis with all other tenants.

Translated into political reality and projected onto e.g. the South African scene this would provide the white people with rigid protection is so far as their language, customs, culture, schools, residential areas and ways of life is concerned, but not on the basis of colour. *Ipso facto* the Zulu, Xhosa, Tswana and other black peoples will enjoy the same protection, as would the Asian and the Coloured communities. Each group will have the right to equal use of such common facilities as transportation, shopping, the marketing of their labour, the benefits of a free market economy, etc. No group will be able to tell any other group what sort of educational system he should follow nor what its religious preferences should be.

The constitution (the rules governing life in the condominium) protects the larger and smaller groups in equal degree and it defines the fundamental rights of all groups (units). Such a constitutional arrangement would eliminate the possibility of any single race, group, religious, community or people dominating any other group.

Should one group gain economic sway there could be no objection since it would occur in a free market economy under conditions of equality. No group will be able to gain superiority simply because of numerical superiority.

There will be, of necessity and in terms of the constitution, joint decision taking on foreign policy, defence and the monetary system. This joint decision taking mechanism can be compared to the management committee of the condominium elected by the various units (tenants).

Although this model has been presented in very simplistic terms it evidently is not a federal structure. It is also not a blend of the Swiss cantonal system and what Professor Arend Lijphart has termed consociation. It is a restructuring of society, both in terms of territory occupied by each group and representation in the management committee (central government) of the condominium, protected by a constitution which is rigid in respect of both group rights and fundamental individual freedoms.

Decisions on matters of common concern, naturally, can only be taken by a body representing all groups i.e. *the entire community*. (In Europe the European Economic Community, the European Parliament and the European Court of Justice is slowly showing the various nations of Europe how it could be done.) Ideally speaking, such a central body or Parliament, should not consist of individual politicians representing a political party or a particular constituency but of *delegations* consisting of experts in various fields, e.g. finance, economics, defence, foreign affairs, power and transportation, etc., *representing* each *group* or *unit.*

On a lower level regional councils would enact rules and regulations for each group e.g. health, housing, education, etc., and should be elected on a one-man one-vote basis for as many constituencies as each group may care to have in its area.

The constitution would forbid the upper, central body, the Southern African Assembly of specialist delegates, to intervene into or make laws which affect the fundamental, constitutionally enshrined rights of each group. Moreover, as protection against tampering with the Constitution, the judiciary should be wholly independent i.e. consist solely of persons appointed by an *elected* supervisory agency representing the legal profession. Only advocates, judges, lawyers or individuals with recognised university law degrees would be able to vote for this agency. In no way should it be possible for the central Parliament or administration, or any other body, to influence the judiciary. (At the moment, in many countries, the Minister of Justice, a politician representing a particular party, is the boss of civil servants who act as attorney-generals, magistrates, etc.) The central or upper Parliament should merely vote a round figure every year for use by the independent judiciary agency who would pay out the salaries to judges or prosecutors and who would administer court procedures, prosecution, defence, judgment and appeal. In short, put justice into the hands of a neutral organization who owe the central government or any political party nothing.

In such a *totally independent legal system* interpretation of laws or regulations of the central or regional representative bodies are guaranteed to be just and fair, so would the judicial interpretation of the constitutionally enshrined rights of groups and individuals. If, in addition, the constitution of such a state (which would embody the legal independence of the judiciary) were to be recognised by say, the permanent members of the UN Security Council and guaranteed by the big five of the West, fundamental group rights would be doubly secured. Any government or party who tampers with the constitution runs the risk of affronting the major guaranteeing powers and a break in diplomatic relations.

Because of freedom of association provided for by the Constitution a dominating influence can only be realised by any one unit in the national political arena if the members of that unit (group) evolves such an attractive and near-utopian open society that all the others would willingly forsake their customs, language, tradition and aspirations to become a member of this particular group. Again, because of the constitutional provision of "freedom of association," the more attractive unit can reject applicants, should it wish to do so. A pattern of group acceptance is not visible in world history of the past 30 years, on the contrary. Instead of becoming more unified, mankind is dividing into more and more autonomous units and groups. UN membership *trebled* between 1945-1975. It would thus be running contrary to current world history if such a movement towards acceptance of integration were to develop **only** in South Africa. In fact, the multi-ethnic form is becoming increasingly common within each nation. [96]

Of course, the practical implementation of the principle of condominium has many pitfalls and there are many uncertainties. But it does not begin to compare, in a country such as South Africa, with the pitfalls of the melting pot, i.e. indiscriminate social, cultural and political integration, based on the principle of one-man one-vote, and a constitution similar to that of, for example, the U.S.A.

As Professor Glaser and Possony have pointed out: "It is easy to agree that barriers between races and racial divisions are undesirable . . . but it does not follow that integration would remove the trouble. The United Nations has never issued a rationale explaining why human rights are better protected by integrationist multi-racial organizations and movements than by

96. Glazer, Nathan: "Ethnicity: A World Phenomenon," in *Dialogue,* United States Information Service, Washington, Vol. 8, 1975, No. 3/4, p. 45.

those representing the interest of specific groups.[97] In 1975 I outlined the pitfalls of a policy of political integration between Black and White for South Africa as follows:

> **THE INTEGRATION MODEL**
>
> The alternative to multinational development most often proposed is the socio-political integration of all peoples in South Africa. Whether the programme of change envisaged is a short-term one, as advocated by the majority of African states normally on the basis of one-man one-vote, popularly known as 'majority rule' or a long-term one, in which not colour but only *merit* would be the basis of political rights, the vision is of a situation in which (ultimately) all people in South Africa will merely be interchangeable units, suddenly shorn of all race, historical and ethnic consciousness, and assimilable in a new common culture with a common group loyalty.
>
> For an evaluation of the alternative of integration, a restatement of four basic considerations is necessary:
>
> **Firstly:** In spite of the post-war migratory surge to the cities and the impact of Western influences on Black culture, the South African population is not homogeneous. According to the standards applied by the first UN conference on the multinational society (Yugoslavia in 1965) South Africa is definitely a multinational and plural society composed of disparate peoples, of whom the Zulu, Xhosa, Whites, Coloureds (of mixed descent), the Tswana and the two Sotho groups are the major components.
>
> **Secondly:** It bears repeating that historically not one of the major (or lesser) groups has an exclusive or prior claim to *all* of South Africa but each group has a moral, historical, legal and constitutional claim to at least a *part* of the country.

97. *Victims of Politics,* op. cit., p. 24.

Thirdly: The White nation cannot return to a European fatherland in the same way as, for example, the Dutch returned to the Netherlands after the independence of Indonesia. After 320 years they know only one homeland, the RSA, and the language used by the majority of Whites (Afrikaans) evolved in Africa, not in Europe. Historically the White South African nation's origins are older than those of the White nations of Australia and New Zealand and about as old as those of the American nation.

Fourthly: The various nations find themselves within the borders of one country, not by choice but as a legacy of British imperialism which turned this part of Africa into one multinational state, where previously separate Kingdoms (Zulu, Xhosa, etc.) and separate republics had existed e.g. the Orange Free State and the *Zuid Afrikaanse Republiek.*

In the light of the foregoing realities, which any responsible administration must perforce take into consideration, the one-man one-vote integration model has been rejected by the white nation for the following specific reasons:

1. The policy of political integration of White and Black and of one-man one-vote -- especially a system based on voting rights according to merit -- has been rejected by virtually every Black African state. Of a general franchise such as is enjoyed by people in Britain, France or West Germany, virtually nothing has remained in Africa. And there is no reason to suppose that the Black majority of South Africa would act differently once they attain power.

The White nation, on the other hand, has had a democratically elected Parliament since 1910, with an independent judiciary, a civil service based on the British model and a relatively free press. Most of the governments of South Africa of the past 60 years could have been unseated by a ten percent swing in the popular vote, and sometimes by as little as a one percent swing.

Socialist Africal political systems are incompatible with those of the Western-oriented White South African nation.

2. The integration model is totally unacceptable to almost the entire White nation. This fact cannot be wished away, nor can the fact that they wield the political and economic power and are numerically the second strongest nation in South Africa after the Zulu.

3. The concept of 'merit' as a basis for the integration model is severely discredited in South Africa for purely practical reasons. The Central African Federation (formerly Northern Rhodesia, Southern Rhodesia and Nyasaland) was established in the early 1950s with a multiracial parliamentary vote along the lines advocated for South Africa by the Afro-Asian world and a considerable number of Western states. South Africa was an interested and close witness of the complete collapse of this model of racial partnership. The reasons for the collapse of the Federation are those that would wreck racial partnership and integration in South Africa -- Black and White consciousness, White and Black nationalism, incompatible socio-cultural systems, the threat to minorities, Black demands for self-determination, for the retention of their own identity, for opportunities to make their own mistakes and achieve their own victories in their own way.

4. Why should the Zulu, Xhosa, Tswana and other Black nations in South Africa be expected to settle for less, or to share political power with other groups in South Africa? Would they, after integration, react any differently to political frustration than their kinsmen in the now defunct Central African Federation?

5. The integration model will run up against serious language, religious and legal problems. Serious clashes have occurred in several countries on the question of language, for example, in Sri Lanka and Belgium. Despite a largely

homogeneous society, Ireland inhabited only by Irishmen, is still a divided land because of religious differences. In view of this, South Africa, with its many disparate peoples, different races, historical lineages and languages would probably be the last place in the world where an integration model would succeed. In addition, the cultural differences involved are staggering, a gap that makes meaningful communication virtually impossible.

6. If history has any meaning, mankind's entire past must be taken as a warning against attempts to force integration upon peoples and races in the country. Never in history has any people *voluntarily* sacrificed their language, customs, culture, standard of living, legal, constitutional and historical rights for the sake of an ideology that has nowhere been applied with any appreciable success in societies segmented by deep social and racial differences. No other people or nation has ever made, or will ever make, such a voluntary sacrifice in similar or even related conditions.

7. The factor of *realpolitik*. Sweden, Norway, Denmark, and Finland once constituted one country -- four peoples of the same colour, same standard of development and socio-cultural background. Yet they found it expedient to separate and the world accepted this division of a relatively homogeneous subcontinent. A more recent example is Singapore opting out of the Malaysian Federation because of ethnic differences. And Germany? The world is not prepared to prescribe that East and West Germany -- one nation until the Second World War -- should integrate. On the contrary, the world has accepted two sovereign Germanies.

8. The UN defines *genocide* as the purposeful elimination or destruction of clearly different racial religious, or cultural groups. Integration must surely lead to the disappearance, rapidly or gradually, of many of South Africa's distinctive

groups, including the white peoples whose roots in Africa go back to 1652 and who are so much part of Africa that the majority speak *Afrikaans,* the only Indo-Germanic language to have originated outside Europe.

9. A major obstacle to the successful implementation of the integration model in South Africa is the question of land. Currently, the Black man's territories are protected by law. Land may not be purchased there by White men. In the Black homelands, White men may not set up any business on a permanent basis. Integration implies that anyone should be able to buy land anywhere at the going price, and set up business and industry where it pays him to do so. Because of the (current) superior economic power and entrepreneurial skill of the White nation, the Asians and the Coloured community, the chances are that within a quarter century there will be no independent Black farmers or landowners to speak of.

10. Deliberate integration on the social and geo-political levels has had major setbacks in practically all plurally structured countries of the world. For example, the influx of non-Whites into traditionally White areas in Europe has led governments and societies to react in a way hardly encouraging to the protagonists of the integration model. The pattern of human relations in South Africa is much more difficult and complex and these setbacks in other countries with less intractable problems are bound to have a negative impact on South Africans, rendering successful implementation of the integration model virtually impossible.

11. The integration model implies the negation of the role of physical (racial) differences in human and group relations. In fact, integration could only have a reasonable chance of success if pronounced physical differences did not matter at all. It is one thing to argue that these

differences *should* not affect social behaviour (and I personally agree that in theory these differences ought not to play a role), but it is quite another thing to ignore the *fact* that they *do* play a very important role in determining group relations, not only in South Africa, but anywhere in the world.

12. It is the *current*, not the unborn, generation which needs to be convinced of the direction of policy, the short-term effects and the ultimate pattern of intergroup relations. It would be totally unrealistic to expect (only) South Africans to ignore the socio-political realities of our day and blindly introduce norms which may acquire some validity several generations from now. To succeed, the integration model would have to recast social behaviour into an idealistic mould, i.e. apply the norms of an idealised and untested future to existing socio-political realities. For integration to be accepted, the current attitudes of South Africans would have to be drastically altered. This might be possible in the case of thousands, perhaps hundreds of thousands; the remaining millions cannot be washed away.

13. Integration would violate the time-honoured right of a nation to determine which elements it is prepared to assimilate. There is no record among civilised peoples of a single treaty, charter or concord comprising a directive to any nation or ethnic group as to what its basic cultural and genetic composition and structure should be. (It is intelectually dishonest for scholars in the United States to suggest that political and economic pressure be brought to bear on white and black in South Africa to integrate, but not to do so in the case of other countries with multi-racial and multi-ethnic communities eg. Burundi, Lebanon, Cyprus, Fiji, New Zealand and others.

Bringing pressure to bear on a people to assimilate basically disparate elements, simply to serve the interest of *other* parties, is patently immoral and contrary to the fundamental tenets of civilised international relations.

14. An unqualified (democratic) dispensation, implying one-man one-vote for the whole of South Africa, would simply mean that sheer weight of numbers would determine the way of life and system of values of the country. Thus one-man one-vote would mean the end of the White nation culturally and politically. Furthermore, while the Whites accept it as perfectly legitimate for each Black group to introduce a one-man one-vote system within its own ethno-national sphere of influence, such a dispensation for the whole of South Africa would destroy the White nation's distinctive political organisation and way of life. This the Whites would naturally resist, and any policy that does not take this basic fact into account is doomed to failure.

15. Those who perceive in selective integration a means to racial peace, lose sight of the fact that in Africa the trend has always been for Black majorities to exploit selective integration for the furtherance of their own group interest. After the achievement of majority rule, previous guarantees of democratic government and equality are almost invariably jettisoned in favour of Black totalitarianism. (Witness the trend in Zimbabwe where even Black political opposition is no longer tolerated and the Whites have become a terrified impotent minority.).

16. Not one of the prerequisites for successful integration exists in South Africa. For instance, there is not even a remote possibility of a permanent Black-White numerical parity and any constitutional system based on political parity would be scrapped as soon as the Blacks become the political majority.

17. The purely theoretical objectives of the integration model cannot be achieved in South Africa. Human dignity

> has become the central cry in the crusade to persuade South Africa to abandon its policy of separate ethnic development in favour of integration. Multinational development, it is alleged, is an affront to human dignity and its aims an assault on human values. The Whites reject this view. They believe that human dignity in a multinational society can be achieved only when each group has attained self-determination. Within his own group each individual may then achieve his own success or make his own mistake, but *never* at the expense of other groups. Human equality does not imply ethnic equality in terms of socio-economic, technological and political development. There can be no disputing the fact that there is none of this type of equality between, for instance, the Swedes and the Kalahari Bushmen. In an ethnically heterogeneous population, majority rule, which for the proponents of integration is synonymous with human dignity, would mean that a minority group would have to change its customs and abandon its culture and vested political interests in order to accommodate the culture, life-style and political needs of a purely numerically determined majority group. [98]

In the ten years which have elapsed since I wrote the foregoing little has happened to change my mind. The Germans and the French are no closer to becoming one nation in Europe. The Dutch still prefer their own language and their own Queen in their own country. They have made no attempt to turn the Benelux countries (Belgium, Luxumbourg en the Netherlands) into one bigger and stronger state. The Scandinavian Peninsula still maintains the separate states of Sweden and Norway. No one has advocated a policy to get rid of the borders between the U.S. and Canada and between the U.S. and Mexico to establish a North American state. The reasons are obvious. The Germans, Belgians and Dutch are

---

98. Cf. *Multi-National Development in South Africa: The Reality,* Department of Information, Pretoria, pp. 76-82.

different nations. So are the Mexicans and Armenians. The black Zulu and Xhosa nations in South Africa are as much nations, culturally and linguistically as the Germans and the French. As nations they are as much different from the White nation, with its own history, culture, religion and language, than the Germans are from the Dutch. The average white Afrikaner and the average Black Zulu are at least as different from each other as the average Mexican from the average American or the average Swede from the average Norwegian.

On the other hand, much has happened elsewhere in the world the past decade, in the Lebanon, India, Cambodia, Cyprus, the Sudan and the Philippines to prove that for white South Africa to jump into the melting pot with the other nations and races in South Africa will result in the whites becoming, in record time, the most popular corpse on the international scene.

I am personally in favour of the new 1984 South African constitution because it improves the political bargaining power of the Indians and the Coloureds, provides them with basic political rights which they did not previously enjoy, and because a close political and economic association between Whites, Coloureds and Indians makes practical political sense. All three are capitalistic, pro-Western and share the two common languages, Afrikaans and English. I am therefore wholly in favour of Coloureds, Indians and Whites sitting in the same Parliament and in the same Cabinet deciding matters of mutual concern such as defence, taxation, foreign policy, transporation, etc. I am wholly in favour of a system which provides each group with equal economic opportunity, sharing the same universities, the same residential areas. My considerations are logically not rooted in racialism, only in what is politically realistic, practical and fair. But when it comes to the various Black nations and the White nation, my view is that even if the Zulu, Tswana and Xhosa had been white, only a separate political dispensation would work if the differences between the White Zulu and the White South African nation is as great as it is today. Call the Zulu the Germans, call the Tswana the Dutch, call the Xhosa the French and you will understand why integration or even political power sharing between the white group and the various black groups is not something which can be achieved by constitutional or any other political means, just as a European Parliament for the French, Germans and Dutch, elected on a one-man one-vote basis is a non-starter.

If some super-power were to draw a line around Europe and impose upon it a constitution of one-man one-vote, it will not work because within that one state the Germans would still be Germans and the Dutch still be Dutch. A thousand years of close proximity have not produced integration in Europe. On the contrary, it has produced political segregation, separate states for its different peoples. And this was without the aggravating factor of racial differences. Some 3,000 killed and 12,000 wounded in Northern Ireland have not brought a unified Ireland closer than it was 50 years ago. What if the Catholics had been black and the Protestants white?

The crux of the matter is that the alternative to the policy of separate ethno-national development must necessarily be *arbitrary* and *artificial* integration. The negative consequences of integration will outweigh those of the current policy. The chances of chaos are infinitely greater. The built-in obstacles to the success of integration are far greater than those in the way of multinational development which recognises realities, such as *natural* divisions among peoples, the role of *historical* forces in group formation, and existing geopolitical arrangements. What is of crucial importance is that once introduced, the integration model cannot be unscrambled, whereas multinational development leaves each ethno-national group the option to negotiate a federal or confederal type of relationship with other groups, provided, of course, the parties will be able to negotiate on equal political terms and not as an impotent minority, as would be the case in an integration system.

I am not applauding the current government policy of South Africa, which is sadly lacking in many respects, paying lip service to its theoretical objectives, too often is implemented in callous, inhumane fashion, and seem unable to distinguish between *race* and *nation*. Thus it would gain credibility if visiting citizens of independent black states were treated like visiting citizens from a white state. No, I am not applauding the South African model of separate development, but what it *could* and *should* be.

Many scholars accept it as axiomatic that the entire black population of South Africa, Coloureds and Indians included would voluntarily and eagerly opt for a one-man one-vote integrated political system for South Africa. Such an assumption is not only wishful thinking but unscientific, moreover, it is racialistic for it presupposes that everyone in South Africa who is not white is automatically black, or considers himself part of the so-called black conscious community. There are black groups in South Africa who hate each other more than they dislike the whites and who are so different that they cannot communicate in the same language. The South African problem is not a clear cut issue between whites and blacks. There are factual and logical reasons for not blindly assuming that all non-whites would go along with an integrated political system. The same reasons for not assuming that the Turkish and Greek community on Cyprus are clamouring for a one-man one-vote situation or that the Druze and Christians in Lebanon, despite a common language and racial characteristics, are eager to embrace each other at the thought of a one-man one-vote solution. Some of the facts and reasons why the non-white community in South Africa may act differently than generally expected when it comes down to a final decision are the following:

1. Integration may be rejected by the smaller Black ethnic groups, because in such a system they will be entirely at the mercy of the numerically stronger Black groups. Only a few generations ago the forefathers of many of the

lesser Black peoples were decimated by, for example, the Zulu and Matabele armies. Individuals may be prepared to accept integration, the communities as a whole certainly are not. If the Matabele in Zimbabwe had known how the Shona leadership of Mr. Robert Mugabe would act after independence they may have thought twice about the new constitution for Zimbabwe.

2. The policy of integration, where tested, was not even acceptable to the masses of the major Black nations. In the 1973 general election in Transkei (one of the homelands of the Xhosa) some 60 percent of the voters cast their secret ballot in favour of the party which supported multinational development i.e. a separate state. In the 1972 Bophuthatswana general election, the first for the Tswana-speaking nation, the party which then supported multinational development received more than 71 percent of the popular vote. While some leaders of the major Black groups may espouse integration, the majority prefer multinational development. A referendum among each group would be necessary to ascertain current attitudes.

3. The integration model will ultimately be rejected by the majority of the 800,000 Indians who are by far the largest Asian community in Africa. The Indians in South Africa enjoy a higher per capita income than any other Asian community in the world. They enjoy religious freedom, participate vigorously in a free-enterprise economy, have a multimillion rand university (the only wholly Indian university outside India) and, unlike in East Africa, are accepted as a permanent segment of the South African population. The mass expulsion of Indians from East Africa and Burma is unlikely to persuade the Indians of South Africa to put themselves at the mercy of a vast Black majority in an integrated South Africa, particularly since current policy protects their languages, customs and

identity. They are capitalist oriented as opposed to African socialism. In a one-man one-vote situation they can only lose.

4. The remaining minority group in South Africa, the two-million strong Coloured (of mixed descent) people have indicated that they may opt for a separate existence, closer to the whites and distinct from the Black groups. It is true that many groups and individual Coloured leaders have advocated closer association with the Black man to form a *Black* (racial) front, but this is probably not the objective of the average Coloured voter. In a major scientific survey conducted by the University of Pretoria in 1972, it was revealed that more than 96 percent of the educated Coloured community in Johannesburg declined to be thought of or described as 'Blacks.' Only a referendum among Coloured voters would reveal if their attitude has changed.

The overriding problem in South Africa is the total dissatisfaction of other racial groups with a dispensation, (no matter how politically logical or historically rooted) decided upon *only* by one group, the Whites. No system has any chance *of lasting* success in plural South Africa unless *all* the groups have a say in what the national socio-political structure ought to be. If a restructuring is to take place, or major constitutional changes are introduced, or a new constitution prepared, *group concensus* is a pre-requisite. Similarly, neither confiliation or the structure of condominium can be achieved without group concensus.

Mention group concensus to the average white politician in South Africa and he has visions of unacceptable power sharing. The terminology is grossly misunderstood. The 1983 referendum to change the constitution of South Africa to bring in an executive president and to allow for Coloureds and Indians to share in the South African Parliamentary system obtained the votes of more than two thirds of the white electorate. But it is not group concensus. There are many ways by which the country can ascertain who the leaders of the various groups are, through an electoral process or other means of counting heads. The first objective would be to identify the leadership. Thereafter delegations from the various groups can meet in consultation and eventually in a constitutional conference

As from 1984 the Coloureds, Indians and Whites are going to be locked in matters requiring group concensus. It remains for the country to get the Black leadership to meet with Whites, Coloureds and Indians as well. Only the intellectually dishonest in South Africa will maintain that the Black people in the White part of South Africa, i.e. living permanently outside their homelands, particularly those homelands which have not sought independence, can be ignored as a political force. The Black people outside the homelands already outnumber the Whites, Indians and Coloureds. But they are not a homogeneous black mass with a common loyalty or a single culture or language. They constitute clearly identifiable groups. These groups, people who are not voters in the black homelands or voters in white South Africa, are the groups who need to be present at any occasion where concensus is sought for future constitutional and political development.

The already independent black states such as Ciskei, Transkei, Bophuthatswana and Venda fall in a completely different category. As independent states, at least in the eyes of the South African government, they would only be present at discussions where Southern African regional affairs are discussed eg. intra-national waterways, soil conservation, customs, postal, rail and air communications, etc. South Africa has already provided for such a forum and such talks have already taken place including the establishment of a Bank for Southern African Development. The apparatus for concensus across national state lines therefore exists. What is non-existent are realistic plans to achieve concensus on the future of the Black groups remaining within the borders of the state now to be run by Whites, Indians and Coloureds.

Conferences on constitutional change are nothing new to South Africa and has only brought greater understanding between groups and individuals. Such a conference was held in 1972 at Jan Smuts House under the auspices of the South African Institute of International Affairs and the findings were later published by MacMillans in London under the title: *Accelerated Development in Southern Africa.* In 1978 the University of Natal hosted other another conference to consider alternative constitutional models for South Africa. The University of Natal Press in 1978 published the findings and discussions under the title: *Constitutional Change in South Africa,* edited by John E. Benyon. In 1977 the Institute for Plural Societies of the University of Pretoria hosted a conference on intergroup accommodation, the biggest international conference of its kind ever held in South Africa. The proceedings were published by MacMillans in London under the title: *Intergroup Accomodation in Plural Societies.* This was followed up the next year by a similar conference in New York and the proceedings were published in 1980 under the title: *Conflict Regulation in Southern Africa,* edited by Professor N.J. Rhoodie.

All the foregoing (and other) conferences were multi-racial and some were attended by experts from all over Asia, Africa, Europe, the U.S.A. and Asia. But what is yet to take place is an official conference on inter-group accommodation arranged by the government for the various groups in South Africa to begin searching for concensus on group rights and constitutional accommodation within the borders of South Africa. No one expects wonders from such a first meeting, but a beginning has to be made and much as one can applaud the academic conferences which I have listed above, a conference under the auspices of the State President's office, remains a *sine qua non* for future peace in South Africa.

CHAPTER XXIV

THE DYNAMICS OF GROUP BEHAVIOUR AND INDIVIDUAL RIGHTS IN POLITICS

Understanding the concept of *Condominium* or *Confiliation* depends upon a real grasp of (i) the dynamics of group behaviour and (ii) the relationship between ethnic communities, groups and individual rights in politics.

In the case of the first this can be achieved by studying, recognising and accepting the simple facts of such behaviour. In the case of the second, there is also a welter of facts but the relationship between the state, the individual and ethnic communities is at the moment still only at the state of political theory, at least in a great many countries of the world. Nonetheless political theory is the starting point of highways which often end in political wisdom and, finally, political implementation.

[i] The Dynamics of Group Behaviour

A society without groups is, practically speaking, virtually non-existent in today's world. It remains, of course, conceivable in theory, such as in Rousseau's *Social Contract* or Aldous Huxley's *Brave New World.* The facts are that in every state of the world today, even in homogeneous Sweden or Norway, there are functional groups, e.g. a parents teachers association and what Glaser and Possony termed total groups, whose doctrines or essences tend to define, shape and limit the personalities of their members, e.g. a religious group. [99]

---

99. *Victims of Politics,* op. cit., p. 49. Cf. Glazer, Nathan: in *Dialogue,* op. cit., p. 36.

In international society nations are groups. Within the nation, for example, the Soviet Union, one can have several different, but homogeneous groups called nationalities. Within those nationalities there can be ethnic groups such as in Spain with the Basque. In a few countries or nations, you may even find nationalities subdivided again by ethnic communities within the border of one state, for example in South Africa with its white nation, divided into Afrikaans and English speaking ethnic communities, its Zulu, Xhosa and Tswana speaking nationalities. In addition, or to complicate matters even more, the different groups belong to different races speaking different languages.

Groups exist because of group interests and preferences, group alliance and identification and the simple human propensity to discriminate. According to Glaser and Possony, the characteristics of groups can be labeled under five main categories: citizenship (people who were born in and owe allegiance to and enjoy the protection of a particular state), racial groups, which requires little explanation, ethnic groups (people who spontaneously identify themselves in terms of ethnic character, language, customs, culture, values, rather than membership in a political state) social and economic classes and, finally, castes. [100]

Of all the factors ethnicity, ethnic diversity, is perhaps the most important.

Of the 157 states whose constitutions I have examined, only 9.1 percent are homogeneous from an ethnic point of view. In more than 63 states the population is divided into five or more significantly differently ethnic communities. In a study on the influence of ethnicity Walter Connor concluded: "The preponderant number of states are multi-ethnic. Ethnic consciousness has been definitely increasing, not decreasing in recent years." [101] As Nathan Glazer also observed: "Ethnicity seems to have become a permanent force in the modern world." [102]

100. Glaser and Possony, op. cit., pp. 65-78.

101. *World Politics,* Vol. 34, No. 3.

102. Glazer, Nathan: op. cit., p. 45. Cf. Rhoodie, Nic: op. cit., pp. 2-7.

Wherever different groups live within the borders of one certain state one finds a universality of group behaviour. The groups reflect a consciousness of kind i.e. identity, revel in their sense of historicity, they openly indicate the primacy of self-interest and claim self-determination and the right to perpetuation of the group. Where groups live in the same state or country, they also reveal typical behaviour patterns in their relation with the other groups. Apart from being ethno-centric they reveal distinct prejudices while almost every group shows a distinction between the in-group and the out-group. In speaking of the other group stereotypes are used. Finally discrimination takes place. [103] Ethnic groups in dominant majority societies generally tend not to co-operate with each other eg. Ulster, Cyprus, etc. [104]

Equality today remains a very utopian concept and this is basically because the weight of ethnicity and the necessity of recognising the rights and aspirations of groups are too often neglected by politicians. As Glaser and Possony quite rightly stated: "It would take a very naive utopian to believe that our segmented world, peopled by human beings involved in ceaseless competition for wealth, honour and prestige, will ever rise above integroup competition and tension. Equally slim is man's chance of creating societies free from one or other form of individual or group ranking, stratification, inequality and discrimination, and where all occupy the same vertical position on the socio-economic totem poll." [105] Even the idea of equal justice is elusive. For in democracies such as Canada and the U.S.A., inequalities persist. As Otis Stephens observed: ". . . it remains doubtful whether the formal expansion of rights (in the U.S.A. and Canada) in accordance with the ideal of equal justice has greatly diminished actual legal inequalities." [106]

---

103. For a survey of groups involved in discrimination and oppression. Cf. Glaser and Possony: op. cit., Parts II and IV.

104. Rabushka, A. and Shepsle, K.: op. cit., pp. 143-147.

105. Op. cit., p. 80.

106. "Equal Justice and Counsel Rights in the U.S.A. and Canada," in Claude, R.: op. cit., p. 161.

The foregoing being the situation the next best position and the objective of political strategy would be to confine discrimination and differentiation to the group itself for within that group the tensions will be more bearable as compared to intergroup discrimination. Hence the concept of condominium has a much better chance of success to achieve social and political stability. In the absence of such stability, of course, no human development is possible.

[ii] Ethnic communities, groups and individual human rights politics

No one will dispute the necessity in any constitutional arrangement for safeguarding the rights and aspirations of the individual. This is a topic of conversation which has penetrated every corner of the earth excepting the totalitarian states such as the USSR and the one-man or one-party dictatorships of the Third World. For the latter, the topic of individual rights is merely to be used *extra territorially* as an exercise in international propaganda. One is almost tempted to pose the hypothesis that at the United Nations, particularly in the General Assembly, more words are spouted on the subject of individual rights by the totalitarian and one-man governments than by the Western democracies and that the passions invoked by delegates are in direct relation to the suppression of rights in their home countries. South Africa, much maligned by Third World and Communist block countries at the UN nonetheless allow a vigorous debate on human rights and individual freedoms in the daily press, in parliament and at national conferences, for example, the conference on human rights in Cape Town in 1979 attended by 339 delegates from sixteen countries. There was no barrier of race, class or politics.[107] Such a conference in any of the Communist block countries is unthinkable as it would be in thirty other one-man dictatorships elsewhere in the world.

107. Forsyth, C.F. and Schiller, J.E., editors: *Human Rights -- The Cape Town Conference,* Juta and Co., Cape Town, 1979.

Having stated the obvious in respect of individual rights it remains necessary to point out that in terms of practical politics greater recognition of the moral and legal status of groups, followed by the implementation of constitutional and legal provisions to safeguard and develop these rights, will go a long way towards easing the strain in states who are struggling to restructure their plural society in an effort to ward off future conflict between the different (and often disparate) groups living within the borders of that one country. The worst will indeed befall any plural society when there is no outlet for the socio-political aspirations of the different ethnic groups and for whom there is no chance of sovereignty because of geographical and economic problems in the partitioning or Balkanization of the country. Such problems produce religious and ethnic strife, a clash of nationalisms of which the one may even be white and the other black, as in the case of South Africa, thereby further complicating matters.

The argument that an individual (liberal or integrationist) approach to the problems of the plural society (crudely put: the "one-man one-vote" or "melting pot" solution) is too limited to achieve success is not confined to white South African academics. The argument is not that there should be no liberal elements in the formula, rather the liberal emphasis on individualism needs at least considerable supplementing or, preferably, the emphasis should be on group rights supplemented by the liberal individualist approach. Vernon van Dyke has pointed out that individual liberalism does not offer a clear basis for the rights of groups. "In some cases the rights that groups exercise are perhaps reducible to individual rights and can thus be brought within the framework of liberal theory, but in other cases the rights belong to groups as corporate units . . . the usual assumption that the consent of the governed is the consent of individuals is open to question, and that the consent that counts may come from groups."[108] In this regard one

108. In *World Politics,* p. 344.

could point to the role of the black group in the 1976 election of Jimmy Carter as President of the United States. Van Dyke's argument is that the communities have rights as units, that in some cases the rights are irreducible and that in principle they may well reflect moral claims.

Elsewhere it has been indicated how Britain conferred legal rights on communities. Also in Belgium. The Belgians speak specifically, in official publications, of assuring "the territorial integrity of the cultural communities." [109]

In respect of the Red Indians community rights are respected and recognized even in the United States. The Indian tribes are considered subordinate and dependent "nations". They enjoy certain powers of sovereignty. [110] Rights of groups are recognized at international level as well. The 1960 constitutions of Cyprus refers specifically to the Greek community and the Turkish community. The Consultive Assembly of the Council of Europe in 1965 called explicitly for the protection of two kinds of rights on Cyprus, rights of all inhabitants and rights of communities. [111]

Concerning the legal rights of communities Van Dyke quotes Woodrow Wilson's statement that not every *person* but every *people* have the right to choose the sovereignty under which to live. He points out: "At most the individual has the right to participate in the decision -- and to leave the group if he does not like the outcome . . . a strong argument can be advanced that self-determination is the right of a group, of a corporate unit." [112] That Van Dyke is correct in his argument can be seen

---

109. Senelle, R.: "The Revision of the Constitution 1967-1971," *Memo from Belgium*, Nos. 144-146, Ministry of Foreign Affairs, Bruxelles, 1972.

110. *Dialogue*, U.S. Information Agency, No. 2, 1973, p. 44. In 1831 in the case *Cherokee Nation versus Georgia*, the U.S. Supreme Court held that the Indians were "domestic dependent nations." Cf. *U.S. News and World Report*, Washington, April 2, 1973, p. 24 and p. 29 also February 25, 1974, p. 60 and June 3, 1974, p. 53.

111. 1965 Sixteenth Ordinary Session, Resolution 290.

112. In *World Politics*, p. 358.

in the fact that after World War II the implementation of self-determination was on a group basis; in the United Nations "people" was defined as the population of a political dependency as a whole.

The assumption that government derives its power from the consent of the governed became open to question. Van Dyke argues, quite correctly, in the opinion of this observer: "But if the population is divided into different communities, each cherishing and wanting to preserve its distinctive identity, why should it be assumed that the consent that counts comes from individuals? Cannot entire communities give or withold consent as collective units?[113] Certainly, this is the case among the Protestants and Catholics in Ireland. In South Africa the seemingly homogeneous white bloc has for fifty years voted overwhelmingly either for English or Afrikaans speaking political parties.

Van Dyke argues that it is necessary that the principle of group *rights* be fully recognized. Some of the advantages which he points out are as follows:

> 1. If, in principle, communities as well as individuals were accepted as right-and-duty-bearing units, the chance would be increased that a coherent and intellectually defensible doctrine or set of doctrines could be developed, which would respond to practical problems... To focus only on the rights of individuals is to focus only on forces making for atomiation and estrangement and to ignore primordial collective sentiment and group loyalties . . .
>
> 2. If ethnic communities as well as individuals were explicitly accepted as right-and-duty-bearing units, it would probably make a difference in their representation in various activities. To be sure, individualism and even the principle of treatment according to merit are

113. Ibid., p. 360.

often modified in practice in favor of group claims, as in affirmative action programs. Nevertheless, individualism and even the principle of treatment according to merit are often modified in practice in favor of group claims, as in affirmative action programs. Nevertheless, individualism gives an advantage to members of the dominant group . . .

3. If ethnic communities as well as individuals were accepted as right-and-duty-bearing units, it should make a difference to the fate of communities that are nondominant and to the psychological health of their members. Individualism, combined with the usual stress on personal merit, is destructive of cultures other than the majority or dominate culture. The schools -- at every level -- are likely to promote the dominant culture and to undermine all others . . . The minority person who adheres to a minority culture is likely to be looked upon as second class and second rate, his culture disparaged as unworthy. The whole attitude is an attack on the existence of the group and the self-respect of its members. It means oppression, and perhaps exploitation as well.

4. It would facilitate affirmative action if ethnic communities were accepted as right-and-duty-bearing units. After all, the discrimination for which affirmative action is compensatory was directed against individuals because of their membership in certain communities, and through them against the community as such. The discrimination was in a sense impersonal; it was not that a given person was to be denied certain opportunities and thus be excluded or kept down; it was rather that the whole community was to be kept in its place . . .

5. A doctrine accepting both individuals and communities as right-and-duty-bearing units is susceptible to universal application, whereas a doctrine focusing on

individuals is not . . . To have a doctrine that responds to the heterogeneity of the world it is necessary to provide a place for (that is, to permit the grant of status and rights to) groups that are intermediate between the individual and the state. Choices can then be deliberately made concerning the relative emphasis on the two principles. Sometimes the emphasis will properly be on individual rights and therefore on equal treatment regardless of ethnic differences. Sometimes the emphasis will properly be on the rights of ethnic communities and therefore on the differential treatment of members and nonmembers. The implication is that the state should not be conceived as a monolithic unity but as an agency for recognizing groups, determining what legal status and rights they shall have, supervising and coordinating their interrelationships, and itself conducting certain kinds of functions in which all have a common interest.

6. If communities as well as individuals were accepted as right-and-duty-bearing units, there would be consequences for both justice and peace.

In principle, the granting of status and rights to ethnic communities on an intermediate basis should extend justice by giving minorities their due and reducing the discrimination and oppression to which they are commonly subjected . . .

In principle, too, the grant of status and rights to communities on an intermediate basis should make for peace -- on the assumption that justice is one of the conditions of peace. But it is unrealistic to expect the prompt achievement of justice even if just rules are accepted. Struggle is likely to be necessary. Hope for justice might actually increase violence, as surer and more rapid change is demanded by some and resisted

> by others. In the long run, however, it seems probable that the interests of peace as well as the interests of justice would be served. [114]

In supporting the arguments of Van Dyke I am also supporting the concept of *condominium as a structure of government for a plural* society.

One recognizes that the main problem concerning human rights in a plural state such as South Africa is the question of reconciling *individual* and *group* rights. Should there be justice between groups such as the white South African community and the various Black communities, the Asians, and the Coloureds, or only justice for each individual? There is no clear cut answer. Government of a plural society such as India, Sri-Lanka, Belgium, Canada, the Philippines, Zimbabwe, Namibia, Cyprus, Fiji, Nigeria and South Africa will always be infinitely more difficult than in homogeneous Costa Rica, Sweden, Norway or Portugal. Yet if a partially rigid constitution along the lines of the principle or condominium could be developed in recognition of the importance of group rights, with flexibility in that part of the constitution concerned with human rights, combined with a pragmatic and democratic decision making power then, relative to the failings and pitfalls of other policies (such as socio-political integration or imposed geo-political fragmentation) such an approach will, at least, establish more congenial circumstances for both individual and group development while maintaining a low national political temperature which would enable the various groups to work out an improved accommodation in a spirit of mutual co-operation.

How the various units of the condominium would be linked to form the ''management committee'' of the condominium can be sorted out only on the basis of concensus. In this upper decision making committee each group would be a potential minority and political or racial domination by one group could be checked.

114. Ibid., p. 364-368.

Finally, human rights can then be approached pragmatically in two ways: group oriented and individual oriented.

In conclusion I wish to emphasize that the proposals contained in this section should not be seen as a *solution* to the problems of group conflict or ethnicity in any plural society. They represent an approach, for just as there are no solutions to the world's problems, so there can be no solutions to the problems of the plural society which is, in many cases, merely a microcosm of the world. Solutions sound seductive but as the French political philosopher Bertrand de Jouvenel observed, in politics solutions are most often a myth,[115] But if there can be no solutions, then at least there can be vast improvements in the quality of life and in intergroup relations in plural societies if the right approach is adopted. The right approach requires that constitutions must reflect the full socio-political and cultural spectrum of a country otherwise they become, like the Cromwellian Protectorate of the 17th century in Britain, and in the words of John Bunyan[116] worthless paper patterns of political procedure.

And The Next Decade?

One can say with more than reasonable certainty that the next twenty years will see more independent states for different peoples, greater ethnic stress in plural societies, a greater emphasis on group rights and less on individual human rights while the devolution, partition, secession and other forms of political fragmentation will continue. The United Nations may have intended otherwise, but its International Covenant on Civil and Political Rights which entered into force March 1976 has coupled group rights demands with self-determination. The covenant actually pleaded with member states to treat different

---

115. de Jouvenal, B.: *The Pure Theory of Politics*, Cambridge University Press, London, 1963.

116. Benyon, J.A.: op. cit., p. 2.

groups of peoples in special ways. Article 27 reads clearly:

> In those states in which ethnic, religious or linguistic minorities exist, persons belonging to such minorities shall not be denied the right . . . to enjoy their own culture, to profess and practice their own religion, or to use their own language.

If this is not encouragement to the French in Canada, to the Basques, Kurds, Corsicans, Eritreans, Christians in Lebanon, Moluccans, Tamils, Flemish, Scots and other separatists, then it is certainly interpreted in this way by their supporters.

An even stronger declaration appears in the Draft Declaration on Race and Racial Prejudice unanimously approved by UNESCO on November 29, 1978. Article 9(2) of the draft reads:

> Special measures must be taken to ensure equality and dignity and rights for individuals and groups whenever necessary . . . to respect the authority of their culture and values . . .

While 94 different groups and peoples found a separate independence since World War II, there have been only three countries which have worked against the trend: the Soviet Union, Vietnam (the Soviet Union's client state in Asia) and Indonesia.

The Soviet Union's action was simply because it is no more no less than the last great imperial empire of our age. After World War II, it swallowed up the former independent states of Lithuania, Latvia and Estonia as well as groups which formed part of Czechoslovakia, Finland, Hungary, Poland and Romania, and Russian troops would have gobbled up Afghanistan by now had it not been for the covert military assistance given to the anti-Soviet factions by certain Western states such as the U.S.A.

Vietnam has conquered both Laos and Cambodia.

Indonesia forcibly and otherwise integrated every territory or part of a territory in its immediate sphere of influence while suppressing cultural, linguistic and religious rights, and ignoring, or trying to ignore, the vast ethnic differences between the peoples of these territories and its own population.

Who will be the next group to attain self-determination and statehood? And where?

There are strong national, liberation movements in East Timor, the South Moluccas, West Iran and even in parts of Sumatra -- all currently part of Indonesia.

South Africa is expected to proceed with the granting of independence to black homelands, despite the failure of the first independent state, Transkei, to receive international recognition because it has international law on its side.[117] Elsewhere in Africa there are a number of multi-national states, the legacy of British and German colonial regimes, where new nations could possibly emerge. The war for Eritrean independence is not going to go away. Armed force had to be used to keep Biafra in the Nigeria federation. A split may yet take place. Namibia, administered by South Africa, will no doubt become independent within the first year after the Russians remove their Cuban-proxy forces from neighbouring Angola. The long standing feud between the coastal people and the merinas on the plateau may yet see Madagascar go the way of Cyprus. In Mauritius the violence of 1968 was an indication of the conflict between Muslims and Creoles.

There is no certainty that the devolution of Pakistan into as many as four separate states will not continue.[118] Jordan could

117. The legal fact of independence does not depend upon the recognition of other states. O'Connel, D.P.: *International Law,* Vol. I (1970), 2nd ed., p. 130 Cf. Brownlie, Ian: *Principles of Public International Law,* 2nd. ed. (1973), p. 76 on *prima facie* evidence of statehood and Booysen, B.; Wiechers, M.; Van Wyk, D.H. and Breytenbach, W.: "Comments on Independence and Constitution of the Transkei" in *South African Yearbook of International Law,* The Verloren van Themaat Centre for International Law, Pretoria, 1976, Vol. II, pp. 1-35.

118. Cf. Harrison, C.F.: *In Afghanistan's Shadow: Baluch Nationalism and Soviet Temptations,* 1981.

end up as the Palistinian homeland since in three quarters of Jordanian territory the Palistinians constitute two thirds of the population. Will the East Indians continue to accept minority political status in Fiji despite their numerical majority? Canada is facing the threat of an independent Quebec. After the death of President Tito in 1980 no one can guarantee that Yugoslavia with her six self governing republics will remain in one place, despite Yugoslavia's impressively structured constitution, not when the Communist Party refuses to recognize the political boundaries between states. And India will have an extremely difficult time holding its disparate nations, religions and ethnic communities together.

Spain, which has already granted considerable autonomy to its Basques is facing separatists movements in the Balaeric and Canary Islands. The Socialists government of President Francois Mitterand of France has granted exceptional autonomy to Corsica which now has its own legislative assembly and government council. This will no doubt serve as a boost for separatist movements in Alsace and Brittany.

Britain has not heard the last word about devolution and the autonomy movements in Scotland and Wales. Cyprus now has a Turkish Cypriot republic as well, already recognized by Turkey. Shri-Lanka is facing huge pressures of race, religion, language and culture. Some 80 percent of the people are Sinhalese Buddhists, the rest are Tamil-speaking Hindus who are bent on self-government and independence.

Belgium is facing almost certain re-structuring and it is doubtful whether even a federal structure for the Flemish and Walloons will be the right constitutional step to take.

In Iran only the Iranian Zoroastrians, Jews and Christians are recognized as minorities[119] and are even allocated one Parliamentary seat each.[120] But nothing is said of the Kurds

119. Constitution of Iran, 1979, article 13.

120. Ibid., article 64.

who are struggling for a separate Kurdistan. In Iraq a concession was made to the Kurds in 1974 when they were granted "autonomy" and in 1976 the number of provinces were expanded to 18 of which three were designated as Kurdish autonomous regions. But on closer inspection it appears autonomy means "as defined by the law," and the Kurds have no say in phrasing the law. The continue to press for true autonomy which can only be achieved in independence.

The splintering of the current crop of countries in the world into more states and countries need not even take 20 years. Look at the rapid proliferation of states which occurred in what is known as the Middle East and Central America. Most of Central American was once joined together as Guatemala. Today it consists of the independent nations of Belize, Costa Rica, El Salvador, Guatemala, Honduras and Nicaragua. All of this fragmentation or Balkanization over a short span of time. Even the United States is uncertain about its foreign trust territories. Those in the Pacific have a population of only 135,000 but are already divided into four self-governing (local) entities: Marshall Islands, Northern Marianas, Palau and the Federated States of Micronesia. In another decade these may be four separate sovereign countries.

If those of us are right who believe that group rights are more important than individual rights when it comes to matters such as language, customs, culture, ethnicity, nationalism, economic and political systems, and generates more power to obtain socio-economic, cultural and political advantages than anything that can be achieved through a human rights campaign, then further political fragmentation of the world is not just a reasonable certainty, it is inevitable.

PART V

BIBLIOGRAPHIES

INTRODUCTION TO THE BIBLIOGRAPHY

This bibliography is divided into four parts. Part I lists those special sets, books, and articles which are most significant in understanding and working with the problems of race, religion and sex classifications in the world's constitutions. This is the "basic" and "select" library on the subject for basic research ahead.

Part II is an *annotated* bibliography of key materials essential to this study, or to any study in this area. But, while important, none of these items meets the test of being "basic". (All of the Part I materials have also been incorporated alphabetically into the Part II listing as well -- with the Part I entries in capital letters).

Part III is a "Negative Bibliography," and a very unusual one. It is a contribution not found in most studies of this type. In the process of doing legal research on such a broad topic as this, numerous entries in indexes and the bibliographies of others have necessarily been checked. Those listed in Part III have been found wanting; they have little value. But, because they might appear attractive to subsequent researchers in this area, they are listed here as a caveat and time-saver.

Because there are so many references to two particular works, a "short-cut" citation has been utilized in this study.

For Blaustein, Albert P., and Gisbert H. Flanz, *Constitutions of the Countries of the World.* 15 volumes, Dobbs Ferry, New York, Oceana Publications, Inc., 1971 -- : use *Blaustein.*

For William A. Veenhoven, editor in chief, *Case Studies on Human Rights and Fundamental Freedoms,* 5 Volumes, The Hague, Nijhoff, 1975: use *Veenhoven.*

BIBLIOGRAPHY: PART I: BASIC

Baudoin, Jean-Louis, and Claude Masse. *"Etude Comparative Et Evolutive des Droits Linguistiques en Belgigue et en Suisse."* Etude E 15. Etudes realiseed pour le compte de la commission D'Enquete sur law situation de la langue Francaise et sur les droits linguistiques au Quebec, 1973 (In French).

Key volume in understanding language rights as protected by the laws of Belgium and Switzerland. By way of contrast, it also provides some information on linguistic rights in Germany, Hungary, and Poland. The bibliography is excellent.

Benyon, J.A., Editor: *Constitutional Change in South Africa,* University of Natal Press, Pietermaritzburg, 1978.

Conference papers of a conference on constitutional change and alternative constitutional models for South Africa. At this multi-racial meeting Southern African experts addressed themselves to constitutions as devices for organising systems of government in a plural society, African constitutionalism, particularly in Kenya and Zambia, structural divisions of power in South Africa, constitutions and political rights and related subjects.

Blaustein, Albert P., and Gisbert H. Flanz. *Constitutions of the Countries of the World.* 15 Volumes with supplementary volume; two historical volumes. Dobbs Ferry, N.Y., Oceana Publications, 1971 -.

Up-to-date (looseleaf) collection of the constitutions of all of the countries of the world in English, together with chronological introductions and annotated bibliographies.

Blaustein, Albert P., and Eric B. Blaustein. *Constitutions of Dependencies and Special Sovereignties.* 6 Volumes. Dobbs Ferry, N.Y., Oceana Publications, 1975 -.

Up-to-date (looseleaf) collections of the constitutions of colonies, dependencies, and such special sovereignties as the Vatican, together with chronological introductions and annotated bibliographies.

Borale, P.T. *Segregation and Desegregation in India.* Bombay, Manaktalas, 1968.

Excellent attempt (but doomed at the start) to analogize the problem of untouchables in India with the problems of blacks in America, but much is learned about segregation practices in India and it does provide some special insights to those familiar with the American problem.

Claude, Richard P., ed. *Comparative Human Rights.* Baltimore, Johns Hopkins University Press, 1976.

Excellent collection of essays on human rights concerns. Emphasis is on public policy as a means of ensuring enjoyment of fundamental freedoms, and case studies echoing that view but dealing with a particular facet of of human rights are included. Those contributions which may be of most interest, in light of this study, are annotated in Part II of the bibliography.

Das Basu, Durga. *Commentary on the Constitution of India.* 6th ed., revised and enlarged. Calcutta, 1973.

Annotations and commentary to the Indian Constitution, with a wealth of analysis and hundreds of case citations. An indispensible reference for any matter dealing with India's Constitution.

Duchacek, Ivo D. *Rights and Liberties in the World Today: Constitutional Promise and Reality.* Santa Barbara, A.B.C. - Clio, 1972.

Essential introductory/handbook for any study on human rights and constitutionalism. While it provides an excellent introduction to the subject, however, it covers too many topics in too few pages (269) to satisfy scholarly needs. After comments on the ''avalanche'' of new constitutions, the author sets up six categories rights and liberties as the basis of his discussions. There are special sections on women's rights, right to one's own language, etc.

Esman, M.J.: *Ethnic Conflict in the Western World,* Cornell University Press, London, 1977.

Essential reading to understand ethnicity, ethnonationalism and ethnic conflict in western societies and the emergence of ethnic solidarity in stable political systems. Should be read in conjunction with Glaser and Moynihan's work *Ethnicity.*

Falch, Jean. *Contribution a L'Etude du Statut des Langues en Europe.* Centre International de Recherches sur le Bilinguisme, Quebec, Les Presses de L'Universite Laval, 1973 (In French).

This volume provides comparisons between various nations on linguistic matters. For example, it compares the laws of the Western states of Belgium and Switzerland with those of the Socialist states of Czechoslovakia and Yugoslavia.

It distinguishes between countries which have several official languages and those which do not make this distinction. It also explains that the difference between language protection via constitutional provisions and those which relegate language matters to statute.

Alanter, Marc. *Competing Equalities: The Indian Experiment With Compensatory Discrimination.* (Forthcoming).

The most up-to-date comprehensive analysis of the ethnic situation and so-called "affirmative action" in India.

Glaser, K. and Possony, S.: *Victims of Politics - The State of Human Rights,* Columbia University Press, New York, 1977.

Indispensable and authoritative overview of infringement of human rights, from discrimination and caste systems to genocide. In analyzing the pathology of discrimination and oppression, Glaser and Possony survey every major nation.

It contains invaluable source material for all those concerned with group and individual human rights.

Heard, Kenneth. *Political Systems in Multi-Racial Societies.* Johannesburg, South African Institute of Race Relations, 1961.

Provides a useful (albeit elementary) introduction to the constitutional framework (and constitutional provisions) in states with multi-racial and multi-ethnic populations.

Imam, Mohammed, ed. *Minorities and the Law.* Indian Law

Institute. Bombay, Tripathi, 1972.

This collection of some thirty papers constitutes the best work on the problem of the plural society which is India. The theme is that the interests of minorities and backward classes must not be sacrificed in the interests of a unified central government. Emphasis is placed upon the scope and extent of constitutional and legal safeguards provided to the minorities. These papers were presented and discussed at a seminar on the topic organized by the Indian Law Institute in New Delhi in April, 1971.

Institut International des Droits de L'Homme. "Enseignement des Droits de L'Homme dans les Universities.' 6 *Revue des Droits de L'Homme* 109 (1973). (In French).

Prepared under the direction of Karel Visak, secretary-general of the International Institute on the Rights of Man, this report was financed by UNESCO, and its authors include leading United Nations experts on human rights.

A lengthy study (222 pages), this report is divided into three parts. It begins with a summary of the present state of teaching and research in the field of human rights. Part Two is devoted to an analysis of "la Methodologie" in human rights study, and Part Three consists of recommendations for future teaching and research.

This is followed by an annex, broken down by region and by country, on human right studies, together with annexes providing questionnaires, resolutions, etc. Annexe 4 contains a related bibliography.

Kloss, Heinz. *The American Bilingual Tradition.* Rowley, Massachusetts, The Newbury House Publishers, Inc., 1977.

A detailed study of American immigration policy and its implications for the rights of nationality group members. Laws to protect and promote ethnic group rights are examined in a historical context. The organization and distribution of minority groups is delineated. An Appendix provides a statistical survey of linguistic groups by state.

Lambert, Richard D., ed., Martin O. Heisler, special ed. *Ethnic Conflict in the World Today.* 433 *The Annals of the American Academy of Political and Social Science* (1977).

Invaluable survey of ethnic "trouble spots"; the articles include general studies on ethnicity and ethnic identity as well as more specialized analyses of ethnic relations in Quebec, Belgium, Northern Ireland, the U.S.S.R., Yugoslavia, China, the Middle East, and Southern Asia. The contributions are brief, and concentrate on constitutional and governmental responses to ethnic conflict. Annotations for the most useful of these articles are included in Part II of the bibliography.

Lijphart, Arend: *Democracy in Plural Societies,* Yale University Press, London, 1977.

Lijphart shows how the political experiences of Austria, Belgium, the Netherlands, Switzerland and, to a more limited extent, Canada and Israel challenges pessimism about democracy in plural societies. He advocates a model of consociational democracy for countries with deep religious, ideological, linguistic, cultural and ethnic cleavages. This book is important for its direct and indirect reference to the consociational model and formal constitutional rules, the stresses inherent in plural societies and pitfalls in constitutional engineering.

McDougal, Myres S., Harold D. Lasswell, and Lung-Chu Chen. "The Protection of Respect and Human Rights: Freedom of Choice and World Public Order." 24 *American University Law Review* 919 (1975).

Refines and categorizes claims made on behalf of respect for individuals. Because the article deals with the sharing of respect in aggregate terms, it frequently touches upon group rights according to sex, religion, language, ethnicity, and race. Slavery and race relations are given detailed attention.

Plural Societies. Published by the Foundation for the Study of Plural Societies, P.O. Box 3566, The Hague, The Netherlands. Quarterly.

Published since 1970, this journal is devoted exclusively to the issues in plural societies. There are several articles in each issue on one or more aspects of the plural society problem -- whether based on race, religion, or language problems.

Rabushka, A. and Shepsle, K.A.: *Politics in Plural Societies,* Charles E. Merrill Publishing Co., Columbus, Ohio, 1972.

Basic reading for understanding the basis of pluralism, ethnic preferences and the political features of the plural society; majority and minority problems, the properties of fragmented societies, theoretical aspects of conflict in the plural society, regularities of politics in plural societies in various countries and the existing democratic instabilities in plural societies.

Revue des Droits de L'Homme. Human Rights Journal.

This quarterly journal has been published by the Institut International des Droits de l'Homme, in Strasbourg, since 1968. It is undoubtedly the principal publication devoted exclusively to this topic and many articles relate directly as well as indirectly to the classification of peoples based on sex, race, religion, and other ethnic classifications.

Rhoodie, Nic., Editor: *Intergroup Accommodations in Plural Societies,* MacMillan Press, London, 1978.

This book is a major contribution to understanding inter-group accommodation, conflict regulation and the socio-political structures which determine policy options in plural societies. The book includes 23 conference papers presented at an international conference on pluralism in Cape Town in 1977. Experts from the Middle East, Europe, the United States and Africa analyzed socio-political trends in general and options for solutions to problems of pluralist accommodation in particular. It contains a mass of fresh empirical data on the contemporary plural scene. All aspects of group rights and intergroup accommodation are dealt with.

Savard, Jean-guy, and Richard Vigneault, eds. *Les Etats Multilingues, Problemes et Solutions/Multilingual Political Systems, Problems and Solutions.* Publications of the International Center for Research on Bilingualism, Quebec, University of Laval Press, 1975.

This collection of twenty papers, presented at a Round Table of the International Political Science Association at Laval University in 1972, explores language and the political process in multi-cultural, multi-racial, and multi-lingual societies in general philosophical terms, in statistical sociolinguistic studies, and finally in specific case studies. Contributors include members of political science, language, and sociology faculties from universities in the United States, Canada, England, Germany, Lebanon, Israel, and Uganda. Most of the articles are well-documented and contain basic bibliographies. Annotations to the most valuable of the articles appear in Part II.

Shiva Rao, B. *The Framing of India's Constitution: Select Documents.* New Delhi, Indian Institute of Public Administration, 1970. 5 Volumes.

The first four volumes of this set present a detailed documentary history of India's Constitution. Volume One deals with the period from the earliest nationalist demands for a constitution to the summoning of the Constituent Assembly in 1946; the second volume contains the reports of the assembly committees. Volume Three is composed of the draft constitution and the minutes of the assembly's drafting committee. The fourth volume reviews reaction to the draft document from provincial governments, scholars, and public figures; included also are revisions of the draft, as finally adopted.

The fifth volume, perhaps the most important, is devoted to an in-depth analysis of government structure and fundamental rights, as set forth in the new constitution.

The entire set is invaluable toward an understanding of the

forces behind the making of India's Constitution.

Turi, Guiseppe. *Les Dispositions Juridico-Constitutionnelles.* Quebec, Centre International de Recherche sur le Bilinguisme, 1977 (Publication B-63).

This is a basic resource volume for the study of linguistic rights. The author has made a complete survey of Blaustein's compilations of the world's constitutions, extracting all constitutional provisions on language rights.

United Nations. Commission on the Status of Woman. *Constitutions, Electoral Laws and Other Legal Instruments Relating to The Political Rights of Women.* Report of the Secretary General. United Nations, New York, 1968. (A/6447/Rev. 1)

While not carefully done, this is none the less the best compilation ever made on the various legal instruments affecting women's rights. It has references to various laws which are not covered in the basic study here. And it would serve as a check on constitutional provisions which are set forth in the major study. A book such as this, more complete and up-to-date, must be part of any further comprehensive study of women's rights.

Note, however, the limitations of this particular report. While it covers such matters as citizenship and voting, it does not include important provisions on either the protection or advancement of women. Conspicuous by their absence are such constitutional provisions as Article 15 (3) of India: "Nothing in this Article shall prevent the State from making any special provision for women and children."

United Nations. *Protection of Minorities.* Special Protective Measures of an International Character for Ethnic, Religious or Linguistic groups. United Nations, New York, 1967. (Sales No. E. 67. XIV. 3)

This brief (58 pages) but important booklet outlines and summarizes important treaties and other international instruments promulgated after both World Wars to protect minority groups. For background information, the lists included on pages seven and eight set forth those treaties which were placed under the guarantee of the League of Nations. Part Two lists and classifies special protective measures under such headings as: Political Representation, Nationality, Language, and Religion.

United Nations. *Racial Discrimination.* By Hernan Santa Cruz. New York, United Nations, 1971. (Sales No. E. 71.XIV.2) Revised and updated version, 1976, New York, United Nations, 1977. (Sales No. E.76.XIV.2) E/CN.4/Sub.2/307/Rev.1.

These United Nations reports are valuable in providing perspective. They furnish historical background (including the role of slavery and colonialism) in the development of racial prejudice and discrimination. There are additional chapters on the meaning and causes of racial discrimination. Only a few pages are devoted to constitutional or legislative provisions or other national action designed to eliminate such discrimination.

Of value to those who approach the problem with a Western orientation is the material on racial discrimination in the economic sphere.

As might be expected in a United Nations publication, there is a disproportionate amount of space devoted to racial policies in Southern Africa.

United Nations. *Yearbook on Human Rights.* United Nations, New York (Published Annually)

Survey of action taken by member nations in the advancement of human rights. Relevant legislative enactments, executive action, judicial decisions, and constitutional provisions are abstracted, and are related to provisions of the Universal Declaration of Human Rights. An indispensible research tool.

UNESCO. *Cultural Rights as Human Rights.* Paris, UNESCO, 1970.

A vital text in a series on cultural policies in specific countries. This is the only one in the UNESCO series which is not limited to the cultural policies of one specific nation. Based on a meeting of experts called to consider the relationship of cultural rights to human rights, the volume is devoted mainly to brief papers and the experts' analyses of these presentations.

Particularly important is the recognition of cultural rights as a new concept based upon the new humanism which has emerged throughout the world.

Van Maarseveen, H.T.J.F., and G.F.M. van der Tang. *On Written Constitutions.* Oceana, N.Y. 1978.

This computer-based study of the world's constitutions uses as its source, Blaustein and Flanz, *Constitutions of the Countries of the World.* The authors have demonstrated the difficulty of classifying constitutions in a meaningful way. The work is useful in comparing the Universal Declaration of Human Rights with specific constitutional provisions; it also provides some gross comparisons of the constitutions with regard to the mention of specific rights in the text of the constitutions. It is generally more useful in posing issues than in providing answers or synthesis.

Veenhoven, William A., ed. in chief. *Case Studies on Human Rights and Fundamental Freedoms: A World Survey. 5 Volumes.* The Hague, Nijhoff, 1975. Referred to throughout this work as *Veenhoven.*

This important work was published for and on behalf of the Foundation for the Study of Plural Societies. This set consists of a series of individual studies dealing with discrimination and classification in countries throughout the world. All of them are important, and all of them are worthy of annotation. But it would be unnecessarily repetitive to prepare separate annotations for each item since they are so well indexed. Thus, Part II of the Bibliography will list each author and title, followed by the name *Veenhoven,* and the volume and page citation. The complete Table of Contents is reproduced as Part IV of the Bibliography.

BIBLIOGRAPHY: PART II: ANNOTATED

Abou, Selim. "Les conditions d'une culture Nationale a partir du Bilinguisme." In: *Multilingual Political Systems.* Quebec, University of Laval Press, 1975, p. 473.

What is the definition of bilingualism? How does one measure or compare the bilingual situation of different nations? Does a bilingual nation always remain bilingual? A long-time observer of Lebanon discusses the French-Arabic linguistic and cultural heritage of that country and the political ideologies which are changing it from bilingualism.

Agunda, Akinola. "Discriminatory Statutory Provisions and Fundamental Rights Provisions of the Constitutions of Botswana, Lesotho, and Swaziland." 89 *South African Law Journal* 299 (1972).

The Constitutions of Swaziland, Lesotho, and Botswana have all been modeled upon the Nigerian Constitution and as such they reflect the influence of the British legal system and the United Nations Universal Declaration of Human Rights. Since the fundamental rights guarantees of the three constitutions are substantially similar, judicial decisions dealing with the construction of such provisions in any one state are automatically of interest and import to scholars and legal practitioners in the others.

Agunda, Akinola, and Oluwadare Agunda. "Judicial Protection of Some Fundamental Rights in Nigeria and in the Sudan before and during Military Rule." 16 *Journal of African Law* 130 (1972).

Criticism of the practice in the Sudan and Nigeria, which constitutionally protects fundamental rights but which then compromises such guarantees through legislation or executive action. (Both constitutions have derogation clauses, which permit legislation inconsistent with constitutional provisions if that legislation is considered reasonable for public safety and security.) It is observed that the fundamental rights guarantees of the two states are somewhat like bikinis, most important for what they do not reveal.

Aithe, D.O. "Fundamental Human Rights Provisions as a Means of Achieving Justice in Society: The Nigerian 'Bill of Rights'." 15 *Malaya Law Review* 39 (1973).

Review of the guarantees of the Nigerian Bill of Rights, which draws heavily from British sources, including the Magna Charta, the Bill of Rights of 1688, and the United Nations Universal Declaration of Human Rights. The role of the judiciary in enforcing these guarantees is stressed.

Aiyar, S.P., and S.V. Raju, eds. *Fundamental Rights and the Citizen.* Bombay and New Delhi, 1972.

The Twenty-fourth Amendment to the Indian Constitution gives Parliament the power to amend any provision of that document, including those provisions having to do with fundamental rights. Reaction to the *Golak Nath* decision, in which the Indian Supreme Court held that any Parliamentary action (including amending the Constitution) which worked in derogation of such fundamental rights guarantees was void, is analyzed.

The articles in this volume debate whether such fundamental rights are entrenched or whether Parliament should be sovereign in such matters.

Akani, Oledeji. "Reflections on Some Recent Constitutional Issues in Nigeria." 3 *Nigerian Law Journal* 102 (1969).

It is pointed out in this essay that the Nigerian Constitution is not the "Supreme Law of the Land," that it can be superseded by executive decree. The Constitution expressly holds that such decrees take precedence over Constitutional provisions. Human rights, too, it is noted then, are also subject to such government by fiat.

Ali, Ahmed. "The Emergence of Muslim Separatism in Fiji." 8 *Plural Societies* No. 1, p. 57 (1977).

While only a brief introductory survey, the article is important because of Fiji's response to demands for representation and power by members of widely divergent ethnic groups.

Al-Marayati, Abid A. *Middle Eastern Constitutions and Electoral Laws.* New York, Praeger, 1968.

A valuable collection of electoral laws not available in the modern *Blaustein* collections.

Ameluxen, Clemens. "Foreign Workers in West Germany." *Veenhoven,* Volume One, p. 113.

Ameluxen, Clemens. "Marriage and Women in Islamic Countries." *Veenhoven,* Volume Two, p. 83.

Annual Report of the Department of Information, Government Printer, Pretoria, 1976.

The Antioch Review, Fall 1971.

The Anti-Slavery Reporter and Aborigine's Friend. Published on an irregular basis by the Anti-Slavery Society for the Protection of Human Rights. London.

This periodical is basic to any comprehensive study of racial, religious, and sex discrimination. There are articles in every issue on one or more types of slavery still being practiced, together with comments on United Nations activities or national legislation designed to counter slavery.

The Anti-Slavery Society for the Protection of Human Rights. Annual Report. 49 Dennison House, 296 Vauxhall Bridge Road, London. SW 1 V 1AE.

Like its publication, *The Anti-Slavery Reporter and Aborigine's Friend,* the Annual Report of the Society provides information on the various forms of slavery and actions being taken to bring about its end.

Asante, S.K.B. "Nation Building and Human Rights in Emergent African Nations." 2 *Cornell International Law Journal* 72 (1969).

This article, first delivered as a lecture at Cornell University Law School, traces the origins of African constitutional human rights provisions from their European and American roots, and compares and contrasts the specific guarantees of English-heritage nations with the more generalized provisions enacted by the former French colonies. Asante casts a realistic eye upon current governmental policies and practices, and acknowledges that some nations fail to respect the guarantees incorporated into their own Constitutions, turning lofty humanistic provisions into empty and barren promises.

Aslanyan, R.G. "Action to Ensure that Soviet Citizens Enjoy Equal Rights and Opportunities." 100 *International Labour Review* 551 (1969).

A study of the Soviet Constitution of 1936, with emphasis upon the effect of its equality provisions upon women and non-Russian Soviet citizens. The closing of the gap in income and education between men of Russian extraction and all other citizens is illustrated through tables.

Aubert, Jean-Francois. *Traite de Droit Constitutionnel Suisse.* Neuchatel, Editions de la Baconniere, 1967.

The most accessible source for gaining an understanding of Swiss constitutional law.

Awolowo, Obafemi. *Thoughts on the Nigerian Constitution.* Ibadan, Oxford University Press, 1968.

Examination of Nigeria as a multi-lingual, multi-cultural state, and the implications such conditions hold for governmental structure. The author notes that unitary governments in such states rarely succeed, and urges adoption of a federal system like those of Canada, Switzerland, or India.

Baar, Carl. "Judicial Behavior and Comparative Rights Policy." In: Richard Claude, ed. *Comparative Human Rights.* Baltimore, Johns Hopkins University Press, 1976, p. 353.

Study of the impact of judicial decisions on human rights policy and practice. The focus of this essay is upon the Supreme Courts of the United States and Canada and their handling of human rights cases brought before them.

Badura, Peter. "Verfassung und Verfassungsgesetz." In: H. Ehmke, ed. *Festschrift fur Ulrich Scheuner.* Berlin, Duncker

& Humblot, 1973, p. 19.

Describes the constitution as the most fundamental expression of a society's legal culture.

Bagley, Christopher. "Sequals of Alienation: West Indian Migrants in Britain." *Veenhoven,* Volume Two, p. 55.

Baker, John R. *Race.* New York and London, Oxford University Press, 1974.

Provides an introduction to racial problems by furnishing both the historical background and the biological basis of the problem. There are useful chapters on the meaning of "species" and "race". Part Three has studies of selected human groups, with emphasis on black peoples.

Baker, R.S. and Dodd, W.E. ed.: *Woodrow Wilson, War and Peace:* Presidential Messages, Addresses and Public Papers, Harper, New York, 1927.

Baldwin, Fletcher N., Jr. "Constitutional Limitations on Government in Mexico, the United States, and Uganda." In: Richard Claude, ed. *Comparative Human Rights.* Baltimore, Johns Hopkins University Press, 1976, p. 76.

General study of the constitutions of these three nations with respect to checks placed upon governmental power. The point is made that the American Constitution makes absolute grants of fundamental rights, while Uganda subordinates and qualifies many of its rights provisions to parliamentary or executive power. Mexico lies somewhere between the two in its response to government power over fundamental rights provisions.

Banerjee, Anil Chandra. *The Making of the Indian Constitution, 1939-1947.* Calcutta, A. Mukherjee and Company, 1948, 3 Volumes.

Authoritative source book for Indian constitutional history. Includes documents -- speeches, position papers, assembly resolutions, etc.

Banerjee, D.N. *Our Fundamental Rights: Their Nature and Extent.* 2d ed. Calcutta, A. Mukherjee and Company, 1968.

Discussion and analysis of fundamental rights, as defined in the Indian Constitution. Emphasis is upon court decisions interpreting the rights provisions of the Constitution. The right to equality, and cultural and educational rights, are given detailed treatment.

Barile, Paolo. "The Particular Value of the Rights of Freedom Set out in the Present Italian Constitution in the Light of Subsequent Trends." In: *Associazione Italiano di Diritto Comparato. Italian National Reports to the IXth International Congress of Comparative Law.* Tehran 1974, Milano 1974. p. 43.

Brief summary of the civil and political rights provisions on the Italian Constitution. No analysis is presented.

Barons, New York.

Bass, Jerome R. "The South-East Asian Chinese: Accommodation without Acceptance." *Veenhoven,* Volume Three, p. 329.

Batshaw, Harry. "A Landmark Decision Against Discrimination in Canada." 4 *Revue des Droits de l'Homme* 207 (1971).

The Canadian Supreme Court ruled that those portions of the Indian Act which prescribed a stiffer penalty for intoxicated Indians than did the ordinary territorial drunkenness statutes contravened Articles One and Two of the Canadian Bill of Rights. Those articles forbade discrimination on racial or ethnic grounds.

More importantly, the Court for the first time stated that the Bill of Rights was to operate as a guiding principle for all legislation, and should serve to invalidate law which contradicts its provisions. This article discusses the legislative and Constitutional implications of the Court's ruling.

BAUDOIN, JEAN-LOUIS, and CLAUDE MASSE. *"Etude Comparative et Evolutive des Droits Linguistiques en Beligue et en Suisse."*

Etude E 15. Etudes realisees pour le compte de la commission d'Enquete sur la Situation de la Langue Francaise et sur les Droits Linguistiques au Quebec, 1973. (In French).

Bay, Christian. *The Structure of Freedom.* Stanford, Stanford University Press, 1970.

Gives theoretical attention to rights and their Constitutional bases.

Beardsley, James E. "The Constitutional Council and Constitutional Liberties in France." 20 *American Journal of Comparative Law* 431 (1972).

Judicial review of legislative enactments is alien to French historical and political tradition. In the Constitution of 1958 provision was made, however, for the establishment of a Constitutional Council; the function of the Council would be to decide whether Parliamentary actions were "in conformity with the Constitution."

The measure of success achieved by this new device is discussed and analyzed in this essay.

Bell, Derrick A. "Racism in American Courts: Cause for Black Disruption or Despair?" 61 *California Law Review* 165 (1973).

Exploration of the treatment of blacks afforded by the judicial system in the United States; the author finds that Constitutional guarantees are, in some circumstances, ignored.

Bennett, G.I. "The I.L.O. Convention on Indigenous and Tribal Populations -- The Resolution of a Problem of *Vires.*" 46 *British Yearbook of International Law* 382 (1972/1973).

This potentially useful article describes briefly the activities and discussion leading to, and conclusions reached, in the International Labor Organization's Convention on Indigenous and Tribal Populations. The convention was undertaken with a view to giving practical help and technical assistance to states in which the disadvantaged economic and social conditions of such groups impedes their integration into society and prevents their participation in and enjoyment of the rights enjoyed by other citizens.

BENYON, J.A. Editor: *Constitutional Change in South Africa,* University of Natal Press, Pietermaritzburg, 1978.

Berinson, Zvi. "Freedom of Religion and Conscience in the State of Israel." 3 *Israel Yearbook of Human Rights* 223 (1973).

Discussion of the limitations on religious practice imposed by government authority in Israel. Israel's Declaration of Independence, which includes a guarantee of religious freedom, is not of Constitutional force, but is merely a pronouncement of the new state's ideals and goals.

In practice, complete religious freedom can be impinged upon by the acts of the Knesset, so long as the legislation operates in promotion of the public welfare, safety, and morals. Singled out for special consideration are marriage and divorce matters, which are completely under the control of religious authorities and the strict control placed upon the raising and butchering of swine.

Bernas, Joaquin G. *A Historical and Juridicial Study of the Philippine Bill of Rights.* Manila, Ateneo University Press, 1971.

Analysis of the fundamental rights provisions of the 1935 Philippine Constitution. Important documents in Philippine Constitutional history, such as the Bill of 1902 and the Autonomy Act of 1916, as included as appendices.

Bertsch, Gary K. "Ethnicity and Politics in Socialist Yugoslavia." 433 *Annals of the American Academy of Political and Social Science* 88 (1977).

Yugoslavia is a true kaleidoscope of ethnic groupings, and such a situation brings about special problems. The political pressures brought about by such ethnic diversity, and the responses to those pressures as reflected in the nation's Constitution and legislation, are detailed in this article.

Beteille, Andre. "The Backward Classes in India." *Veenhoven,* Volume Three, p. 499.

Beteille, Andre. *Social Inequality.* Middlesex, England, Penguin Books, 1972.

A collection of essays on social class and stratification. Race, caste, and other forms of social distinctions are described by leading scholars.

Binder, Leonard, ed. *Politics in Lebanon.* New York, John

Wiley, 1965.

Discussion of Lebanon as a pluralist society and its political institutions as reflective of its multi-ethnic nature. Chapters are devoted to the Maronite Christians and to Arab Nationalism, but the focus is on Lebanon's institutions as reflective of democratic ideals.

In light of the recent civil war in Lebanon, the analysis is somewhat dated.

Bingaman, Anne. *A Commentary on the Effect of the Equal Rights Amendment on State Laws and Institutions.* California Commission on the Status of Women, 1975.

Analysis of the impact ratification of the Equal Rights Amendment would have on California's educational institutions, family and labor laws, and marital property provisions. The author concludes that many state laws would have to be modified or repealed in order that discrimination against women can be eliminated.

Biscaretti di Ruffia, Paolo. *Introduzione al Diritto Costituzionale Comparato.* 2d ed. Milano, Dott. A. Giuffre Editore, 1970.

A limited, preliminary attempt at a comparison of constitutions.

Black, Edwin R.: *Divided Loyalties,* McGill Queen's University Press, Montreal, 1975.

BLAUSTEIN, ALBERT P. and GISBERT H. FLANZ, *Constitutions of the Countries of the World.* 15 Volumes with supplementary volume: Two historical volumes. Dobbs Ferry, N.Y., Oceana Publications, 1975.

Boguszak, Jiri. "The Problem of Constitutional Regulation of Personal and Political Rights." 25 *Bulletin of Czechoslovak Law* No. 8, p. 46, (1967).

The Czechoslovakian Constitution's human rights provisions are examined and criticized in this essay. Enactment of further human rights guarantees as Constitutional provisions is advocated. The author places much hope in the newly-created Constitutional Court, and cites the Yugoslav example as a model of a workable separatist Constitution which places appropriate emphasis upon guarantees of civil and political rights.

Boguszak, Jiri. *Teorie Statu a Prava.* 2 Volumes. Prague, Orbis, 1967.

Provides a Communist view of constitutional theories.

BORALE, P.T. *Segregation and Desegregation in India.* Bombay, Manaktalas, 1968.

Bourdeaux, Michael. "The Persecution of Christians in the U.S.S.R." *Veenhoven,* Volume Four, p. 535.

Brazeau, Jacques. "L'usage des Langues dans les Activites de Travail." In: *Multilingual Political Systems.* Quebec, University of Laval Press, 1975, p. 303.

Should French be the required language of the workaday world in Quebec and francophonic Canada? Although there has been agitation for such a policy in recent years, there has been almost no research on the actual use of languages in this setting. Brazeau reports on a survey undertaken by the Gendron Commission to study the use of language in both spoken and written internal and external communication between superiors and their subordinates. He supports a mandatory bilingual education for all children in Quebec as a long-range solution and favors increased recruitment of linguistic minorities in public employment as an important intermediate step in reducing language conflicts in Canada.

Brazeau, J. and Cloutier, E.: "Interethnic relations and the language issue in Canada," in Esman, M.: *Ethnic Conflict in the Western World,* Cornell University Press, London, 1977.

Breytenbach, W.J. "Inter-Ethnic Conflict in Africa." *Veenhoven,* Volume One, p. 309.

Breytenbach, W.: "The Protection of Minority Rights in Africa," in Rhoodie, Nic,: *Integroup Accommodation in a Plural Society,* MacMillan Press, London, 1978.

Bridge, Susan: "Some Causes of Political Change in Modern Yugoslavia," in Esman, M.J.: *Ethnic Conflict in the Western*

World, Cornell University Press, London, 1977.

Brinton, Joseph Yeates. *The Constitution of the Congo.* American Society of International Law, 1965.

Translation of and short commentary on the 1964 Constitution of the Democratic Republic of the Congo.

Brodin, Eric. "The Lapps of Sweden." *Veenhoven,* Volume Four, p. 29.

Brossard, Jacques. *L'accession a la Sourerainete et le Cas du Quebec.* Montreal, les Presses de l'Universite de Montreal, 1976.

Handbook of the legal, political, and Constitutional implications of Quebec's contemplated secession from the Canadian federation. Historical precedents (Ireland, Biafra, the American Confederacy) are cited, and the effect of seccession upon the economic health of Quebec is heavily emphasized. (In French).

Brown, Barbara A., Thomas I. Emerson, Gail Falk, and Ann Freedman. "The Equal Rights Amendment: A Constitutional Basis for Equal Rights for Women." 80 *Yale Law Journal* 871 (1971).

Excellent in-depth look at sex discrimination in the United States worked around the context of the proposed Equal Rights Amendment. This article outlines past and present limits on women's rights, and explains the potential effect of the Amendment's ratification on legislation and practice.

The legislative history of the E.R.A. is included as an appendix.

Bruegel, J.W. "A Neglected Field: The Protection of Minorities." 4 *Revue des Droits de l'Homme* 413 (1971).

This essay surveys and reviews twentieth century efforts in the international community to protect European linguistic and ethnic minorities. The impact of such documents as the League of Nations Minorities Protocols, the 1945 Potsdam Agreement, the United Nations Universal Declaration of Human Rights, and the European Convention on Human

Rights are assessed. National constitutions and their provisions are not mentioned, but it is suggested that interest expressed by the international community in protecting the rights of minorities will influence states toward proper treatment of minority group members.

Brunet, Michael: "Continentalism and Quebec Nationalism," *Queen's Quarterly,* Vol. 76, 1970.

Bucci, P. Vincent. *Chiese e Stato: Church-State Relations in Italy within the Contemporary Constitutional Framework.* The Hague Nijhoff, 1969.

Case studies of church-state conflicts in postwar Italy, with emphasis on issues of religious freedom and clerical jurisdiction over marriage and divorce. The place of the Lateran Treaty in Italian Constitutional law and history is examined.

Buchner-Uhder, Willi. *Socialist Human Rights in the German Democratic Republic.* Berlin, 1968.

Review of constitutional and statutory sources of the "human rights" enjoyed by the citizens of the GDR. Such rights include the right to work, the right to recreation, and the right to material assistance in case of illness, accident, or old age. An appendix consolidates these human rights provisions from statutes, government decrees, and other non-constitutional sources.

Budiarjo, Carmel. "The Abuse of Human Rights in Indonesia." *Veenhoven,* Volume Three, p. 209.

Buergenthal, Thomas. "Implementing the United Nations Racial Convention." 12 *Texas International Law Journal* 87 (1977).

This study focuses on the practices of the Committee on the Elimination of Racial Discrimination which was established under the Convention to supervise its implementation.

Buergenthal, Thomas. "International and Regional Human Rights Law and Institutions: Some examples of their interaction." 12 *Texas International Law Journal* 321 (1977).

A very brief article, which concerns itself with the relationships and interactions between United Nations-sponsored human rights efforts and the work of regional and specialized organizations. Since the focus is on such relationships rather than upon the substantive results achieved, the article is of limited value for our purposes.

Bulletin of Czechoslovak Law, Volume 8. Union of Czechoslovak Lawyers, Prague Faculty of Law (1967).

Provides valuable insight into the Czech liberalization period of 1967-68. Each of the twenty-three articles in the volume touches upon some aspect of human rights, and all are sophisticated in their analysis -- the rhetoric commonly associated with Communist scholarship is almost entirely absent. Those articles which are of most interest with regard to Czech Constitutional provisions are annotated separately.

It is revealing that the *Bulletin* published through 1968, then ceased publication until 1971. When it reappeared, it was with a new director and editorial board.

Burdeau, Georges. ''Zur Auflosung des Verfassungsbegriffs.'' In: *Der Staat,* p. 389 (1962).

The author sees Constitutions as essentially empty of real significance.

Butler, William J., and Georges Levasseur. *Human Rights and the Legal System in Iran.* Geneva, International Commission of Jurists, 1976.

Report on the criminal justice system and the secret police (SAVAK) in Iran. It is stressed that Constitutionally-guaranteed freedoms may be impinged upon by police or legal action, as the power of the Shah is absolute, and the Shah controls all state organs.

Calvert, Harry. *Constitutional Law in Northern Ireland.* London, Stevens and Sons, Ltd., 1968.

Analysis of the Government of Ireland Act of 1920, which serves as a Constitution for the six counties which make up Northern Ireland, and of later statutes and court decisions which are also of importance for Ulster.

The 1920 Act is particularly scrutinized with regard to its

provisions for regional and local government; human rights aspects are barely mentioned.

Camargo, Pedro Pablo. "The Right to Judicial Protection: 'Amparo' and other Latin American Remedies for the Protection of Human Rights." 3 *Lawyer of the Americas* 191 (1971).

Excellent essay on the Latin-American "amparo" -- a remedy similar to the Anglo-American *habeas corpus,* but which is broader in scope. Discussion centers upon the evolution of "amparo" in Mexican law, its spread to other Latin American states, and its importance, as reflected in the constitutions of most of those nations. Camargo envisions an expansion of the "amparo" remedy to include all invasions of civil or human rights, by whatever authority.

Carlyle, A.J.: *Political Liberty, a History of the Conception in the Middle Ages and Modern Times,* Oxford University Press, Oxford, 1963.

Carter, Gwendolyn M., ed. *Five African States: Responses to Diversity.* Ithaca, Cornell University Press, 1963.

Somewhat dated social, constitutional, and political history of Dahomey, the Congo, Rhodesia, South Africa, and Cameroon. These states all struggled with the problem of different ethnic and cultural groups in a central government; the various constitutional responses to the problem are stressed throughout the study.

Carter, Gwendolyn M., ed. *National Unity and Regionalism in Eight African States.* Ithaca, Cornell University Press, 1966.

Excellent sourcebook on the peoples and governmental systems of Nigeria, The Congo, Gabon, Central African Republic, Niger, Chad, Ethiopia, and Uganda. Emphasis is placed upon tribal, religious, and cultural minorities, and means of protecting the rights and interests of minority group members are discussed.

Chakravarti, N.R.: *The Indian Minority in Burma,* Oxford University Press, London, 1971.

Chari, V.K. Thiruvenkata. "The Courts and the Constitution in

India.'' In: R.N. Spann, ed. *Constitutionalism in Asia.* Bombay, Asia Publishing House, 1964.

Discussion of Articles 36 to 51 of the Constitution, which are not judicially enforceable, but which provide policy considerations to guide governmental actions.

Charton, Nancy. ''Ethnicity and its Significance for Local Government and Constitutional Planning in the Republic of South Africa.'' 6 *Studies in Comparative Local Government* No. 2, p. 44 (1972).

Very fine statistical survey of ethnic membership of South Africa's politicians and public servants -- the ethnically-based electoral bloc of the Afrikaner is noted. Suggestions are made for the decentralization of governmental authority, so that non-Afrikaners, blacks, coloureds, and Asians may participate more fully in local government.

Chaudhary, A.G. ''The Scope of Article Two of the 1962 Constitution.'' 1-2 *Pakistan Supreme Court Law Quarterly* 271 (1967/69).

An elucidation of the due process provisions of the 1962 Pakistan Constitution. Included is a discussion of the evolution of the concept of due process, from the Magna Charta to the West German and Indian Constitutions.

Article Two of the Pakistan Constitution operates to bar arbitrary legislative and executive exercises of power. Unlike some other fundamental rights provisions, which extend only to citizens, Article Two protects all persons within the nation's borders, offering them the umbrella of due process protection.

Christol, C.Q., and Helmut Bader. ''Legal Rights of the Alien in Austria, with special Reference to the U.S. Citizen.'' 7 *International Lawyer* 289 (1973).

An outline of the constitutional rights and guarantees provided the alien in Austria. The article touches upon general fundamental rights provisions of the Austrian constitution as well.

CLAUDE, RICHARD P., Ed. *Comparative Human Rights.* Baltimore, Johns Hopkins University Press, 1976.

Claude, Richard P. "The Threshhold Problem for Human Rights Research." 6 *Human Rights Journal* 169 (1977).

Compilation and analysis of source materials for scholarly research into human rights concerns. Claude emphasizes that the prospective researcher must take care to assure that his sources are both accurate and reliable, and notes that many self-serving documents on human rights are issued by governments and government agencies. A country-by-country bibliography of reliable source material is included.

Claude, Richard P. "The Western Tradition of Human Rights in Comparative Perspective." 14 *Comparative Juridicial Review* 4 (1977).

A valuable examination, in historical and philosophical terms, of the evolution of the great "liberal democracies" -- Britain, France, and the United States -- with emphasis on human rights elements in those nations' constitutions and legislation. Claude traces the stages of institutional development in the three nations, and shows that human rights concerned evolved in parallel with governmental structure and organization.

Codding, George: *Federal Government of Switzerland,* Boston, Houghton Mifflin Co., 1961.

Cole, Sonia. *The Races of Man.* London, Trustees of the British Museum (National History), 1965.

Illustrated summary providing background material on racial classifications. The emphasis is biological.

Coleman, Howard David. "The Problem of Anti-Semitism under the International Convention on the Elimination of All Forms of Racial Discrimination." 2 *Revue des Droits de l'Homme* 609 (1969).

This essay examines the form of discriminating known as anti-Semitism; it defines the term, explains its scope, and demonstrates how racially-based anti-Semitism falls within the ambit of the International Convention on the Elimination of All Forms of Racial Discrimination.

Collette, N.J. "Malaysia's Forgotten People: Education, Cultural Identity and Socio-Economic Mobility Among South Indian Plantation Workers." *Veenhoven,* Volume Five, p. 101.

Columbia Human Rights Law Review, Volume 8, No. 1 (Spring-Summer, 1976).

This entire volume is devoted to an International Symposium on "Law and the Status of Women"; lawyers and jurists presented reports on issues of concern to women as dealt with in Brazil, Egypt, France, Ghana, India, Indonesia, Iran, Jamaica, Kenya, Peru, the Philippines, Sweden, Togo, the United States, and Yugoslavia.

Each monograph follows a uniform outline and discusses, in turn, general political and civil rights; rights relating to marriage and the family; penal laws; health and family planning concerns, particularly the right to abortion and voluntary sterilization; education; and employment. Many of the contributions contain excerpts from applicable statutes, and several include bibliographies.

An extremely valuable source for ascertaining, virtually at a glance, the rights of women in the fields outlined above.

Columbia Law School. "Symposium on the Status of Women." 20 *American Journal of Comparative Law* 585 (1972).

The text of this very valuable symposium contains surveys on the status of women in Great Britain, Sweden, Norway, France, the Soviet Union, and Israel. Also included is a study of "The status of Married Women under customary law in Senegal."

Congress Monthly, Vol. 45, No. 3 March/April 1978.

Connor, Walker. "Nation-Building or Nation-Destroying?" 24 *World Politics* No. 3, p. 319 (1972).

According to Connor, only 12 contemporary states can be considered ethnically homogeneous. In nearly a third of the cases (29.5 percent), the largest group comprises less than half of the state's population. And in 53 states (40.2 percent), the poplulation is divided into at least five significant ethnic groupings.

Cooray, Joseph A.L. *Constitutional Government and Human Rights in a Developing Society.* Colombo, 1969.

Monograph on Ceylon (now Sri Lanka) and its constitutional history. Human rights are discussed in general terms only, and little is said about judicial enforceability of human rights guarantees.

Corpus Constitionnel: Recueil universel des Constitutions en Vigueur. Leiden, E.J. Brill, 1968 -.

Excellend compendium of constitutional materials, together with introductions by recognized scholars. Incomplete. Editors have only completed countries up to "E" alphabetically.

Corry, Stephen. "Towards Indian Self-Determination in Colombia." *Veenhoven,* Volume Three, p. 33.

Cortes, Irene R. "Population and Law: The Fundamental Rights aspects in the Philippine Setting." 48 *Philippines Law Journal* 303 (1973).

The text of a lecture delivered at the University of the Philippines College of Law; it deals with the constitutional and legal actions and views taken on the subject of population (i.e., growth, control, etc.), in the Philippines and elsewhere. Some of the topics covered include marriage laws; right to privacy and population control; religion and population control; family planning and individual rights.

Cortes, Irene R. "Women's Rights Under the 1973 Philippine Constitution." 4 *Lawasia* No. 2, p. 118 (1973). (Same article also in 50 *Philippines Law Journal* 1 (1975(.

The 1973 Constitution does much to eliminate some of the obvious discriminatory elements of the older Constitution. This article points out, however, that the Constitution's guarantee of equality to all is far from realization. Examples of Civil Code legislation which act in derogation of Constitutional guarantees are detailed.

Coulson, N.J. "The State and the Individual in Islamic Law." 6 *International and Comparative Law Quarterly* 49 (1957).

This is an examination of the effect that Islamic law, philosophy, and tradition have had on the notion of defined liberties of the individual in the Constitutions and legislation of Islamic states. A bit outdated, but still valuable nonetheless for its insights.

Crawford, J.R. "The Working of Rhodesian Declaration of Rights." 83 *South African Law Journal* 337 (1966).

Rhodesia's 1961 Constitution includes a Declaration of Rights closely modeled upon the 1960 Nigerian Constitution and thus, ultimately, upon the European Convention on Human Rights. The Constitution, however, specifically exempts all pre-existing legislation from requirements imposed by the Declaration. Consequently, arbitrary and discriminatory practices which have been set in motion by pre-Constitutional legislation have been legitimated, and thus are forever closed to Constitutional challenge. This article gives several examples of the impotence and frustration faced by petitioners when faced with the official recalcitrance embodied in the 1961 Constitution.

Daily Telegraph, London.

Danelski, David J. "A Behavioral Conception on Human Rights." 3 *Law in Transition Quarterly* 63 (1966).

An examination of human rights, with the thesis that in order for a person to be accorded basic rights and dignity, he must first be perceived as a person. Human rights are distinguished from civil rights, which attach merely because of the operation of law.

Das, S.R. Mohan. "Discrimination in India." *Veenhoven,* Volume Two, p. 157.

DAS BASU, DURGA. Commentary on the Constitution of India. 6th ed., Rev'd and enlarged. Calcutta, 1973.

Das Gupta, Jyotirindra. "Nation, Region, and Welfare: Ethnicity,

Regionalism, and Development Politics in South Asia." 433 *Annals of the American Academy of Political and Social Science* 125 (1977).

General study of minority groups in South Asia, particularly India.

Das Gupta, S.K. "Racial Discrimination and Human Rights." 15 *Journal of the Indian Law Institute* 440 (1973).

A short critique on the ineffectiveness of United Nations measures against racial discrimination. Nations are urged to implement and enforce policies of non-discrimination.

de la Garza, Rudolph O. "Mexican Americans in the United States: The Evolution of a Relationship." *Veenhoven,* Volume Five, p. 259.

Denisov, A. "Some Theoretical Problems of the Constitutional Structure of the Soviet State (On the Thirtieth Anniversary of the U.S.S.R. Constitution of 1936)" 5 *Soviet Law and Government* No. 4, p. 20 (1967).

In this explication of the purpose of the 1936 Soviet Constitution, Denisov contrasts that document, which he holds to be reflective of the interests of all the Soviet peoples, with the Constitutions of bourgeois societies. The latter, it is posited, are mere tools in the hands of a powerful minority, and are wielded in order to more fully exploit the masses.

Deshpande, V.S. "Rights and Duties under the Constitution." 15 *Journal of the Indian Law Institute* 94 (1973).

A discussion of India's system of democratic socialism. The purpose of India's constitution, according to Deshpande, is to introduce and effectuate socially desirable goals. Rights and duties, it is warned, do not exist in isolation, but against the fabric of reality. The tone of the piece is patronizing, as if aimed at children.

de Jouvenal, B.: *The Pure Theory of Politics,* Cambridge University Press, London, 1963.

de Silva, K.M. "Discrimination in Sri Lanka." *Veenhoven,* Volume Three, p. 71.

Deutsch, Karl W. "The Political Significance of Linguistic Conflicts." In: *Multilingual Political Systems.* Quebec, University of Laval Press, 1975. p. 7.

The neglect of linguistic conflicts has had grave social consequences, which extend even to the physical loss of life. Deutsch sets forth several theories about language conflicts for consideration by the political community and suggests possible solutions for the development of effective language policies which will aid political science in fulfilling two of its major tasks; namely, the protection of human life, and the defense of the autonomy and dignity of the individual.

de Villiers, Cas. "Colour Discrimination and Policy Evolution in South Africa." *Veenhoven,* Volume Five, p. 327.

Dialogue, US Information Service, Washington, 1975.

Dialogue, US Information Agency, Washington, 1973.

Djordjevic, Jovan. *Novi Ustavini Sistem.* Belgrade, 1964.

An excellent study providing background on the Yugoslav Constitutions from 1945 through 1963.

Djordjevic, Jovan. "The Yugoslav Constitution and New Individual Rights and Freedoms." In: *Scritti in onore di Gaspare Ambrosini.* Volume 1. Milano, 1970. p. 595.

Survey of the fundamental rights guarantees incorporated into the Yugoslav constitution of 1963. Among the rights enumerated is the right of minority group members to use their own language and retain their own culture.

Doehring, Karl. "Non-Discrimination and Equal Treatment under the European Human Rights Convention and the West German Constitution with Particular Reference to Discrimination against Aliens." 18 *American Journal of Comparative Law* 305 (1970).

In Article 3 of the West German Constitution equal treatment of all persons is mandated with regard to all state activities; even when no fundamental or constitutionally enunciated right is involved, the West German is protected against arbitrariness by officials. The corresponding provision of the European Convention on Human Rights, Article 14, prohibits discrimination only where those rights guaranteed by the Convention itself are at issue.

German constitutional practice has long permitted distinctions to be made on the basis of citizenship; the Human Rights Convention, though, specifically imparts fundamental rights to all persons regardless of alienage or citizenship, and indeed cites discrimination on the basis of citizenship or alienage as impermissible.

Here Doehring compares and contrasts the texts of the German and European documents, paying special attention to protection of the rights of non-nationals.

Donneur, Andre P. "La Solution Territoriale au Probleme de Multilinguisme." In: *Multilingual Political Systems.* Quebec, University of Laval Press, 1975. p. 209.

There are two solutions for the problems created by the coexistence of several languages within a nation: the principle of personality and the principle of territoriality. Donneur makes a comparative study of Switzerland and Belgium who chose territoriality, and Canada, which chose personality, in solving multilingual problems in the areas of public administration, education, private services, and commerce and work.

Dressler, Alfred. "Human Rights in Constitutional Theory." 25 *Bulletin of Czechoslovak Law* No. 8, p. 56 (1967).

This analysis of the United Nations Universal Declaration of Human Rights focuses on its applicability to socialist states, and points out that the socialist concept of the individual's *duty* to the state makes enactment of many of the Declaration provisions (on freedom of emigration, for example) impracticable.

A brief summary of Czech constitutional history is included, with an emphasis upon the historical importance accorded protection of linguistic and cultural minorities in this multiethnic state.

Dreyer, June Teufel. "Ethnic Relations in China." 433 *Annals of the American Academy of Political and Social Science* 100

(1977).

Though ethnic minorities comprise only six percent of China's population, they inhabit some of China's most strategically valuable and resource-rich lands. This article traces historically the ways in which the Chinese government, from the beginning of the twentieth century to the present day, has perceived and treated such minorities.

Dryden, P.K. "Annotated Bibliography of Political Rights of African Women." 7 *African Law Studies* 27 (1972).

A valuable source for sociologically-oriented studies of the role of African women in their states. Law Reviews are sadly underrepresented in this bibliography, which concentrates on sociological and political science articles and monographs. United Nations materials relating to women's rights are also included, but most of these date back to the early 1950's, and their present authority can be called into question.

Duchacek, Ivo D. *Power Maps: Comparative Politics of Constitutions.* Santa Barbara, California, A.B.C. - Clio, 1973.

Useful summary of comparative data on the world's constitutions in a limited number of selected areas. Breakdowns are provided on such topics as preambles, powers to declare and conduct wars, emergency powers, etc. There are also data on different kinds of parliaments and presidential systems, a comparison between rigid and flexible constitutions and other useful materials. It is only of secondary value, however, in a study of racial, religious, and sex discrimination

DUCHACKE, IVO D. *Rights and Liberties in the World Today: Constitutional Promise and Reality.* Santa Barbara, A.B.C. - Clio, 1972.

Dunn, James A., Jr. "The Revision of the Constitution of Belgium: A Study in the Institutionalization of Ethnic Conflict." 27 *Western Political Quarterly* 143 (1974).

Brief but excellent history of the Flemish-Walloon conflict and the movement toward federalization of Belgium along ethnic and linguistic lines. Recent revision of the national constitution to satisfy demands for decentralization by the Flemish and the problems inherent in the designation of Brussels as a bilingual city are discussed.

Dunner, Joseph. "Anti-Jewish Discrimination Since the End of World War II." *Veenhoven,* Volume One, p. 65.

Dushnyck, Walter. "Discrimination and Abuse of Power in the U.S.S.R." *Veenhoven,* Volume Two, p. 445.

Dushnyck, Walter. "Human Rights in Communist Ruled East-Central Europe." *Veenhoven,* Volume One, p. 377.

Eckstein, Susan. "Occupational Inequality in Urban Mexico." *Veenhoven,* Volume Two, p. 357.

Elsen, S., and P. Coogan. "Men, Women, and the Constitution and the Equal Rights Amendment." 10 *Columbia Journal of Law and Social Problems* 77 (1973).

The text of a symposium, which discusses the history of sex discrimination in the United States and the development of the Equal Rights Amendment. The discussion is couched in constitutional terms.

Engold, Izhak. "The Problem of Jewis Law in a Jewish State." 3 *Israel Law Review* 254 (1968).

Here the presence and influence of Halacha (Jewish religious law) upon the secular state of Israel are discussed. Religious groups favor a return to the Halacha as part of the establishment of a Jewish religious nation, and even some non-religious Israelis see in the Halacha a cultural value akin to that of the Hebrew language, and so favor its adoption.

Problems of jurisdiction with regard to the Halacha are considered, and examples of the application of religious law by Israeli civil court judges are cited.

ESMAN, M J : *Ethnic Conflict in the Western World,* Cornell University Press, London, 1977.

Esperson, Ole. "Denmark and the European Convention ofHuman Rights." 18 *American Journal of Comparative Law* 293 (1970).

The Danish government has maintained that, with a few minor exceptions, the nation's existing laws do not impinge upon the guarantees set forth in the European Convention of Human Rights. This essay illustrates the influence which the Convention has engendered in Danish judicial and administrative practice.

Ewing, Winifred Crum. "Discrimination in Great Britain." *Veenhoven,* Volume One, p. 509.

Ewing, Winifred Crum. "Human Rights in Northern Ireland." *Veenhoven,* Volume Five, p. 33.

FALCH, JEAN. "Contribution a l'Etude du statut des langues en Europe." Centre International de Recherches sur le Bilinguisme, Quebec, less presses de l'Universite laval, 1973. (In French).

Faruki, Kemal A. *The Evolution of Islamic Constitutional Theory and Practice.* Karachi, National Publishing House, Ltd., 1971.

This volume discusses the influence of *shar'ia* (religious law) upon governments of Muslim secular rulers, from Islam's beginnings in the Seventh Century to the 1920's. The title is somewhat misleading, as national constitutions are discussed only peripherally.

The Federalist, No. 84, Modern Library ed., 1937.

Feldbrugge, F.J.M. "Law and Political Dissent in the Soviet Union." 26 *Current Legal Problems* 241 (1973).

Focuses on political protest in the Soviet Union and ignores issues of race, religion, and nationality. Some persons accused of political crimes have openly proclaimed the incompatibility of the Criminal Code with the guarantee of freedom of opinion and expression found in Article 125 of the Soviet Constitution -- to no avail.

Filesi, Teobaldo. "Orientations et revisionnisme constitutionnel dans les Nouveaux Etas d'Afrique, Specialement dans les Etats d'expression Anglaise au sud su Sahara." In: *Les Constitutions et Institutions Administratives des Etats Nouveaux.* Brussels, Incidi, 1965. p. 512.

Article discusses former British colonies in Africa after

independence.

Fischer, Georges. "Les Etats Multiriciaux." 5 *Human Rights Journal* 535 (1972).

Written in French, this article explores the basic problems of selected multi-racial states. It begins with several definitions, then attempts to classify types of groups. The body is devoted to the situation in the United States, India, England, and Malaysia. The reader, however, questions the choice since the situation in the West is so different from that of the Asian countries which are also discussed.

Fishman, Joshua A., and Haya Fisherman. "The Official Langguages of Israel: Their Status in Law and Police Attitudes and Knowledge Concerning Them.' In: *Multilingual Political Systems.* Quebec, University of Laval Press, 1975. p. 497.

An official language is one that is used by a government and promoted through the power of the state, but it is not necessarily the national language. Prior to 1948 the official languages in what is now Israel were English, Arabic, and Hebrew. After the establishment of the state of Israel Hebrew was named as the official language; English became optional; and Arabic, though official in name, was increasingly ignored. The authors document the past and present statutory law and, in a survey of police, show the confusion created by the differences in theory and practice.

Fisk, Winston M. 'The Constitutionalism Movement in Yugoslavia: a Preliminary Survey." 30 *Slavic Review* 277 (1971).

Introduction to the Yugoslav Constitution, unique among Communist constitutions because of the provisions it makes for a federalist system. In Yugoslavia the provinces exercise an extraordinary degree of self-determination -- the point is made that profound ethnic sentiments of the Croats, Serbs, and other ethnic minorities played a part in influencing the establishment of such a system.

Fitzgibbon, Russel H. "Constitutional Development in Latin America: A Synthesis." In: Asher N. Christensen, ed. *The*

Evolution of Latin American Government. New York, Henry Holt and Co., 1951. p. 210.

Traces foreign influences upon Latin American constitutions.

Forsyth, C.F. and Schiller, J.E.: ed.: *Human Rights - The Cape Town Conference,* Juta & Co., Cape Town, 1979.

Fort, E.: ''Some Education and Imperatives Regarding the Peaceful Pursuit of Intergroup Accommodation in a Plural Society,'' in Rhoodie, Nic, *Intergroup Accommodations in Plural Societies,* Macmillan Press, London, 1978.

Franck, Thomas M. *Comparative Constitutional Process: Cases and Materials.* New York, Praeger, 1968.

Textbook, which examines the actions of various common law states with regard to such topics as interstate commerce, judicial review, due process, etc. One chapter, a short one, is devoted to civil/political/human rights material.

Friedrich, Carl J. *The Impact of American Constitutionalism Abroad.* Boston, Boston University Press, 1967.

Brief but important work on the influence of American constitutional ideals and practices upon foreign states. Friedrich discusses the impact of the American system on notions of Presidentialism, Federalism, and Human Rights, the latter including an analysis of judicial review, as practiced in the United States and imported for use overseas.

Friedrich, Carl J. *Limited Government: A Comparison.* Englewood Cliffs, N.J., Prentice-Hall, 1974.

Aspects of constitutionalism, discussed by one of America's leading authorities. Chapter Six is devoted to constitutional aspects of human rights protection.

Friedrich, Carl J. ''The Politics of Language and Corporate Federalism.'' In *Multilingual Political Systems.* Quebec, University of Laval Press, 1975. p. 227.

A philosophical paper on the relationship of language to nationality, the role of federalism in multi-lingual societies, cultural autonomy, and the principles of territoriality and personality. Austria-Hungary, Yugoslavia, and Estonia are cited as models.

Friedrich, Carl J. "Some Reflections on Constitutionalism for Emergent Political Orders." In: Herbert J. Spiro, ed. *Patterns of African Development.* Englewood Cliffs, N.J., Prentice Hall, 1967. p. 9.

Deals with the applicability of western political ideas in the constitutions of developing countries.

Friedrich, Carl J.: "Political Theory of New Democratic Constitutions," in A.J. Zurcher, ed.: *Constitutions and Constitutional Trends Since World War II,* New York University Press, New York, 1951.

Friedrich, Carl J. "Some Reflections on the Meaning and Significance of Constitution-Making in Our Time." In: Henry Steele Commager, ed. *Festschrift fur Karl Loewenstein.* Tubingen, J.C.B. Mohr, 1971. p. 119.

The author sees some importance in the role of constitutions in state formation.

Gablentz, Otto Heinrich von der. *Einfuhrung in die Politische Wissenschaft.* Koln and Opladen, Westdeutscher Verlag, 1965.

Deals with the several types of constitutions; distinguishes "formal" from "genuine" constitutions.

Gajendragadkar, P.B. *The Constitution of India; its Philosophy and Basic Postulates.* Nairobi, Bombay, London, 1969.

A reprint of the Gandhi memorial lectures at the University of Nairobi. Much of the material concerns the fundamental rights and minorities provisions of the Indian Constitution. The brevity of the work (less than 100 pages) makes it an attractive introduction to India's Constitution, especially since multi-volume works on the Constitution abound.

Galanter, Marc. "The Abolition of Disabilities -- Untouchability and the Law." In: J. Michael Mahar, ed. *The Untouchables in Contemporary India.* Tucson, University of Arizona Press, 1972. p. 227.

Historical treatment of legal responses to untouchability problem, going back to British practices.

GALANTER, MARC. Competing Equalities: The Indian Experiment with Compensatory Discrimination. (Forthcoming).

Galanter, Marc. "Equality and Preferential Treatment: Constitutional Limits and Judicial Control." 14 *Indian Yearbook of International Affairs* 257 (1965).

An important article describing the judicially-imposed limitations on the overly-broad language on special preferences in Articles 15 and 16 of the Indian Constitution.

Galizia, Mario. "The Declarations of Rights and their Place in the History of Italian Constitutional Law." In: *Associazione Italiano di Diritto Comparato. Italian National Reports to the IXth International Congress of Comparative Law.* Tehran, 1974, Milano, 1974. p. 33.

Limited historical sketch of the influence of the French and American declarations of Rights on Italian sympathies and political ideals. The constitutions of Italian nation-states which were adopted as a result of the 1848 ferment, and the impact of fascism with respect to constitutional rights provisions are discussed.

Gastil, R.D.: "The Rights to Self-Determination: Definition, Reality and Ideal Policy," in Rhoodie, Nic: *Intergroup Accommodation in a Plural Society,* Macmillan Press, London, 1978.

Gastil, Raymond. "Comparative Survey of Freedom." 17 *Freedom at Issue* 3 (1973).

Survey grades each nation on the basis of the political and civil liberties enjoyed by its people. Nations are categorized on a scale of 1 to 7, 1 indicating the highest degree of freedom, and 7 reflecting a complete lack of freedom. On this basis all states of the world are classified either as "free," "partly free," or "not free." Interesting idea, but the bases for the analysis and the conclusions are not shown.

Gaur, Santosh Kumar. "Safeguards to Stateless Linguistic Minorities." 2 *Lawyer* 61 (1970).

Many of India's component states contain members of various

language groups within their borders, but recognize and grant official status only to the tongue spoken by the majority of their citizens. Those who speak other languages are thereby disadvantaged in education and employment, and state governments do little to assist them in adjusting to life in a linguistically foreign community.

Gaur suggests that the various state governments address themselves to the problems presented by the stateless linguistic minorities and that they champion the rights of such peoples by giving special subsidies and encouraging cultural and education independence. Harking back to the India-Pakistan partition, Gaur warns of the bitterness and strife that may ensue if the needs and rights of these neglected peoples are not tended to.

Geertz, Clifford: "The Integrative Revolution," in *Old Solcieties and New States: the Quest for Modernity in Asia and Africa,* Free Press of Glencoe, New York, 1963.

Geographical Magazine, Washington, June, 1976, January 1984.

Ghouse, Mohammad. "Judicial Control of Protective Discrimination." 11 *Journal of the Indian Law Institute* 371 (1969).

Discussion of the definitions of "socially backward class" and caste, within the meaning of Article 15(4) of the Indian Constitution. Since "backward class" is nowhere defined in the Constitution, defining it is a matter of governmental policy; each state has the power to define "backward class," which would trigger with respect to such persons the special protection provisions of Article 15 (4).

Ghouse, Mohammad. "Minority Rights under the Indian Constitution." 36 *Supreme Court Journal* 67 (1967).

A discussion of Articles 29 and 30 of the Indian Constitution. These articles guarantee the educational and cultural rights of linguistic and ethnic minority groups, including the rights to establish and administer educational institutions.

Gilbertson, E.R. "Women and the Equal Protection Clause." 20

Cleveland State Law Review 351 (1971).

Article points out the inadequacy of the Fourteenth Amendment in providing for the equal protections of women. It highlights the attitudes which courts have.

Ginsberg, Morris: *On Justice in Society,* Ithaca Cornell University Press, 1965.

Historical view of discrimination on the basis of sex. Excellent for any examination of sex discrimination in the United States, but rather dated with regard to Equal Rights Amendment discussion.

Glazer, Nation: "Ethnicity: A World Phenomenon" in *Dialogue,* US Information Service, Washington, Vol. 8, 1975, No. 314.

GLASER, K and POSSONY, S.: *Victims of Politics -- The State of Human Rights,* Columbia University Press, N.Y., 1977.

Glayden, J. "The Transnational Protection of Ethnic Minorities" 13 *Canadian Yearbook of International Law* 25 (1974)

Discussion of ethnicity from a sociological and policy viewpoint; examples of ethnic consciousness are taken not only from Canada but from Europe, Africa, and Asia. The work of the United Nations in this area is briefly discussed.

Gonzales, Neptali. *Philippine Constitutional Law.* 3d ed. Manila, 1969.

A general textbook/casebook on the subject.

Gotlieb, Allan, ed. *Human Rights, Federalism, and Minorities.* Toronto, 1970.

An important collection of essays by political leaders (Pierre Trudeau) and distinguished scholars (Tarnopolsky, John Humphrey) concerning the protection of human rights in the federalist system of Canada. Emphasis is upon cultural and language rights of the French-speaking Canadian and, indeed, several of the articles are in French.

Graefrath, Bernhard. *The Economic, Social, and Cultural Human Rights in the German Democratic Republic.* Berlin, Publications of the GDR Committee on Human Rights, 1970.

Summary of economically and culturally-based human rights

enjoyed by citizens of the German Democratic Republic. An appendix placed the United Nations international Covenant on Economic, Social, and Cultural Rights and East German Constitutional provisions and statutes side-by-side in order to demonstrate the latter's compliance with the declarations and goals of the former.

Greenland, Jeremy. "Ethnic Discrimination in Rwanda and Burundi." *Veenhoven,* Volume Four, p. 95.

Greenwood, D.J.: "Continuity in change, Spanish Basque Ethnicity as a Historical Process," in Esman, M.: *Ethnic Conflict in the Western World,* Cornell University Press, London, 1977.

Greeley, A.: "The Rediscovery of Diversity," *The Antioch Review,* Fall, 1971.

Grementieri, Valerio, and Nicolo Trockner. "The Protection of Human Rights in Constitutional Law: Italy." In: *Associazione di Diritto Comparato. Italian National Reports to the IXth International Congress of Comparative Law.* Tehran, 1974, Milano, 1974. p. 491.

Discussion of remedies against infringement of civil and political rights under Italian Law. The importance of judicial review by the nation's Constitutional court is stressed.

Grigoryan, L. and Y. Dolgopolov. *Fundamentals of Soviet State Law.* Moscow, Progress Publishers, 1971.

Chapter II of this work deals with Communist theories on the idea of Constitutions.

Grove, D. John. *The Race vs Ethnic Debate: A Cross-National Analysis of Two Theoretical Approaches.* Denver, Center on International Race Relations, 1974.

Monograph contrasting the "assimilation' and "pluralistic" theories of multi-ethnic societies. Heavily laden with statistics; also good for its summarization of current work in the field.

Groves, Harry E. *The Constitution of Malaysia.* Singapore, Malaysia Publishers, Ltd., 1964.

Discussion and analysis of the Malaysian Constitution of 1957, as amended when the Federation of Malaya became Malaysia in 1962. Included is a short chapter on fundamental rights and freedoms, but the bulk of the work focuses on governmental structure and operations, as provided for in the Constitution.

Guggenheim, Malvina H. "The Implementation of Human Rights by the U.N. Commission on the Status of Women: A Brief Comment." 12 *Texas International Law Journal* 239 (1977).

A brief paper tracing the actions of the Commission on the Status of Women. It arrives at the conclusion that the Commission's creation of resolutions and Conventions on Women's Rights contribute significantly to the development of international law, but that its efforts should now be devoted to the implementation and enforcement of the rights it helped to foster.

Guggenheim, Malvina. "Re: Human Rights." 6 *New York University Journal of International Law and Politics 427* (1973).

This brief article concerns itself with the procedures of the Economic and Social Council on the Human Rights Commission and the Subcommission on Prevention of Discrimination and Protection of Minorities. The scope of its authority and the remedies suggested are limited.

Gupta, U.N."Constitutional Paramouncy of Fundamental Rights: Methods for Enforcement." 40 *Supreme Court Journal* 43 (1969).

A discussion of the *Golak Nath* case. The Court's decision in the case -- that Parliamentary action cannot amend the fundamental rights guarantees of the Indian Constitution -- is criticized. Gupta favors the adoption of a system similar to the French, where a Constitutional Council hands down advisory opinions on the constitutionality of legislation, rather than the Anglo-Indian system of judicial review.

Haden-Guest, Anthony: "The King of Fiat: Living with Terrorism." New York Magazine, May 1, 1978.

Hahlo, H.R., and Ellison Kahn. *The Union of South Africa: The Development of Its Laws and Constitution.* London, Stevens and Sons, Ltd., 1960.

History of South Africa, with emphasis on evolution of its legal and constitutional principles. Racial laws and apartheid are not emphasized, and are given only cursory treatment -- the bulk of the volume deals with contract law and conflict of laws problems.

Haksar, Urmila. *Minority Protection and International Bill of Human Rights.* Bombay, Allied Publishers, 1974.

Concerned exclusively with the problem of minority protection in its relation to the International Bill of Human Rights. United Nation protection of minority rights is seen as an extension of minorities problems going back to World War I and beyond.

Hamilton, David, and Mara Whitcombe. "Discrimination in Ethiopia." *Veenhoven,* Volume Three, p. 275.

Hanby, Victor J. "Indians in American Cities." *Veenhoven,* Volume Two, p. 343.

Hanby, Victor J. "The New Indianism and the Menominee of Wisconsin." *Veenhoven,* Volume One, p. 191.

Harbottle, Michael, and Eirwen Harbottle. "Cyprus: The Greek and Turkish Confrontation." *Veenhoven,* Volume Four, p. 497.

Harding, J. and Hogrefe, A.: "Attitudes of White Department Store Employees Toward Negro Co-Workers." 8 *Journal of Social Issues,* 1952.

Harlitz, Nils. *Elements of Nordic Public Law.* Stockholm, P.A. Norstedt and Sons, 1969.

General discussion of constitutional law and administrative development in Denmark, Finland, Iceland, Norway, and Sweden. Human rights concerns are touched upon in Chapter 9, "The Public and the Individual."

Harris, George S. "Ethnic Conflict and the Kurds." 433 *Annals of the American Academy of Political and Social Science* 112 (1977).

This article discusses the predicament of the Kurds, an ethnic minority spread throughout Turkish, Iranian, and Iraqi lands. The inability of the Kurds to establish their own state, and their impotence as a force of power in states in which they are a statistically significant minority, are analyzed here.

Harrison, Charles. "Uganda: The Expulsion of the Asians." *Veenhoven,* Volume Four, p. 287.

Hazard, John N. "Communist Constitutionalism in a New Form." 4 *Studies in Comparative Communism* 107 (1971).

Discussion of a 1971 Draft for a Chinese Constitution. In the Constitution Mao is named as chief of state, and Lin Piao is designated as his successor. The observation is made that the Chinese draft constitution is closely modeled on the Stalinist 1936 Soviet Constitution.

HEARD, KENNETH. Political Systems in Multi-Racial Societies. Johannesburg, South African Institute of Race Relations, 1961.

Heisler, Martin O. "Managing Ethnic Conflict in Belgium." 433 *Annals of the American Academy of Political and Social Science* 32 (1977).

Historical summary of ethnic division between Flemish and Walloons in Belgium. Religious and linguistic bases for such division are discussed and analyzed.

Heming, John: *Red Gold,* Harvard University Press, Cambridge, 1978.

Henkin, Louis. "National and International Perspectives in Racial Discrimination." 4 *Revue des Droits de l'Homme* 263 (1971).

Racial discrimination is a common practice, it is conceded here, and Professor Henkin of Columbia University attempts to explain the failure of international efforts to halt such discrimination by pointing out that governments rarely act with positive force against inequality. Indeed, he notes, racial or ethnic discrimination can be a cornerstone of national policy (citing South Africa and Cyprus as examples); it is suggested that most governments are particularly loath to enforce racial equality by outlawing private discriminatory actions, and that values of national autonomy often operate to discourage concerned nations from interfering in the affairs of states whose policy it is to discriminate.

Hewitt, Christopher. "Majorities and Minorities: a Comparative Survey of Ethnic Violence." 433 *Annals of the American Academy of Political and Social Science* 150 (1977).

A comparative study of ethnic divisions which have escalated into open rioting or warfare, and an analysis of the cause of such violent outbreaks.

Hingorini, L. "Minorities in India and their Rights." 5 *Revue des Droits de l'Homme* 479 (1972).

A brief look at Indian Constitutional treatment of minorities; it forms an excellent accompaniment to the many outstanding full-length studies in this area.

Horgen, James: "Adhdam Tribe Inservitude," *Geographical Magazine,* Washington, June, 1976.

Holborn, L.W., Gwendolyn M. Carter, and J.H. Herz, eds. *German Constitutional Documents since 1871: Selected Texts and Commentary.* New York, Praeger, 1970.

Comparative study of various areas of Constitutional concern (governmental structure, the role and power of the legislative, fundamental rights), which illustrates how those spheres were dealt with in Weimar, Nazi, and post-war Constitutional documents. Comparison is facilitated by the editors' practice of placing texts from each Constitution in juxtaposition.

Horowitz, Donald. "Cultural Movements and Ethnic Change." 433 *Annals of the American Academy of Political and Social Science* 6 (1977).

General discussion of ethnicity in the 1960's and 1970's, with reference to African and European unrest and ethnic conflict.

Horrell, Muriel. *Legislation and Race Relations.* Johannesburg,

South African Institute of Race Relations, 1971. With mimeographed supplementary materials.

Supplementing Constitutional provisions on racial separation, this book summarizes important legislation and regulations which affect race relationships. It is broken down by topic.

Hosken, Fran P. *Genital Mutilation of Women in Africa.* Munger Africana Library Notes, Pasadena, California Institute of Technology, 1976.

Overly brief (21 pages) summary of sex practices violative of women's rights in African nations. Points up failure of United Nations to publicize problem or take any action against such practices.

Hottel, Althea K., ed. "Women Around the World." 375 *Annals of the American Academy of Political and Social Science.* Philadelphia, 1968 (entire volume).

A discussion of the political, economic, and social status of women throughout the world. Participation by women in the political process, particularly in the exercise of the franchise, is most closely examined. Articles on women in Peru, Japan, Western and Eastern Europe, the Middle East, Sub-Saharan Africa and Southeast Asia are included.

Huillier, F.O.: "Histoire et droits de l'homme," 6 *Revue des droits d l' homme* 81, 1973.

Howard Law Journal. "Symposium on the International Law of Human Rights.' 11-12 *Howard Law Journal* 257 (1965).

This entire issue of the *Howard Law Journal* is comprised of papers and lectures given at the Symposium. Contributions on human rights in India, Israel, Japan, the Soviet Union, the United States, Nigeria, Sierra Leone, and South Africa are included; constitutional aspects of the topics are stressed. Some of the articles may be dated.

Humphrey, John P. "The International Bill of Rights: Scope and Implementation." 17 *William and Mary Law Review* 527 (1976).

Brief look at the birth and development of the concept of an International Bill of Rights. Specific attention is paid to the movement toward such an international document afforded by the United Nations International Covenant on Economic, Social, and Cultural Rights and the International Covenant on Civil and Political Rights.

Hug, Abul Fazl. "Constitution-Making in Bangladesh." 46 *Pacific Affairs* 59 (1973).

Constitutional history of Bangladesh, with emphasis on the part played by various political factions in the establishment of the government. The author notes that Bangladesh's problems in creating a constitution were minimized in that the people were generally of one language and culture, and that minority group membership was statistically insignificant.

Hyer, Paul V. "The Mongolian Nation within the People's Republic of China." *Veenhoven,* Volume One, p. 471.

Imam, Mohammed. *The Indian Supreme Court and the Constitution: A Study of the Process of Construction.* Lucknow, 1968.

Summary of Supreme Court cases in several areas, including religious freedom, equality, and minority rights. A good general guide to the activities of the Supreme Court, though somewhat dated. The Indian Constitution, with explanatory notes and commentary, is reprinted as an appendix.

IMAM, MOHAMMED, Ed. *Minorities and the Law.* Indian Law Institute. Bombay, Tripathi, 1972.

Institut International des Civilisations Differentes. *The Constitutions and Administrative Institutions of the New States.* Brussels, 1965.

A series of discourses and reports (with appropriate documentation) of legal, political, social, and economic aspects of the Constitutions and administrative institutions of newly-independent states. A fifth general report, this volume is concerned with "perspectives of democracy."

INSTITUT INTERNATIONAL DES DROITS DE L'HOMME. "Enseignment des droits de l'homme dans les universities." 6 Revue des Droits de l'Homme 109 (1973) (In French).

International League for the Rights of Man. "The Violation of

Human Rights in India." *Veenhoven,* Volume Five, p. 473.

Isaacs, H.R.: "The Ex-Untouchables," in Mahar, J.M. ed.: *The Untouchables in Contemporary India,* University of Arizona Press.

Isajiw, Wsevolod W.: "Definitions of Ethnicity," in *Ethnicity,* Vol. I, 1974.

Jain, M.P.: "Safeguard to Minorities: Constitutional Principals, Policies and Framework," in M. Inman: *Minorities and the Law.*

Jagchid, Sechin. "Discrimination Against Minorities in China." *Veenhoven,* Volume Two, p. 389.

Jahan, Rounag. "Women in Bangladesh." *Veenhoven,* Volume Five, p. 533.

Jaksch, W.: *Europa's Weg Nach Potsdam,* Verlag Wissenschaft und Politik, Cologne, 1967.

Jicinsky, Zdanek. "Problems of the Socialist Concept of Civil Rights and its Development." 25 *Bulletin of Czechoslovak Law* No. 8, p. 29 (1967).

An astonishingly frank discussion of human rights guarantees in Socialist countries. Jicinsky postulates that freedoms had been limited by the social and cultural "backwardness" of the masses in most Socialist states prior to revolution. Czechoslovakia, however, is seen as a state of culturally advanced peoples and thus "political rights and freedoms under Socialism must be constitutionally conceived as the rights of the individual citizen." The fullest enjoyment of political rights (freedom of speech, the press, etc.) is exhorted.

Joncic, K. *The Yugoslav Constitution and Relations Between the Nationalities.* Belgrade, Editor Medjunrodna Stampa-Interpress 1967.

Attempts to explain the treatment of nationalities in Yugoslavia under various Constitutional arrangements.

Journal of the International Commission of Jurists, Vol. 18, June, 1977.

Kaikus, B.A. "The Role of Islamic Law in Pakistan Polity."

1-2 *Pakistan Supreme Court Law quarterly* 253 (1967/69).

An illuminating discussion of the influence of religious law in Pakistan. Kaikus holds that the government should operate as a reflection of the letter and spirit of the *Shar'ia* (religious law).

"The Islamic State is an ideological state and only those who believe in that ideology can be allowed to control its policy." Civil rights recognized by Islamic law and the traditional criminal penalties (particularly amputation of the hand for theft offenses) are discussed.

Kalenska, Marie. "Protection of Human Rights in Employment." 25 *Bulletin of Czechoslovak Law* No. 8, p. 208 (1967).

It is acknowledged here that Czech constitutional labor and employment guarantees are far from being realized -- the low status and salaries of many women in the workforce is acknowledged. Kalenska states that full realization of social rights in employment is dependent upon full enjoyment of political freedoms in a system where expression of political and civil rights if fully protected.

Karlsson, Paul H. "Sources for African Constitutional Studies." 5 *African Law Studies* 57 (1971); 6 *African Law Studies* 123 (1972).

Excellent bibliography of sources for studies in African Constitutionalism. Included are citations to the constitutions themselves and to important constitutionally-based legislation as well as references to scholarly journal articles and books. The bibliography is organized by country.

Kastari, Paavo. "Guarantees of Fundamental Rights and the Constitutional Principle." 13 *Jahrbuch des Offentlichen Rechts Neue Folge* 437 (1964).

Brief and cursory comparative study of judicial review as a means of enforcing constitutional fundamental rights provisions in America and Europe.

Katre, S.M. "The Case for India." In: *Multilingual Political Systems.* Quebec, University of Laval Press, 1975, p. 553.

India's language problems are compounded by the great number of languages spoken (even though they fall into only four major language families); the extremely high rate of adult illiteracy; the government's stated and legislated goals of replacing English with Hindi as the official language and establishing regional languages; and the necessity of creating textbooks and other curriculum materials to achieve these goals.

Kauper, Paul, and Rudolf Halberstadt. "Religion and Education in West Germany: A Survey and an American Perspective." 4 *Valparaiso University Law Review* 1 (1969).

The publicly-supported confessional (sectarian) school has roots which extend deep into German history. Existence of such schools, where faculty and teaching materials are oriented toward a particular denominational philosophy, was guaranteed by, among others, the Prussian Constitution of 1850 and the Weimar Constitution. Article 140 of the West German Federation's *Grundgesetz* (Constitution) likewise provides for the establishment and support of such schools through tax revenues.

The German system of confessional schools and public subsidy of religious education is scrutinized with an eye toward the prohibitions implicit in the establishment clause of the American Constitution's First Amendment. American aid to parochial schools for supplemental and non-educational services, and the constitutionally-based attacks on such practices, are examined.

Khol, Andreas A. "The Influence of the Human Rights Convention on Austrian Law." 18 *American Journal of Comparative Law* 237 (1970).

When ratifying the European Convention for the Protection of Human Rights and Fundamental Freedoms, the Austrian Parliament explicitly elevated that document to Constitutional status; thus, individuals whose rights and freedoms (as defined in the Convention) are infringed upon may appeal to Austria's Constitutional Court for relief.

Legal scholars in Austria have evidenced concern, however, that peculiarly Austrian legal institutions and processes might be emasculated by a too-broad interpretation of the Convention's provisions. It is emphasized here that Austria did not participate in the drafting of the Convention, and some feel reluctant to bind its courts in adhering to a document over whose terms and language the nation had no control.

Kili, Suna. *Turkish Constitutional Developments and Assembly Debates on the Constitutions of 1924 and 1961.* Istanbul, Robert College Research Center, 1971.

Brief Constitutional history of Turkey, with a summary of Parliamentary debates on draft constitutions. The Constitutions of 1876, 1921, 1924, and 1961 are included as appendices.

Kinsella, Noel A. "The Canadian Model for the Protection from Discrimination." 4 *Revue des Droits de L'Homme* 270 (1971).

Federal legislation aimed at combating racial, religious and sex discrimination (particularly in employment) is summarized here. Enforcement and grievance procedures also are outlined. Interestingly, most major Canadian anti-discrimination legislation was enacted in the mid-1950's -- a full decade before the United States Congress got around to the task.

Kirkwood, John. "Constitutional Change in Ceylon: A Peaceful Revolution." 3 *Lawasia* No. 1, p. 194 (1972).

Deals with Ceylon's new Constitution, in which the Republic of Sri Lanka was declared.

Kliesch, Enno. *Der Einflusz des franzosischen Verfassungsdenkens auf Afrikanische Verfassungen.* Hamburd, 1967.

The former French colonies in Africa are close modeled after the French Constitution of 1958. The enormous influence of the French upon these documents is discussed.

KLOSS, HEINZ. The American Bilingual Tradition. Rowley,

Massachusetts, Newbury House Publishers, Inc., 1977.

Kloss, Heinz. "Democracy and the Multinational State." In: *Multilingual Political Systems.* Quebec, University of Laval Press, 1975, p. 29.

Western democracy holds three important principles: equality of the individual or group before the law; government by the people; and the ideal of one-man, one-vote. Kloss asks and attempts to answer three questions: (1) Is it possible to have full equality of language in countries which have two or more major ethnic groups? (2) Does full equality of language automatically mean full equality between these groups: (3) Can equality between these groups be effected without violating the one-man, one-vote principle?

Kovacs, I. *New Elements in the Evolution of Socialist Constitutions.* Budapest, 1968.

Comparative study of the Marxist-Leninist states and their constitutional documents. Emphasis is placed upon governmental structure (as reflected in the constitutions) and upon the universal elements and philosophical touch-stones that all such documents have in common. A good general source.

Kuhrig, Herta. *Equal Rights for Women in the German Democratic Republic.* Berlin, Publications of the GDR Committee for Human Rights, 1973.

Those provisions of the East German Constitution which affect the status and rights of women, and statutes which have been enacted to protect and preserve those rights, are annotated and compiled in this volume. The annotations are prefaced by a brief commentary by the author, who touts East Germany's achievement in providing total equality between men and women, particularly in the fields of education and employment.

Kunstadter, Peter, ed. *Southeast Asian Tribes, Minorities and Nations.* Princeton, New Jersey, Princeton University Press, 1967. 2 volumes.

Anthropologically-oriented study of minority, ethnic, and tribal groups in India, China, Malaysia, Thailand, and Indochina.

Several of the contributions discuss how governments in Asia deal with minority groups and minority group concerns.

Kunz, Frithjef. "The Constitutional Basic Rights in the Field of Socialist Labour." 1968 *Law and Legislation in the German Democratic Republic* (Special Edition) 51 (1968).

A draft of a new Constitution for East Germany, in which the basic rights of the worker in Socialist society (right to equal pay, right to disability benefits, and the right to recreation) are included as Constitutional guarantees. In all Socialist states, however, the state imposes upon the individual a corollary duty to work, and the Constitution also reflects this mode of thought.

Kuo, Warren. "Oppression and Persecution in Communist China." *Veenhoven,* Volume Three, p. 303.

Kuper, Leo. *The Pity of it All: Polarisation of Racial and Ethnic Relations.* Minneapolis, University of Minnesota Press, 1977.

Following an introductory note on the problem, "From Reformism to Genocide," four case studies are analyzed: Algeria, Burundi, Rwanda, and Zanzibar.

Kuper, Leo, ed.*Race, Science, and Society.* Paris, UNESCO, 1975

An excellent study of the effects of racism on history, culture, and politics. Case studies and sociological examinations predominate in this volume, which features an explanatory introduction by editor Kuper. Contributers include Claude Levi-Strauss, Andre Beteille, and Otto Klineberg.

UNESCO'S *Four Statements on the Race Question* is included in the appendix.

Kyriakides, Stanley. *Cyprus: Constitutionalism and Crisis Government.* Philadelphia, 1968.

This Constitutional history of Cyprus focuses primarily on post World war II constitutional plans and the adopted constitution of 1960. Much attention is drawn to summary and analysis of the perpetual strain between Greek and Turkish Cypriots, and the inevitable eruptions into violence that have ensued. Blame is placed on the 1960 Constitution for failing to avert alienation and frustration of the Turkish minority, since the constitutional guarantees of minority participation in government have been largely ignored or exploited by the Greek Cypriots. The author rejects the proposed solution (which has since become a reality) of a divided state.

Lador-Lederer, J. Joseph. *International Group Protection: Aims and Methods in Human Rights.* Leyden, Sijthoff, 1968.

Sociologically-based analysis of human rights concerns with an emphasis on the protection of linguistic and ethnic minorities. Efforts of non-governmental organizations to guarantee human rights are chronicled.

Laffin, John. "The Arabs as Slavers." *Veenhoven,* Volume Four, p. 431.

la Garza, R.O. and Arcieniega, T.A., eds.: *Chicanos and Native Americans -- The Territorial Minorities,* Prentice Hall, New Jersey, 1973.

Lahav, Phina. "The Status of Women in Israel -- myth and Reality." 22 *American Journal of Comparative Law* 107 (1974).

Provides an excellent look at the position of women in Israel, and is a good source for any study of sex discrimination in that state.

LAMBERT, RICHARD D., Ed. Martin O. Heisler, special ed. *Ethnic Conflict in the World Today.* 433 *Annals of the American Academy of Political and Social Science* (1977).

Lannung, Hermod. "The Rights of Minorities." In: *Melanges Offerts a Polys Modinos.* Paris, A. Pedone, 1968. p. 181.

Review of international efforts to protect the rights of minorities, especially the European Convention on Human Rights.

Laponce, J.A. "Relating Linguistic to Political Conflicts: The Problem of Language Shift in Multilingual Societies." In: *Multilingual Political Systems.* Quebec, University of Laval

Press, 1975. p. 185.

According to the author's theory, languages become specialized in the mind of a multilingual person according to roles and stratified according to knowledge and preference; within society, men specialize in their roles and stratify their power relationships. Laponce suggests that political scientists study the effects of language shifts on the individual's self-esteem, social effectiveness, and position in the political structure in order to find the best solution for a multilingual state which wishes to both maintain linguistic diversity and reduce ethnic-linguistic conflicts.

Laponce, J.A.: ''The Protection of Minorities by the Electoral System,'' *Western Political Quarterly,* Vol. 10, No. 2, June 1957.

Laskin, Bora. ''Constitutionalism in Canada: Legislative Power and a Bill of Rights.'' In: Bernard Schwartz. *The Fourteenth Amendment: Centennial Volume.* New York, New York University Press, 1970, p. 172.

Constitutional history of individual rights legislation in Canada. The role of the judiciary in interpreting legislative enactments in light of Canada's non-entrenched Bill of Rights is extensively discussed.

Lavaroff, D.G., and G. Peiser. *Les Constitutions Africanes.* Paris, A. Pedone, 1961.

Collection of Africa's black Francophonic Constitutions (in French) at the time independence was granted by the French government. Useful for comparative purposes with regard to present-day constitutions.

Lee, Changsoo. ''Ethnic Discrimination and Conflict: the Case of the Korean Minority in Japan.'' *Veenhoven,* Volume Four, p. 263.

Lefever, Ernest: ''Limits of Government in the Third World,'' in Rhoodie, Nic., ed.: *Integroup Accommodations in Plural Societies,* Macmillan Press, London, 1978.

Leguebe, Jacques. ''The Harkis: From Involvement to Exile.''

Veenhoven, Volume Three, p. 517.

Leguebe, Jacques. "Mozambique under Frelimo Rule." *Veenhoven,* Volume Four, p. 1.

Leng, H.S. "Ethnic Politics in Malaysia." *Veenhoven,* Volume Three, p. 1.

Lent, John A., ed. *Cultural Plurality in Malaysia: Polity, Military, Mass Media, Education, Religion, and Social Class.* Center for Southeast Asian Studies, Northern Illinois University, 1977 (Special Report No. 14).

This uneven collection of six disparate papers meets its objective of furnishing "an analysis of the current impact of changing institutions on the evolving patterns of cultural pluralism and social class formation in Malaysia." Useful for its background information, but lacking real value in a Constitutions study.

Leon-Portilla, Miguel. "Endangered Cultures: The Indian in Latin America." *Veenhoven,* Volume One, p. 177.

Le Page, R.B. "Polarizing Factors -- Political, Cultural, Economic - Operating on the Individual's Choice of Identity through Language Use in British Honduras." In: *Multilingual Political Systems.* Quebec, University of Laval Press, 1975. p. 537.

This study of 280 schoolchildren growing up in an area of British Honduras where Spanish, Creole, Mayan, English, and Carib are spoken, attempts to explore the dynamics of community development by examining children of a specific society at their formative ages.

Lerner, Natan. *The Crime of Incitement to Group Hatred.* New York, World Jewish Congress, 1965.

Worldwide survey of constitutional provisions and legislation which make incitement of racism, anti-Semitism, or other prejudice criminal. Included also in the discussion are United Nations documents on human rights and racial tolerance.

Levak, Albert E. "Discrimination in Pakistan: National, Provincial, Tribal." *Veenhoven,* Volume One, p. 281.

Lieberson, Stanley and James F. O'Connor. "Language Diversity in a Nation and its Regions." In: *Multilingual Political Systems.* Quebec, University of Laval Press, 1975. p. 161.

This study expands on a previous one by the same authors; it is, like the other, an attempt to reduce to mathematical terms data about the distribution of the mother tongues in a nation and its political subdivisions. They believe that such studies will show the probabilities of maintaining a multilingual nation and its potential for splintering into two or more separate countries.

LIJPHART, AREND: *Democracy in Plural Societies,* Yale University Press, London, 1977.

Lillich, Richard B. "The Problem of the Applicability of Existing International Provisions for the Protection of Human Rights to Individuals who are not Citizens of the Country in which they Live." 70 *American Journal of International Law* 507 (1976).

A brief editorial commentary explaining how the topic of alien rights was brought under the jurisdiction of the United Nations Sub-Commission on the Prevention of Discrimination and Protection of Minorities.

Lincoln-Douglas Debates. Lincoln at Freeport, August 27, 1858.

Linz, Juan J. "Politics in a Multi-Lingual Society with a Dominant World Language: The Case of Spain." In: *Multi-Lingual Political Systems.* Quebec, University of Laval Press, 1975. p. 367.

The language which is commonly called Spanish the world over is actually Castilian, one of the four languages of Spain. The Spanish government has never given serious thought to the issue of multi-lingualism, and official census or other statistical data have never included information on language use. Linz explores the history of multi-lingualism in Spain, with an emphasis on regional stirrings for greater recognition of the Catalan, Galician, and Basque languages; he suggests that in the future Spain will be forced to consider its language problems.

Livingston, William S., ed. *Federalism in the Commonwealth: a Bibliographical Commentary*. London, Cassell, 1963.

An inadequate treatment of the variety of Constitutional development in the several nations that comprise the Commonwealth.

Loewenstein, Karl. "Constitutions and Constitutional Law in the West and in the East." 30 *Indian Journal of Political Science* 203 (1969).

General comparative study, by a distinguished scholar, on Socialist and Western constitutional documents. Discussion centers on the respect accorded fundamental rights protections, procedures for amendment, and the availability of judicial review under both Socialist and non-Socialist systems.

Loewenstein, Karl: "Reflections on the Value of Constitutions in our Revolutionary Age," in Zurcher, A.J. ed.: *Constitutions and Constitutional Trends Since World War II,* New York University Press, N.Y., 1951.

Luca, Costa. "Discrimination in the Arab Middle East." *Veenhoven,* Volume One, p. 211.

Luchaire, Francois. "Les Constitutions et les Institutions administratives des Etats norveaux: Aspect Juridique." In: *Les Constitutions et les Institutions Administrative des Etats nouveaux*. Brussels, Incidi, 1965. p. 600.

A sympathetic treatment of Constitution-making in the new states, with the emphasis on francophonic Africa.

MacKenzie, W.J.: "Representation in Plural Societies," *Political Studies,* Vol. 2, No. 1, February, 1954.

Mackey, William F., and Albert Verdoodt. *The Multinational Society*. Rawley, Massachusetts, Newbury House Publishers, Inc., 1975.

A collection of essays of varied quality and interest. Although there is little agreement on definitions, some of the articles, especially those on Yugoslavia, are genuinely useful. The articles were originally papers delivered at a Ljubljana,

Yugoslavia, seminar.

Mackey, William F. ''Puissance, attraction et pression des Langues en Contact: Modeles et Indices.'' In: *Multi-lingual Political Systems.* Quebec, University of Laval Press, 1975. p. 119.

The examples of India and Ireland in attempting to legislate language policy form the backdrop for this study. Mackey seeks to identify and measure the elements of linguistic power and to show what happens, in statistical terms, when two or more languages conflict. He feels that empirical data concerning demography, global dispersion of languages, mobility, economy, idealogy, and culture will be most valuable in future legislation.

Mahapatra, L.K. ''Group Discrimination in Orissa.'' *Veenhoven,* Volume Four, p. 43.

Mahar, J.M., ed.: *The Untouchables in Contemporary India,* University of Arizona Press, Tucson, 1972.

Maier, Georg. ''Peru: Portrait of a Fragmented Society.'' *Veenhoven,* Volume One, p. 155.

Makielski, S.J., Jr. ''America's Minorities.'' *Veenhoven,* Volume Three, p. 435.

Ma'oz, Moshe. ''Homogeneity and Pluralism in the Middle East; The Case of Lebanon.'' *Veenhoven,* Volume Three, p. 181.

Ma'oz, Moshe: ''Islamic-Arabism versus pluralism; the failure of integroup accommodation in the Middle East,'' in Rhoodie, Nic: *Integroup Accommodation in Plural Societies,* Macmillan Press, London, 1978.

Mascarenhas, Anthony. ''Bangladesh: a Profile of Twentieth-Century Genocide.'' *Veenhoven,* Volume Five, p. 239.

Marrow: *Changing Pattern of Prejudice,* Philadelphia: Chilton, 1962.

Marshall, Richard, ed. *Aspects of Religion in the Soviet Union,* University of Chicago Press, Chicago, 1971.

Mason, Philip. *Race Relations.* New York and London, Oxford

University Press, 1970.

Following a brief summary on the biological aspects of race, the author discusses the race aspects of some early societies and then devotes the important chapter (Chapter 7) to selected modern situations.

Masriya, Y. "A Christian Minority: The Copts in Egypt." *Veenhoven,* Volume Four, p. 77.

Masterman, Sue, and Anton Koene. "The Netherlands: Truly Plural?" *Veenhoven,* Volume Three, p. 153.

Mathur, H.M. "India's Tribal Minorities: Bringing Them into the Mainstream of National Life." 5 *Plural Societies* No. 2, p. 25 (1974).

Extremely useful little article, outlining and listing the different tribes, racial types, tribal languages, etc.

Mazrui, Ali A. "The Racial Boundaries of the English Language." In: *Multilingual Political Systems.* Quebec, University of Laval Press, 1975. p. 61.

In this article the author compares the use and spread of Arabic, a language that may be termed "communalistic" because its speakers tend to belong to the same ethnic group, with English, which claims speakers from all ethnic groups and races. It is suggested that, since English is in use throughout Africa, that some linguistic reforms in that language on that continent might be appropriate.

McDougal, Myres S. "Human Rights and World Public Order: Principles of Content and Procedure for Clarifying General Community Policies." 14 *Virginia Journal of International Law* 387 (1974).

Inquiry into the possibility of improving the intellectual procedures for the clarification and specification of the substantive content of human rights in particular instances of application. Although this article is primarily concerned with procedure and theoretical perspective, it also assists in obtaining an understanding of present human rights documents. The appendices are especially valuable; they provide a veritable checklist of human rights provisions for national or international documents.

McDougal, Myres S., Harold D. Lasswell, and Lung-Chu Chen. ''Freedom from Discrimination in Choice of Language and International Human Rights.'' 1 *Southern Illinois University Law Journal* 1151 (1976).

One of a series of articles by these authors, this essay concerns itself with the deprivations imposed upon certain peoples because of their linguistic identity. It is international in scope and outlook.

McDougal, Myres S., Harold D. Lasswell, and Lung-Chu Chen. ''Human Rights for Women and World Public Order: the Outlawing of Sex-based Discrimination.'' 69 *American Journal of International Law* 497 (1975).

A look at the creation and present status of certain international prescriptions intended to foster equality between women and men.

McDougal, Myres S., Harold D. Lasswell, and Lung-Chu Chen. ''Nationality and Human Rights: the Protection of the Individual in External Areas.'' 83 *Yale Law Journal* 900 (1974).

This is an in-depth study of ''the claims of individuals for membership in a territorial community''; that is to say, nationality or citizenship.

McDougal, Myres S., Harold D. Lasswell, and Lung-Chu Chen. ''The Protection of Aliens from Discrimination and World Public Order: Responsibility of States conjoined with Human Rights.'' 70 *American Journal of International Law* 432 (1976).

An excellent article, which concerns itself with ''the deprivations . . . imposed upon individuals on the ground that they do not possess the 'nationality' of the imposing state. By nationality we refer to the 'characterizations' states make of individuals for the purpose of controlling and protecting them . . .''

McDougal, Myres S., Harold D. Lasswell, and Lung-Chu Chen. "The Protection of Respect and Human Rights: Freedom of Choice and World Public Order." 24 *American University Law Review* 919 (1975).

McDOUGAL, MYRES S., HAROLD S. LASSWELL, and LUNG CHU CHEN. "The Right to Religious Freedom and World Public Order: The Emerging Norm of Nondiscrimination." 74 *Michigan Law Review* 856 (1976).

An excellent study on the problems and laws relating to religious freedom and toleration on both the international and domestic levels. It deals extensively with documentary (including constitutional) expressions on the subject.

McRae, Kenneth D. "The Concept of Consociational Democracy and its Application to Canada." In: *Multilingual Political Systems.* Quebec, University of Laval Press, 1975. p. 245.

A philosophical discussion of "segmented pluralism" or "consociationalism" as practiced in the Netherlands, Austria, Belgium, and Switzerland, where there exist a combination of strong social fragmentation and political efficiciency and stability. The author suggests that "consociationalism" might be a solution to Canada's language problems.

McRae, Kenneth D. *Switzerland: Example of Cultural Co-Existence.* Toronto, Canadian Institute of International Affairs, 1964.

Useful comparative view from a Canadian perspective.

McWhinney, Edward. "The 'Quiet Revolution' in French Canada and its Constitutional Implications for Canadian Federalism." 19 *Jahrbuch des Offentlichen Rechts Neue Folge* 331 (1970).

Canadian federalism is here perceived as a loose and flexible system, able to deal with pressures put upon it by special interest groups or minorities (such as the Quebecois). In this analytical study, current problems of national/provincial relations are examined, with an eye toward reconciliation of those problems through increased provincial autonomy.

Medina, Manuel. "Spain: Regional, Linguistic and Ideological

Conflict.'' *Veenhoven,* Volume One, p. 133.

Meisel, John. ''Political Styles and Language -- Use in Canada.'' In: *Multilingual Political Systems.* Quebec, University of Laval Press, 1975. p. 317.

French Canadians -- as compared with English-speaking Canadians -- are generally considered to be more interested in personal politics than in political parties and broad political issues; more concerned with local and provincial politics than with federal politics; and less confident of their influence on political decision-making. This study of 2767 persons who participated in a 1968 post-election survey seeks an explanation for these supposed differences in political attitudes and behavior.

Meisler, Stanley. ''Holocaust in Burundi, 1972.'' *Veenhoven,* Volume Five, p. 225.

Memo from Belgium, Ministry of Foreign Affairs, Bruxelles, 1972.

Mensah-Brown, A.K., ed. *African International Legal History.* New York, United Nations Institute for Training and Research, 1975.

Ethnic problems are intelligently analyzed in Chapter 3, a legal and historical survey by Antony Allott on boundaries in Africa. The author points out how colonial-based boundaries disregarded tribal and ethnic considerations.

Meyer, Perry. ''Human Rights Declarations and their Place in the History of Constitutional Law: a Quebec Perspective.'' 8 *Revue Juridique Themis* 275 (1973).

Critique of the Canadian ''Bill of Rights,'' which has the same status as any ordinary federal statute. Enactment of a new bill of rights, ''entrenched,'' and enforceable through the mechanism of judicial review, is urged.

Micaud, Charles A. ''Bilingualism in North Africa: Cultural and Socio-Political Implications.'' 27 *Western Political Quarterly* 92 (1974).

Discussion of language in Tunisia, Morocco, and Algeria,

where Arabic has been deemed the official tongue, but where facility in French is considered vital for social and economic advancement. The point is made that, among young people, Arabic is falling into disuse and French is becoming the language of choice.

Mickenberg, Neil H. "Aboriginal Rights in Canada and the United States." 9 *Osgoode Hall Law Journal* 119 (1971).

This article summarizes leading Canadian and American cases that have grappled with the question of aboriginal land title. Since both nations share a common Colonial heritage, the manner in which Indian rights have been addressed by these governments is remarkably similar. Both nations recognize the right of land possession in aboriginal peoples, but both also hold that this possessory right is inferior to any claims upon the land made by the sovereign.

Minattur, Joseph: "Protective Discrimination and the Rule of Law," in Mohamed Imam, *Minorities and the Law.* Bombay, Tripathi, 1972.

Minority Rights Group. *Reports.* Benjamin Franklin House, 36 Craven Street, London WC2N 5NG

Series of excellent monographs, each dealing with another of the world's minority groups and its problems. A list of the reports follows:

1. Religious minorities in the Soviet Union.
2. The two Irelands: the double minority -- a study of inter-group tensions.
3. Japan's minorities: Burakumin, Koreans, and Ainu.
4. The Asian Minorities of East and Central Africa.
5. Eritrea and Southern Sudan: aspects of wider African problems.
6. The Crimean Tatars, Volga Germans and Meskhetians: Soviet treatment of some national minorities.
7. The position of Blacks in Brazilian society.
8. The Africans' Predicament in Rhodesia.
9. The Basques and Catalans.

10. The Chinese in Indonesia, the Philippines and Malaysia.
11. The Biharis in Bangladesh.
12. Israel's Oriental Immigrants and Druzes.
13. East Indians of Trinidad and Guyana.
14. The Rom: the Gypsies of Europe.
15. What future for the Amerindians of South America?
16. Problems of a Displaced Minority: the new position of East Africa's Asians.
17. India and the Nagas.
18. The Montagnards of South Vietnam.
19. The Namibians of South-West Africa.
20. Selective Genocide in Burundi.
21. Canada's Indians.
22. Race and Law in Britain and the United States.
23. The Kurds.
24. The Palestinians.
25. The Tamils of Sri Lanka.
26. The Untouchables of India.
27. Arab Women.
28. Western Europe's Migrant Workers.
29. Jehovah's Witnesses in Central Africa.
30. Cyprus.
31. The Original Americans: U.S. Indians.
32. The Armenians.
33. Nomads of the Sahel.
34. Indian South Africans.
35. Australian Policy towards the Aborigines.

Mittal, J.K. "Right to Equality in the Indian Constitution." Part I: 1970 *Public Law* 36 (1970); Part 2: 1972 *Public Law* 232 (1976).

A comprehensive analysis of all forms of equality under the Indian constitution. Part 1 traces the background of the equality provisions; Part 2 discusses the principles laid down by the Supreme Court and examines recent cases.

Modeen, Tore. "The Situation of the Finland-Swedish Population in the Light of International Constitutional and Administrative Law." 16 *McGill Law Journal* 121 (1970).

During the eighteenth and nineteenth centuries Finland was nominally under the political control of Russia, but its autonomous institutions were Swedish in nature, and Swedish was the official state language. In this century, however, ethnic Finns dominate the nation, and the Swedish-speaking people constitute an extraordinarily vocal minority.

In a welfare state such as Finland, Swedish-language schools (including universities) are maintained at public expense, and a Swedish-speaking brigade of the armed forces has been established. All state civil servants must demonstrate a reasonable degree of facility in both languages. It is noted that the provision of services for the Swedish minority has not proved too great a financial burden for the state to bear.

Mohammed Suffian bin Hashim, Tan Sri. *An Introduction to the Constitution of Malaysia.* Kuala Lumpur, 1972.

Constitutional history, with an analysis of constitutional provisions as enacted.

Molnar, Thomas. "Malaysia: Observations in a Bi-racial Society." 1 *Plural Societies* No. 1, p. 41 (1970).

Provides a useful, albeit brief, introduction to the multiracial character of Malaysia.

Montagu, Ashley. *Statement on Race.* London, Oxford University Press, 1972.

An annotated analysis of UNESCO's *Four Statements on the Race Question.* Excellent explication and annotation of the UNESCO pronouncements -- an invaluable tool to assist in the understanding of the statements.

Morris, H.R. and James S. Read. *Uganda -- The Development of its Laws and Constitution.* London, Stevens and Sons, 1966.

Constitutional history of Uganda: an analysis of the provisions of the Constitution is also included. A survey of the major provisions of Ugandan civil and criminal law complete the volume.

Morrisson, C.C., Jr. "Margin of Appreciation in European Human Rights Law." 6 *Revue des Droits le l'homme* 263 (1973).

This essay examines some of the internal workings of the European Human Rights Commission and one of the major techniques used by the Commission in arriving at its decisions. This technique, termed "margin of appreciation," is reviewed, from its inception to its development in the jurisprudence of the Commission. The avowed "purpose of the article is to arrive at some normative conclusions about the utility of the technique and its proper application to human rights cases."

Moskowitz, Moses. *The Politics and Dynamics of Human Rights.* Dobbs Ferry, New York, Oceana Publications, Inc., 1968.

This discussion of human rights in a global and nationalistic context contains chapters on "Pluralism and Diversity," "The Rights of Man and the Fate of Minorities," and "The International Color Bar." Constitutional provisions dealing with human rights concerns are used to illustrate the author's presentation.

Mubako, Simbi V. "Racialism and the Erosion of the Rule of Law in Rhodesia." 4 *Eastern Africa Law Review* 191 (1971).

Constitutional, legislative, and administrative efforts by the Smith government to consolidate the power of the white minority in Rhodesia are discussed. It is noted that the 1969 Rhodesian constitution ties suffrage and legislative representation to income and wealth, thereby barring the vast majority of black Rhodesians from the franchise.

Mukerjee, Bhuperi N. "World Constitutions and Population: A Preliminary Survey of World Constitutions." 16 *Journal of the Indian Law Institute* 675 (1974).

A study of how the Constitutions of 133 states deal with the problem of population -- whether, for instance, birth is encouraged or discouraged.

Provisions which provide for infant day care, protection of the unborn, and equal rights for women are examined. Appendices and tables are included.

Mullard, Chris. "Racism in Britain: Management Concepts, 1948-1975." *Veenhoven,* Volume Five, p. 197.

Munch, Fritz. "Einfuhring in die Verfassungsvergleichung." 33 *Zeitschrift fur Auslandisches Offentliches Recht und Volkerrecht* No. 1, p. 126 (1973).

An excellent bibliographic source on comparative constitutional law.

Munzel, Mark. "The Manhunts: Ache Indians in Paraguay." *Veenhoven,* Volume Four, p. 351.

Murphree, Marshall W., and Donald G. Baker. "Racial Discrimination in Rhodesia." *Veenhoven,* Volume Five, p. 375.

Nair, V. Narayanan. "Protective Discrimination' -- the Supreme Court Retreats?" 41 *Supreme Court Journal* 33 (1969).

A discussion of Article 15(4) of the Indian Constitution, which permits special protections for persons who are socially and educationally backward. Though caste may be one element in determining "backwardness," it is not in itself determinative of that status. Court cases concerning the reservation of a specified number of places in universities and professional schools for members of the so-called "backward classes" are summarized.

Nakayama, Isao. "On Fundamental Clauses of the Human Rights in the Constitution of Japan." 21 *Osaka University Law Review* 17 (1974).

Discussion of the fundamental rights provisions of the Japanese Constitution as the product of World War II and American influence. Reference is also made to the West German Constitution, and comparisons between the two documents are drawn.

Nanda, Ved P. "Racial Discrimination and the Law: recent Legislation in Great Britain, Canada, and the United States." In: Richard Claude, ed. *Comparative Human Rights.* Baltimore

Johns Hopkins University Press, 1976. p. 214.

Review of civil rights legislation in the 1950's to 1970's, aimed at putting an end to governmental and private racial discrimination. It is the author's conclusion that the "laissez-faire" attitude to racial discrimination only fosters racial hatred, and urges that governments adopt policies of "affirmative action" in order that discriminatory practices can be stopped.

Narasimhan, C.V. "The United Nations and Racial Discrimination." In: Bernard Schwartz. *The Fourteenth Amendment: Centennial Volume.* New York, New York University Press, 1970.

Survey of principal United Nations instruments against racial discrimination, including the Universal Declaration of Human Rights and *Four Statements on the Race Question.*

Naudin, Pierre. "The Violation of Human Rights in Uganda." *Veenhoven,* Volume Five, p. 415.

National Review, N.R., January 20, 1978.

Nelson, Sarah. "Discrimination in Northern Ireland: The Protestant Response." *Veenhoven,* Volume Four, p. 405.

New York Magazine, May 1, 1978.

New York Times, June 3, 1977.

New York Times, March 25, 1978.

New York Times, March 27, 1978.

Nikoki, Pavle: "Baxid Characteristics of the System of Delegates," *Review of International Affairs,* Vol. XXV, April, 1974.

Nobel Symposium 7: International Protection of Human Rights. Asbjorn Eide and August Schon, eds. New York, Wiley and Sons, 1968.

Record of the proceedings of the Seventh Nobel Symposium, held in Stockholm in October 1967. The majority of the presentations center upon transnational protection of and concern for human rights (such as the role of the United Nations and the impact of the International Covenants on Human Rights).

Nogel, R.J. "Human Rights and Uganda's Expulsion of its Asian Minorities." 3 *Denver Journal of International Law and Politics* 107 (1973).

The Ugandan situation is outlined in order to illustrate the failure of traditional international law to provide mechanisms for protecting individual rights within the domestic activities of a sovereign state. It is suggested that humanitarian intervention can help ensure protection of human rights in such circumstances,.

Nordlinger, Eric A. "Military Governments in Communally Divided Societies: Their Impact upon National Integration.' *Veenhoven,* Volume Three, p. 533.

Nwabueze, Benjamin O. *Constitutionalism in the Emergent States.* London, C. Hurst and Co., 1973.

Study of the evolution of constitutional government in Commonwealth nations, with emphasis upon Africa in general and Nigeria in particular. Problems of governmental structure, executive power are examined. The issue of secession is extensively discussed.

Oded, Arye. "The Southern Sudan Civil War." *Veenhoven,* Volume Four, p. 227.

O'Kane, Joseph P. "Islam in the New Egyptian Constitution." 26 *Middle East Journal* 137 (1972).

Review of public sentiment and political pressures with regard to proposed Constitutional articles. One such suggested provision would announce Egypt's status as an "Islamic State" and would acknowledge dependence on the *shar'ia* (religious law) as a source for legislation. The government's concern in promoting full equality for women, notwithstanding Islamic law and tradition, is noted.

Okoth-Ogendo, H.W.O. "National Implementation of International Responsibility: Some Thoughts on Human Rights." 10 *Eastern African Law Journal* No. 1, p. 1 (1974).

Particular problems which arise in the African experience when attempting to implement human rights protections are examined in this article.

Orbis, Foreign Policy Institute, University of Pennsylvania, March, 1967.

Ornstein, Allan C. "Affirmative Action and American Universities." *Veenhoven,* Volume Five, p. 347.

Otuteye, Seth C. "Constitutional Innovation in French West Africa -- the Experience of Guinea and the Ivory Coast." 10 *University of Ghana Law Journal* 16 (1973).

This essay focuses on the structure and functions of the governments of Guinea and Ivory Coast under their new Constitutions.

Otzen, Katharina. "Discrimination and preferment in the Federal Republic of Germany." *Veenhoven,* Volume Two, p. 31.

Outrata, Vladimir. "Some Notes on the Implementation of the Covenants on Human Rights and Its Control." 25 *Bulletin of Czechoslovak Law* No. 8, p. 293 (1967).

Another analysis of the United Nations' Universal Declaration of Human Rights. Outrata warns that multi-national human rights covenants will never be practicable until the nations involved have a common understanding of the language utilized in such covenants ("right to work" is cited as an example of a term which has different meanings in different nations).

The proposal of a United Nations High Commission for the implementation and enforcement of the Declaration is severely criticized.

Palley, Claire. "Constitutional Devices in Multi-Racial and Multi-Religious Societies." 19 *Northern Ireland Legal Quarterly* 377 (1968).

Sociologically-oriented examination of institutions and practices utilized by multi-ethnic states in order to concentrate or de-centralize political power. Various types of governmental structure -- the federation, the confederation, the centrist -- are examined, as is the effect of such structures on minority rights and interests. The Constitutional provisions of such multi-ethnic states as Cyprus, Belgium, and the

United States are scrutinized.

Palley, Claire. *The Constitutional History and Law of Southern Rhodesia.* Oxford, Clarendon Press, 1966.

Impressive historical study of Rhodesian Constitutional development. Extensive analysis of the present constitution and its provisions is included, as are numerous appendices.

Palley, Claire. "Law and the Unequal Society: Discriminatory Legislation in Rhodesia under the Rhodesian Front from 1963 to 1969." 12 *Race* 15, 139 (1970).

Review of legislation in Rhodesia which had the purpose and effect of ensuring continuing domination by the white minority over the black and mixed-race majority. Enactments aimed at depriving non-whites of land, educational opportunity, and political participation are summarized. The article, published in two parts, leans heavily on sociological studies and findings.

Paradis, Jerome B. "Language Rights in Multicultural States: a Comparative Study." 48 *Canadian Bar Review* 651 (1970).

Constitutional provisions dealing with language use in Switzerland and Belgium are studied. The two European states are examined with an eye toward the future of Canada, where the Quebecois have been pressed for greater recognition of the French language, and for the protection of the language rights of French-speaking citizens. The author stresses that, just as the linguistic preference of Canada's French-speaking people must be respected, so must the rights of Quebec's English-speaking minority be rigorously protected.

Patel, Brundaban. "The Scope and Meaning of the Right to Freedom of Religion under the Indian Constitution." 127 *Modern Review* 370 (1970).

Explication of the "free exercise" clause of the Indian Constitution. Religious exercise is deemed to be subject at all times to considerations of "public order, morality, and health," thus investing the state with much power to control and regulate religious practice.

Patra, Atul Chandra. "Multilingual Legislation." 10 *Journal of the Indian-Law Institute* 661 (1968).

A summary of the "official language" legislation of the Indian states. The Constitutional provisions of other multi-lingual nations (Switzerland, Canada, etc.) are discussed as well.

There is an interesting section on the evolution from Latin to French to English as the language of legal practitioners and the courts in England.

Peaslee, Amos J. *The Constitution of Nations.* 3d ed., by Dorothy Peasley Xydis. The Hague, Nijhoff, 1965-1970. 4 Volumes.

Definitive work in English prior to *Blaustein and Flanz* on the world's constitutions. Useful in checking on older constitutions.

Pescatore, Pierre. "The Protection of Human Rights in the European Communities." 9 *Common Market Law Review* 73 (1972).

This communication was written for the Parliamentary Conference on Human Rights organized by the Council of Europe on October 18-20, 1970. It was submitted on behalf of the Court of Justice of the European Community in order to give a concise outline of the Court's attitude on the problem of the protection of human rights.

Peselj, Branko M. "Recent Codification of Human Rights in Socialist Constitutions." 11 *Howard Law Journal* 342 (1965).

An article written for the 1965 Symposium on Human Rights held at Howard University. It examines the theories upon which Socialist Constitutions deal with human rights.

Emphasis is placed upon the provisions covering human rights protection contained in the Czech and Yugoslavian Constitutions.

Pipes, Richard: "Introduction: The Nationality Problem," *Handbook of Major Soviet Nationalities,* Zer Katz, Rosemarie Rogers, Frederic Harned, eds., The Free Press, New York, 1975

Pirzada, Syed Sharifuddin. "Fundamental Rights in Pakistan."

1-2 *Pakistan Supreme Court Law Quarterly* 27 (1967/1969).

A history of the fundamental rights enactments in Pakistan, up to the adoption of the 1962 Constitution. The Constitutional provision which allows the fundamental rights guarantees of the Constitution is to be superseded in times of emergency is discussed, and important court decisions interpreting the guarantees of the 1962 Constitution are reviewed.

Plamenatz, John. "Diversity of Rights and Kinds of Equality." In: *Equality . . . Nomos IX.* New York, 1967. p. 79.

The article, and the entire volume, deal with equality from the theoretical and ethical standpoints exclusively.

Plourde, Gaston. *Options Politiques Fundamentales de L'Etat Plurilingue.* Quebec, Les Presses de l' Universite Laval, 1972.

Concerned primarily with linguistic rights. Various political arrangements for protecting linguistic and cultural groups are surveyed, with interesting comments on colonial and dependency status and significance of that status on implementation of such rights.

PLURAL SOCIETIES. Published by the Foundation for the Study of Plural Societies, P.O. Box 3566, The Hague, The Netherlands. Quarterly.

Political Studies, Vol. 2, No. 1, February, 1954.

Portell-Villa, Herminio. "Cuba: The New Dominant Caste." *Veenhoven,* Volume Three, p. 369.

Possony, Stefan T. "Anti-Semitism in the Russian Orbit." *Veenhoven,* Volume Two, p. 405.

Possony, Stefan T. "From Gulag to Guitk: Political Prisons in the U.S.S.R. Today." *Veenhoven,* Volume One, p. 1.

Potocny, Miroslav. "The Principle of Self-Determination of Peoples (Article 1 of the International Covenants on Human Rights)" 25 *Bulletin of Czechoslovak Law* No. 8, p. 310 (1967).

Discussion of the principle of self-determination, as reflected in United Nations documents and as espoused in conclaves of the non-aligned countries.

Prinz, Friedrich: "A Model of a Multi-National society as developed in Austria-Hungary before 1918,'' in Rhoodie, Nic: *Intergroup Accommodation in Plural Societies,* Macmillan Press, London, 1978.

Prins, J. ''The World's Plural Societies: an Introduction.'' *Plural Societies,* The Hague, Holland, Vol. I, 1970.

Proehl, P.O. *Fundamental Rights Under the Nigerian Constitution, 1960-1965.* UCLA, African Studies Center, 1970.

Monograph on the impact of the 1960 Nigerian Constitution on human rights practices.

RABUSHKA, A. AND SHEPSHLE, K.: *Politics in Plural Societies,* Charles E. Merrill Publishing Co., Columbus, Ohio, 1972.

Radvanova, Senta. ''Protection of Matrimony, Maternity, and Family.'' 25 *Bulletin of Czechoslovak Law* No. 8, p. 184 (1967).

An examination of Constitutional and legislative protection of women and the family unit. As in all socialist states, the right to day care for children is constitutionally guaranteed.

Rakowska-Harmstone, Teresa. ''Ethnicity in the Soviet Union.'' 433 *Annals of the American Academy of Political and Social Science* 73 (1977).

Agitation for change among non-Russian Soviet citizens forms the basis of this report. The author points out the long-standing domination of every aspect of Soviet society by persons of Russian descent, and contrasts this with the current impetus toward ethnic ''self-assertion'' by other Soviet peoples.

Ramachandran, V.G. *Fundamental Rights and Constitutional Remedies,* 2d ed. Lucknow, 1968.

This study of the Indian Constitution's fundamental rights provisions focuses on judicial review as a remedy for state-initiated discrimination or infringements upon freedom. It is not a casebook -- the leading cases are commented upon but not reprinted or quoted.

Rana, M.S. *Writings on the Indian Constitution, 1861-1972.* Delhi, 1973.

A bibliography of books, articles, and monographs on Indian

Constitutional history and practice. Sources are broken down by Constitutional article for post-1948 works -- helpful for those researching specific provisions of the Indian Constitution.

Rappard, W.E. *La Constitution Federale de la Suisse.* Neuchatel, Editions de la Baconniere, 1948.

The definitive work on the Constitution of Switzerland.

Read, James S. "Bills of Rights in 'the Third World': Some Commonwealth Experiences." 6 *Verfassung und Recht Ubersee* 21 (1973).

Comparative analysis of bills of rights enacted by Asian and African Commonwealth nations during the 1960's. Emphasis is placed on the judicial enforceability of civil and political rights guarantees provided for in the constitutions and legislative enactments of these Third World states.

The Reality of Multi-National Development, Department of Information, Pretoria, 1975.

Report of Colonel Patrick Montgomery, Secretary, Anti-Slavery Society, 1970. Summarized in the *Daily Telegraph,* London August 18, 1970.

Retzlaff, Ralph H. "The Problem of Communal Minorities in the Drafting of the Indian Constitution." In: R.N. Spann, ed. *Constitutionalism in Asia.* Bombay, Asia Publishing House, 1964. p. 55.

A good brief survey of the legislative history behind India's failure to solve the Muslim problem through Constitutional means.

REVUE DES DROITS DE L'HOMME. (Human Rights Journal). Published by the Institut International des Droits de l'Homme, Strasbourg. Quarterly.

Rhoodie, E.M.: *Penal Systems of the Commonwealth,* Cape Town, H & R Academica Publishers, 1967.

RHOODIE, NIC., Editor: *Integroup Accommodation in Plural Societies,* Macmillan Press, London, 1978.

Rigo, Sureda, A. *The Evolution of the Right of Self-Determination:*

A Study of United Nations Practice. Leyden, Sijthoff, 1973.

This study concentrates on United Nations responses to agitation on the part of colonies or ethnic groups within nations for a greater measure of self-determination. Discussion is organized by country for ready reference. United Nations support of the concept of self-determination is analyzed.

Robinson: Jacob: *Were the Minorities Treaties a Failure?* New York, 1943.

Roche, George. "The Balancing Act: Quota Hiring in Higher Education." *Veenhoven,* Volume Four, p. 135.

Roome, K.P.S. "Discrimination in By-Laws." 86 *South African Law Journal* 319 (1969).

An examination of discriminatory statutes passed by South African provincial legislatures.

Rosenne, Meir. "Some Legal Aspects of the Struggle for the Rights of Jews in the Soviet Union." 9 *Israel Law Review* 588 (1974).

A brief essay commenting on the Soviet Union's discriminatory treatment of Jews, particularly with respect to emigration.

Roumani, Maurice M. "The Case of the Jews from Arab Countries: A Neglected Issue." *Veenhoven,* Volume Five, p. 69.

Roussillion, C. "Cultural Pluralism, Equality of Treatment, and Equality of Opportunity in Lebanon." 98 *International Labour Review* 225 (1968).

A brief history of the immigrations of the peoples into the area that is now Lebanon is coupled with a discussion of the Constitutional provisions that reflect the plural nature of Lebanese society. Emphasis is placed on the delicate balance between Christian and Islamic sects and the inevitable power struggles that accompany such a situation.

Roy, W.T. "Hostages to Fortune (A Socio-Political Study of the Anglo-Indian Remnant in India)" 5 *Plural Societies* No. 2, p. 55 (1974).

Brief introduction to the Indian "marginal man" resulting

from British-Indian miscegenation. This is a subculture discriminated against both by the British and the Indians.

Rowley, C.D.: *The Destruction of Aboriginal Society,* Penquin, Harmondsworth, England, 1972.

Rozek, Edward J. "The Problems of National Minorities in the Soviet Union." *Veenhoven,* Volume Four, p. 461.

Rozenbaum, I.A. "Separation of Church from State in the U.S.S.R." 11 *Soviet Law and Government* 154 (1972).

Analysis of the place religion holds in the Soviet System. It is emphasized here that the government of the U.S.S.R. guarantees freedom of religious thought to all its people, but must also retain an attitude of neutrality where religion is concerned (nothing must be done to foster or encourage the practice of religion). Religious activity is subject, however, to any legitimate exercise of the state's police power.

The author also points out that espousal of atheism is a prerequisite for membership in the Communist party or any Communist youth organization.

Rubinstein, Ammon. "Law and Religion in Israel." 2 *Israel Law Review* 380 (1967).

The extent to which religion permeates secular aspects of life in Israel is examined in this essay. It is pointed out that even though jurisdiction over marriage, divorce, and inheritance is vested in religious bodies, Israel has managed to remain a secular nation, and has been justly proud of its guarantee of religious freedom to all its citizens.

Rustow, Dankwart A. "Language, Nations, and Democracy." In: *Multilingual Political Systems.* Quebec, University of Laval Press, 1975. p. 43.

The ideal of linguistic nationalism is to have political boundaries which coincide with language boundaries. This paper is an overview of the development of modern languages and modern states from pre-colonial times through today's modern era. Rustow concludes with some examples of nations which are trying to solve the problem of linguistic statehood and a plea for more comparative study of devices which they have used.

Rycroft, W. Stanley. "The Protestant Churches and Religious Freedom in Latin America." 8 *Journal of Church and State* 264 (1966).

A former Protestant missionary in Latin America notes the dramatic increase of non-Catholic Christian denominations on that continent during the last half-century. It is noted, however, that a state's guarantee of religious freedom may extend only to belief and may not include a corresponding guarantee of freedom to worship. In several nations -- Chile, for example -- religious toleration has come years or decades after a Constitutional provision recognizing the right of religious freedom has been adopted.

Safilios-Rothschild, Constantina. "Sex Discrimination: Theory and Research." *Veenhoven,* Volume Five, p. 135.

Said, A.A. and Simmons, L.R.: eds. *Ethnicity in International Context,* Transaction Books, New Brunswick, N.J., 1976.

Salzberg, John, and Donald D. Young. "The Parliamentary Role in Implementing International Human Rights: A U.S. Example." 12 *Texas International Law Journal* 251 (1977).

The United States Congress is utilized as an example of the role a legislative body may play in the implementation and protection of human rights, on both the domestic and international levels.

SAVARD, JEAN-GUY, and RICHARD VIGNEAULT, Eds. *Les Etats Multi-Lingues/Multilingual Political Systems: Problems and Solutions.* Publication of the International Center for Research on Bilingualism. Quebec, University of Laval Press, 1975.

Scali, John, Philip Hoffman, Daniel Patrick Moynihan, and Leonard Garment. "The United Nations and Human Rights; the American Viewpoint." *Veenhoven,* Volume Five, p. 563.

Schacter, Oscar. "How Effective are Measures Against Racial Discrimination?" 4 *Revue des Droits de l'Homme* 293 (1971).

This excellent study contains no materials on constitutional measures to combat discrimination; it examines generally, however, the phenomenon of race discrimination. The psychological and cultural effects of discrimination upon minority group members and those in the majority are discussed and analyzed.

Schlemmer, Lawrence. "Institutional Inequality and Differentiation: an Evaluation of Race Discrimination in South Africa." *Veenhoven,* Volume Five, p. 291.

Schluter, Bernhard. "The Domestic Status of the Human Rights Clauses of the U.N. Charter." 61 *California Law Review* 100 (1973).

An exploration of the relationship between the human rights provisions of the United Nation's Charter and the constitutions and statutes of member states. The impact of the Charter provisions on the laws and behavior of sovereign states is discussed.

Schmitt, David E. "Discrimination and Conflict in Northern Ireland." *Veenhoven,* Volume Five, p. 1.

Schoneburg, Karl-Heinz. "Constitution and Society." 1968 *Law and Legislation in the German Democratic Republic* 19 (special issue) (1968).

Valuable for East German Constitutional theory.

Schreiber, Anna P. "The Status of Women in the United States and the Scandinavian Countries." In: Richard Claude, ed. *Comparative Human Rights.* Baltimore, Johns Hopkins University Press, 1976. p. 251.

Review of social and economic factors which lead to unequal status between men and women in the United States, Norway, and Sweden. Emphasis is placed on the still-strong impact of the traditional wife-mother role as a factor in women's lower economic and occupational status, although it is noted that such concepts are changing, particularly in the United States.

Schreuer, Christoph. "The Impact of International Institutions on the Protection of Human Rights in Domestic Courts." 4 *Israel Yearbook of Human Rights* 60 (1974).

Examination of the effect of international rights pronouncements (particularly the Universal Declaration of Human Rights) upon matters before the domestic courts of signatory states. It is pointed out that many governments look upon the Universal Declaration as a statement of goals and ideals rather than as a document with the force of law. West Germany is cited as having relied heavily on the Declaration in several court decisions involving construction of its own Constitution.

Schuler, Edgar A., and Kathryn Schuler. *Public Opinion and Constitution-Making in Pakistan,* 1958-1962. East Lansing, Michigan, Michigan State University Press, 1967.

Study of the impact of two English-language daily newspapers upon the drafting and adoption of the Pakistan Constitution of 1962.

Schwartz, Bernard. *The Fourteenth Amendment: Centennial Volume.* New York, New York University Press, 1970.

Collection of essays celebrating the hundredth anniversary of the ratification of the Fourteenth Amendment. Stress is placed upon expansion of the Amendment's force under the aegis of the Warren Court, but space is also devoted to equal protection and due process-type provisions of foreign constitutions. Annotations of those essays relevant to this study are also included in this bibliography.

Schwartz, Harry. "Freedom and the Communist Constitutions." In: Bernard Schwartz. *The Fourteenth Amendment: Centennial Volume.* New York, New York University Press, 1970. p. 196.

This article postulates that the provisions guaranteeing civil and political rights in the Communist nations are merely empty promises, and that government officials in those states have no intention of permitting their citizens to enjoy such rights.

Seervai, H.M. *Constitutional Law of India: a Critical Commentary.*

2d ed. Bombay, 1975. 2 Volumes.

This study and analysis of India's Constitutional provisions has a strong emphasis on the human rights and fundamental freedoms portions of the Constitution. Virtually the entire first volume of this two-volume work is devoted to a discussion of equality, freedom, and religious, cultural, and educational rights.

Seidman, R.B. "Judicial Review and Fundamental Freedoms in Anglophonic Independent Africa." 35 *Ohio State Law Journal* 820 (1974).

A study of the manner in which the Constitutions of Anglophonic African nations entrust protection of fundamental freedoms to the legal order. Seidman concludes that such mechanisms are doomed to failure, because the courts have been ineffective in enforcing fundamental rights guarantees.

Senelle, R.: "The Revision of the Constitution 1967-1971," *Memo from Belgium,* Nos. 144-146, Ministry of Foreign Affairs, Bruxelles, 1972.

"Sex Discrimination and the Equal Protection Clause: Do We Need a Constitutional Amendment." (Comment) 84 *Harvard Law Review* 1499 (1971).

An excellent discussion of the need for an amendment to the United States Constitution forbidding discrimination on the basis of sex.

Shapira, Amos. "The Status of Fundamental Individual Rights in the Absence of a Written Constitution." 9 *Israel Law Review* 497 (1974).

A look at the relationship between Israel's unusual situation with regard to a written constitution and individual rights. Particular focus is placed upon the courts as the agency entrusted with the protection of fundamental rights and freedoms.

Sharma, Din Dayal. "Equality of Status between Men and Women: Constitutional Experiment and Judicial Experience." 34 *Supreme Court Journal* 51 (1966).

Discussion and analysis of Article 15 of the Indian Constitution, which empowers Parliament to make any provision necessary to the protection and advancement of women: discrimination "only" on the basis of sex is prohibited. Cases in which the courts have gone to great lengths to show that discrimination was not based solely on sex (and was therefore permissible) are summarized.

Sharma, Indra D. *Modern Constitutions at Work.* New York, Asia Publishing House, 1962.

Somewhat superficial attempt at comparative constitutional analysis.

Sharma, V.D., and F. Woolridge. "Some Legal Problems Arising from the Expulsion of Ugandan Asians." 23 *International and Comparative Law Quarterly* 397 (1974).

View of the Ugandan move expelling its citizens of Asian descent as a violation of both international agreements and the state's own constitution. The international reaction to the incident is also discussed.

Shelton, Dinah. "Human Rights Within Churches." 6 *Revue des Droits de l'Homme* 487 (1973).

Though not concerned directly with constitutions, this general study of the means by which organized religious groups discriminate on racial or sex grounds is excellent.

Sheppard, Claude-Armand. *Study E19.* Prepared for la Commission D'Enquete sur la Situation de la Langue Francaise et sur les Droits Linguistiques au Quebec. Quebec, 1974.

This study is in three parts. The first section is devoted to the Canadian situation in regard to language used in law, business, etc. The second part deals with "jurisdiction" over language and language problems in Canada. Section Three is a comprehensive study of the law affecting the linguistic and cultural entities of Yugoslavia. In French.

Sheridan, L.A., and Harry E. Groves. *The Constitution of Malaysia.* Dobbs Ferry, New York, Oceana Publications, 1967.

Annotated edition of the Malaysian constitution. An index

to constitutional provisions, organized by topic, is included.

SHIVA RAO, B. *The Framing of India's Constitution: Select Documents.* New Delhi, Indian Institute of Public Administration, 1970. 5 Volumes.

Shoup, Paul: *Communism and the Yugoslav National Question,* Random House, New York, 1968.

Sigler, Jay Adrian. "Research Resources on Comparative Rights Policies." In: Richard Claude, ed. *Comparative Human Rights.* Baltimore, Johns Hopkins University Press, 1976. p. 286.

Survey and review of scholarly literature in the field of human rights.

Simon, Walter B. "Occupational Structure, Multilingualism and Social Change." In: *Multilingual Political Systems.* Quebec, University of Laval Press, 1975. p. 87.

Language conflicts which are but one facet of class and cultural conflicts have increased with the urbanization and industrialization of society. Simon believes that their importance has been underrated by social scientists, and he proposes a detailed outline for a study of the relationships between social class, language conflicts, and political idealogy.

Singh, Suresh, ed.: *Tribal Situation in India:* IAAS, 1972.

Sivan, Emmanuel. "The Kabyls: An Oppressed Minority in North Africa." *Veenhoven,* Volume One, p. 261.

Sivan, Emmanuel. "The Kurds: Another Perspective." *Veenhoven,* Volume Two, p. 137.

Smith, Alan H. "Prevention of Discrimination under Kenya Law." 20 *International and Comparative Law Quarterly* 136 (1971).

The Kenyan Constitution prohibits discrimination on racial or tribal grounds, but elaborate constitutional distinctions are made between the rights enjoyed by Kenyan citizens, citizens of British Commonwealth nations, and aliens. This commentary briefly examines the relevant articles of the Kenyan Constitution, and discusses recent cases which have dealt with the construction and effect of such constitutional provisions.

Smith, Stanley Alexander de. *The New Commonwealth and Its Constitutions.* London, Stevens and Sons, 1965.

Rather dated examination of Commonwealth nations and their written constitutions. Emphasis is placed upon safeguards for minority rights and fundamental rights guarantees (bills of rights).

Snider, Nancy L.: "Malaysian Noncommunal Political Parties," in Johan A. Lent, ed., *Cultural Pluralism in Malaysia: Polity, Military, Mass Media, Education, Religion and Social Class.* DeKalb, Illinois: Northern Illinois University Center for Southeast Asian Studies, 1977.

Solaun, Mauricio. "Black-White Relations in Iberian America: on the 'Miscegenated-Infused' Racial System." *Veenhoven,* Volume Three, p. 469.

South Africa Official Yearbook of the Republic of South Africa, Perskor Printers, Johannesburg, 1976.

South African Yearbook of International Law, University of South Africa, Pretoria, 1976.

Southern African Comparative and International Law Journal, Institute of Foreign and Comparative Law, University of South Africa, Pretoria. 1976.

Srinivas, M.N. and Sanwal, R.D.: "Some Aspects of Political Development in the North-Eastern Hill Areas of India." In: K. Suresh Singh, ed. *Tribal Situation in India:* IAAS, 1072.

Spann, R.N., ed. *Constitutionalism in Asia.* Bombay, Asia Publishing House, 1964.

Series of seminar papers in which much emphasis is placed on the problems of communal minorities.

Spiro, Herbert J. *Government by Constitution: the Political Systems of Democracy.* New York, Random House, 1959.

Although essentially a textbook, this volume contains useful ideas for the writing of constitutions.

Stajgr, Frantisek. "Protection of Human Rights in Civil Proceedings." 25 *Bulletin of Czechoslovak Law* No. 8, p. 233 (1967).

An examination of the Czech Code of Civil Procedure and its provisions which deal with due process.

Stasz, Clarice. "Gender Discrimination." *Veenhoven,* Volume Four, p. 317.

Strong, C.F. *A History of Modern Political Constitutions: An Introduction to the Comparative Study of their History.*

Spann, R.N., ed.: *Constitutionalism in Asia,* Asia Publishers, New York, 1965.

Subba Rao, Shri K. "The Philosophy of the Indian Constitution." 4 *Eastern Journal of International Law* 173 (1972).

A good introduction to the Indian Constitution, particularly as it relates to fundamental rights and protection of the "backward classes." The author is the former Chief Justice of the Supreme Court of India, and he prefaces his discussion of fundamental rights concerns with an analysis of Indian federalism.

Suzuki, Jiro, and Mickey Sakamoto. "Discrimination Against Foreigners of Japanese Descent in Japan." *Veenhoven,* Volume Two, p. 247.

Szabo, Imre. *Cultural Rights.* Leiden, A.W. Sijthoff, 1974.

Translated from the original Hungarian, this volume, by a member of the Hungarian Academy of Sciences, suffers from Eastern European over-emphasis on word definitions. It is extraordinarily dull. What it does do, however, is to provide some insights on Eastern European thinking absent from most of the literature on human rights.

Szabo, Imre, ed. *Socialist Concept of Human Rights.* Budapest, Akademiai Kiado, 1966.

General theoretical study of human rights as perceived in Socialist societies and reflected in the constitutional provisions of the U.S.S.R. and Eastern European states. Mention is also made of United Nations human rights documents (such as the U.N. Charter) as tools to protect enjoyment of human rights by citizens in member states.

Tamarin, Georges R. "Israeli Society: Authoritarian Traditionalism Versus Pluralist Democracy." *Veenhoven,* Volume Two, p. 101.

Tarnopolsky, Walter Surma. *The Canadian Bill of Rights.* 2d ed. revised. Toronto, Carlton Library, McClelland and Stewart Ltd., 1975.

Comprehensive analysis of human rights in Canada, with special sections on language rights and chapters on the recognition of ethnic and regional differences.

Tarnopolsky, Walter Surma. "The Effectiveness of Constitutional Guarantees and Other Governmental Declarations on Human Rights and Fundamental Freedoms." 5 *Proceedings of the International Symposium on Comparative Law* 117 (1968).

Criticism is leveled at the Canadian Bill of Rights for its failure to clearly delineate a mechanism whereby aggrieved persons could petition to full enjoyment of their rights. It is also suggested in this presentation that supplemental anti-discrimination legislation be adopted in order to ensure adherence to the Bill's guarantees.

Tatz, Colin. "Pessimism in Australian Race Relations." *Veenhoven,* Volume One, p. 445.

Thomas, Claudius C. "Constitutional Theory and Practice in the West Indies." 15 *Jahrbuch des Offentlichen Rechts Neue Folge* 683 (1966).

Comparative analysis of Constitutions in Britain's West Indies dependencies. The point is made that the islands' constitutions were granted by Britain, and that all amendments to such documents must be made by Act of Parliament or an Order in Council.

Thomssen, J.J.: *La Constitution Belge Annottee,* Brussels, 1879.

Thomson, Dale C.: "Quebec and the Bicultural Dimension," *Academy of Political Science. Proceedings* Vol. 32, No. 2, 1976.

Thompson, Richard. "Discrimination and the Maoris in New Zealand." *Veenhoven,* Volume Three, p. 565.

Tilly, Charles, ed. *The Formation of National States in Western Europe.* Princeton, Princeton University Press, 1975.

Excellent collection of monographs on the building of the great European national states; the contributors focus of the role of the military, the effect of the food supply, the growth of governmental bureaucracies, and the impact of social structure on the emergent states. Economic considerations are also analyzed.

Todorovic, Mijalko: *Yugoslav Constitution and Relations between the Nationalities,* Ed. Medjunarodna: Stampa-Interpress, Belgrade, 1967.

Touret, Barnard. *L'Amenagement Constitutionnel des Etats de Peuplement Composite.* Quebec, Les Presses de L'Universite Laval, 1973.

A quite useful analysis of factors causing cultural heterogeneity. Race, language, ethnicity, and religion are seen as differentiating forces. Solutions to conflicts created by these forces are examined, particularly territorial solutions. The book advocates greater regional autonomy and guarantees of collective rights for certain groups.

Terrelli, Maurice, and Renee Baudouin. *Les Droits de l'Homme et les Libertes Publiques.* Par les Textes. Montreal, Quebec University Press, 1972.

A study of human rights, in French, based upon selected provisions of certain past and present constitutions. Useful in providing significant features of such constitutions as those of France during and after the 1789 Revolution, and Germany under the Weimer government and the Nazi regime. The second and third parts of the volume are devoted to international documentation.

Time, July 17, 1964 and April 9, 1965.

Tripathi, P.K. "Secularism: Constitutional Provision and Judicial Review." 8 *Journal of the Indian Law Institute* 1 (1966).

A discussion of Articles 25 and 26 of the Indian Constitution. India wanted to avoid the American trend toward complete toleration in permitting nonconforming religious practice. The result: the present Indian Constitution guarantees religious freedom, but religious practice is at all times subject to state scrutiny and regulation.

Toure, Sekou: *Toward Full Reafricanization,* Presence Africaine, Paris, 1959.

Triska, Jan F. *Constitutions of Communist Party States.* Stanford, Stanford University Press, 1968.

Useful survey of Communist constitutions, but now somewhat dated.

Turack, D.C. "Freedom of Movement and the Travel Document." 4 *California Western International Law Journal* 8 (1973).

Deals tangentially with the International Convention on the Elimination of All Forms of Racial Discrimination, with regard to freedom of movement and freedom to emigrate, etc.

TURI, GIUSEPPE. *"Les Dispositions Juridico-Constitutionnelles."* Quebec, Centre International de Recherche sur le Bilinguisme, 1977. (Publications B-63).

UNITED NATIONS. Commission of the status of women. *Constitutions, Electoral Laws and Other Legal Instruments Relating to the Political Rights of Women.* Report of the Secretary-General. United Nations, New York, 1968 (A/6447/Rev. 1.)

United Nation Economic and Social Council, Commission of Human Rights: *Study of the Problem of Discrimination Against Indigenous Populations,* E/CN 4/Sub 2/L.622, July 17, 1975.

United Nations. *Human Rights: A Compilation of International Instruments of the United Nations.* New York, United Nations, 1973.

Consolidation of all Human Rights documents issued under the aegis of the United Nations in the quarter-century since the promulgation of the Universal Declaration of Human Rights.

United Nations. "Law and the Status of Women: An International

Symposium." New York, 1977. 8 *Columbia Human Rights Law Review* No. 1, p. 1 (1977).

Following an introductory chapter, fifteen articles, each discussing law and the status of women in a different country, are set forth. Some of the nations profiled include Sweden, France, Egypt, Kenya, Peru, and Iran.

UNITED NATIONS. *Protection of Minorities* Special Protective Measures of an International Character for Ethnic, Religious, or Linguistic Groups. United Nations, New York, 1967. (Sales No. E.67.XIX.3)

United Nations. *Racial Discrimination.* by Hernan Santa Cruz. New York, United Nations, 1971. (Sales No. E.71.XIV.2). Revised and updated version, 1976, New York, United Nations, 1977. (Sales No. E.76.XIV.2) . E/CN.4/Sub.2/307/Rev. 1.

United Nations. *Report on Slavery.* By Special Rapporteur Hans Egen. 19 U.N.E.S.C.O.R., Annexes (Agenda Item 8), U.N. Doc. E/2673 (1955).

A concise summary of information supplied by both member and non-member governments in an attempt to get a clear view as to the extent to which slavery and practices resembling slavery exist in the world today.

Slavery, serfdom, debt bondage, exploitation of children, and "purchase" of wives are among the topics explored.

United Nations. *Report on Slavery.* By Special Rapporteur Mohamed Awad. New York, United Nations, 1967. E/4168. Revised.

This update of the 1955 report consolidates information received from governments, specialized agencies, and non-governmental organizations on the subject of slavery. These data frequently make reference to Constitutional revisions and statutes on the subject.

The report is particularly useful with regard to women's rights, since under United Nations definitions marriage arrangements without consent of both parties and marriage of very young girls are considered to be forms of involuntary servitude.

United Nations. *Report on Slavery.* By Special Rapporteur Mohamed Awad. United Nations, New York, 1971. E/CN.4/ Sub 2/322.

Another update of an earlier report. Focus of this study is upon measures which might be taken to implement and enforce international conventions on the abolition of slavery. The possibility of cooperation by police and security forces of member nations in helping combat slavery is also examined.

United Nations, Seminar on the Multi-National Society, 1965, ST/TAO/HR/23.

United Nations. *Seminar on the Promotion and Protection of the Human Rights of National, Ethnic, and other Minorities.* Ohrid, Yugoslavia, 25 June - 8 July, 1974. New York, United Nations, 1974.

This pamphlet is not nearly so valuable as the title would indicate. While the discussants are all able and knowledgeable, Eastern European and Yugoslavian problems are overemphasized. Nonetheless, attention was drawn to the fact that many constitutions profess human rights, including those of minorities, but that such principles are often violated in actual practice.

United Nations. *Study of Discrimination in the Matter of Religious Rights and Practices.* By Arcot Krishnaswami. New York, United Nations, 1960. E/CN4/Sub 2/200/Rev. 1.

While this text does not furnish any statistical or systematic information on religious freedoms and practices in the different countries of the world, it provides the valuable function of ''defining'' the dimensions of religious practices. It discusses the scope of freedom to maintain or change religion, the scope of freedom of manifest religion and the scope of permissible limitations upon such freedoms. There is also a good philosophical discussion on individual and collective aspects of freedom.

United Nations. *Yearbook on Human Rights.* United Nations, New York (published Annually).

UNESCO. *Cultural Rights as Human Rights.* Paris, UNESCO, 1970.

UNESCO. *Four Statements on the Race Question.* Paris, UNESCO, 1969.

A compilation of UNESCO's 1950, 1951, 1964, and 1967 statements on race and race prejudice. In all the statements the economic and social causes and consequences of racism are stressed. The unifying theme of all four statements -- that racial differences are, ultimately, irrelevant -- is brought forth clearly in this brief volume.

UNESCO. *Study of the Problem of Discrimination Against Indigenous Populations.* Report of Jose R. Martinez Cobo. Geneva, E/CN.4/Sub.2/622. July 1975.

Every study on indigenous populations necessarily involves questions of racial discrimination. The indigenous populations are, for the most part, victims of white colonialism. Indians throughout South America, the Maoris of New Zealand, the Lapps of Finland, etc., are all in this category. This is a rather disjointed report, but it does have a useful collection of data, enriched by reports and comments from various governments which have minority indigenous populations.

UNESCO. *Women, Education, Equality: A Decade of Experiment.* Paris, UNESCO Press, 1975.

Report on the progress of three UNESCO-sponsored programs (in Upper Volta, Nepal, and Chile), all aimed at promoting educational and employment opportunities for women.

The United Nations and Human Rights. Eighteenth Report of the Commission to Study the Organization of Peace. Dobbs Ferry, New York, Oceana Publications, Inc., 1968.

Review of existing United Nations Human Rights documents, with an emphasis on the Universal Declaration of Human

Rights. Included is an analysis of the documents by Professor Louis B. Sohn; the documents themselves are appended to the text.

A good general introduction to the efforts of the United Nations in the context of human rights protection.

United States Department of State. *Country Reports on Human Rights Practices.* Reports submitted to the Committee on International Relations, U.S. House of Representatives, and Committee on Foreign Relations, U.S. Senate, February 3, 1978. Washington, Superintendent of Documents, 1978.

These reports were prepared for Congress in accordance with sections of the Foreign Assistance Act of 1961. There is a brief summary of human rights practices of roughly 100 of the 160 countries of the world. For some reason, not explained in the report, South Africa, Argentina, Chile and Brazil are among those omitted. While the reports are very brief, they do make reference to the status of women and occasionally to matters of religious practice.

United States. *Human Rights Reports.* Prepared by the Department of State and submitted to the Subcommittee on Foreign Assistance of the Committee on Foreign Relations, United States Senate. March, 1977. 95th Congress, 1st Session.

Human Rights conditions in 83 countries are examined.

United States. *Human Rights and U.S. Policy: Argentina, Haiti, Indonesia, Iran, Peru, and the Philippines.* Reports submitted to the Committee on International Relations, U.S. House of Representatives, December 31, 1976. 94th Congress, 2d Session

Department of State report on human rights in six selected nations.

United States. *Human Rights in the International Community and in U.S. Foreign Policy, 1945-1976.* Prepared for the Subcommittee on International Organizations of the Committee on International Relations, U.S. House of Representatives, July 24, 1977. 95th Congress, 1st Session.

Study examines evolution of international human rights and considers U.S. foreign policy and its relationship to human rights.

US News and World Report, Washington, April 2, 1973, February 25, 1974 and June 3, 1974.

United States. *The Status of Human Rights in Selected Countries and the U.S. Response.* Prepared for the Subcommittee on International Organizations of the Committee on International Relations, U.S. House of Representatives, July 25, 1977. 95th Congress, 1st Session.

Reports on human rights conditions in fifteen selected nations, with the United States response to such conditions.

"Uppsala Colloquium on the Right to Leave and Return." 5 *Israel Yearbook of Human Rights* 276 (1975).

Thoughtful compilation and discussion on the right of emigration and subsequent return to one's native land. Article 13(2) of the Universal Declaration of Human Rights proclaims such as a right, and the European Convention for the Protection of Human Rights and Fundamental Freedoms has also construed free emigration as a fundamental right.

The articles concentrate on European nations, particularly those which are signatories to the Convention, and the U.S.S.R. and its satellites. Reference is made to relevant constitutional and legislative provisions.

Van Boven, Theodor C. "Some Results on Special Problems Relating to Human Rights in Developing Countries." 3 *Revue des Droits de l'Homme* 383 (1970).

Step-by-step outline of factors which must be considered when analyzing constitutional provisions for the protection of human rights in developing countries.

Van den Berghe, Pierre. *Race and Racism: A Comparative Perspective.* New York, John Wiley and Sons, Inc., 1967.

Case studies of Mexico, Brazil, the United States, and South Africa as multi-racial societies. Social factors which militate for or against racial integration are examined, as are historical and cultural biases. Governmental institutions are scrutinized for the parts they play, intentionally or not, in encouraging racist sentiments.

Van der Kroef, Justus: "Pattern of Intergroup Accommodation in South East Asia: Is Democratic Pluralism Possible?" in Rhoodie, Nic: *Intergroup Accommodation in Plural Societies, Macmillan Press, London, 1978.*

van der Kroef, Justus M. "The Papuans of Irian Java (West New Guinea)." *Veenhoven,* Volume Two, p. 219.

van der Kroef, Justus M. "Race and Class in Indonesia: Patterns of Discrimination and Conflict." *Veenhoven,* Volume Four, p. 193.

van der Vet, A.C.W. "Dutch Tolerance on Trial: Holland on the Brink of Conflict." *Veenhoven,* Volume Five, p. 433.

Van Dyke Vernon: "Justice as Fairness for Groups," *American Political Science Review,* Vol. 69.

Van Dyke, Vernon. "One Man, One Vote, and Majority Rule as Human Rights." 6 *Revue des Droits de l'Homme* 447 (1973).

Outline of some of the ways in which various countries restrict voting and majority rule and, as a consequence, discriminate against some of their citizens. Particular attention is paid to South Africa and Rhodesia.

Van Dyke, Vernon: "Human Rights and the Rights of Groups," *American Journal of Political Science,* Vol. 18, 1974.

Van Dyke, Vernon: "The Individual, The State and Ethnic Communities in Political Theory," *World Politics,* Princeton University Press.

Van Dyke, Vernon: "Communities in Political Theory," *World Politics,* op cit.

van Haegendoren, Maurits. "Ethno-Linguistic Cleavage in Belgium." *Veenhoven,* Volume Two, p. 1.

Van Niekerk, Barend. "The Dream of Liberty -- Bills of Rights for the Bantustans." 90 *South Africa Law Journal* 403 (1973).

An examination of the idea, expressed by Chief Gatsha

Buthelezi, of entrenching in "constitutions of liberty" basic human and civil rights for South Africa's Bantu peoples, and possible ways of achieving this goal.

Van Maarseveen, H.Th. J.F., and G.F.M. Van der Tang. *On Written Constitutions.* Oceana, N.Y., 1978.

Vasil, R.K. "Communalism and Constitution-Making in Fiji." 45 *Pacific Affairs* 21 (1972).

Constitutional history of Fiji, from its last years of dependency upon Britain to its first years as an independent state. Discussion centers upon the division of legislative seats among members of the three major ethnic groups -- Indians, native Fijians, and persons of European descent. Though Indians constitute a majority of Fiji's population, a Constitution which enabled political power to be entrenched in the hands of the Fijians and the Europeans was ultimately adopted.

Vasil, R.K. "Ethnic Discrimination in Fiji: An Indian View." *Veenhoven,* Volume Two, p. 191.

VEENHOVEN, WILLIAM A., Ed. in Chief. *Case Studies on Human Rights and Fundamental Freedoms: A World Survey.* 5 Volumes The Hague, Nijhoff, 1975. Referred to throughout this work as *Veenhoven.*

Veiter, Theodor. "Commentary on the Concept of 'National Minorities'." 7 *Revue des Droits de l'Homme* 273 (1974).

A brief look at the development, and various aspects of the definition of the concept of a 'national minority.'

Verzijl, J.H.W., ed. *Human Rights in Historical Perspective.* Haarlem, the Netherlands, 1958.

Compilation of historically significant human rights documents. Included, among others, are the Magna Charta, the Habeas Corpus Act, the American Bill of Rights, the United Nations Universal Declaration of Human Rights, and the European Convention on Human Rights and Fundamental Freedoms.

Vidyarthi, L.P. "Inter-Group Conflict and Tension in Contemporary India.'' *Veenhoven,* Volume Three, p. 121.

von Taubinger, L.M. ''Suffering and Struggle of the Kurds.'' *Veenhoven,* Volume One, p. 241.

Wagatsuma, Hiroshi. ''Political Problems of a Minority Group in Japan: Recent Conflicts in Buraku Liberation Movements.'' *Veenhoven,* Volume Three, p. 243.

Wagley, Charles and Martin Harris. *Minorities in the New World.* New York, Columbia University Press, 1958.

Somewhat dated historical examination of six minority groups in the Western Hemisphere -- Indians in Mexico and Brazil, Blacks in Martinique and the United States, the French in Canada, and American Jews. The study was sponsored by UNESCO.

Walker, Connor: ''Nation Building or Nation Destroying,'' *World Politics,* Vol. 34, 1972.

Wasby, Stephen, ed. *Civil Liberties.* Lexington, Massachusetts, Lexington Books, 1976.

An examination of civil liberties in specified contexts -- the media, abortion, privacy, religious practice -- in the United States. Included are discussions of the Supreme Court as a maker of policy and a study of the role of the ACLU and other civil liberties interest groups.

Watts, R.L. ''Asian Multicultural Federations.'' In: *Multilingual Political Systems.* Quebec, University of Laval Press, 1975. p. 561.

Federal political systems would seem to be the solution for the problems of integration and separatism in multilingual, multi-cultural societies. This comparative study of the treatment of central institutions, political parties, and official language policies shows how the theory has succeeded or failed in India, Pakistan, and Malaysia.

Weis, Paul. ''Recent Developments in the law of Territorial Asylum.'' 1 *Revue des Droits de l'Homme* 378 (1968).

The Commission on Human Rights of the United Nations decided as early as 1947 to ''examine at an early opportunity the question of the inclusion of the right of asylum of refugees from persecution.'' Asylum has come under the Commission's jurisdiction, and the reasons for which asylum is usually sought are examined in this essay.

Wenner, Manfred W. ''The Politics of Equality Among European Linguistic Minorities.'' In: Richard Claude, ed. *Comparative Human Rights.* Baltimore, Johns Hopkins University Press, 1976. p. 184.

Study of minority groups in the multi-lingual nations of Europe, and examination of efforts to guarantee to such minorities the right to function in their own tongue. Constitutional provisions in such nations as Belgium and Switzerland which evidence concern for minority linguistic groups are studied.

Western, John S. ''Discrimination in Australia and New Zealand.'' *Veenhoven,* Volume Two, p. 301.

Western Political Quarterly, Vol. 10, No. 1, June, 1957.

Wetherall, William, and George A. DeVos. ''Ethnic Minorities in Japan.'' *Veenhoven,* Volume One, p. 333.

Wheare, K.C. *Modern Constitutions.* London, Oxford University Press, 1966.

Constitutional theory and philosophy as analyzed by a leading British scholar. After discussing how constitutions may be classified, the author compares and contrasts modern-day constitutional documents in various ways. The most interesting chapter is devoted to what a constitution should contain.

Wheare, K.C.: *Federal Government,* Oxford University Press, 1964.

Wickramanayake, D. ''The Caste System in Sri Lanka.'' *Veenhoven,* Volume Two, p. 179.

Wickramanayake, D.: ''Harijan Terror in India.'' *Plural Societies,* No. 3. Autumn, 1975.

Wilson, William J. ''The Changing Context of American Race Relations: Urban Blacks and Structural Shifts in the Economy.'' *Veenhoven,* Volume Five, p. 175.

Wolf-Phillips, Leslie. *Constitutions of Modern States.* New York, Praeger, 1968.

The Introduction, entitled "A Note on the Classifying of Constitutions" is useful in comparing different constitutional discrimination provisions.

Wood, James E., Jr. "Religious Liberty in Ecumenical and International Perspective." 10 *Journal of Church and State* 421 (1968).

In this essay, written in celebration of the twentieth anniversary of the United Nations Universal Declaration of Human Rights, it is noted that true religious freedom has become possible only within the last two centuries. Recent United Nations and ecumenical documents supporting the principle of religious freedom are summarized and discussed.

Worrall, Denis. "Government in the Plural Society: The South Africal Model." *Veenhoven,* Volume Two, p. 285.

Ybema, Seerp Bernhard. *Constitutionalism and Civil Liberties.* Juridicial Studies of the University of Leiden, Volume 12, Leiden, 1973.

Comparative study of constitutional fundamental rights provisions in Canada and the United States. Judicial review as a means of ensuring state and local compliance with constitutional guarantees is lauded.

Yinger, J. Milton. "Discrimination Against American Blacks." *Veenhoven,* Volume One, p. 39.

Zolberg, Aristide R. "Transformation of Linguistic Ideologies: The Belgian Case." In: *Multilingual Political Systems.* Quebec, University of Laval Press, 1975. p. 445.

In this essay Zolberg divides the linguistic and political history of Belgium into four chronological phases:a unilingual francophonic state with limited political participation; a bilingual state with expanding political participation; a plural monolingual state with universal suffrage; and, finally, a movement away from linguistic issues with increased emphasis on economic development, social equity, and political participation in the wider European community.

Zubrzycki, Jerzy. "Cultural Pluralism and Discrimination in Australia: With Special Reference to White Minority Groups." *Veenhoven,* Volume Three, p. 397.

Zurcher, A.J. ed.: *Constitutions and Constitutional Trends Since World War II,* New York University Press, New York, 1951.

Zwerin, Michael. *A Case for the Balkanization of Practically Everyone.* London, Wildwood House, 1976.

Subtitled "the new nationalism," this volume ostensibly treats problems of group rights in Europe and advocates separatism as the solution. It is written in a light vein and, while it lacks a sound scholarly basis, it does point up the major issues involving the Occitans in Southern France, Basques, Gypsies, Bretons, Mohawk Indians in the United States, Catalans, and Lapps.

BIBLIOGRAPHY: PART III: NEGATIVE

Abbott, Simon, ed. *The Prevention of Racial Discrimination in Britain.* London, Oxford University Press, 1971.

Adebiy, S.D. *Fundamental Human Rights in Nigeria: Some Decided Cases and Future Problems.* British Institute of International and Comparative Law, London, Commonwealth Law Series, 1965.

Adler, J.E. "Judicial Review of Administrative Action in East Africa and England." 10 *East Africa Law Journal* No. 1, p. 17 (1974).

Aiyar, S.H. "The Basis of the Constitution of Sri Lanka." 5 *Lawyer* 191 (1973).

Akiwowo, Akinsola. "Tribalism and Nation Building in Nigeria." 37 *Il Politico* 79 (1972).

Almond, Gabriel A., and G. Bingham Powell, Jr. *Comparative Politics, a Developmental Approach.* Boston, Little, Brown and Company, 1966.

Amato, Giulano. "Structure and Subject of the Constitution." In: *Associazione Italiano di Diritto Comparato. Italian National Reports to the IXth International Congress of Comparative Law.* Tehran, 1974; Milano, 1974. p. 505.

Andrews, William G., ed. *Constitutions and Constitutionalism.* 2d ed. Princeton, N.J., D. van Nostrand Company, Inc., 1963.

Arles, J.P. "Untouchability in India and Equality of Opportunity and Treatment." 101 *International Labour Review* 291 (1970).

Austin, Granville. *The Indian Constitution: Cornerstone of a Nation.* Oxford, Oxford University Press, 1966.

Baldwin, F.N., Jr. "A Constitutional Comparison: Mexico, the United States, and Uganda." 10 *California Western Law Review* 82 (1973).

Baxter, Craig. "Constitution-Making: the Development of Federalism in Pakistan." 14 *Asian Survey* 1074 (1974).

Bentsi-Enchill, Kwamena. "The Cononial Heritage of Legal Pluralism." 1 *Zambia Law Journal* No. 2, p. 1 (1969).

Beyme, Klaus von. *Die Verfassunggebende Gewalt des Volkes, Demokratische Doktrin und Politische Wirklichkeit.* Tubingen, J.C.B. Mohn (Paul Siebeck), 1968.

Bhuckony, Somdath. *Our Constitution.* Port Louis, Mauritius, 1971.

Bihari, Otto. "Constitutionalism and Legality." 6 *Acta Politica* 99 (1964).

Biscaretti Di Ruffia, Paolo, and Stefan Rozmaryn. *La Constitution comme loi Fondamentale dans les Etats de l'Europe Occidentale et dans les Etats Socialistes.* Torino, G. Giappichelli, 1966.

Black, Edwin R. *Divided Loyalties.* Montreal, McGill-Queen's University Press, 1975.

Blondel, Jean. *An Introduction to Comparative Government.* London, Weidenfeld and Nicolson, 1969.

Bonenfant, Jean-Charles. *L'etat et les Valeurs Humaines Essentialles.* Series IV, Memoires de la Societe Royale du Canada, Volume II, 1973.

Bonenfant, Jean-Charles. *Les Influences Etatsuniennes sur la Conception Canadienne des Droits des de l'Homme.* Series IV, Memoires de la Societe Royale du Canada, Volume 11, 1973.

Bright, Jagat S. *Handbook of World Constitutions.* 2d rev. ed. Delhi, The Universal Book and Stationery Co., 1971.

Brunet, Michel. "Continentalism and Quebec Nationalism." 76 *Queen's Quarterly* 511 (1970).

Bryce, James. "Flexible and Rigid Constitutions." In: James Bryce. *Studies in History and Jurisprudence,* Volume 1, Oxford, The Clarendon Press, 1901. p. 145.

Burdeau, Georges. *Droit Constitutionel et Institutions Politiques.* 16th ed. Paris, R. Pichon et R. Durand-Auzias, 1974.

Cagatay, N. and S.S. Hussain. "The Concept of Equality and Brotherhood in Islam." In: *International Islamic Conference, Rawalpindi, 1968. Proceedings,* Volume 1, p. 113.

Carl, B.M. "Erosion of Constitutional Rights of Political Offenders in Brazil." 12 *Virginia Journal of International Law* 159 (1972).

Carlston, Kenneth S. *Social Theory and African Tribal Organization.* Urbana, University of Illinois Press, 1968.

Caulk, R.A. "Religion and the State in Nineteenth Century Ethiopia." 10 *Journal of Ethiopian Studies* No. 1, p. 23 (1972).

Chalidze, Valery N. *To Defend these Rights: Human Rights and the Soviet Union.* Translated from the Russian by Guy Daniels.

Chiarelli, Giuseppe. "Elasticita della Constituzione." In: *Studi di Diritto Costituzionale in Memoria di Luigi Rossi.* Milano, Dott. a. Giuffre, 1952. p. 43.

Chalmers, Donald. "Human Rights and What is Reasonably Justifiable in a Democratic Society." 3 *Melanesian Law Journal* 92 (1975).

Codding, George. *Federal Government of Switzerland.* Boston, Houghton Mifflin Co., 1961.

Cotta, Sergio. "La Notion de Constitution dans ses Rapports avec la Realite Sociale." In: *L'Idee de Philosophie Politique.* Paris, Presses Universitaires de France, 1965. p. 147.

Crabb, J.H. "The Environment and Nature of the Legal System of Congo-Kinshasa." 1966 *Wisconsin Law Review* 1125 (1966).

Dareste, F.R. *Les Constitutions Modernes.* rev. ed. by J. Laferriere and J. Delpech. 6 Volumes. Paris, 1928-1934.

Dasgupta, P. "The Ghana Constitution: an Assessment." 9 *Africa Quarterly* 220 (1969).

Davis, Helen M. *Constitutions, Electoral Laws and Treaties of States in the Near and Middle East.* rev. ed. Durham. Duke University Press, 1953.

del Carmen, R.V. "The Philippine Juridicial System under the New Constitution and Marital Law." 9 *Texas International Law Journal* 143 (1974).

Dennewitz, Bodo, ed. *Die Verfassungen der Modernen Staaten.* 4 Volumes. Hamburg, Hansicher Gildenverlag, 1947-1949.

Derett, J.D.M. "Hindu Empires." In: *Les Grands Empires.* 31 *Recueil de la Societe Jean Bodin* 565 (1973).

Derett, J.D.M. "Religion, Law and the State in India." 22 *Recueil de la Societe Jean Bodin* 417 (1969).

Djurovic, Dragoljub. "Constitutional Changes in Yugoslavia." 5 *Journal of Constitutional and Parliamentary Studies* 184 (1971).

Dodd, Walter Farleigh. *Modern Constitutions: A Collection of Fundamental Laws of Twenty-two of the Most Important Countries of the World, with Historical and Bibliographical Notes.* 2 Volumes. Chicago, University of Chicago Press, 1969.

Eggleston, E.M. "Prospects for United Nations Protection of the Human Rights of Indigenous Minorities." 1970-1973 *Australian Yearbook of International Law* 68 (1975).

Engholm, G.F., and A.A. Mazrui. "Violent Constitutionalism in Uganda." 2 *Government and Opposition* 585 (1967).

English, J.C. "Law and State in Contemporary Islam: the Cases of Malaysia and Pakistan." 5 *Indian Sociological Bulletin* 86 (1968).

Ercman, Sevinc. "The Problem of Discrimination and Measures Which Should be taken for its Elimination." 20 *Annales de la Faculte de Droit d'Istanbul* 237 (1970).

Finer, Herman. *The Theory and Practice of Modern Government.* 4th ed. London, Methuen and Company, Ltd., 1965.

Finer, S.E. *Comparative Government.* London, Allen Lane, The Penquin Press (Pelican ed), 1974.

Fitzgerald, Gerald E., ed. *The Constitutions of Latin America.* Chicago, Henry Regnery Company, 1968.

Fitzgibbon, Russell H. *The Constitutions of the Americas.* Chicago, Chicago University Press, 1948.

Foligno, Dario. "The Right to Respect for Private Life and the Home and the Right to Equality of Aliens, in the Practice of the Italian Constitutional Court." In: A.H. Robertson, ed. *Privacy and Human Rights.* Manchester, Manchester University Press, 1973. p. 115.

Franck, Thomas M. "Some Legal Problems of Becoming a New Nation." 4 *Columbia Journal of Transnational Law* No. 1, p. 13 (1965).

Franz, Gunther, ed. *Staasverfassungen, eine Sammlung wich-*

tiger Verfassungen der Vergangenheit und Gegenwart in Urtext und Ubersetzung. 2d ed. Munchen, R. Oldenbourg, 1964.

Gaur, S.K. "The New Frontiers of Cultural and Educational Rights of Minorities." 13 *Indian Advocate* No. 1 and 2, p. 41 (1973).

Gebethner, S. "Polish Report (On Recognition and Putting into Effect of Economic and Social Rights)" In: *La Reconnaissance et la Mise en Oeuvre des Droits Economiques et Sociaux.* Actes du Colloque International de Droit Compare. Brussels, 1972. p. 321.

Ghai, Yash P. "Constitutions and the Political Order in East Africa" 21 *International and Comparative Law Quarterly* 403 (1972).

Ghori, A.S.K. *The Evolution of Islamic Constitutionalism in Pakistan.* Karachi, 1972.

Ghouse, Mohammad. "Safeguards of Linguistic Minorities" 7 *Journal of Constitutional and Parliamentary Studies* 20 (1973).

Glickman, H. "Traditional Pluralism and Democratic Process in Mainland Tanzania." 1969 *Journal of Asian and African Studies* 165 (1969).

Godchot, Jacques. *Les Constitutions du Proche et du Moyen Orient.* Paris, Sirey, 1957.

Goitein, S.D. "Minority Self-Rule and Government Control in Islam." 31 *Studia Islamica* 106 (1970).

Gonidec, P.F. *Constitutions des Etats de la Communaute.* Paris, Sirey, 1959.

Gotlieb, A.E. "Canada and the Refugee Question in International Law" 13 *Canadian Yearbook of International Law* 3 (1976).

Goy, R.H.M. "The International Protection of the Cultural and National Heritage." 1973 *Nederlands Yearbook of International Law* 117 (1973).

Griffin, E.C. "The Universal Suffrage Issue in Japanese Politics, 1918-1925." 31 *Journal of Asian Studies* 275 (1972).

Gyandoh, S.O., Jr., and J. Griffiths. *A Sourcebook of the Constitutional Law of Ghana.* Accra, University of Ghana Press,

1972.

Hajenko, F. "Violation of Workers' Rights in the U.S.S.R." 17 *Bulletin of the Institute for the Study of the U.S.S.R.* No. 6, p. 17 (1970).

Hassan, H. "The International Protection of Human Rights: an Approach to Interpretation." 19 *Buffalo Law Review* 35 (1969).

Hassan, H. "The Word 'Arbitrary' As Used in the Universal Declaration of Human Rights; 'Illegal' or 'Unjust'?" 10 *Harvard International Law Journal* 225 (1969).

Hauriou, Maurice. *Precis de Droit Constitutionnel.* 2d ed. Paris, Librairie du Recueil Sirey, 1929.

Hazard, John N. "Constitutions and Revolutionary Socialism." In: Henry Steele Commager, ed. *Festschrift fur Karl Loewenstein.* Tubingen, J.C.B. Mohr (Paul Siebeck), 1971. p. 191.

Heggoy, A.A. "Algerian Women and the Right to Vote: Some Colonial Anomalies." 64 *Muslim World* 228 (1974).

Hennis, Wilheim. *Verfassung und Verfassungswirklichkeit, ein deutsches Problem.* Tubingen, J.C.B. Mohn (Paul Siebeck, (1968).

Hesse, Konrad. *Die Normative Kraft der Verfassung.* Tubingen, J.C.B. Mohn (Paul Siebeck), 1959.

Hickling, R.H. "Recent Constitutional and Legal Developments in Thailand." 3 *Hong Kong Law Journal* 215 (1973).

Huber, Hans. "Probleme des ungeschriebenen Verfassungsrecht. In: *Rechts Theorie - Verfassungsrecht - Volkerrecht, Ausgewahlte Aufsatze,* 1950-1970. Bern, Verlag Stampfli und Cie AG, 1971, p. 329.

Hug, Mahfuzul. "Some Reflections on Islam and Constitution-Making in Pakistan, 1947-1956." 5 *Islamic Studies* 209 (1966).

Jain, P.C. *Law and Religion: a Comparative Study of the Freedom of Religion in India and the United States.* Allahabad, 1974.

Jais, Ch. K.R. "Equal Protection of Laws and the Problems of the Poor." 3 *Singapore Law Review* (1971/1972).

Jellinek, Georg. *Allegemeine Staaslehre.* rd ed. Berlin, Verlag von O. Haring, 1914.

Jellinek, Georg. *Verfassungsanderung und Verfassungswandlung,* Berlin, Verlag von O. Haring, 1906.

Kagi, Werner. *Die Verfassung als rechtliche Grundordnung des Staates, untersuchungen uber die Entwicklungstendenzen im modernen Verfassungsrecht.* Zurich, Ploygrafischer Verlag A.G., 1945.

Kahn, Ellison. "Some Thoughts on the Competency of the Transkeian Legislative Assembly and the Sovereignty of the South African Parliament." 80 *South African Law Journal* 475 (1963).

Kapoor, S.K.: "Constitutional and International Status of Sikkim." 6 Lawayer 236. (1974)

Kastari, Paavo. "Le Caractere normatif et le Preeminence hierarchique des Constitutions." 1966 *Revue Internationale de Droit Compare* 831 (1966).

Keeney, K.J. "Civil Rights of the Clergy." 32 *Jurist* 66 (1972).

Klokocka, Vladimir. "Verfassungsprobleme im socialistischen Staassysteem." 1966 *Der Staat* 71 (1966).

Koopmans, T., ed. *Constitutional Protection of Equality.* Leyden, Nijhoff, 1975.

Kopp, Ferdinand O. "Das Verfassungsverstandnis in den socialistischen Staaten." In: *Recht und Staat, Festschrift fur Georg Kuchenhoff,* 1972. p. 573.

Kotok, V.F., and N.P. Farberov. *Konstitusionnoe pravo socialistischeskich stran.* Moscow, 1963.

Krader, Lawrence. "Mongols -- the Governed and the Governors." In: 22 *Recueil de la Societe Jean Bodin* 512 (1969).

Kurtz, Donn M. "Political Integration in Africa: the Mali Federation." 8 *Journal of Modern African Studies* 405 (1970).

La Palombara, J. "Values and Idealogies in the Administrative Evolution of Western Constitutional Systems." In: R. Braibaati, ed. *Political and Administrative Development.* Durham, Duke University Press, 1969. p. 166.

Leibholz, Gerhard. "Constitutional Law and Constitutional Reality." In: Henry Steele Commager, ed. *Festschrift fur Karl Loewenstein.* Tubingen, J.C.B. Mohr (Paul Siebeck),

1971, p. 305.

Lee, Han-Key. "Constitutional Developments in South Korea." 4 *Hong Kong Law Journal* 41 (1974).

Legum, Colin. "Tribal Survival in the Modern African Political System." 5 *Journal of Asian and African Studies* 102 (1970).

Le Mong, Nguyen. "Contribution a la theorie de la constitution souveraine par la peuple." 1970 *Revue du Droit Public et de la Science Politique en France et a l'Etranger* 923 (1970).

Lerner, Natan. "Anti-Semitism as Racial and Religious Discrimination under United Nations Conventions." 1 *Israel Yearbook of Human Rights* 103 (1971).

Le Vine, V.T. *The Cameroons: From Mandate to Independence.* Berkeley and Los Angeles, University of California Press, 1964.

Lichtman, Richard. "The Facade of Equality in Liberal Democratic Theory." 12 *Inquiry* 170 (1969).

Loewenstein, Karl. *Political Power and the Governmental Process.* 2d ed. Chicago and London, University of Chicago Press, 1965.

Mackinnon, Victor S. *Comparative Federalism.* The Hague, Martinus Nijhoff, 1964.

Mahmood, M. *The Constitution of the Islamic Republic of Pakistan.* Lahore, 1973.

Martin, Robert. *Personal Freedom and the Law in Tanzania.* Nairobi, 1974.

Ma'sumi, M.S.H. "The Islamic Concept of Human Rights." 11 *Islamic Studies* No. 3, p. 211 (1972).

Mayer-Tasch, P.C., and Ion Contiades, eds. *Die Verfassungen der Nichtkommunistischen Staaten Europas.* 2d ed. Munchen, Verlag C.H. Beck, 1975.

McBain, Howard Lee, and Lindsay Rogers. *The New Constitutions of Europe.* New York, Doubleday Page and Company, 1922.

McDougal, Myres, Harold Lasswell, and Lung-chu Chen. "Non-Conforming Political Opinion and Human Rights: Transnational Protection Against Discrimination." 2 *Yale Studies in World Public Order* 1 (1975).

McInnis, Edgar. *Canada.* New York, Holt, Rinehart, and Winston, 1961.

McWhinney, Edward. "Comparative Federalism and Bicultural Constitutionalism in Canada." 1 *International Journal of Legal Research* 9 (1966).

Melody, T.P. "The Right to be Educated in the New Africa." In: R.F. Drinan, *The Right to be Educated.* Washington, 1968, p. 204.

Mirkine-Guetzevitch, Boris. *Les Constitutions Europeennes.* 2 Volumes. Paris, Presses Universitaires de France, 1951.

Mittal, J.K. "Fundamental Rights, Directive Principles, and Recent Constitutional Changes." 4 *Allahabad Law Review* 128 (1972).

Mittal, J.K. "The Right to Hold Property and the Deprivation of Property." 4 *Allahabad Law Review* 128 (1972).

Montagu, Ashley. *Man's Most Dangerout Myth; The Fallacy of Race.* London, Oxford University Press, 1964.

Natium, Fasil. "The Enigma of Eritrean Legislation." 9 *Journal of Ethiopian Law* 307 (1973).

Nigeria, Federal Republic of. *Reports of the Constitution Drafting Committee,* 2 Volumes. Lagos, Federal Ministry of Information Printing Division, 1976.

Nisser, C.G. "Swedish Report (On Recognition and Putting into Effect of Economic and Social Rights). In: *La Reconnaissance et la Mise en Oeuvre des Droits Economiques et Sociaux. Actes du Colloque International de Droit Compare. Brussels, 1972.*

Nwabueze, B.O. *Judicialism in Commonwealth Africa.* London, C. Hurst and Company, 1977.

Olivier, N.J.J. "The Governmental Institutions of the Bantu Peoples in Southern Africa." In: 22 *Recueil de la Societe Jean Bodin* 215 (1969).

Oyewole, Anthony. "The Role of the Courts in the Process of National Integration in Nigeria." 12 *Journal of Administration Overseas* 136 (1973).

Picker, J.M. "Law and the Status of Women in the United States." 8 *Columbia Human Rights Law Review* 1139 (1977).

Plamenetz, John. "Privacy and Laws Against Discrimination." 51 *Rivista Internazionale de Filosofia del Diritto* 443 (1974).

Puget, Henry. *Les Constitutions de l'Asie et de l'Australasie.* Paris, Editions de l'Epargne, 1965.

Quebec, Government of. *The Position of the French Language in Quebec.* (Report of the Commission of Inquiry on the Position of the French Language and on Language Rights in Quebec.) 3 Volumes. Book 1: *The Language of Work: the Position of French in Work and Consumer Activities of Quebecers;* Book 2: *Language Rights;* Book 3: *The Ethnic Groups -- other Ethnic Groups and the Enhancement and Development of French in Quebec.* Montreal, 1972-1973.

Rabinowicz, Aharon M.K. "Human Rights Problems in the United States and Israel." 34 *Jewish Social Studies* 207 (1972).

Ramolefe, A.M.R., and A.J.G.M. Sanders. "The Structural Pattern of African Regionalism." 4 *Comparative and International Law Journal of Southern Africa* 155, 293 (1971); 5 *Comparative and International Law Journal of Southern Africa* 30, 171, 299 (1972).

Ristic, P. "Yugoslavian Report (On Recognition and the Putting into Effect of Economic and Social Rights)" In: *La Reconnaissance et la Mise en Oeuvre des Droits Economiques et Sociaux.* Actes du colloque International de Droit Compare, Brussels, 1972.

Rodriguez, A.I. *A Compilation of the Political Constitutions of the Independent Nations of the World.* 3 Volumes. Washington, D.C., Government Printing Office, 1907.

Rogge, Hartwig, Henning von Wedelm and Brun-Otto Bryde, eds. *Verfassungstexte.* Hamburg, Institut fur Internationale Angelegenheiten der Universitat Hamburg, 1972-.

Rozmaryn, Stefan. "Quelques questions de la Theorie des Constitutions Socialistes." In: *Liber Amicorum baron Louis Fredericq,* Volume II. Gent, Story-Scientia, 1965, p. 881.

Rupp von Brunneck, Wiltraut. "Admonitory Functions of Constitutional Courts; Germany: The Federal Constitutional Court." 20 *American Journal of Comparative Law* 387 (1972).

Rutgers, G.R. "The Dutch Report (On Recognition and the Putting into Effect of Economic and Social Rights)" In: *La Reconnaissance et la Mise en Oeuvre des Droits Economiques et Sociaux.* Actes du Colloque International de Droit Compare, Brussels, 1972.

Saario, V. "The Constitution as a Guarantee of Human Rights in Finland." In: *Rene Cassin, Amicorum Discipulorumque Liber.* Paris, 1969. p. 267.

Salas, Rafael M. "The Philippines in the Field of Human Rights." 11 *University of the East Law Journal* No. 1, p. 1 (1968).

Saleem Khan, M.A. "The Religion and the State in Iran: a Unique Muslim Country." 2 *Islam and the Modern Age* No. 3, p. 67.

Sarbah, John Mensah. *Fanti National Constitution.* London, Frank Cass and Company, Ltd., 1968.

Sartori, Giovanni. "Constitutionalism: A Preliminary Discussion." 56 *American Political Science Review* 853 (1962).

Schambeck, Herbert. "Der Verfassungsbegriff und seine Entwicklung." In: *Festschrift fur Hans Kelsen zum 90. Geburtstag.* Wien, Deuticke, 1971, p. 211.

Scheuner, Ulrich. "Fundamental Rights and the Protections of the Individual against Social Groups and Powers in the Constitutional System of the Federal Republic of Germany." In: *Rene Cassin Amicorum Discipulorumque Liber III.* Paris, 1971, p. 253.

Scholler, Heinrich. "The Purpose and Structure of the Ethiopian Constitution." *Ethiopian Contributions to the IXth International Congress of Comparative Law* Tehran 1974, Addis Ababa, 1974.

Schwarzenberger, Georg. "Equality and Discrimination in International Economic Law." 25 *Yearbook of International*

Affairs 163 (1971).

Sen, S.C. "The Constitution of Bangladesh and a Short Constitutional History." 7 *Verfassung und Recht in Ubersee* 257 (1974).

Secretariat of the Asian-African Legal Consultative Committee. *Constitutions of African States.* 2 Volumes. New Dehli -- Dobbs Ferry, N.Y., Oceana Publications, Inc., 1972.

Secretariat of the Asian-African Legal Consultative Committee. *Constitutions of Asian Countries.* New Dehli-Bombay, Tripathi Private Ltd., 1968.

Shava, Menashe. "Legal Aspects of Change of Religious Community in Israel." 3 *Israel Yearbook of Human Rights* 256 (1973).

Sheppard, Claude-Armaud. Synthese S6. *Regimes Linguistiques Canadiens et etrangers.* Quebec, 1974 (Prepared for La Commission d'Enquite sur la situation de la langue Francaise et sur les Droits Linguistiques an Quebec [in French]).

Shoup, Paul. *Communism and the Yugoslav National Question.* New York, Random House, 1968.

Silverman, Jerry M. "Local Government and National Integration in South Vietnam." 47 *Pacific Affairs* 305 (1974).

Simmonds, R.L. and M.L. Barlar. "Equal Protection and Problems of the Poor." 3 *Singapore Law Review* 1 (1971/1972).

Simpson, G.E. and J.M. Yinger. *Racial and Cultural Minorities: An Analysis of Prejudice and Discrimination.* 3d ed. New York, Harper and Row, 1965.

Singh, Bakshish. "The Supreme Court in Indian Society." 9 *Civil and Military Law* 178 (1973).

Smith, S.A. de. *Constitutional and Administrative Law.* London, Penquin Books, 1971.

Smith, S.A. de. "Legislatures under Written Constitutions." In: Sir Alan Burns, ed. *Parliament as an Export.* London, 1966, p. 208.

Staron, S. "State-Church Relations in Poland." 21 *World Politics* 575 (1969).

Stockli, Walter A. *Church, State, and School in Switzerland and the United States: A Study in Comparative Constitutional Law.* Berne, Herbert Lang and Company, Ltd., 1970.

Swamy, E.K. *Glimpses of World Constitutions and Judiciaries.* Allahabad, Kitab Mahal Private, Ltd., 1966.

Szabo, Jozsef. ''Comparative Constitutional Law: Its Possibility and Limits.'' 21 *Oesterreichische Zeitschrift fur offentliches Recht,* No. 1-2, p. 133 (1971).

Tambiah, M.W. ''The Commonwealth and its Citizens.'' 3 *Colombo Law Review* 20 (1972).

Tandon, M.P. ''Constitutionality of the Hindu Marriage Act, 1975.' 5 Allahabad Law Review 75 (1973).

Thalmann-Antenen, Helene. ''Equal Pay: the Postition in Switzerland.'' 104 *International Labour Review* 275 (1971).

Thomson, Dale C. ''Quebec and the Bicultural Dimension.'' 32 *Academy of Political Science: Proceedings* 27 (1976).

Tizzano, Antonio. ''Regional Integration in Africa.'' In: *Somali National Reports to the IXth International Congress of Comparative Law.* Tehran, 1974, Milano, 1974, p. 47.

Todorovic, Mijalko. ''Yugoslavia's New Constitution.'' 25 *Review of International Affairs* 7 (1974).

Topornin, B.N., ed. *Konstitutsii Zarubezjnich Socialisticheskich gosudarstv Evropi.* Moscow, Isdatelstvo ''Progress,'' 1973.

Topornin, B.N. ''Vstupitelnaja statiya.'' In: *Konstitutsii Zarubezjnich Socialisticheskich gosudarstv Evropi.* Moscow, Isdatelstvo ''Progress,'' 1973, p. 7.

Tripathi, G.P. ''The Right Against Exploitation under the Indian Constitution.'' 4 *Allahabad Law Review* 73 (1972).

Ts'ao, Wen-Yen. *The Constitutional Structure of Modern China.* Westport, Connecticut, Hyperion Press, Inc., 1974.

Vangsnes, Kari. ''Equal Pay in Norway.'' 103 *International Labour Review* 379 (1971).

Vierdog, E.W. *The Concept of Discrimination in International Law, with Special Reference to Human Rights.* The Hague, 1973.

Vigoriti, Vincenzo. "Admonitory Functions of Constitutional Courts; Italy: The Constitutional Court." 20 *American Journal of Comparative Law* 404 (1972).

Wade, E.C.S., and G. Godfrey Phillips. *Constitutional Law.* 7th ed. London, Longmans, 1965.

Wickramanayake, D. "Harijan Terror in India." 6 *Plural Societies* No. 3, p. 17 (1975).

Wimmer, Norbert. *Materiales Verfassungsverstandnis.* Wien - New York, Springer-Verlag, 1971.

Wormuth, Francis D. *The Origins of Modern Constitutionalism.* New York, Harper and Brothers, 1949.

Wright, Theodore P., Jr. "The Muslim League in South India since Independence: A Study in Minority Group Political Strategies." 60 *American Political Science Review* 579 (1966).

Yugoslavia. *The Legal Status of Religious Communities.* Belgrade Institute of Comparative Law, Collection of Yugoslav Laws, Volume 15, 1971.

Index

Of Subjects, Names of People, Organisations, Places, States, Countries, Religions and Language Groups, Races and Ethnic Minorities.

INDEX